HIP HOP SAMPLES
A HISTORICAL ANTHOLOGY

REVISED EDITION

Edited by

Glen Garrett

California State University–Northridge

cognella™
San Diego, CA

First published in the United States of America in 2010 by Cognella, a division of University Readers, Inc.

Trademark Notice: Product or corporate names may be trademarks or registered trademarks, and are used only for identification and explanation without intent to infringe.

14 13 12 11 10   1 2 3 4 5

Printed in the United States of America

ISBN:978-1-935551-70-6

www.cognella.com 800.200.3908

Contents

Introduction

By Glen Garrett

Given its universal popularity and its troubling effects, hip hop is a vital cultural language that we all better learn. To ignore its genius, to romanticize its deficits, or to bash it with undeserving generalities is to risk the opportunity to engage our children about perhaps the most important cultural force in their lives.
—Michael Eric Dyson
Holler If You Hear Me, p. 138

A COLLEGE COURSE REVOLVING around the study of Hip Hop—its emergence, development, and subsequent importance—could arguably be a valuable addition to the course offerings of almost any department in today's college or university. Hip Hop courses can most often be found in Ethnic Studies, Women's Studies, Music, Art and Dance departments, logically. But certainly English, Political Science, Sociology, Business, Comparative Religion, Philosophy and arguably even Criminal Science departments could effectively use the study of Hip Hop and its history as a springboard to the study of their respective disciplines, as well as an effective way to capitalize on students' interest. Likewise, in almost any department in the college or university, there is still likely to be some impassioned opposition to the study of Hip Hop in the academic environment. Hip Hop, if nothing else, has always been highly controversial, and for a number of different reasons. Like many of its cultural and musical predecessors—again for various reasons—it has often been viewed as threatening by the older generation and the *status quo*. Embedded in the study of Hip Hop and its artists are most of the major problems and debates of our time. It is this very controversy, and the subsequent debate that these opposing views often inspire, that makes the study of Hip Hop so rewarding and academically valuable.

Hip Hop culture is now at least 30 years old, and there is no denying that its influence is pervasive in every corner of our society. Hip Hop, of course, is much more than just the medium by which rappers express their ideas. It is the culture and lifestyle from which the ideas are germinated as well. Hip Hop shines a fresh light on some very old problems, as well as redefining and unearthing more than a few new ones. Hip Hop exposes both the decadence and desperation of the urban ghettoes' dirtiest street corners, as well as the greed and corruption of corporate boardrooms. Hip Hop expresses both the *naiveté* of youthful optimism and the jaded opportunism of those pandering sensationalism and gratuitous sex and violence. Hip Hop's products and styles generate billions of dollars from recordings, fashion, advertising, movies, television, and every other form of capitalism's traditional pillaging of art and culture. At the very same time, Hip Hop can be seen inspiring social and political revolutions, Afro-centric religions, and the counter-culture in general. Hip Hop started in the mid 70s, as the latest expression of the generation gap, the outrage of the economically oppressed, and the eternal desire of young people to party and rebel against the hypocrisy of their parent's values. And, like all of its many predecessors—and much to the dismay of the *status quo*—Hip Hop was quickly and efficiently marketed to and appropriated by middle-class white teens as a way to vicariously experience the *outside* world, the very outside world from which their parents had been trying so hard to protect them. In the process, these expressions of a youthful and rebellious counter-culture always seem to eventually become mainstream "pop culture." Studying the history of how Hip Hop's *four elements* have traveled, to some extent separately, through the gristmill of American show business, art and entertainment, is a particularly revealing study of American cultural values. There are many parallels in the histories of American music, dance and art styles from previous generations.

Bakari Kitwana, in his book, *The Hip Hop Generation,* has arbitrarily defined the "Hip Hop Generation" as anyone born between 1965 and 1984. (1.p.xiii). Obviously, almost all of today's college students are going to be younger than that. That makes them, one hopes, not the "post-Hip-Hop generation," but the "second Hip Hop generation." At any rate, today's college students, unlike those of Kitwana's "generation," didn't grow up with Hip Hop as the culture itself was maturing. Instead, they grew up consuming it after it had already morphed into a mainstreamed record business commodity. Hip Hop, in its first thirty years, has indeed undergone some profound changes and developments, and it has definitely broadened its scope and audience. Hip Hop is global now and is popular in many cultures and many languages. The influence of Hip Hop culture is much larger than the Rap category of the record business. Rappers or MCs tell us what to wear, what to drink, how to talk, what to think and how to reinterpret our world. Rappers in the Middle-East rap in Arabic about their politics and predicaments. Preschool kids in white middle-class neighborhoods take Hip Hop dance classes. Our first African-American president, Barack Obama, while slightly older than Kitwana's "generation," was elected with a graffiti-inspired poster and took his wife to Spike Lee's *Do the Right Thing* on their first date. One of the newer members of the Supreme Court, Sonya Sotomayor, is a Puerto Rican woman from the Bronx. In much the same way that the first Hip Hop generation didn't seem to appreciate the civil rights struggles of their elders, perhaps today's college students are not really aware of the struggles in Hip Hop's own history. Hip Hop is hollering at us from across the abyss of the gender and generation gaps, and though we may be put off at first by the deafening volume and thunderous echo, we are obliged to listen; because if we do, we often find the message all too familiar. Hip Hop is old enough and important enough now, that it deserves some historical perspective and certainly more academic attention.

The most obvious and perhaps most important truth to be garnered from the study of Hip Hop's history, is the old saying that history often repeats itself. Actually, according to William Jelani Cobb, it doesn't repeat itself—"but it is prone to extended paraphrases." (*To the Break of Dawn,* p.43). That's close enough. Hip Hop, at first glance, appears to be radically new, but it's an obvious continuation of a recurring cycle in American cultural history that began with "minstrelsy" and continued with ragtime, the Blues, jazz, swing, rock n' roll, disco, etc. All of these forms of art and entertainment were initially viewed as dangerous and revolutionary, but were eventually understood to be merely part of a cyclical cultural evolution. All of the above started as honest expressions of disenfranchised minorities, particularly African-Americans. Then, after proving to be popular and powerful forms of communication, these forms of expression were then sentimentalized and exploited for their popularity amongst young, primarily white, youth who wanted to identify with the minorities' predicament. The jazz poet Gil Scott Heron is often mentioned as a forerunner and early influence of rap. Particularly, his recording of "The Revolution Will Not Be Televised" is most often singled out. Perhaps more to the point, however, would be his recording called "It Ain't No New Thing," which recounts the story of the recurrent practice of Afro-American music being exploited by the mainstream media. As each new generation tries in some way to separate itself from the hypocrisy of their parents, they look for a new form of expression, the validity of which is often determined, literally, by how offensive their parents find it. Even before the roaring 20s, there was Hip Hop prototype Jelly Roll Morton, who flaunted his extravagant wardrobe, his excessive "bling" (including a diamond in his teeth). He also notably bragged about his purported prowess with "bitches and whores" (notice the historical spelling). The Blues and Hip Hop both share roots that come from the "toasts" and "legends" developed and perpetuated by prison culture. Hip Hop? "It Ain't No New Thing." Vanilla Ice and the Beastie Boys are the Hip Hop generation's version of Pat Boone or the Osmond Brothers. Grandmaster Flash turned down the opportunity to record the first rap record because he didn't think the essence of what he did could be captured on a recording, and because he was afraid his work would be copied and stolen. Similarly, in 1916, Freddie Keppard turned down an opportunity to make the first jazz record for essentially the same reasons. The struggles of Ice-T, N.W.A. and 2 Live Crew with censorship and the first amendment are the latest versions of the struggles of Lenny Bruce, Allen Ginsburg, William S. Burroughs, Larry Flynt, and countless others who have fought for an artist's right to disgust, titillate and otherwise exploit our basest nature. All of Hip Hop's cultural predecessors have been ridiculed and riddled with the same criticisms we see leveled at Hip Hop today. Studying the history of Hip Hop should only whet one's appetite to study its forbearers in other kinds of Afro-American entertainment. And, when better understood, it should provide an understanding that better connects us with previous and future generations—rather than separating us.

This collection of writing about Hip Hop is intended to provide a general history and backdrop of information that could easily be adopted as a textbook for a Hip Hop course in several different departments. There is plenty of historical information included in these pieces, and most of the important moments and personalities in Hip Hop's history are covered. The intent, however, is not necessarily to provide a comprehensive history, but to tell the story with different voices. The beauty of this anthology is that it covers the subject from a variety of viewpoints, including those of writers with wildly varying styles and agendas. With that aim in mind, it was deemed valuable to allow some limited amount of overlap from article to article. It is also expected that the lecturer or professor may need to augment the material with his or her lectures. Some of the writing is academically dry and rather meticulous. On the other hand, some of the writing has an almost "fanzine" kind of sensationalism. Some of the writing is intended to be objective history, and some of it is intended to be an impassioned defense against Hip Hop's critics. The author's background, point of view and motivation should always be kept in mind as the reader moves from selection to selection. While some of Hip Hop's most famous writers are unfortunately not represented here, the authors that do contribute to this anthology include many of Hip Hop's most respected journalists and historians. It is, of course, hoped that each selection will inspire further discussion, debate and research, and perhaps even a complete reading of the source from which the article was drawn.

The first two selections in the anthology are intended to introduce the subject and the parameters of the discussion, as well as to outline the current dilemma in which Hip Hop now finds itself. There is a short discussion of Hip Hop's most prevalent criticisms and defenses and an attempt at defining a Hip Hop aesthetic.

The next three selections describe Hip Hop's roots and emergence from the squalor of the Bronx in the 1970s. The following three selections describe Hip Hop's emergence as a national and global phenomenon. The fourth section describes Hip Hop's maturation as serious art and lucrative commerce, and finally, the last section points out Hip Hop's diversity and crossover potential. If Duke Ellington were alive, he would probably gleefully point out that like the music he loved, Hip Hop also defies categorization.

PART ONE

Aesthetics

The Hip Hop Wars

By Tricia Rose

Tricia Rose teaches twentieth-and twenty-first-century African-American culture, music, and gender issues at Brown University. Besides *The Hip Hop Wars* she is also the author of the seminal *Black Noise*.

The introduction to Tricia Rose's book *The Hip Hop Wars* makes the perfect introduction to our anthology of Hip Hop writings as well. Rose describes her book as "a sometimes polemical, always passionate assessment of where we are, what's wrong with the conversation we are having about Hip Hop, why it matters and how to fix it." (page 29). The two basic tenets of her introduction are first, that the commercial success of contemporary rap records has severely limited the scope and subject matter of Hip Hop. This may be true to the extent that Hip Hop may have lost its role as the platform for the discussion and resolution of African-Americans' problems. In the process, Hip Hop may have become merely another avenue to perpetuate negative racial caricatures and stereotypes and exploit white people's fascination for images of African-American crime, gangsters, drugs and misogyny. These negative images, Rose maintains, not only adversely affect the progress of African-Americans on their journey towards true equality, but also reinforce the negative stereotypes held by the white community. Sometimes, unfortunately, these images reinforce the myth that African-Americans may ultimately be the cause of their own problems. The second theme of her introduction is that the debate we are having over Hip Hop and its role, not only in the African-American community, but in society in general, has become so polarized and emotional that finding and defending some sort of middle ground is becoming increasingly more difficult.

The real value of this piece is not necessarily to be found in the answers she offers up in her book, so much as her accurate and perceptive assessment of the current predicament and the questions it poses—questions that we may find ultimately unanswerable, but unquestionably engaging. The most important question she asks is, of course, "How do these negative images sold under the auspices of a Hip Hop 'reality' affect the everyday reality of life in the ghetto?" Does the seductive glamour of success in the record business inspire and promote crime, drugs, gangs and misogyny, or do our rap stars merely document the ugly truth of the world they represent? Some form of this same question has probably been argued since the muses and the early Greeks first started discussing the role of art and music in our world. There is truth on both sides of the argument, of course. There is no question that as consumers, we are drawn to the sensationalism of sex and crime and that the industry exploits that—as well as our collective curiosity about the ugly, hidden truths of ghetto life—by exaggerating and glorifying many of the gory details. The real question is: How seriously should we take all of this? Is "gangsta" rap ultimately any more dangerous than horror movies or comic books or heavy metal, or any of the other cultural forms that have been accused of destroying the moral fabric of our society? Is "gangsta" rap to be interpreted as literal truth, or is it just another metaphor for the beguiling "other world" that we all want to experience vicariously? These questions are actually quite complex, and Rose would argue that the polarization of opinions on both sides tends to over-simplify the issue rather than unraveling its complexity. Unfortunately, attacks on rap records and Hip Hop have become excuses to attack youth culture (primarily black youth culture) in general. In the 1950s, rock and roll was blamed for the moral decay of what some viewed as a threatening new generation. In the 1920s, it was jazz. All of those kids have grown up. They have unceremoniously discarded some of their parents' values and mores, while tenaciously retaining others. The question remains, is our world ultimately better or worse because of these youthful rebellions and the changes they bring?

More specifically, Rose's introduction also describes in detail the technological and corporate changes of the 1990s that have enabled, or perhaps been the direct cause of, the commercialization of Hip Hop. The result, Rose argues, has been a narrowing range of themes, a depletion of meaningful content, and the exploitation of negative images. One might call this a general "dumbing down," or pandering to popular taste. Rose gives us five key factors she believes are responsible for the current "toxic conditions." She also lists what she calls the Hip Hop Top Ten. The public debate about Hip Hop, she says, always revolves around these ten arguments: Five criticisms and five defenses. Each of these eventually becomes a separate chapter in her book, and all of them are excellent topics for thought, research and discussion.

"INTRODUCTION" FROM *THE HIP HOP WARS*

I'd like to say to all the industry people out there that control what we call hip hop, I'd like for people to put more of an effort to make hip hop the culture of music that it was, instead of the culture of violence that it is right now. There's a lot of people that put in a lot of time, you know the break-dancers, the graffiti artists, there's people rapping all over the world. … All my life I've been into hip hop, and it should mean more than just somebody standing on the corner selling dope—I mean that may or may not have its place too because it's there, but I'm just saying—I ain't never shot nobody, I ain't never stabbed nobody, I'm forty-five years old and I ain't got no criminal record, you know what I mean? The only thing I ever did was be about my music. So I mean, so, while we're teaching people what it is about life in the ghetto, then we should be teaching people about what it is about life in the ghetto, me trying to grow up and to come up out of the ghetto. And we need everybody's help out there to make that happen.

—Melle Mel, lead rapper of and main songwriter for the seminal rap group Grandmaster Flash and the Furious Five, in an acceptance speech during the group's induction into the Rock and Roll Hall of Fame, March 2007

HIP HOP IS in a terrible crisis. Although its overall fortunes have risen sharply, the most commercially, promoted and financially successful hip hop—what has dominated mass-media outlets, such as television, film, radio, and recording industries for a dozen years or so—has increasingly become a playground for caricatures of black gangstas, pimps, and hoes. Hyper-sexism has increased dramatically, and homophobia along with distorted, antisocial, self-destructive, and violent portraits of black masculinity have become rap's calling cards. Relying on an ever-narrowing range of images and themes, this commercial juggernaut has played a central role in the near-depletion of what was once a vibrant, diverse, and complex popular genre, wringing it dry by pandering to America's racist and sexist lowest common denominator.

This scenario differs vastly from the wide range of core images, attitudes, and icons that defined hip hop during its earlier years of public visibility. In the 1980s, when rap's commercial value began to develop steam, gangsta rappers were only part of a much larger iconic tapestry. There were many varieties of equally positioned styles of rap—gangsta as well as party, political, afrocentric, and avant-garde, each with multiple substyles as well. However, not only were many styles of rap driven out of the corporate-promoted main stream, but since the middle to late 1990s, the social, artistic, and political significance of figures like the gangsta and street hustler substantially devolved into apolitical, simple-minded, almost comic stereotypes. Indeed, by the late 1990s, most of the affirming, creative stories and characters that had stood at the defining core of hip hop had been gutted. To use a hip hop metaphor, they were driven underground, buried, and left to be dug up only by the most deeply invested fans and artists.

Gangstas, hustlers, street crimes, and vernacular sexual insults (e.g., calling black women "hoes") were part of hip hop's storytelling long before the record industry really got the hang of promoting rap music. Gangstas and hustlers were not invented out of whole cloth by corporate executives: Prior to the ascendance of corporate mainstream hip hop, these figures were more complex and ambivalent. A few were interesting social critics. Some early West Coast gangsta rappers—N.W.A., and W.C. and the Maad Circle, for example—featured stories that emphasized being trapped by gang life and spoke about why street crime had become a "line of work" in the context of chronic black joblessness. Thwarted desires for safe communities and meaningful work were often embedded in street hustling tales.

Eventually, though, the occasional featuring of complicated gangstas, hustlers, and hoes gave way to a tidal wave of far more simplistic, disproportionately celebratory, and destructive renderings of these characters. Hip hop has become buried by these figures and the life associated with them.

This trend is so significant that if the late Tupac Shakur were a newly signed artist today, I believe he'd likely be considered a socially conscious rapper and thus relegated to the margins of the commercial hip hop field. Tupac (who despite his death in 1996 remains one of hip hop's most visible and highly regarded gangsta rappers) might even be thought of as too political and too "soft." Even as he expressed his well-known commitment to "thug life," his rhymes are perhaps too thoughtful for mainstream "radio friendly" hip hop as it has evolved since his death.

This consolidation and "dumbing down" of hip hop's imagery and storytelling took hold rather quickly in the middle to late 1990s and reached a peak in the early 2000s. The hyper-gangsta-ization of the music and imagery directly parallels hip hop's sales ascendance into the mainstream record and radio industry. In the early to middle 1990s, following the meteoric rise of West Coast hip hop music producer Dr. Dre and of N.W.A., widely considered a seminal gangsta rap group, West Coast gangsta rap solidified and expanded the already well-represented street criminal icons—thug, hustler, gangster, and pimp—in a musically compelling way. This grab bag of street criminal figures soon became the most powerful and, to some, the most "authentic" spokesmen for hip hop and, then, for black youth generally.

For the wider audience in America, which relies on mainstream outlets for learning about and participating in commercially distributed pop culture, hip hop has become a breeding ground for the most explicitly exploitative and increasingly one-dimensional narratives of black ghetto life. The gangsta life and all its attendant violence, criminality, sexual "deviance," and misogyny have, over the last decade especially, stood at the heart of what appeared to be ever-increasing hip hop record sales. Between 1990 and 1998, the Recording Industry Association of America (RIAA) reported that rap captured, on average, 9–10 percent of music sales in the United States. This figure increased to 12.9 percent in 2000, peaked at 13.8 percent in 2002, and hovered between 12 and 13 percent through 2005. To put the importance of this nearly 40 percent increase in rap/hip hop sales into context, note that during the 2000–2005 period, other genres, including rock, country, and pop, saw decreases in their market percentage. The rise in rap/hip hop was driven primarily by the sale of images and stories of black ghetto life to white youth: According to Mediamark Research Inc., increasing numbers of whites began buying hip hop at this point. Indeed, between 1995 and 2001, whites comprised 70–75 percent of the hip hop customer base—a figure considered to have remained broadly constant to this day.[1]

I am not suggesting that all commercial hip hop fits this description, nor do I think that there is no meaningful content in commercial hip hop. I am also not suggesting that commercially successful gangsta-style artists such as Jay-Z, Ludacris, 50 Cent, T.I., and Snoop Dogg lack talent. It is, in fact, rappers' lyrical and performative talents and the compelling music that frames their rhymes—supported by heavy corporate promotion—that make this seduction so powerful and disturbing. They and many others whose careers are based on these hip hop images are quite talented in different ways: musically, lyrically, stylistically, and as entrepreneurs. The problems facing commercial hip hop today are not caused by individual rappers alone; if we focus on merely one rapper, one song, or one video for its sexist or gangsta-inspired images we miss the forest for the trees. Rather, this is about the larger and more significant trend that has come to define commercial hip hop as a whole: The trinity of commercial hip hop—the black gangsta, pimp, and ho—has been promoted and accepted to the point where it now dominates the genre's storytelling worldview.

The expanded commercial space of these three street icons has had a profound impact on both the direction of the music and the conversation about hip hop—a conversation that has never been *just* about hip hop. On the one hand, the increased profitability of the gangsta-pimp-ho trinity has inflamed already riled critics who perceive hip hop as the cause of many social ills; but, on the other, it has encouraged embattled defenders to tout hip hop's organic connection to black youth and to venerate its market successes as examples pulling oneself up by the bootstraps. The hyperbolic and polarized public conversation about hip hop that has emerged over the past decade discourages progressive and nuanced consumption, participation, and critique, thereby contributing to the very crisis that is facing hip hop. Even more important, this conversation has become a powerful vehicle for the channeling of broader public discussion about race, class, and the value of black culture's role in society. Debates about hip hop have become a means for defining poor, young black people and thus for interpreting the context and reasons for their clearly disadvantaged lives. This is what we talk about when we talk about hip hop.

THE STATE OF THE CONVERSATION ON HIP HOP

The excessive blame leveled at hip hop is astonishing in its refusal to consider the culpability of the larger social and political context. To many hot-headed critics of hip hop, structural forms of deep racism, corporate influences, and the long-term effects of economic, social, and political disempowerment are not meaningfully related to rappers' alienated, angry stories about life in the ghetto; rather, they are seen as "proof" that black behavior creates ghetto conditions. So decades of urban racial discrimination (the reason black ghettos exist in the first place), in every significant arena—housing, education, jobs, social services—in every city with a significant black population, simply disappear from view. In fact, many conservative critics of hip hop refuse to acknowledge that the ghetto is a systematic matrix of racial, spatial, and class discrimination that has defined black city life since the first half of the twentieth century, when the Great Black Migration dramatically reshaped America's cities. For some, hip hop itself is a black-created problem that promotes unsafe sex and represents sexual amorality, infects "our" culture and society, advocates crime and criminality, and reflects black cultural dysfunction and a "culture of poverty." As hip hop's conservative critics would have it, hip hop is primarily responsible for every decline and crisis worldwide except the war in Iraq and global warming.

The defenses are equally jaw-dropping. For some, all expression in commercialized hip hop, despite its heavy manipulation by the record industry, is the unadulterated truth and literal personal experience of fill-in-the-blank rapper; it reflects reality in the ghetto; its lyrics *are the result of poverty itself*.[2] And my favorite, the most aggravating defense of commercial hip hop's fixation on demeaning black women for sport—"well, there *are* bitches and hoes." What do fans, artists, and writers mean when they defend an escalating, highly visible, and extensive form of misogyny against black women by claiming that there *are* bitches and hoes? And how have they gotten away with this level of hateful labeling of black women for so long?

The big media outlets that shape this conversation, such as Time/Warner, News Corporation, Bertelsmann, General Electric, and Viacom, do not frame hip hop's stories in ways that allow for a serious treatment of sexism, racism, corporate power, and the real historical forces that have created ghettos. When well-informed, progressive people do get invited to appear, on news and public affairs programs, they wind up being pushed into either "pro" or "con" positions—and as a result, the complexity of what they have to say to one side or the other is reduced. Although the immaturity of "beef" (conflict between rappers for media attention and street credibility) is generally considered a hip hop phenomenon, it actually mirrors much of the larger mainstream media's approach to issues of conflict and disagreement. Developing a thoughtful, serious, and educated position in this climate is no easy task, since most participants defend or attack the music—and, by extension, young black people—with a fervor usually reserved for religion and patriotism.

WHY WE SHOULD CARE ABOUT HIP HOP

The inability to sustain either a hard-hitting, progressive critique of hip hop's deep flaws or an appreciation for its extraordinary gifts is a real problem, with potentially serious effects that ripple far beyond the record industry and mass-media corporate balance sheets. We have the opportunity to use the current state of commercial hip hop as a catalyst to think with more care about the terms of cross-racial exchanges and the role of black culture in a mass-mediated world. Indeed, we should be asking larger questions about how hip hop's commercial trinity of the gangsta, pimp, and ho relates to American culture more generally. But, instead, we have allowed hip hop to be perceived by its steadfast defenders as a whipping boy (unfairly beaten for all things wrong with American society and blamed as a gateway to continued excessive criticisms of black people's behavior) and charged by its critics as society's career criminal (responsible for myriad social ills and finally being caught and brought to trial). Not much beyond exhaustion, limited, and one-sided vicious critique, and nearly blind defense is possible in this context. Very little honest and self-reflective vision can emerge from between this rock and hard place.

Why should we care about hip hop and how should we talk about it? Serial killer, whipping boy, whatever, right? It's just entertainment—it generates good ratings and makes money for rappers and the sputtering record industry, but it doesn't matter beyond that. Or does it? In fact, it matters a great deal, even for those who don't listen to or enjoy the music itself. Debates about hip hop stand in for discussion of significant social issues related to race, class, sexism, and black culture. Hip hop's commercial trinity has become the fuel that propels public criticism of young black people. According to some critics, if we just got rid of hip hop and the bad behavior it supports (so the argument goes), "they'd" all do better in school, and structurally created racism and disadvantage would disappear like vapor. This hyper-behavioralism—an approach that overemphasizes individual action and underestimates the impact of institutionalized forms of racial and class discrimination—feeds the very systematic discrimination it pretends isn't a factor at all.

The public debates about hip hop have also become a convenient means by which to avoid the larger, more entrenched realities of sexism, homophobia, and gender inequality in U.S. society. By talking about these issues almost exclusively in the context of hip hop, people who wouldn't otherwise dare to talk about sexism, women's rights, homophobia, or the visual and cultural exploitation of women for corporate profit insinuate that hip hop itself is sexist and homophobic and openly criticize it for being so. It's as if black teenagers have smuggled sexism and homophobia into American culture, bringing them in like unauthorized imports.

This conversation about the state of hip hop matters for another reason as well: We have arrived at a landmark moment in modern culture when a solid segment (if not a majority) of an entire generation of African-American youth understands itself as defined primarily by a musical, cultural form. Despite the depth of young black people's love of the blues, jass, and R&B throughout various periods in the twentieth century, no generation has ever dubbed itself the "R&B generation" or the "jazz generation," thereby tethering its members to all things (good and bad) that might be associated with the music. Yet young people have limited their creative possibilities, as well as their personal identities, to the perimeters established by the genre of hip hop. No black musical form before hip hop—no matter how much it "crossed over" into mainstream American culture—ever attracted the level of corporate attention and mainstream media visibility, control, and intervention that characterizes hip hop today. It is now extremely common for hip hop fans of all racial and ethnic backgrounds, especially, black fans, to consider themselves more than fans. They're people who "live and breathe hip hop every day."

This level of single-minded investment, forged in the context of sustained blanket attacks on hip hop music and culture, makes objective critique nearly impossible. Of course, this investment is itself partly a response to the deep level of societal disregard that so many young, poor minority kids experience. As Jay-Z says in the remixed version of Talib Kweli's "Get By," "Why listen to a system that never listens to me?" For anyone who feels this way about anything (religion, patriotism, revolution, etc.), critical self-reflection is hard to come by. The more under attack one feels, the greater the refusal to render self-critique is likely to be. But such fervor is also the result of market manipulation that fuels exaggerated brand loyalty and confuses it with black radicalism by forging bonds to corporate hip hop icons who appear to be "keeping it real" and representing the 'hood. In turn, the near-blind loyalty of hip hop fans is exploited by those who have pimped hip hop out to the highest bidder. Members of the hip hop generation are now facing the greatest media machinery and most veiled forms of racial, economic, sexual, and gender rhetoric in modern history; they need the sharpest critical tools to survive and thrive.

Another reason this conversation is important is that the perceptions we have about hip hop—what it is, why it is the way it is—have been used as evidence against poor urban black communities themselves. Using hip hop as "proof" of black people's culpability for their circumstances undermines decades of solid and significant research on the larger structural forces that have plagued black urban communities. The legacy of the systemic destruction of working-class and poor African-American communities has reached a tragic new low in the past thirty years.

Since the early 1980s, this history has been rewritten, eclipsed by the idea that black people and their "culture" (a term that is frequently used when "behavior" should be) are the cause of their condition and status. Over the last three decades, the public conversation has decidedly moved toward an easy acceptance of black ghetto existence and the belief that black people themselves are responsible for creating ghettos and for choosing to live in them, thus absolving the most powerful segments of society from any responsibility in the creation and maintenance of them. Those who deny the legacy of systematic racism or refuse to connect the worst of what hip hop expresses to this history and its devastating effects on black community are leveling unacceptable and racist attacks on black people.

The generalized hostility against hip hop impinges on the interpretation of other visible forms of black youth culture. For instance, black NBA players are tainted as a group for being part of the hip hop generation stylistically, no matter their personal actions. The few who have committed violent or criminal acts "prove" the whole lot of them worthy of attack. In a league that has mostly black players and mostly white fans, this becomes a racially charged (and racially generated) revenue problem. Such group tainting does not occur among white athletes or fans. The National Hockey League, a league that is predominantly white (in terms of both fans and players) and experiences far more incidents of game-related violence (they take timeouts to brawl!) is rarely described as problematically violent. Indeed, no matter how many individual white men get in trouble with the law, white men as a group are not labeled a cultural problem. At a more local level, hip hop gear, while considered tame—even cute—on middle-class white wearers, is seen as threatening on black and brown youth, who can't afford not to affiliate with hip hop style if they are going to have any generational credibility.

In short, the conversation about hip hop matters a great deal. Our cultural perceptions and associations have been harmful to black working-class and poor youth—the most vulnerable among us. The polarized conversation also provokes the increasing generation gap in the black community—an age gap that, in past eras, was trumped by cross-generational racial solidarity. But I wonder, too, if the effects of corporate consolidation—and of the new generational and genre-segregated market-niche strategies that dismantled the multi-generational and cross-genre formats that defined black radio in the past—have exaggerated, if not manufactured, the development of a contentious generational divide in the black community.

Who is hurt by our misunderstandings of hip hop? Surely, all of American society is negatively affected by both the antagonism leveled against it and the direction that commercial hip hop has taken. If we continue to talk about black people and race generally in near-parodic terms, our nation will not overcome its racial Achilles' heel; the American democratic promise, as yet unfulfilled, will end up an irreparable, broken covenant. The current state of conversation about hip hop sets destructive and illiterate terms for cross-racial community building. The people *most* injured by the fraught, hostile, and destructive state of this conversation are those who most need a healthy, honest, vibrant (not sterile and repressed) cultural space: young, poor, and working-class African-American boys and girls, men and women—the generation that comprises the future of the black community. They have the biggest stake in the conversation, and they get the shortest end of the stick in it.

In this climate, young people have few visible and compassionate yet unflinchingly honest places to turn to for a meaningful appreciation and critique of the youth culture in which they are so invested. The attacks on black youth through hip hop maintain economic and racial injustice. Many working-class and poor black young people have come up in black urban communities that have been dismantled by decades-long legacies of policy-driven devastation of such communities. This devastation takes many forms, including urban and federal retreat from affordable housing, undermining of antidiscrimination laws that were designed to end structural racism, police targeting, racially motivated escalations of imprisonment, and reductions in support for what are still mostly segregated and deeply unequal public schools. Very little of this history is common knowledge, and critics avoid serious discussion of these factors, focusing instead on rappers and the ghettos they supposedly represent.

The defenses of hip hop are also destructive. The same media that pump commercial hip hop 24/7 fail to take the time to expose the crucial contexts of post-civil rights era ghetto segregation for hip hop's development. Rappers and industry moguls who profit enormously from hip hop's gangsta-pimp-ho trinity defend their empires purportedly in the interests of black youth. The constant excuses made about sexism, violence, and homophobia in hip hop are not just defenses *of* black people via hip hop; they are hurtful *to* black people. Corporate media outlets empower these businessmen-rappers, underpromote the more sophisticated rhymes, and play down the vigorous and well-informed analysis and criticism. Many fans consume lopsided tales of black ghetto life with little knowledge about the historical creation of the ghetto; some think the ghetto equals black culture. These decisions not only dumb down the music but minimize fan knowledge and constrain the conversation as a whole.

The public conversation is both an engine for and a product of the current state of commercial hip hop. Driven by one-dimensional sound bites from the polarized camps—a format designed to perpetuate a meaningless and imbalanced form of "presenting both sides"—this conversation is not only contributing to the demise of hip hop but has also impoverished our ability to talk successfully about race and about the role of popular culture, mass media, and corporate conglomerates in defining—and confirming—our creative expressions.

Versions of what has happened to hip hop that include both the ways that hip hop reflects black and brown lived experience and creativity *and* represents market and racial manipulation have been, thus far, destined for media obscurity. It is as if the real sport of our conversation about hip hop is mutual denial and hostile engagement. Intelligent, nuanced dialogue has been drowned out by the simple-minded sound bites that sustain this antagonistic divide.

Advocates and supportive critics have made a valiant effort to participate in this conversation in complex, subtle, and meaningful ways. Many writers, journalists, poets, scholars, and activists have made important contributions to the popular, literary, and scholarly treatments of hip hop. Michael Eric Dyson, Davey D, bell hooks, Mark Anthony Neal, Patricia Hill-Collins, Cornel West, Adam Mansbach, Jeff Chang, Dream Hampton, Scott Poulson-Bryant, Oliver Wang, Nelson George, Gwendolyn Pough, Imani Perry, Jeffery Ogbar, Paul Porter, Greg Tate, Marcyliena Morgan, Lisa Fager Bediako, Angela Ards, Kevin Powell, George Lipsitz, Robin Kelley, Bakari Kitwana, Joan Morgan, and Kelefah Sanneh have all offered insightful reflections on and analyses of hip hop in their respective fields. Several others have contributed blogs and other web commentaries that try to sort through the current state of hip hop in a productive way. But these writers and scholars are not being relied upon to frame the mainstream conversation.

The terms of this conversation need our direct attention because they keep black youth and progressive thinkers and activists locked into one-sided positions and futile battle. If we fail to address its contradictions, denials, and omissions, we will become subjected to and defined by the limits of the conversation rather than proactive participants in shaping it. I want to delineate the key features—the broadest strokes—of this conversation, since the micro-struggles in which hip hop gets embroiled usually cover up the larger terms that perpetuate tiresome and disabling conflict.

This conversation is an integral part of the current state of commercial hip hop. But to properly situate the conversation, we need to account for the larger forces driving the changes in hip hop. Why has the black gangsta-pimp-ho trinity been the vehicle for hip hop's greatest sales and highest market status? Why did a substyle based on hustling, crime, sexual domination, and drug dealing become rap's cultural and economic calling card and thus the key icon for the hip hop generation? Familiar answers like industry manipulation and racism contain important truths but gloss over five key factors that have worked synergistically to create these toxic conditions:

- New technologies and new music markets
- Massive corporate consolidation
- Expansion of illicit street economies
- America's post-civil rights appetite for racially stereotyped entertainment
- Violence and sexually explicit misogyny as "valued" cultural products

Together, these five factors explain the complicated forces that have grossly distorted the legacy of hip hop while also contributing to the conversation about it. Whereas the final three are discussed in the context of the various debates about hip hop that I examine in the chapters that follow, the first two—the role of new technologies and new music markets and the unprecedented impact of massive corporate consolidation—have a systemic effect on the entire field of discussion, and so their inclusion in this introduction is warranted. For now, let us simply note that the debates that have played out in the hip hop wars mask the full depth of the corporate and economic circumstances that redirected commercial hip hop, with an especially dramatic turn taken in the middle to late 1990s.

NEW TECHNOLOGIES, NEW MUSIC MARKETS

Hip hop came of age at the beginning of a new technological revolution. After the late 1970s, when hip hop emerged onto the public scene, all forms of media technology exponentially expanded. Network television met stiff competition as cable televisions' hundreds of niche market-driven cable stations increased market share, especially as music became a predominantly visual medium (MTV and BET served as major anchors for this shift). Our listening format changed from records to CDs and computer technology. Advanced recording and digital technology became widely accessible to independent artists, producers, and consumers, changing the way music was made, purchased, consumed, shared, distributed, and stolen. Today, cell phones are MP3 players, with downloads and ringtones representing yet another expansion of the music market. These changes have made room for additional independent record labels and more local music production and distribution (at less cost and greater profits), thereby sustaining genres that might have been impossible to maintain solely with local support before this revolution took place.

Hip hop, like nearly all black musical forms that preceded it, began as a commercially marginal music that was subjected to segregated treatment and underfunding. It was characterized by smaller production and promotion budgets along with the assumption that the rap audience would be a youthful segment of African-Americans—an already proportionately small consumer market—and an even smaller percentage of whites and other ethnic groups. During the 1980s, when rap artists were developing commercial appeal, traditional but highly irregular sales measures were still being used—measures that especially underrepresented fan interest in unconventional music. As *New York Times* writer Neil Strauss described it: "Until 1991 the pop music charts were notoriously unreliable. Paying off record store employees with free albums, concert tickets, and even vacations and washing machines was the standard music-business method of manipulating record sales figures. Even the Billboard magazine charts, considered the most prestigious in the business, were compiled from the store managers' oral reports, which were inaccurate to begin with and easily swayed."[3]

In 1991, Soundscan, a sales measurement system that tracks album purchases at their point of sale, was introduced. Although new methods of sales figure manipulation were eventually developed by record industry sales executives, new and explosive information emerged with the advent of Soundscan: Two renegade genres, hard rock and rap, came in at the top of the charts, showing the greatest actual sales and outstripping mainstream pop acts. Two weeks after the advent of Soundscan, Paula Abdul's "Spellbound" was "replaced at the top by the Los Angeles rap group N.W.A.'s 'Efil4zaggin',' which had appeared on the chart at No. 2 the previous week."[4]

Soundscan initiated a dramatic reconsideration of what the record industry believed mainstream youth wanted to purchase; the results indicated that large numbers of young white consumers (whose consumption drove pop chart positions) wanted to hear gangsta-oriented rap music and would support it heartily. This encouraged an increase in record label investment in hip hop production, distribution, and promotion on radio, especially for gangsta rap. Radio was considered the big breakthrough for hard-edged rap. Veteran radio and music programmer Glen Ford—co-owner and (from 1987 to 1994) host of *Rap It Up*, the first nationally syndicated radio hip hop music program—draws crucial connections between the new data about consumption and the new corporate strategy for promoting gangsta rap:

> By 1990 the major labels were preparing to swallow the independent labels that had birthed commercial hip hop, which had evolved into a wondrous mix of party, political and "street"-aggressive subsets. One of the corporate labels (I can't remember which) conducted a study that shocked the industry: The most "active" consumers of Hip Hop, they discovered, were "tweens," the demographic slice between the ages of 11 and 13. The numbers were unprecedented. Even in the early years of Black radio, R&B music's most "active" consumers were at least two or three years older than "tweens." It didn't take a roomful of PhDs in human development science to grasp the ramifications on the data. Early and pre-adolescents of both genders are sexual-socially undeveloped—uncertain and afraid of the other gender. Tweens revel in honing their newfound skills in profanity; they love to curse. Males, especially, act out their anxieties about females through aggression and derision. This is the cohort for which the major labels would package their hip hop products. Commercial Gangsta Rap was born—a sub-genre that would lock a whole generation in perpetual arrested social development.[5]

In 1993, Bill Stephney, a well-respected musician, producer and promoter known for his ground-breaking work with political rap group Public Enemy, saw older teens being targeted as well. "It's a function of the culture," Stephney noted in connection with industry decisions that had driven hard rap's triumph over the FM airwaves. "You now have the prime 18-to 24-year-old demographic people who grew up only on rap music, whether they be black, Latino or white, Radio has decided they want to target this generation, and that rap music is the music they're gonna program. … The radio stations have had to play it; advertisers have had to deal with it; and corporate America has understood it."[6] In the context of new technologies and the expansion of media markets, this new interest in gangsta rap as a mainstream profit stream moved swiftly into a multitude of markets and related products.

MASSIVE CORPORATE CONSOLIDATION

During this same period, the consolidation of mass-media industries, aided by ongoing government deregulation, began to pick up steam. Regulations designed to prevent monopolization were overturned and large-scale consolidation in and across various media industries took place in a very short period of time. Consolidation within a given industry (when one or two record companies merge) gave way to single corporations with dominant holdings in all mass media, from newspapers, television, and musical venues to publishing houses, movies, magazines, and radio stations. As late as the early 1980s, these industries operated relatively independent of one another and encompassed many internally competitive companies. Media scholar Ben Bagdikian put it like this:

> In 1983, the men and women who headed the fifty mass media corporations that dominated American audiences could have fit comfortably in a modest ballroom. The people

heading the twenty dominant newspaper chains probably would form one conversational cluster to complain about newsprint prices … the broadcast network people in another … etc. By 2003, five men controlled all these media once run by the fifty corporations of twenty years earlier. These five, owners of additional digital corporations, could fit in a generous phone booth.[7]

Five conglomerates—Time/Warner, Disney, Viacom, Newscorporation, and Bertelsmann (of Germany)—now control the vast majority of the media industry in the United States. (General Electric is a close sixth.) Viacom, for example, owns MTV, VHI, and BET, along with CBS radio, which operates 140 radio stations in large radio markets. The four biggest music conglomerates (each made up of many record companies) are Warner Music, EMI, Sony/BMG, and Universal Music Group. Together they control about 70 percent of the music market worldwide and about 80 percent of the music market in America. A multitude of artists have contracts with the companies that fall within these vast media categories. While rappers seem to be on a wide variety of labels and in different and competing camps and groups of subaffiliated artists, in fact many artists labor underneath one large corporate umbrella. For example, Warner Music (which falls under Time Warner) has more than forty music labels including Warner Brothers (where rappers such as Crime Mob, E-40, Talib Kweli, and Lil' Flip are signed); Atlantic (where rappers such as Flo Rida, Webbie, Twista, Trick Daddy, Plies, Diddy, and T.I. are signed), Elektra, London-Sire, Bad Boy, and Rhino Records, to name just a few. Even a high-profile "beef" such as the one between rappers The Game and 50 Cent looks somewhat tamer when one considers that The Game, whose music is distributed by Geffen, and 50 Cent, whose music is distributed by Interscope, are both included under the Universal Music Group parent company.[8]

Mass-media consolidation was rendered even more profound for the record industry after the Telecommunications Act of 1996. Although it enabled dramatic consolidation of ownership within the radio industry, the music industry's key promotional and sales-generating venue, the Telecommunications Act was described by many of its supporters as a telephone industry bill designed to allow Baby Bell phone companies to get into long-distance service, spur competition, and deregulate cable rates. Included in this sweeping act, though, was a nearly buried provision that lifted all ownership caps for radio-station broadcasters across the nation and permitted companies to operate as many as eight stations in the largest markets. Previously, broadcasters could own only forty stations nationwide, and only two in a given market. But now, with such limited restrictions, wealthy and powerfully connected investors, were able to snap up a dizzying number of radio stations in an incredibly short period of time. By the end of 1996, ownership of 2,157 radio stations had changed hands. And as of 2001, 10,000 radio transactions worth approximately $100 billion had taken place.[9]

Until this point, a relatively large network of small-to medium-sized local radio-station owners were accountable to the public and its local musical, cultural, religious, newscasting, community, and political needs. Now, our public airwaves are profoundly dominated by a small number of very large national and international corporations. According to a study published by the Future of Music Coalition, "Ten parent companies dominate the radio spectrum, radio listenership and radio revenues. … Together these ten parent companies control two-thirds of both listeners and revenue nationwide." Clear Channel is the mightiest of them all, owning a dramatic 1,240 radio stations nationwide, thirty times more than previous congressional regulation allowed. With more than 100 million listeners, Clear Channel reaches over one-third of the U.S. population.[10]

This consolidation has affected radio programming in many ways, including a higher consolidation of playlists within and across formats, higher levels of repetition of record industry—chosen songs, homogenized and in some cases automated programming, and the near erasure of local, non-record-industry-sponsored artists. Large corporations profit from maintaining high levels of efficiency and consistency, which help them maintain the widest possible market share. Both efficiency and consistency of product encourage cuts in local staffing as well as in idiosyncratic programming such as local acts and news that cannot be packaged and rebroadcast elsewhere. Commercially established major-label acts, because of their visibility and notoriety, are easily packaged for a national audience and easily transportable across regions. Thus they dominate their genre-specific playlists across the country.

Officially speaking, record stores are the primary sales venue for recorded music; in reality, radio stations and music video programs provide the bulk of music promotion and sales. Radio and music video airplay are at the heart of artist visibility and record industry profits. Record companies try to convince owners and radio and music video program directors to play their artists' music in elaborate and ever-evolving ways. Consolidation of radio-station ownership focused and consolidated the record industry's "promotional" contracts with independent promoters, who do the radio-and television-station schmoozing and bribing on behalf of the record companies to encourage them to add their clients' songs to the stations' playlists. Instead of having to develop promotional relationships with hundreds of independent program directors, now record companies can negotiate with fewer corporate program directors who determine the playlists for dozens of stations around the country.

Industry-wide consolidation had a distinctive impact on black radio, and this in turn dramatically influenced the direction of commercial hip hop. Counting just those formats that emphasize hip hop/contemporary R&B (sometimes dubbed "hot urban" stations, with a target demographic of 12-to 24-year-olds), we find that Clear Channel, Radio One, and Emmis Radio have an astounding number of major urban markets covered. "Urban" is a euphemism for black music genres and markets. The stations listed below represent the depth of corporate consolidation of stations dedicated to playing hip hop on urban radio stations. Keep in mind that these lists comprise only the names of "hot urban"/hip hop-focused stations; other black urban music formats such as Rhythmic Adult Contemporary (with a target demographic of 18-to 34-year-olds) and Urban Adult Contemporary (with a target demographic of 29-to 45-year-olds) feature some hip hop but much more soul and R&B. Many of these other formatted stations are controlled by the same key players, however.

Clear Channel owns stations with the "hot urban"/hip hop and R&B format in nearly all major cities, many with large black populations, including Boston (94.5 WJMN), Chicago (107.5 WGCI), Columbus (98.3 WBFA), Detroit (98 WJLB), Memphis (97 WHRK), New Orleans (93.3 WQUE), New York (105.1 WWPR), Norfolk/Virginia Beach (102.9 WOWI), Oakland/San Francisco (106 KMEL), Philadelphia (99 WUSL), and Richmond (106.5 WBTJ). Emmis Radio owns 106 KPWR in Los Angeles and 97 WQHT in New York.

Radio One, the other major player in the hip hop radio market, is black owned and controls at least fifty-three urban music stations in sixteen markets, fourteen of which are hip hop focused. Radio One founder Catherine Hughes, who began as the owner of a small black radio station, carried out the legacy of black radio as a local community service operation—one among many of her roles and capacities. Despite this legacy, Radio One—given its need to remain profitable in the context of massive consolidation—has supported the record industry's drive to promote the consolidation of programming that includes destructive caricatures of black people. Radio One owns major hip hop stations in Atlanta (107.9 WHAT), Baltimore (92.3 WERQ), Cincinnati (101.1 WIZF), Cleveland (107.9 WENZ), Columbus (107.5 WCKX), Dallas (97.9 KBFB), Detroit (102.7 WHTD), Houston (97.9 KBXX), Indianapolis (96.3 WHHH), Philadelphia (100.3 (WPHI), Raleigh-Durham, NC (97.5 (WQOK), Richmond (92.1 WCDX), St Louis (104.1 WHHL), and Washington, D.C. (93.9 WKYS).

Consolidation had an especially negative impact on black radio news programming that went beyond the drastic reduction of news on all radio stations. Historically, black radio news programs played a powerful role in gathering and disseminating information about black social-justice issues that were largely omitted from other radio program formats. Such programs comprised a vital communication network for the civil rights movement, for example. Bruce Dixon, managing editor of the *Black Agenda Report*, describes the historical role of black radio as "a transmitter and conveyor, as the very circulatory system of public consciousness in African-American communities." The deep reductions in local news programming and journalism felt nationwide in commercial radio have cut into a crucial form of black social activism not easily replaced by other news media. Indeed, it could be argued that the absence of local news reports on such activism, coupled with the expansion of destructive and simple-minded fare, has negatively affected African-American public consciousness—specifically, by reducing black community knowledge about crucial issues.[11]

The consolidation of radio-station ownership not only raised the stakes for getting radio stations to play record companies' designated songs; it also resulted in greater airplay on a wider network of stations. The history of payola—paying to get your song played on the radio—is long and storied. The refusal of most people in the industry to publicly admit to it has rendered payola a shadowy but still powerful force, plied in sophisticated ways to evade payola-inspired laws. It is a crime for a radio-station employee to accept any sort of payment to play a song unless the radio station informs listeners about the exchange. Thus, record companies' direct method of paying for airplay has been replaced by the indirect method of payoff. Independent promotion firms (called "indies") are hired by record companies to "do promotion" at radio stations. As reporter Eric Boehlert explains: "In exchange for paying the station an annual promotion budget ($100,000 for a medium size market) the indie becomes the station's exclusive indie and gets paid by the record companies every time that station adds a new song. (Critics say it's nothing more than a sanitized quid pro quo arrangement—station adds a song, indie gets paid.)"[12]

In the case of urban music, considered by some the wild west of an industry widely perceived as corrupt and volatile, the money is less likely to go toward the radio's budget than to end up in the program director's hands—either as cash or in some other form of gifting. This arrangement takes place in both radio and music video programming, despite public denials from corporate executives. Reports that the practice is prevalent have been made by many industry insiders, nearly all of whom want to remain anonymous. In 2001, Eric Boehlert asked an urban industry insider whether payoff-taking is widespread. The latter replied: "What do you mean 'widespread'? It's all the [urban] stations everywhere."[13]

Paul Porter—a former radio and BET video programmer who, with Lisa Eager Bediako, co-founded Industry Ears, a nonprofit, nonpartisan, and independent organization that focuses on the impact of media on communities of color and children—has spoken openly about how payola works both at radio stations and at music video stations like BET:

> During my first week as program director at BET, I set up the playlist, deciding which videos would be played and how often. I cut the playlist from four hundred titles to a mere eighty because they had been playing any videos a record company sent over. Some industry executives were elated because their videos got more airplay; the others were furious. And if you were a record label executive, you needed to make sure I was happy. Almost everybody in this industry takes money. If they have the power to put a song on the radio or a video on television, they've been offered money to do it—and they've taken it. Maybe it's only been once or twice. But they've done it[14]

Porter admits to taking cash payments for adding songs and videos (which was standard operating procedure). He also reveals how the high cost of music videos raised sales expectations and thus expanded payoffs:

> Videos became so expensive. I just started noticing all the pressure when it came to adding videos, everybody wanted to be on BET since MTV wasn't playing anything black in those days. It started small, with sending you and your girl to Miami for the weekend first class, nice hotels, tickets to Knicks playoff games, offers to big ticket concerts in Europe. Then it just became money, flat-out straight money. I went to work in New York for two years and when I came back to BET in '99 as program director, the second week I was there I was staying in Hotel George and I got a call from the promoter who said, "Hey man, I'm sending you this package," it was for Arista records, right, and I'm like "cool," I've never met the guy blah blah blah—I got a FedEx on Saturday, I got fifteen grand! In an envelope![15]

In this era of massive corporate mergers, corrupt record industry promotional methods in collusion with radio stations are empowered and consolidated while independent black local musical culture and radio are subsumed or dismantled. Commercial hip hop is driven by this Byzantine system; gangstas, pimps, and hoes are products that promotional firms, working through record companies for corporate conglomerates, placed in high rotation.

While the swift consolidation and hyper-marketing of the hip hop trinity haven't entirely killed off more diverse portrayals, they have substantially reduced their space and their value. As a result, such portrayals are now harder to see, less commercially viable, and less associated with prestige and coolness. Veteran "conscious rapper" Paris was quoted as saying: "*What* underground? Do you know how much good material is marginalized because it doesn't fit white corporate America's ideals of acceptability? Independents can't get radio or video play anymore, at least not through commercial outlets, and most listeners don't acknowledge material that they don't see or hear regularly on the radio or on T.V."[16]

Throughout *The Hip Hop Wars*, when I use the phrase "commercial hip hop," I am not referring to any artist signed to a record company. In this market environment, nearly all artists who want to survive have to sign up to one label or another. "Commercial hip hop," then, refers to the heavy promotion of gangstas, pimps, and hoes churned out for mainstream consumption of hip hop.

Powerful corporate interests that dominate radio, television, record production, magazines, and all other related hip hop promotional venues are choosing to support and promote negative images above all others—all the while pretending that they are just conduits of existing conditions, and making excuses about these images being "reality."

Challenges that emphasize the role of corporate power are on the rise. In the face of sustained protests and opposition by individuals and interest groups such as Al Sharpton, the Enough Is Enough campaign, Spelman alum and Feminist Majority member Moya Bailey, and Industry Ears, mass-media executives have remained remarkably silent. In May 2007 Marcus Franklin reported in *USA Today* that Universal chairman Doug Morris and president Zach Horowitz declined repeated requests to discuss the issue, as did Warner chairman and chief executive Edgar Bronfman, Sony chairman Andrew Lack, chief executive Rolph Schmidt-Holtz, and EMI Group CEO Eric Nicoli.[17]

Cowardly silence aside, these executives could not have transformed commercial hip hop into a playground for destructive street icons alone. Clearly, the corporate takeover of commercial hip. Hop has also been facilitated, directly or indirectly, by artists (especially those who have become moguls and entrepreneurs) who gleefully rap about guns and bitches, liberal and conservative critics and academies, and journalists who uncritically profile these artists and hip hop fans of all races, classes, and genders. This shift was not instable; it was *allowed to* happen. We must be more honest in thinking about how black ghetto gangsta-based sales are the *result* of marketing manipulation and the *reflection* not only of specific realities in our poorest black urban communities but also of the *exploitation* of already-imbedded racist fears about black people.

"Mainstream" white America, black youth, black moguls (existing and aspiring), and big mass-media corporations together created hip hop's tragic trinity, the black gangsta, pimp, and ho—the cash cow that drove the big mainstream crossover for hip hop. Unless we deal with this part of the equation and see the dynamic as both new and very old—unless we acknowledge that racialized and sexualized fantasies and the money they generate for corporate mass media helped elevate this trinity in hip hop—well be back here again in no time, to a different black beat.

In the following chapters, readers will find the Hip Hop Top Ten: the top-ten arguments about hip hop, five from each side of the polarized debate. One way or another, the public debates about hip hop always come back to these ten issues. In each chapter, I will explore one of these favorite claims against and defenses of hip hop, challenging excesses, myths, denials, and manipulations as well as identifying the elements of truth that each argument contains.

Hip Hop's Critics
1. Hip Hop Causes Violence
2. Hip Hop Reflects Black Dysfunctional Ghetto Culture
3. Hip Hop Hurts Black People
4. Hip Hop Is Destroying America's Values
5. Hip Hop Demeans Women

Hip Hop's Defenders
6. Just Keeping It Real

7. Hip Hop Is Not Responsible for Sexism
8. "There Are Bitches and Hoes"
9. We're Not Role Models
10. Nobody Talks About the Positive in Hip Hop

There are two kinds of traps set by these popular, polarized, and partially true positions. I've already talked about their lack of complexity. But there is another trap: the hidden mutual denials on opposing sides of the debate. Indeed, the fact that critics and defenders share many underlying assumptions about hip hop only mires us more deeply within this conversation. In Chapter 11, I explore these mutual denials and discuss how they work to mask underlying attitudes shared by both sides. They direct our attention away from the ugly truths about ghetto fantasies and corporate influences, but also away from the kinds of progressive solutions that could nourish hip hop, open up opportunities for poor youth, and contribute to affirming multiracial vision.

Extraordinary creativity and possibility continue to come up through the narrow spaces that still remain. Not only do some artists find lyrically creative and community-affirming ways to make well-worn stories about street life seem renewed, but many brilliant artists and local community activists continue to write and perform rich, dynamic stories and trenchant political commentary, the likes of which listeners almost never hear on commercial radio. I will identify these marginalized but crucial artists and activists in Chapter 12. Among them are filmmaker Byron Hurt, director of the extraordinary film *Hip Hop: Beyond Beats and Rhymes,* who challenges fans as well as hip hop artists and their corporate representatives in powerful and progressive ways; Raquel Cepeda, whose fascinating film *Bling: A Planet Rock* connects U.S. consumption of diamonds to exploitation and violence and poverty in Sierra Leone; and rappers Lupe Fiasco and Jean Grae, whose music is funky, lyrically sophisticated, vibrant, and progressive. These filmmakers and artists are rarely promoted. They are given little airtime in mainstream media, and thus many readers might think they simply don't exist, might believe that the mainstream corporate rappers, producers, and promoters who support and excuse hip hop's most destructive elements are all there is to hip hop.

Hurt, Cepeda, Fiasco, Grae, and many others are part of the solution because they are developing hip hop generation—based progressive terms for the conversation about hip hop and encouraging community—affirming terms of creativity. Equally important, they are finding ways to critique hip hop without bashing the entire genre, to support hip hop without nourishing sexist, homophobic, or racist ideas or promoting economic exploitation of the communities from which hip hop comes.

Finally, if my point about our being trapped in the false oppositions sustained by our polarized conversation on hip hop has any value, it will generate some version of the following questions: What do we do next? How do we—those who have progressive visions and appreciate hip hop's gifts—participate, judge, critique, reject, and support hip hop? How can we help hip hop's youngest fans become conscious of what they are being fed and of its impact on them and their communities? How can we change the conversation and the terms of play in hip hop itself? Which position should we take up vis-à-vis hip hop, and on what should it be based?

To answer these questions, I conclude with six ideas for guiding progressive hip hop creativity and participation. So many of us are caught between rejecting hip hop and embracing it, while turning a blind eye to what has become the genre's greatest profit engines. The terms of embrace and rejection we often settle on are not clear, nor do they help us shape a progressive vision that can transform what we have now into what we might want to see in the future.

These ideas represent community-inspired standards marked by a balanced, loving, socially and politically progressive vision of creativity and black public thought, action, and reaction. Developing this vision isn't a repression of anger or sexuality or of artists telling their truths. On the contrary, it is a vehicle for encouraging creativity that does not revolve around hurling insults and perpetuating social injustices. Countless times, in these hip hop wars, hip hop media mogul Russell Simmons has defended the right of artists to "speak from their hearts," to tell their own truths. But do they tell all their truths in hip hop? And to what ends, to serve whom? Surely, no one wants artists to speak from a false place, but the heart is not a predetermined place: It is a cultivated one.

Communities have always set limits on the depths of self-destructive iconography, language, and action that will be allowed. This isn't a matter of invoking police or government action. It is about taking cultural control of ourselves in a society that has long been involved in the destruction of black self-love, dignity, and community survival. Operating in the larger progressive interests of the black community—and society at large—is the aim. But to fulfill this aim, we have to consolidate and illuminate the actions of those who are working toward community-sustaining goals and promote the key principles about how self-expression can be cutting-edge, angry, loving, honest, sexy, meaningful, and *empowering,* no matter the subject. Black music has always been a central part of this affirming, truth-telling process, but in this so-called post-civil rights era, it is up against new pressures and requires new strategies.

We cannot truly deal with what is wrong in hip hop without facing the broader cultures of violence, sexism, and racism that deeply inform hip hop, motivating the sales associated with these images. Yet, those of us who fight for gender, sexual, racial, and class justice also can't *defend* the orgy of thug life we're being fed simply because "sexism and violence are everywhere" or because corporations are largely responsible for peddling it. We can explain and contextual why hip hop seems to carry more of this burden, but we can't defend it. Even if sexism and violence are everywhere (and, sadly, they are), what I care most about is not proving that hip hop did or did not invent sexism, or the gangsta figure, bitch, ho, thug, or pimp, but showing how the excessive and seductive portrayal of these images among black popular hip hop artists is negatively affecting the music and the very people whose generational sound is represented by hip hop.

The destructive forms of black, racist-inspired hyper-masculinity for which commercial hip hop has become known make profound sense given the alchemy of race, class, and gender in U.S. society. But we shouldn't sit idly by or celebrate the fixation with the black pimp, his ornate pimp cup, and the culture of sexual, economic, and gender exploitation for which this persona stands. Understanding and explaining are not the same as justifying and celebrating, and this is the crucial distinction we must make if we stand a fighting chance in this perpetual storm. The former—understanding and explaining—are an integral part of solving the problems with hip hop; the latter—justifying and celebrating—are lazy, reactionary, dangerous, and lacking in progressive political courage. Yes, hip hop's excesses will continue to be used as a scapegoat; but we must develop our own progressive critique, not just stand around defending utter insanity because our enemies attack it. The mere fact that our enemies attack something we do does not make our actions worthy of defense.

We must fight for a progressive, social justice—inspired, culturally naunced take on hip hop—a vision that rejects the morally hyper-conservative agenda and the "whatever sells works for me" brand of hustlers' neo-minstrelsy that have become so lucrative and accessible for the youth in poor black communities today. *The Hip Hop Wars* is a sometimes polemical, always passionate assessment of where we are, what's wrong with the conversation we are having about hip hop, why it matters, and how to fix it. Too many people on both sides of this debate seem to have lost their collective minds, taking a grain of truth and using it to starve a nation of millions.

I hope this book will help galvanize progressive conversation and action among the thousands of current and aspiring artists, fans, parents, teachers, and cultural workers—black, white, Latino, Asian, young and old, of all backgrounds, from all places and spaces. I am even hoping that various industry workers and record and television executives will read this book, see themselves as part of the solution, and work harder to develop community-enabling ways to stay in business. This book is for everyone who feels uneasy about commercial hip hop—some who know that something is really wrong but can name it; others who are working to make hip hop the kind of cultural nourishment it can be but are getting very little help to fix it; and still others who remain sidelined, worried that jumping into the fray means being forced to take impossible sides in an absurdly polarized battle.

NOTES

1. This statistic was calculated on the basis of RIAAs consumer profile reports of 1998 and 2006.
2. Adrienne P. Samuels, "Russell Simmons: The Godfather Takes a Stand," *Ebony* magazine, July 2007, p. 79. In this article Simmons is quoted as saying: "Poverty created these conditions and these conditions create these words."
3. Neil Strauss, "Are Pop Charts Manipulated?" *New York Times,* January 25, 1996.
4. Stephen Holden, "Billboard's New Charts Roil the Record Industry," *New York Times*, June 22, 1991.
5. Glen Ford, "Hip Hop Profanity, Misogyny and Violence: Blame the Manufacturer," *Peninsula Peace and Justice Center,* May 7, 2007, available online at www.peaceandjustice.org/article.php/20070507114621137/print.
6. Quoted in Havlock Nelson, "Rapping Up '93," *Billboard,* November 27, 1993.
7. Ben H. Bagdikian, *The New Media Monopoly* (Beacon Press, 2004), p. 27.
8. Ibid. See also the transcript of the PBS documentary *Merchants of Cool* featuring charts of media consolidation, available online at www.pbs.org/wgbh/pages/frontline/shows/cool.
9. Mark Fratrik, "Radio Transactions 2001: Where Did All the Deals Go?" *BIA Financial Networks* (2002), p. 8; Eric Boehlert "One Big Happy Channel?" Salon.com, June 28, 2001.
10. Peter DiCola and Kristin Thomson, "Radio Deregulation: Has It Served Citizens and Musicians? A Report on the Effects of Radio Ownership Consolidation Following the 1996 Telecommunications Act," Future of Music Coalition, November 18, 2002, p. 3.
11. Bruce Dixon, "Making Real Change: Taking on Black Commercial Radio," *Black Agenda Report,* May 21, 2008.
12. Eric Boehlert, "Payola City," Salon.com, July 24, 2001.

13. Ibid.
14. Paul Porter, "Same Song," unpublished manuscript.
15. Author Interview with Paul Porter, May 24, 2008.
16. Ford, "Hip Hop Profanity, Misogyny and Violence."
17. Marcus Franklin, "Music Execs Silent as Rap Debate Rages," *USA Today,* May 11, 2007, available online at www.usatoday.com/life/music/2007-05-11-3355380428_x.htm.

OBJECTIVE QUESTIONS

1. The body of the article is preceded by a quote from_____. Who is he?

2. The author speculates that if Tupac Shakur were a newly signed artist today, he _____.

3. Through 2005, RIAA reported that rap represented what percentage of music sales in the United States? How does this compare to other music business genres? What percent of the Hip Hop consumer base is white?

4. What is the "trinity" of commercial Hip Hop?

5. To many of Hip Hop's critics, "alienated, angry stories about life in the ghetto" are not meaningfully related to African-American's problems; rather, they are seen as _____.

6. According to the author, what is the most aggravating defense of commercial Hip Hop's fixation on demeaning black women for sport?

7. How does the author define "beef"?

8. "It is as if the real sport of our conversation about Hip Hop is _____ and _____."

9. What are the five factors that the author says "have worked synergistically to create these toxic conditions," and have "distorted the legacy" of Hip Hop?

10. In 1991, _____, a sales measurement system that accurately tracks album purchases at their point of sale, was introduced. What was the result?

11. In 1990, one of the major labels conducted a study that concluded that the most active consumers of Hip Hop were_____.

12. In 1983, the men and women who headed the mass media corporations that dominated American audiences could have fit comfortably in a modest ballroom. By 2003, [they] could fit in _____.

13. With more that _____ listeners, Clear Channel reaches over _____ of the U.S. population.

14. _____ is a euphemism for black music genres and markets.

15. What are Tricia Rose's Hip Hop Top Ten?

16. Besides the thousands of artists, fans, parents, teachers and cultural workers that she hopes to inspire, who else does the author hope will read her book and "see themselves as _____"?

QUESTIONS FOR FURTHER THOUGHT, RESEARCH, AND DISCUSSION

1. Tricia Rose writes: "Hip Hop is in a terrible crisis." What is the crisis she is alluding to and why is it important that we face it? Or is it all that important?

2. How, why and to what extent has the discussion about Hip Hop been broadened to a discussion about the issues of race, poverty, politics, gender and generation?

3. In what ways does Rose think that Hip Hop fans are different from the consumers of previous styles of African-American music? Do you agree?

4. Tricia Rose argues that blacks and whites are still often judged very differently for the same behaviors. Can you give or find other examples?

5. Why was there no noticeable "generation gap" in the African-American community until the 1970s, or was it always really there?

6. Discuss in detail the end result of the Telecommunications Act of 1996. Discuss the historical role that black radio news programs played during the civil rights struggle.

7. Watch and write a critique of the documentary film *Hip Hop: Beyond Beats and Rhymes*.

8. Pick any of Tricia Rose's Hip Hop Top Ten and write an essay.

9. Tricia Rose writes: "Communities have always set limits on the depths of self-destructive iconography, language, and action that will be allowed." Do you agree?

10. Do you agree with Rose about the current state of Hip Hop and its possible negative effect? If so, what do we do?

11. Do you know of any other instances when the consolidation or dissolution of power in the record industry or media profoundly changed the way we listened to and consumed music?

Word of Mouth

By William Jelani Cobb

William Jelani Cobb is Associate Professor of History at Spellman College. He is a contributing writer at *Essence* magazine, and his criticism has also appeared in the *Washington Post, Emerge*, and *The Progressive*.

William Jelani Cobb's book is subtitled *A Freestyle on the Hip Hop Aesthetic*. Trying to describe the aesthetic nature of any form of artistic expression, even in free style, is a very ambitious undertaking. There is probably nothing more elusive than attempting to draw aesthetic parameters around any style or form of artistic expression. Most artists seem to work from their own set of rules—rules they often make up as they go along. As any art form itself grows and matures, its intrinsic values and notions of beauty naturally change and evolve correspondingly.

Many of Hip Hop's aesthetic values were inherited from the blues, funk and other older forms of African-American culture, to be sure, but the essence of what makes Hip Hop unique is that often, its aesthetic values are in direct reaction against the older and prevailing values. The beauty of the "bombed" subway car and the perfectly drawn "tag" are examples. The expertly mixed "break" beat and the sublimely "rocked" party would be a couple more. The aesthetic of Hip Hop glorifies the "outlaw hero" and anti-authoritarianism. It is an aesthetic of confrontation and competition, posturing and signifying. It is "art so strong it hurts people," as Claudio Bruno once described his graffiti show in Italy. In an earlier chapter of the book, Cobb points out that nothing is rarer than a Hip Hop record about heartbreak, unrequited love, or the guilt of unfaithfulness—all common themes in the blues and "soul" music.

Nothing is more prevalent in capitalistic America than the aesthetic of "sales." What sells is, by this definition, beautiful and, by extension, perhaps even meaningful. It should also be obvious that the "art" of Hip Hop is quite different—though not unrelated—to the "shrink-rapped" products one finds in the CD rack at Wal-Mart. Fortunately, artistic expression is not best judged by how well it mirrors or illuminates its own era, but ultimately, by how well it transcends it. Hip Hop has quite easily transcended its provincial roots in the Bronx and has proven its global relevance. Hip Hop records that are more than 25 years old are still often played and can still make us think and give us pause. Hip Hop as a form of artistic expression has certainly transcended its time and original locale. If we believe in the ghetto value system that says that respect is more important in the "hood" than money, then there will always be rappers willing to discard the aesthetic of sales in a search of more relevance and a broader palette of ideas than the business may be currently promoting. While to a certain extent the creation of the music business and the music press, the ongoing dichotomy between the "conscious" and the "commercial" rappers only exemplifies the inherent contradictions in trying to reward the production of sincere artistic expression in a capitalistic society. This dilemma is not new or unique to Hip Hop. It is important to bear in mind, however, that the originators of Hip Hop—like the first blues singers and jazz musicians—were not making career moves, but were merely trying to have fun and find some meaning in a situation that appeared at first glance to be hopeless. Old school Hip Hoppers were merely trying to beautify a landscape that they found in ruins with a little fresh spray paint, create some new and different beats that weren't on the radio, and invent some slick new moves to impress the girls.

The aesthetic of graffiti, more that anything else, is an aesthetic designed not so much to awaken the complacent and those immersed in denial, but to celebrate and advertise the importance and meaning of their lives. In this chapter, Cobb focuses primarily on the levels of meaning in Hip Hop lyrics. Cobb identifies several characteristic aesthetics in Hip Hop. Again, some of these are inherited and some are unique. First is the aesthetic of "cool" which has long been a staple in the aesthetics of the blues and jazz. It is an aesthetic commonly trampled on by white rockers, but an aesthetic given new meaning by the stoic and apparent unemotional delivery of many rappers. Secondly, the author identifies an aesthetic of freedom and exuberance, exemplified by the importance of "free style," or spontaneity and improvisation. Once again, these qualities have long been staples of African American culture and survival, but the new levels of opportunity and self-esteem that supposedly resulted from civil rights era struggles give new meaning and irony to the necessity for African-Americans to be clever, creative, and adaptable. The third characteristic aesthetic the author identifies is the "battle," or confrontation. Many authors have compared rappers to boxers. To proclaim and ultimately prove one's dominance and greatness is not only inherent in blues and jazz culture, but it is an absolute necessity for survival in prison. It is also one of the most recurrent themes in Hip Hop history. Cobb also identifies what he calls the three components of the Hip Hop aesthetic: "Beat," "lyrics" and "flow." After comparing "flow" to the enigmatic and ineffable quality in jazz we call swing, the author lists the common poetic and literary devices in Hip Hop lyrics and gives examples of how they have been effectively used.

"WORD OF MOUTH" FROM *TO THE BREAK OF DAWN*

Rapper grips mic tight
Drums explode in throat's barrel
Lyrics leap from lips
—Joel Dias-Porter

STEP IN THE ARENA

HEMINGWAY DEFINED COURAGE as grace under pressure. In the black tradition, though, grace under pressure is the definition of *cool*—which leads us to the understanding that *coolness is a form of individual courage*. No wonder, then, in Yoruba art, the quality of mystic coolness (*itutu*) is often represented by the color blue—suggesting that existential calmness, and therefore courage, is at the heart of the blues tradition. In the hip hop arena, the battle, the ritual exchange of freestyle barbs, requires mental poise, grace under verbal fire, and composure—literally. Here we witness the rapid-fire calculation of speed chess combined with the language virtuosity of a poetry recital.

The concept of the hip hop baffle is the obvious extension of "the dozens" snapping, riffing, breaking, jonin', dissin': the ritual insults of the black vernacular tradition. The folklorist Roger D. Abrahams pointed out that

> the practice of mother-rhyming (the dozens) has been observed in various Afro-American communities as well as in a number of groups in Africa, including the Yoruba, Efik, Dogon, and some Bantu tribes.

And inside this sphere of formalized disrespect, coolness is the ultimate virtue because he who loses his temper loses face, the contest of wits, and sometimes teeth. Mel Watkin's history of black comedy *On the Real Side* points out that

> when confirmed to friends and familiar circumstances [the dozens] was viewed much like a basketball or baseball game, as competitive sport. If, however, one of the limitations was ignored—say, someone appeared with his girlfriend and his manhood was questioned—the game could escalate into hostility and violence.

To battle in hip hop—or in the dozens—is to put one's name on the line and test one's self in the crucible of verbal conflict. The freestyle is the crucial element of hip hop, but also is a cornerstone of black culture that is in consistent rebellion against the strictures of form and convention. Thus what the MC calls freestyle the jazz musician calls improvisation—literally confronting structure with a riff on time. The kinesthetic genius of an NBA baller lies in his ability to construct *physical* freestyles, rebelling against the step-dribble-shoot simplicity of structure with an improvised use of body and time. This emphasis upon freedom of form emerges in direct relation to a group of people whose history has been defined by physical and time constraints. *Free* style—as in opposite of *slave* style, understood? Beyond all else, the ability to freestyle, the ability to verbally snap the larynx of rival MC in the crucible of the battle, is what separates the grown men from the juveniles. Doubt hip hop's literary merit if you wish, but James Baldwin never had to essay head-to-head against Norman Mailer, Eldridge Cleaver, or William Styron while sitting at the desk next to him.

Lyrical improvisation has its origins in the worksongs from which the blues sprung. Classics like "Wake Up Dead Man" or "Berta, Berta" were improvised songs built around the percussion of the hammer falling on the railroad track being laid. But the hip hop freestyle is spoken—not sung—and there is less room for verbal error in speech. The AAB structure common in blues is directly connected to the improvised nature of many of these songs; repetition of the first line gives the singer a moment to come up with the rhyming punchline in the third. But the freestyle rapper gets no breathers. The MC is in constant, literal dialogue with not only the audience but also their collective sense of timing and expectation.

Ralph Ellison—whose own word craft was informed by the temporal sensibilities he developed as a musician—riffed on the uses of time in the prologue to *Invisible Man*, a statement that also speaks to the nature of the MC craft.

> Once I saw a prizefighter boxing a yokel. The fighter was swift and amazingly scientific. His body was one violent flow of rapid rhythmic action. He hit the yokel a hundred times while the yokel held up his arms in stunned surprise. But suddenly the yokel, rolling about in the gale of boxing gloves, struck one blow and knocked science, speed and footwork cold as a well-digger's posterior … the yokel has simply stepped inside his opponent's sense of time.

Nelson George once observed that the *battle royale* in the opening pages of *Invisible Man* bore a relationship to hip hop's element of battle. But the parallel of the pugilist to the MC also exists on a level beyond simple metaphors. It makes sense that Muhammad Ali, the boxer with the most highly cultivated and idiosyncratic understanding of time inside the ring, was also the lyrical forerunner of the MC outside it. Jay-Z pointed this out when announcing his retirement as a rapper:

> People compare rap to other genres of music, like jazz or rock 'n' roll. But it's really most like a sport. Boxing to be exact. The stamina, the one-man army, the combat aspect of it, the ring, the stage, and the fact that boxers never quit when they should.

In hip hop we find Mike Tyson immortalized in verse like the gladiators of old (you never saw Sinatra, for instance, singing about Rocky Marciano, but you did see Joe Louis valorized in Richard Wright, Cab Calloway, and Paul Robeson's collaboration "King Joe Blues"). Sonny Liston lived his life as a blues epic born in the Arkansas backwater, the thirteenth child, his date of birth was etched into a tree that was struck by lightning and shattered, leaving him a man without known beginnings. If Liston had not been born, the blues would've had to invent him. Tyson, though, was pure hip hop metaphor: raised in Brownsville, the crumbling precinct at the center of Crooklyn's mythology, rolling into the ring accompanied by the organized cacophony of Public Enemy's "Welcome to the Terrordome" or Redman's demented funk "Time for Some Action." And it was no coincidence that Tyson found himself in the company of hip hop personas Tupac Shakur and

Suge Knight—Pac was, in fact, leaving a Tyson fight the night he was gunned down on the Vegas strip.

In his prime, Roy Jones, Jr.—a rapper in his own right—*fought* in an improvisational style that almost seemed like the ring equivalent of a freestyle verse, which is one reason you find innumerable references to him in hip hop, but virtually none for that gentleman pugilist Lenox Lewis or the ring evangelist Evander Holyfield. The rapper and the prizefighter share the common themes of improvisation and requisite composure in the face of incoming fire. Boxing is physical entrepreneurship for the dead-broke—an arena where one's fists are the equivalent of venture capital. Hip hop is verbal offense and defense raised to the level of high art. And both the pugilist and the MC share a common charge in their professions: protect yourself at all times.

Down in the diminished wards of the City where some hearts run as cold as the (651) area code, disrespect is a form of larceny and worthy of capital punishment. The axiom holds that if you look at what people pursue in excess then you're usually looking at what they were once deprived of. In the city, respect is worth more than money—because respect is what will allow you to keep dollars in your pocket and not in the possession of those who would trespass against you. In hip hop—and inside the broken histories of black men in America—respect is the gambling with the most valuable commodity available one's rep and the respect that flows from it.

Proverbs 22 will tell you that a good name is rather to be chosen than great riches, but in this arena one's rep is one's wealth. In the days of yore, heads battled for *names*—where losing MCs were stripped of their accumulated glory by being forces to assume a new MC name. And in the MC battle, victory belongs to the slickest dealer of disrespect. Take this tendency to treat insult as a blood felony and then pair it with the wit, invention, and genius of the Negro verbal tradition and the result is either a high-stakes art competition, where victory belongs to him of the swiftest tongue, or a prelude to black homicide. Or both, simultaneously.

There is a genealogy of conflict in hip hop, a lineage that connects the new school to the old school and the old school to whatever cam before that. Kool Moe Dee versus Busy Bee, MC Shan versus KRS-One, LL Cool J versus Kool Moe Dee, Canibus versus LL, Common versus Cube—all the way down to the fratricidal conflicts of Big versus Pac and the citywide civil warfare of Nas versus Jay-Z and Ja Rule vs 50 Cent. And, to cop a line from De La Soul, the *stakes is high*. The verbal manslaughter KRS-One committed on "South Bronx" and "The Bridge Is Over" ended Shan's career and put the whole Queens MC delegation on artistic probation. Coming off the canvas from his rounds with LL, Canibus joined the U.S Army—thinking it safer to handle live ammunition than hot microphones.

Elders to the game will point to the ancestral clash of Kool Moe Dee and Busy Bee at Harlem World in 1983 as the template for what was to come. True indeed, as KRS-One has pointed out, that battle was not simply a lyrical contest, but it was a clash of competing styles, differing approaches to the art of rapping, a smoke-filled referendum on the direction hip hop was to take. Moe Dee's lyrical decapitation of Busy Bee marked the triumph of the serious, poetic lyricist over the flamboyant showman, but that stylistic conflict has played itself out down to the current era, animating MC battles ad infinitum. The stake is always the same: the individual rep; the regard of the avenues, corners, and roads where you and your peoples dwell; and the stylistic evolution of hip hop. If one is to take the art form in new direction, you must defeat and exile its roster masters first. Regicide as a job requirement.

Nas gave light to this reality, explaining the genesis of his conflict with Jay-Z on "Last Real Nigga Alive":

> *In the middle of that, Jay tried to sneak attack*
> *Assassinate my character, degrade my hood*
> *cause in order for him to be the don, Nas had go*
> *the Gam-b-i-n-o rules. I understood.*

Thus the conflict of rival poets earns comparison to the rub out of a rival boss in the tradition of Gotti's bullet-riddled ascension over Paul Castellano.

In the early years, the battle could be more metaphor than reality. At the zenith of their hostilities, Kool Moe Dee and LL could be photographed together at the same industry parties. For a period in the late 80s, Big Daddy Kane and Rakim were to hip hop what Frazier and Ali had been to boxing a decade earlier, what the Yankees and Dodgers were to New York in the 1950s-two antagonists so dissimilarly gifted that they were defined by each other's talents: The slow-flowing meditative Ra contrasting with the compact densely structured lyrical assaults of Kane. Rakim, the ascetic spiritualist from the Strong Island suburbs, Kane the flat-topped hedonist hailing from the heart of Flatbush.

But the battle devolved from figurative to liberal in the early 1990s and by the time Dr. Dre attacked TV host Dee Barnes for interviewing Cube on her show *Pump It Up* the nature of lyrical conflict had changed irrevocably. Ice Cube, the ex-*Nigga with an Attitude* had traded barbs with the remaining NWA members on "No Vaseline" and "100 Miles and Running," but the 1991 Barnes assault initiated an era of physical antagonism that extended not only to one's microphone nemesis, but also to the journalists who covered the music. NWA quickly dissolved into lyrical fratricide with Dre's assault on founder Eazy-E shortly after he left the Ruthless Records label. By the time Bronx native Tim Dawg's anemic assault on NWA's "Step To Me" reached airwaves the MC skirmishes had begun to metastasize into coastal, and ultimately lethal, conflicts.

The ascent of the squad of MCs attached to Death Row Records and the grumblings the New York MCs had been vanquished by upstarts from the left coast gave particular significance to Notorious B.I.G.'s 1994 debut, *Ready to Die*. Those same dynamics applied to Nas's blistering debut, *Illmatic*, released that same year. The burly bard from Brooklyn anointed himself king of New York on the strength of *Ready to Die*—in the face of competition from cross-borough rivals like Nas, and the Wu-Tang standouts Raekwon and Ghostface Killah. The year 1996 witnessed both the release of Jay-Z's *Reasonable Doubt* and the murder of Tupac Shakur—a loss that changed the balance of power between the coasts. Shakur had been the most noted icon not only of West Coast hip hop, but of the music at large. Though it would take some years for the hopes to be born out, *Reasonable Doubt* heralded the arrival of another MC that showed all the potential of restoring the East Coast to its former glory. B.L.G.'s death five months after Shakur's effectively closed a chapter in which the battle had drifted far away from its roots: two turntables, one microphone; two MCs, one title, and the freestyle exchange of artistic insult. Hip hop had driven at full speed down a dead-end street and now the only route available was to move backward. The extended wake of their deaths saw the continuation of conflict among artists. But the Shakur and B.I.G parables were at least part of the reason that subsequent conflicts-most notably Jay-Z and Nas-remained lyrically lethal, not literally so.

The ability to freestyle reached the point of diminishing returns in the era of the MC as commercial vehicle-despite, or perhaps because of the momentary rush of attention the form received after the success of the 2002 Eminem biopic *8 Mile*. Freestyle is to hip hop as street ball is to the NBA. Just as asphalt legend has it that proving grounds of Harlem's Rucker League, there is no shortage of triple-platinum-level rappers who would get *took* in the freestyle arena. This is the age-old conflict of glitz against guts, played out the elemental tools of the hip hop trade: two turntables and a microphone. An arena where speaking a previously written rhyme-as opposed to going *extemp* from the top of the head-is treated as kindly as marking a card in a back-alley poker game. This relationship to the freestyle battle aesthetic is one of the reasons why Ice Cube, who is central to the history of hip hop, but is not and never was a *battle* rapper per se, lacked the skill to funk with Common's classic incendiary "I See the Bitch in You." Incensed by a line about West Coast on "I Used to Love H.E.R.," Common's metaphorical ode to hip hop, Ice Cube responded with an assault titled "Westside Slaughterhouse." Pulling no punches Cube made a pun of his opponent's original stage name, charging.

> *You used to love her*
> *Now mad 'cause we fucked her*
> *Pussy-whipped bitch*
> *With no common sense*

In hip hop terms, Cube's salve was standard fare for verbal conflict, but nowhere near the thermonuclear reply that was "I See the Bitch in You." The point, however was that Cube and Common existed on different Planes of the MC craft—Cube primarily as a deft lyricist and songwriter and Common as an extension of the verbal gladiator tradition that stretched back to the days of old. (Conversely, at that point in their careers, Common's record as a songwriter was not nearly as impressive as Cube-who as a teen had ghostwritten virtually all of NWA's classic *Straight Outta Compton*.)

And yet the battle—as central as it is to hip hop—is only one element of what makes a great MC. Rare is the artist who was capable of operating in both of these arenas with equal adroitness. The songwriting artist with battle skills is the hip hop equivalent of ballplayer whose game is as tight on Madison Square Garden's hardwood as it is on Harlem's asphalt. Or the boxer who both hits hard and is hard to hit. It's worth nothing, however, that after the turning-point release *Like Water for Chocolate*, Common was essentially reincarnated as an artist in the songwriter-lyricist mode. The Common who conceived of the conceptually bold if poorly executed *Electric Circus* in 2002 was a millennium away from the mic-ripping artist who first blew out of the Windy City a decade earlier. Taken together, lyricism and battle skills were indispensable elements of greatness, but did not constitute the total package. For the MC, the mechanics of the *how* one raps have proven to be as important as the content and circumstances under which one says it.

BENEATH THE SURFACE

Those who dismissed hip hop at the outset as musically monotonous missed the point. Hip hop has its musical roots in the breakbeat or "the bridge"—the most kinetic section of a record. The first rappers floated their vocals over synchronized "bridges" provided by the DJ who had mastered the ability to repeat the most kinetic section of song ad infinitum. Instead of having a bridge within a bridge—which might have sounded less *monotonous* to the uninitiated—the variation lay within the realm of the lyricist. The primary question on the floor is what a given MC can do artistically within a 4/4 measure. And the answers to this question, as we'll see, are myriad. Though the genre will always be dismissed by many as brash, monotonous noise, the truth is that hip hop has undergone an astounding array of lyrical and musical transformations.

Early hip hop featured simple syncopation—matching beats, or more specifically *pulses* to syllables—and that explains why early rappers often paused between syllables (hip ... hop ... you ... don't ... stop) and generally rapped slower than their lyrical descendants. Given the fact that early crews were built around the DJ, not the rapper, very few individual lyricists got the chance to fully demonstrate-or cultivate-their mic skills. Instead, they worked in routines where each line of a verse might be broken down and distributed to one of four or five rappers in the crew. The rapper's place in hip hop was still evolving and they treated songs the way soul singers treated duets—basically dividing the lyrics down the middle and singing the hooks in the chorus. Given the fact that the early rhyme crews were larger than the subsequent MC cliques (the Furious Five, the Fantastic Five, the Funky Four Plus One, etc.), their approach to a song also echoed 70s soul groups like the Temptations or the Four Tops where each person contributed a different timbre to a song. It was no coincidence that these early crews often featured harmonized hooks where all four or five MCs joined in—regardless of their questionable singing abilities. The Cold Crush Brothers' early routines were not all that far removed from doo-wop. The Fantastic Five harmonized their way through entire stanzas before dissolving into rhyme:

> *We're the fantastic romantic five*
> *We're the crew that makes you come alive*
> *So when you're rockin' to the sound*
> *That the five are laying down*
> *Just dance, boogie scream and shout*
> *'cause we won't hesitate to turn it out.*

Rapping and singing were so closely related at the outset that acts like the Force MDs, who eventually came to public attention as R&B singers, actually started out as rappers. (The group was originally called the Force MCs.) "White Lines"—Grandmaster Flash and the Furious Five's anti-coke anthem—was not only important in its thematic content, but also in terms of its structure. Many of the early hip hop songs—like Kurtis Blow's "Christmas Rappin"—featured beginning-to-end, uninterrupted rhyme sessions. By contrast, "White Lines" not only featured a hook that divided the song into different sections, but also contained a structural innovation. The hook was, on alternate lines, harmonized by the five MCs or spoken by a narrator:

> *Ooooh ... White Lines*
> *Vision dreams of passion*
> *Blowin through my mind*
> *And all the while I think of you*
> *Pipe cries*
> *A very strange reaction*

For us unwind
The more I see the more I do
Something like a like a phenomenon
Baby
Tellin your baby to come along, but white lines ... .blow away
Blow! Rock it! Blow!

Again, Flash is the first-person reference for this development:

> The Kool Here style at the time was basically freelance talking, not necessarily syncopated to the beat. The Three of them—Cowboy, Kid Creole and Melle Mel—came up with a style called back and forth, where they would be MC-ing to the beat that I would play. I'll take a sentence that hopefully the whole wide world knows: "Eeny Meeny Miny Mo, catch a piggy by the toe." So they devised it where Cowboy might say "Eeny meeny," and the Creole would say, "Miny" and then Mel would say, "Mo." So they would kind of bounce it around.

Big Daddy Kane made a similar point, highlighting the close connection between R&B singing and early hip hop:

> R&B is black music; before rap, that's all we had. When you really look at the origin of rap, "Rapper's Delight" is [performed] over "Good Times," an R&B song. When cats came out, they mainly rapped over R&B tracks. Cold Crush, Fantastic and Master Don and the Def Committee, these cats, when they performed were singing. The Force MDs [originally] were a rap group, but when they were doing their routines they were singing. The only time they rapped is when they would freestyle one by one, but the majority of their routine was singing. So that whole melodic thing has always played an important part in hip hop from the beginning.

It would take time to realize that the rapper's approach to a song was different that of a singer—no matter how many traits the two shared—and that there would be no room for four-part harmony in hip hop. By the early nineties, the harmonic tradition in hip hop had been so long neglected that Bone Thugs-N-Harmony's vocalist approach to the hip hop song could be seen as an innovation rather that a throwback to the styles of old.

Run DMC made use of the back-and-forth style, trading single lines and couplets on classics like " Here We Go" and "Peter Piper"—which is essentially a duet, rapped the way Tammi and Marvin sang "Ain't Nothin' Like the Real Thing" or "Ain't No Mountain High Enough." But by the time *Raising Hell* hit the streets in 1986, the rhyme routines were on their way out. In their absence, the vocal inflection of the rapper (or his *flow*) could come to the fore.

As group routines broke down into sequential rhyme sets, the individual rapper had more input of how he would say a particular line. Not only did he have more lines to work with, he no longer had to be concerned about whether or not his inflection would disrupt the timing of the next MC down the line. And the mechanics of what we now call *flow* quickly evolved. At its heart, flow is an individual time signature, the rapper's own idiosyncratic approach to the use of ime. Flow has two basic characteristics: the division of syllables and the velocity at which they ire spoken.

The rhyme is mathematic: A set of twelve syllables can be broken into combinations such as 4/4/4, 6/4/2, or 8/2/2, and the skilled rapper is most often trying his best to organize his syllables in the least predictable arrangement. And this is why even the slickest of MC lyrics look sterile on the page. Rakim once predicted that an imitator was liable to break his jaw trying to recite one of the master's lines in his absence. Flow is the Rosetta Stone of lyrical understanding. Since there is seldom the same number of syllables or words from one line to the next, the rapper doesn't *speak* at the same speed from one line to the next. This is lyrical long division. Rapping through a standard sixteen-bar combination, the MC has to manage an equal number of changes in pitch, inflection, and delivery—all while maintaining breath control. The craft comes down to this: the trickiness of enunciation, the constant variation of speed, the tongue-twisting elongation or contraction of words. The MC is the mathematician.

The term *flow*—and all its metaphysical implications—didn't come along by accident. The aim is to be fluid, liquid, protean in one's approach to sound. Water and blood flow, liquids take the shape of their vessels—in this case, the vessel is the particular beat composition that the MC is rhyming to. In the lexicon of the avenue, to do a solid is to show a sign of strength or commitment, but on the mic, it is not a mater of strength, but finesse.

Flow is as elemental to hip hop as the concept of *swing* is to jazz. And like the jazz musician who deliberately plays an eighth note behind or ahead of the measure, flow is the science of funking with one's expectations of time. In some instances, the pure aesthetic sheen of an MC's flow is enough to get him past all but the most severe critics. Snoop Dogg's has based his entire career on the uniqueness of his flow, not the density of rhyme or impact of his punchlines. Jay-Z's tailor-made flow is so casual and conversational that he sounds more like he's talking than rapping. Ghostface Killah's "crying style" of MCing involves tapering the end of his phrases like an overwrought man on the verge of tears, while Method Man, his crewmate in the nine—MC Wu-Tang Clan outfit has a trademark flow involving the exaggerated extension of key vowels. The hyper active, dense line of OutKast's Andre 3000 and Big Boi are wrought with double entendres and clever wordplay, all done at a speed just past the casual comprehension of the listener.

Now compare that emotionalism with the deliberate monotonists Guru and Rakim who approach the rhyme like actors who deliberately deadpan. The hallmark of the B-list actor is the limited palette of facial expressions, the failure to make use of his or her own physically. But for the talented actor—a William Hurt or a Meryl Streep—that same emotional reserve is a refined technique. The gifted rapper sounds distinct in terms of timbre, use of unusual vocabulary—or common vocabulary in unusual ways—tonal variation, and timing.

Like its ancestral inspiration, the blues, the hip hop lyric is built around a series of second lines, or what is known in the craft as the punchline. So an entire hip hop song can be structured in terms of (first) premise statements followed by secondary punchlines. And no, it's not a coincidence that MCs borrowed a term traditionally associated with comedy because both the craft of rhyming and joke-telling require a flawless sense of timing—not to mention the fact that the punchline in both blues and hip hop is frequently a clever phrase designed to elicit laughter from the listener.

The lyrical punchline, like its comedic counterpart, is where all the elements of the previous lines come together. It is the line that confounds the expectations that are established in the premise line. A traditional blues lyric may state

I'm a big fat mama with meat shaking on my bones

And then repeat:

Lord, I'm a big fat mama with meat shaking on my bones

But that is sterile statement of the obvious until the singer breaks it down that

Ev'ry time I shake this meat, some skinny girl lose her home
(Ida Cox, "Four Day Creep," 1939)

In this case, the punchline is technically the third line sung in an AAB song structure, but it is the second line in terms of content. Now, a classic Big Daddy Kane premise and punchline hold that

I won't say I'm the baddest or portray that role
But I'm in the top two and my father's getting old

Generally speaking, the MC uses flow to disguise the precise location where the punchline will drop (or what it is) in the same way that comedians hide the conclusion of their jokes. But any number of rappers violate these ideals, kicking rhymes with an *anti-flow.* Some use deliberately predictable cadence as means of illustrating the punchline—if the listener knows exactly where the line's punctuation will be, the rapper then has to up the ante in terms of its creativity and impact. MCs like Rass Kass, Canibus, Eminem, Lord Finesse, and his late Harlemite collaborator Big L were masters of this approach. The listener is clear almost from the outset about *where* the punchline will be, but the real question is *what* exactly it will be in terms of content. This verbal tactic is the reason that early DJs started the tradition of dropping the audio at the end of every fourth or eighth measure—to literally give the MC breathing room, to allow him to drop his punchline a capella for maximum impact. On his classic "La Di Da Di," Slick Rick—a comedic performer by nature—had his partner Doug E. Fresh drop the fourth bar to deliver his sharpest line in a song about a mother and daughter literally fighting over his amorous attentions:

I tried to break it up
I said "Stop it, leave her."
She said "If I can't have you
She can't either."

The final phrase uttered by the jealous mother is said without musical accompaniment.

In the original proving grounds of the art form, the freestyle battle and the live-on-the-street performance, the punchline was indispensable to getting a crowd open. And under those raucous circumstances, the nuances of flow might be easily lost on the audience. Both Finesse and Big L—along with punchline kings like Rass Kass, Talib Kweli, Common, Wordsworth, and Chino XL—were direct descendants of that lineage of early playground MCs. The difference between them and their mic-gripping forbears though is that there were different criteria in the modern era, where a rapper could gain a national audience without ever matriculating through the boulevard ranks. At the same time, the rise of hip hop as commercial music made the distinction between

MC as rhyme-spitter and the MC as songwriter that much more clear. Thus began an entire lineage of MCs like Lord Finesse, Rass Kass, Supernatural, Canibus, Big L, and the legendary Mikey D, whose microphone skills were beyond question but who was not able to compose *songs* that were nearly as compelling as their individual rhymes. In short, the intricacies of content and flow that were so essential to success in the venues where hip hop was born were necessary but by no means sufficient in the new era.

Flow is not about *what* is being said so much as *how* one is saying it. And while any list of the greatest MCs would include at least two of the preceding names, a list of the greatest songwriters in the tradition probably would not. A Tribe Called Quest's "Electric Relaxation," for instance, contained almost no notable punchlines, but is still regarded as a classic within the genre. And it is ironic that none of the catalog of artists listed above is known for compelling lyrical flow (and in the case of Talib Kweli, his tongue-twisting, stutter-step flow has been cited as a reason why his brilliant work has not gotten its due acclaim).

This is not an either/or scenario: commercially recognized artists like a Jay-Z and less-hailed but nonetheless blistering wordsmiths like Black Thought and Guru have the capacity to issue slick punchlines with distinctive, magnetic flows. When Jay-Z confessed on his Black Album that he'd "dumbed down for his audience and double his dollars" he was essentially talking about de-emphasizing his punchlines—since punchlines are often evasive similes and double entendres, by diminishing them the listener didn't have to think as much. Obviously not every commercially successful song in the genre has been the result of lyrical simplification, but it takes a particular kind of talent to walk that line. (He went on to issue the revealing compliment that "If skills sold/ truth be told/I'd probably be/lyrically Talib Kweli.")

The most successful artists in the field have been able to wed the witty punchline to other artistic techniques—flow in particular. As flow evolved and developed in the 1983–1992 era, so also did the structural elements of the art of MCing. Rhyme styles evolved most dramatically in the 1980s, where MCs went from the basic AAAA or ABAB rhyme schemes that had been standard to dense, multi-layered compound rhymes that augmented a rapper's flow. The *art* of MCing also began to increasingly incorporate the standard techniques of literature and poetry: alliteration, metaphor, assonance, onomatopoeia, personification, and hip hop's most prominent literary characteristics, simile, double entendre, and comparison. Run DMC's 1983 classic "Sucker MCs" inaugurated a new era in hip hop's history, but started with this couplet:

> *Two years ago, a friend of mine*
> *Asked me to say some MC rhymes.*

By the end of the decade, though, listeners had come to expect a level of lyrical complexity that made the opening lines to "Sucker MCs" sound almost Seussian. In the early 1990s, Big Daddy Kane's practiced nonchalance reigned supreme as he issued lines on "Set It Off" like:

> *Attack, react exact the mack'll move you with*
> *A strong song as long as you groove to this.*

The fact the Kane was using the same AA rhyme scheme as Run DMC was obscured by the fact that he brought an unprecedented level of internal rhyme to the field—and ran through his lines far more quickly than his predecessors. Every single word in his couplet—with the exception of the articles and a single preposition—rhymes with another word. Not only did it become more difficult generally to tell when a particular punchline would be dropped, it became a guessing game as to which set of words it would rhyme with. The listener is no longer waiting to hear the rhyme phrase at the end of the second line, but also the rhymes at the beginning and middle of it.

The self-professed lyrical legend LL Cool J announced his musical presence with 1984's "I Need a Beat" and simultaneously introduced a broader vocabulary palette into rap music. Sounding like he'd raided every entry in as SAT prep book, LL's reliance on polysyllabic words and uncommon allusions on the original version of 1985's "Rock the Bells"—along with T La Rock's "It's Yours"—pioneered a rhyme approach that avenue denizens termed "computer style." And the wider array of words created a wider set of lyrical possibilities. Cool J's verbal repertoire shone on riffs like:

> During this episode vocally I explode
> My title is the king of the FM mode
> See, my volume expands to consume
> And my structures emote a lyrical heirloom.

Before this point, it would have been highly unlikely that a rapper would use the words connoisseur, tympanic, impresario, pestilence, plateau, subpoena, conjecture, cranium, plagiarism, metabolism, auditory, eradicate, adversary, membrane, jugular, manuscript, and virtuoso in a single song, as LL did so boldly on the remix version "Rock the Bells."

In the mid-1980s acts like the ultra Magnetic MCs and Eric B. & Rakim were responsible for dilating the thematic possibilities of the hip hop record. Rhyme—with the notable exception of pioneers like Afrika Bambaataa's Soul Sonic Force—had been literal and concrete, in the hands of Kool Keith of the Ultras or Rakim, subject matter became abstract, metaphysical, bordering upon the science fictional. The sonic collage that underpinned the Ultras sublime "Ego Trippin" was augmented by Kool Keith and Ced Gee's vague non sequiturs and random allusions. The casual gravel of Rakim's unmistakable baritone stylings on "Eric B. Is President" or "Check Out My Melody" compelled the listener to dig the slick metaphysic the MC was laying down.

But Run DMC's string of commercial successes with singles like "Sucker MCs," "King of Rock," "My Adidas," and "Rock Box" introduced into hip hop the age-old conflict of art versus commerce. The rhyme schemes NWA employed on *Straight Outta Compton* were not nearly as advanced as a representative Kane or Rakim line, but the West Coast gangstas dwarfed them in sales. Too Short's "Freaky Tales" high-lighted the bass-and-synth oriented sound that would come to characterize West Coast hip hop, but his rhyme scheme was elementary.

The conflict between the aesthetic and the economic is the most recurrent theme in KRS-One's body of work over the past seventeen years. KRS-One's obsession with marketing-free MCing made sense given the reality that the two highest selling artists of the decade were Vanilla Ice and MC Hammer, neither of whom warranted a second look-or, truthfully, a first one—for their rhyming abilities.

Jay-Z's highlighted this theme on *The Black Album*, rapping,

Truth told, I wanna rhyme like Common Sense
But I did 5 mill—I ain't rhymed like Common since.

The point being that the multi-layered meanings, wordplay, and wit that made Common's name as an MC pushed the artistic boundaries of hip hop forward, but the market demands—and rewards—simplicity. Both Jay-Z and Eminem—like Tupac and Biggie before them—managed to straddle the line between that which was sellable and that which was artistically credible, but even Jay-Z had to concede alliteratively that he "dumbed down his lyrics and doubled his dollars."

Classic Kane showcased his trademark high-velocity enunciation on his 1989 "Wrath of Kane" (a work that was impressive on wax, not so much in person. On stage, Kane needed an oxygen tank by the time he got to the second verse.) His approach to the rhyme was the artistic equivalent of running wind sprints in a labyrinth.

Go with the flow, my rhymes grow like an afro
The entertainer Kane'll gain and never have no
Problem, I could sneeze, sniffle or cough
e-e-even if I stutter I'ma still come off.

But more importantly, Kane had picked up the habit of breaking lines in the middle of a sentence, a technique called *enjambment* among the literary crowd. The idea that "Kane will never have no problem" may be a single thought, but it occupies two different lines. Kane used enjambment frequently as a verbal tactic:

Line by line, chapter after chapter
Like a pump on the street I gotta rap to
Those who chose to oppose, friend or foes
I all dispose and blow 'em out like afros.

Kane was the cleanup rhymer on Marley Marl's famous "Symphony" and had the misfortune of following Kool G. Rap, who was probably the the only rapper at the time who could match Kane on the level of rhyme density, verbal speed, and clever allusion. It may be debated eternally among hip hop aficionados as to who should have had the distinction of rhyming last over Marley's indelible keyboard-driven track. For the MC analyst, Kane and G. Rap's mic duel was a closer contest than the fabled bout between Marvelous Marvin Hagler and Sugar Ray Leonard in 1987.

The MC craft also came to utilize alliteration as a means of organizing rhymes. In 1988, Kool Moe Dee spat an alliteratively classic battle rhyme at the zenith of his hostilities with LL riffing on his rival's initials as

Lower level, lack luster, last least, lip lover,
lousy lame, late lethargic, lazy lemon, little logic
lucky leech, liver lipped, laborious louse from a loser's lips
living limbo, lyrical lapse, low life with the loud raps, boy.

Pharoahe Monch decided to forego the standard definition of rhyming on "Hell" from his under-heralded solo debut, *Internal Affairs:*

> *Follow for now, for no formidable fights have been formed as yet*
> *Pharoah fucks familiar foes first, before following female MCs fiercely*
> *Focus upon the face that facts can be fabricated to form lies*
> *My phonetics alone forced feeble MCs into defense on the fly—feel me?*

Rakim's "Follow the Leader" was an alliterative masterpiece. Here Rakim laced his cosmic allusions with staccato consonant combinations.

> *Music mixed mellow maintains to make*
> *Melodies for MCs motivates the breaks.*

In addition to alliteration, MCs had utilized personification at least as far back as 1982 when Melle Mel offered a deft example of the technique on "New York, New York."

> *A castle in the sky, one mile high*
> *Built to shelter the rich and greedy*
> *Rows of eyes, disguised as windows*
> *Lookin DOWN on the poor and the needy*

Mel speaks as if the building itself is looking down on impoverished people in the streets—mimicking the attitudes of the overlords who constructed them.

But given the thematic orientation of later hip hop, the personification would take on a deliberate boulevardian edge. Thus Nas on his 1996 sophomore release *It Was Written* breathes life into a Desert Eagle, semi-automatic nine-millimeter:

> *Always I'm in some shit, my abdomen is the clip*
> *The barrel's my dick—uncircumcised*
> *They pull me back and cock me*
> *I bust off when they unlock me.*

Tupac's "Me and My Girlfriend" from *Don Killimunati* extends the same theme, making his gat into his significant other.

> *Nigga, my girlfriend may be 45, but she still live*
> *One shot making Niggas heartbeat stop*
> *My girlfriend blacker than the darkest night*
> *When Niggas act bitch-made she got the heart to fight.*

Lloyd Banks's contribution to G-Unit's "8 More Miles" is a coke's-eye narration of the drug hustle:

You could sniff me, cut me, I'll turn you into a junkie
I'm the number one seller in the whole fucking country
Wall street niggas, they cop me on the low
White boys, they don't call me coke, they call me blow.

On *Return of the Boom Bap* (1993) KRS-One satirized the hip hop obsession with get-high with "I'm a Blunt," a song personifying a marijuana-filled blunt trying to avoid being smoked by a succession of rappers—ultimately being passed around to then-presidential candidate Bill Clinton.

As the form evolved, the artistic watermark for the exceptional MC rose higher and higher. MCs began experimenting with both simple and extended metaphors. De La Soul's classic 1989 *Three Feet High and Rising* featured the single "Potholes in My Lawn," an abstract metaphor tying suburban yard woes to the wholesale imitation of their artistic style. Large professor, the South Queens producer and MC whose "Live at the Barbeque" brought an adolescent Nas to national attention, was also responsible for "A Friendly Game of Baseball" (1991), in which the routine brutality of New York City police is likened to a spectator sport. In his telling, RBI's are "real bad injuries," not runs batted in, and the game is measured in endings, not innings.

When the outfielder guns you down,
You're out and off to the dugout underground.

Brooklynite wordsmith Masta Ace paid tribute to that same theme in 2003 with "Unfriendly Game," in which the illicit drug hustle is detailed in the form of a football game. In four double-entendre laden bars, Ace lays out the playbook:

Your offense gotta be cats with no conscience
No nonsense Niggas, with no options
Who know how to carry that rock
Make the hand off and run off the block.

The meaning in his line is that the drug hustler relies upon workers not burdened by a moral conscience, but in the athletic world, the player who is able to score at will and without hesitation is lauded as having "no conscience." The reference to having "no options" means that the drug seller has no viable alternatives, but it also refers to the play-option pass in football. The latter two lines make use of the alternate meanings of the term "rock," which is avenue terminology for both crack and a ball used in sports, "hand off," which is both a play in football and the means by which low-level hustlers make hand-to-hand drug sales, and "run off the block," which could be either following one's blockers to gain rushing yardage or literally running off the block when the police arrive.

GZA, the under-heralded lyricist of the Wu-Tang Clan breathed new life into the cliché of the city existing as a "concrete jungle" with "Animal Planet" from *Legend of the Liquid Swords*—a song on which he imagined the cast of characters in his neighborhood as animals and pondered how those animal traits played themselves out in the urban eco-system.

Shouldn't gamble with a cheetah and not expect to get beat
You silly goose, you know he move fast on his feet

Now you're neck deep in depth with a bunch of lone sharks
So you move on a colony of ants with aardvarks.

Duke Ellington famously declared that "music is my mistress" and that same sentiment animated what is probably the most respected extended metaphor in the history of hip hop, Common's "I Used to Love H.E.R.," in which he relays his relationship to hip hop as an on-again, off-again romance.

I met this girl when I was ten years old
And what I loved most, she had so much soul
She was old school when I was just a shorty
Never knew throughout my life she would be there for me.

Speaking in terms reserved for a lost love, Common narrates the rise of hip hop as the tale of a local girl whose entertainment career leads her to forget where she comes from ("Now I see her in commercials, she's universal"). What made Common's metaphor so widely hailed was the skill he utilized in conveying what had, by that point, become a very widely held view of the art form. And, on the real, the metaphor was so slickly composed that the entire second layer of meaning might have gone unnoticed to the casual listener had he not included the final line, "Who I'm talking about, y'all, is hip hop." The significance of the developing use of metaphor and extended metaphor in hip hop is hard to overstate. As with any artistic evolution, the aesthetic stakes in the form grew higher with time. The presence and utilization of time-honored literary techniques—the same stuff being pored over in Intro to English Lit classes made it increasingly difficult to defend the argument that hip hop did not qualify as art. Unapologetic and audacious as it was, hip hop had been clear about this debate from the gate. But the developing body of work had begun to make that clear to the blinkered crowds that had initially cut their eyes at this newly birthed approach to music.

By the mid-1980s, artists had begun drafting less common literary techniques and welding them into their approach to self-expression. Epistolary form, for example, involves a narrative that is told in the form of letters being exchanged. LL Cool J's *Radio* (1985) featured the moralistic "Dear Yvette," an open letter charting the abundant trysts of a fast local girl. On *Illmatic* Nas delivered the epistolary gem "One Love"—a one-sided correspondence between the poet and a recently incarcerated friend. He Monday-morning-quarterbacks the missteps that resulted in the jail bid and gives him the headlines of events in their common 'hood before speaking of his aspirations for him when they're reunited on the outside. Tupac's *Me Against the World* contained "Dear Mama," a missive to his mother detailing the depth of his love for her, despite the trials that lay in their history together. He ends telling her

There's no way I could pay you back
But my plan is to show you that I understand.

Masta Ace's 2003 *Disposable Arts* featured the comic "Dear Diary," in which his diary a record of his fears and self-doubts, writes *him* a letter advising him to "write your rhymes in the shower—you're washed up." In 2000 Eminem produced the haunting "Stan," a two-way exchange in which a fan gradually reveals his deteriorating mental state and the rapper responds to him—really to his fans at large and his critics as well—telling him to distinguish between entertainment and reality.

Alliteration, personification, and metaphor came to be common in the genre, but comparison, double entendre, and simile became the central literary techniques of the hip hop lyricists—and for clear reasons. If the freestyle battle was to establish a contrast between two vocalists than the use of comparison. At its core, the battle really was little more than a form of artistic comparison. The whole purpose of an analogy is to simplify a complex relationship—*this* (the complex thing) is like *that* (the simpler one).

In hip hop, the use of simile and analogy was from the outset used to illustrate the preternatural talents of the vocalist or the indisputable wackness of his rhyme competitor. Thus, Cypress Hill lead rapper B-Real's assertion that "you trying to step up to me for some action/that's like Mike stepping to Papa Joe Jackson" is part of a long tradition of telling one's peers that verbal resistance is futile. This (a wack MC approaching me) is like *that* (a small-boned androgynous performer challenging his abusive blue-collar dad). Vintage LL similied himself to a heavyweight champ saying "I'm like Tyson, icin' I'm a soldier at war/making sure you don't try to battle me no more." Talib Kweli forewarned any prospective foes that "I'm like shot clocks, blood clots and interstate cops—my point is, your flow gets stopped"—cleverly conflating several different implications of the word "flow."

Busta Rhymes, verbalizing on the remix for Pharoahe Monch's incendiary "Get the Fuck Up," dismissed a rival by saying:

> *The bitch in you coming out and you're showing it*
> *Like when the British civil service gave secrets to the Soviets.*

Mos Def offered a classic line on the cut "Definition," from the Black Star project, claiming that the duo had "accurate assassinship" before pointing out that "me and Kweli close like Bethlehem and Nazareth." In a different vein, Nas on *Illmatic* advertised his prodigious weed consumption by stating

> *You couldn't catch me in the streets without a ton of reefer*
> *That's like Malcolm X catching the jungle fever.*

The ultimate homage to an MC's skill is the rewind. Only the most basic of MCs can be taken at face value; the true artist strives to craft rhymes that, like a taut cinematic thriller, you understand better the second time around. And this effect can be achieved in a number of ways—an intricate flow, filled with unexpected rhyme phrases may induce repeat listening. But more often than not, MCs prefer to drop lines with layered meanings that filter up to the surface live seconds after the line was spoken—when the listener is already grappling with the next rhyme phrase. This explains why simile is so frequently paired with another of the MC's trademark lyrical tools—the double entendre.

On "Dooinit" form the *Resurrection* LP, Common offers this example:

> *I stay focused like Gordon Parks when it's sorta dark*
> *For niggas flooded with ice, my thought is the ark.*

His simile is combined with an internal rhyme and *two* double entendres—focus as mental concentration and as the means a photographer uses to achieve clarity in an image. Ice serves as a reference to both frozen water and diamonds. But by the time these multiple interpretations become apparent, Common is already off to other subjects. And thus the listener rewinds. Nas on *Illmatic* issued the politically incorrect simile–double entendre saying "my style switches like a faggot." Lord Finesse informed the world that "my style is tricky—like spelling Mississippi." On the classic "Raw," Big Daddy Kane constructed a simile connected to a homonym saying of his competitors that

> *None of them can see me*
> *I leave' em whinin' like their names were Bebe and CeCe.*

The fact that the ebonic enunciation of *whining* is almost indistinct form the gospel singers last name, *Winans*, allowed Kane to get away with an otherwise unworkable line.

While the goal of the simile is to literally express similarities between two objects or ideas, hip hop lyricism also makes use of comparisons that serve the exact opposite purpose—to highlight the *distinctions*, often between an artist and his or her inferior counterpart. In the palette of hip hop literary techniques, comparison is, in fact, behind only metaphor and simile as the method of choice. Given the simple fact that hip hop has been both explicitly and implicitly about competition since the days when the first MC dropped the first rhyme, it makes sense that comparison—especially of one's rhyming repertoire—would occupy a central niche. Phife's declarations that he "got more rhymes than the Winans got family," is grand comparison to those who know the size of that gospel-singing clan. And that point might be outdone only be KRS-One's assertion that he "got more rhymes than there's Jamaicans in Brooklyn"—you don't need a census tract to know that there's a whole lot of Jamaicans in Brooklyn.

When Jay-Z informed his listeners that "the boy got more sixes than first grade," he was talking about 600 series Mercedes Benzes, not school-aged children. G-Unit's Lloyd Banks dropped a similarly numerical theme, claiming that he "Got more four five's and nines than a deck of cards," playing on the caliber of his 45 and 9 millimeter handguns. Young Z schooled would-be contenders that he rolls with "more niggas than the NAACP"—at last count, the National Association for the Advancement of Colored People had half a million members. In that same vein, Lord Finesse announced in a classic freestyle:

> *It's better that you chill and max with me*
> *I'm sending out warnings quicker than a fax machine.*

While Big L, Finesse's partner in the revered Diggin in the Crates crew, rhymed that:

> *I keep the women screaming and fiendin' for cool shit*
> *My rhymes are phat and your are thin as a pool stick.*

Jean Grae played on the dual meanings of the term "credit" in saying that because her skills have gone unrecognized there's "more credit due to me than a store that doesn't exchange." Grae was also responsible for a line in which she declared herself "more necessary than violence on the Amistad."

M-1 of Dead Prez explained that "I be what John Wilkes Booth was to Lincoln." Wordsworth combined a slick double entendre with his comparison, pointing out that conflicts with him "result in more cast appearances than a thousand actors." In that same vein, Big Pun rhymed:

> *My prerogative to chase girls who look provocative*
> *Terror Squad rock ice whiter than Yugoslavians.*

In so doing he deliberately compared the clarity of his diamonds with the fair skin of Eastern Europeans.

Hip hop utilizes literary technique even down to its most fundamental level: the use of rhyming phrases. That rhyme is a literary technique in itself so obvious that it is overlooked. But the MC goes beyond operating on the most basic approach to rhyme-linking a single syllable to one that sounds similar to it—and employs the variations of rhyme types: oblique rhyme, double and triple rhyme, assonance, identical rhyme, and internal rhyme. Check Obie Trice's debut album, *Cheers.* On the intro track, "Average Man," the Detroit-based bard drops a swift double rhyme and follows it with a triple rhyme.

> *I'm no gangster—I'm an average man*
> *But damn if I let 'em do me savage man*
> *Before that, I'm strapped and will challenge him*
> *Cock back and the gat will damage them.*

Double rhyme entails matching two syllables to two similar sounding syllables and triple rhyme involves the same approach to three syllables. The words "average" and "savage" in the first couple constitute a double rhyme, but in order to make it work the MC has to elide the first word down to two syllables: "av'rage." The words "challenge" and "damage" are oblique rhymes—meaning words that do not rhyme, but are enunciated in such a way as to manufacture a rhyme, but they are each attached to the proper rhymes *him* and *them*. Jay-Z worked that same technique on "Moment of Clarity."

> *Pop died, didn't cry didn't know him that well*
> *Between him doing heroin and me doing crack sales.*

The words *well* and *sale* rhyme obliquely, purely because the artist chose to blend the short *e* in "well" into a long *a* sound so the word was pronounced more like "wail."

When Jay-Z announced that "Truth be told, I wanna rhyme like Common Sense/(But I did five mil) I ain't rhymed like Common since," he was not only speaking of the corrupting influence of the dollarism on art and making deft use of homonyms, but also utilizing a technique called *identical rhyme*—the use of two words that are pronounced the same but spelled differently and carry different meanings. Kanye West uses the same identical rhyme approach on "Never Let You Down" from *College Dropout*, but follows it with a double entendre:

I can't complain what an accident did to my left eye
'cause look what an accident did to Left Eye
First Aaliyah, now Romeo must die.

The phrases "left eye" and "Left Eye" refer to his face—which was damaged in a car accident—in the first instance and the lyricist Lisa Lopez—who was killed in a car accident—in the second. He then refers to the death of R&B singer Aaliyah and the film she starred in, *Romeo Must Die*. But it wasn't a coincidence that the television actor Romeo Santana had also been murdered in the previous year. Obie Trice on *Cheers* also utilizes identical rhyme:

They say to increase the peace
The only piece that increase
Is the type that deletes your peeps.

The MC deliberately conflates peace, the absence of conflict, with piece, the street reference for a weapon. As in the kind of "piece" that deletes the presence of one's people.

Yet even as rhyming complexity evolved as a hallmark of hip hop lyricism, it was—at least to many on the music's periphery—overshadowed by the broad palette of words that artists chose to employ in their lyricism. To be precise: rap's insistent, widespread, and unrepentant usage of cuss words distinguished it from virtually every other popular music since the advent of rock and roll. It also gave fuel to those who would offhandedly dismiss the art form. In its early expressions, especially those captured on wax, the curse word was the rare exception. As late as the mid 1980s Craig G—who later earned a rep as a freestyler supreme—lamented on "Shout":

On the mic I don't curse, that is the worst
I don't wanna catch beef every time I converse

Schoolly D's "PSK"—short for Park Side Killers—contained the word "fuck" and the critic and pioneer hip hop scribe Nelson George talked about how chilling the song was in its description of casual violence. The lyrical god Rakim never cursed on his classic material, and only used the word *nigga* on the cut "Know the Ledge" on the soundtrack of the film *Juice*—and even then he was rhyming in the person of the film's antagonist, Bishop (which also happened to be Tupac Shakeur's breakout role). It might've been the recognition of the change in the expectations of the MC that inspired Ra to say on the Jay-Z/Dr. Dre/Rakim collaboration, "The Watcher":

You could try copin'
I seen enough shit to leave your frame of mind broken.

As late as 1988 Kane had to issue a disclaimer before cussin:

If you were loungin' around it's time to get up
Pardon my expression, but I'ma tear shit up.

(Admittedly he did say later on that same cut that you could "fuck around with Kane and come out black and blue.") The standards for lyrical audacity changed in the latter part of the 1980s, amplified in part by NWA's early releases and Ice Cube's multiple *motherfuckers* per minute ratio on *Amerikkka's Most Wanted*. Classic Cube inaugurated a song with the observation:

> *Goddamn another fucking payback with a twist*
> *The motherfuckers shot, but the punks missed*

Ultimately, the shift meant little in terms of the mechanics of rhyming—*fuck* rhymes with *truck* no better or worse than *stuck* does—but the new language ensured that the music would not be inter-generational. Any honest reading of the musical history of black America would yield that the sentiments expressed in hip hop were not new—they were simply the first generation that could speak them without the euphemism of metaphors. On another level, the four-letter vocabulary that increasingly entered the rap lexicon served to place their poetry on the level of the context that it was more often than not attempting to describe. For what it matters, Paul Lawrence Dunbar, who caught grief from certain quarters of the afrostocracy for his use of Negro dialect in his poems, could've understood the criticisms leveled at rappers for their language liberties. As it stood, hip hop became the only music in which one might routinely hear technical nouns like *motherfucker*. But like it or not, the addition of profanity-laced lyrics echoed the ways in which some ideas were expressed. This was either evidence of either degeneracy or democracy. Or both. And on that level, maybe *fuck* did rhyme better than any of its milder substitutes.

And beyond utilizing specific literary techniques within a song, hip hop increasingly developed lyricism in which the song was the technique. That is to say songs that contain themes that in turn dictate how the song can be expressed. A prime example of this thematic approach is Mos Def's "Mathematics," in which the entire song is a form of algebraic expression with lines like:

> *I got 16 to 32 bars to rock it*
> *But only 10% of profits*
> *Ever see my pockets.*

"Two Words," the collaboration of Kanye West, Mos Def, and Freeway, featured three MCs organizing their verses such a way that each two words expressed a complete thought or a complete premise for the next two words of the rhyme. Jay-Z's "22 Twos" from *Reasonable Doubt* was structured such that the words *to, two,* and *too* appeared twenty-two times in the first sixteen bars and too appeared twenty-two times in the first sixteen bars and 50 Cent's "21 Questions" posed that number of interrogative statements in the body of the song. Notorious B.I.G. constructed the hustler's how-to guide "Ten Crack Commandments" in such a way that the song could be divided into ten distinct themes.

Not all of these songs were based on numerical progressions. Nas scripted "Rewind," which, in keeping with the title, relayed a violent chain of events in reverse order, complete with inverted quotes like "Go he there." Masta Ace strung alphabetic lines together on "Alphabet Soup"—a song where single letters are deployed creatively to narrate the tale of a carjacking gone awry.

On virtually every level of the form—from the timing and cadence of rhymes to the level of technical sophistication in their construction—hip hop remained in dialogue with ancestral poetic and musical traditions. And at the same time, the MC remains at the foreground of those traditions, expanding their application to a new set of musical practices. In reality, though, the lyrical construction of the art was only one level on which the evolution of the art and this ancestral dialogue occurred. The other level involved the actual *content* of the work itself.

OBJECTIVE QUESTIONS

1. What the MC calls free style, the jazz musician calls _____—literally "confronting structure with a riff on time."
2. What is the common structure of blues lyrics?
3. Jay Z pointed out that "people compare rap to other genres of music, like jazz or rock 'n' roll, but it's really most like a _____."
4. Who was Ray Jones Jr.?
5. What is the significance of the battle between Kool Moe Dee and Busy Bee at Harlem World in 1983?
6. For a period in the late 80s, Big Daddy Kane and Rakim were to Hip Hop what _____.
7. For the MC, _____ have proven to be as important as the content and circumstances under which one says it.
8. The Cold Crush Brothers' routines were not all that far removed from _____.
9. By the early 90s, the harmonic tradition in Hip Hop had been so long neglected that _____ could be seen as an innovation rather than a throw-back to the styles of old.
10. At its heart, it is an individual time signature, the rapper's own idiosyncratic approach to the use of time:_____.
11. Jay Z alliteratively confessed on his *Black Album* that he had "_____ for his audience and _____."
12. The author identifies at least eight common poetic and literary devices in Hip Hop. What are they, and what do they mean?
13. Breaking lines in the middle of a sentence is a technique called _____.
14. Who was the cleanup rhymer on Marley Marl's famous "Symphony"?
15. According to the author, the most recurrent theme in KRS-One's body of work over the past seventeen years has been_____.
16. What is epistolary form?
17. According to the author, what is the purpose of an analogy?
18. What is the ultimate homage to an MC's skill?
19. The author identifies six different types of rhyme. What are they? Give examples.
20. Like it or not, the addition of profanity-laced lyrics echoed the ways in which some idea were expressed. This was evidence of either_____ or _____ . Or both.

QUESTIONS FOR FURTHER THOUGHT, RESEARCH, AND DISCUSSION

1. What does the word "aesthetic" mean? How has it changed over time?
2. Analyze one or more of your favorite Hip Hop recordings using the poetic devices listed in this chapter.
3. Read and discuss the importance of Ralph Ellison's novel *The Invisible Man*.
4. The author states that the standards for lyrical audacity changed in the latter part of the 1980s and that the Hip Hop generation was the first African-American generation that could speak without the euphemism of metaphor. Do you agree?
5. Discuss the role of artistic expression in a capitalistic society.
6. Do you think that profanity and vulgar speech are necessary to express the true meaning of ghetto life?
7. Discuss the relationship of "beat" poets and comedians like Allen Ginsberg, William S. Burroughs, and Lenny Bruce to Hip Hop history.

PART TWO

Roots

Sipple Out Deh

By Jeff Chang

Jeff Chang is a well-established and respected Hip Hop journalist who has written for *The San Francisco Chronicle*, *The Village Voice*, *Vibe*, *The Nation*, *URB*, *Rap Pages*, *Spin*, and *Mother Jones*. He was a founding editor of *Colorlines Magazine*, senior editor of Russell Simmons's 360hiphop.com, and cofounder of the influential label Sole-Sides. You can visit him at www.cantstopwontstop.com.

Can't Stop Won't Stop, by Jeff Chang, is probably the definitive and most comprehensive history of Hip Hop written to date. Chapter two, included here, attempts to trace the roots of Hip Hop back to Jamaica. Chang writes, "jazz had New Orleans; the blues had the Mississippi delta, and Hip Hop had Jamaica." The similarities shared by Hip Hop as it emerged from the Bronx and Jamaican culture go way beyond big street dances with powerful sound systems. The irony is that even though Kool Herc came to the Bronx from Jamaica, Jamaican culture and music were not popular or fashionable in the Bronx until years after Hip Hop emerged. Reggae music and dreadlocks were looked down upon and Herc tried hard to lose his Jamaican accent. There is no denying, however, that the curious mixture of music, corrupt politics, religion, gangs and drugs that were found in Jamaica in the 60s and 70s appears to be a precursor to a similar blend that later emerged from the Bronx. The invention of the "dubplate" or simply "dub" is unquestionably the most important Jamaican contribution. The idea of "dub," for Chang, takes on a huge and broad metaphorical significance, a metaphor that he develops throughout the entire volume. The "dub" becomes the 'B' side, the "other" side of the story, or the hidden truth. It also is analogous to the invisible and parallel spirit world that *rastas* believe simultaneously inhabits the same space we live in, but in another dimension. There is also the glorification of the legendary outlaw hero Rhygin, the subject of the cult movie *The Harder They Come*, and his mysterious graffiti tags and eventual martyrdom. All of this takes place in the most impoverished urban ghettoes imaginable, plagued by "cleansing" arson fires, where pop culture meets the third world. The similarities are obvious and undeniable. The amount of direct influence of Jamaican street culture on Hip Hop in the Bronx, however, is still debatable.

Chang's writing style is also somewhat remarkable. He describes history, not necessarily chronologically, but in a series of overlapping and interlocking "loops," circles, or ciphers. He also writes with a kind of "insider" tone, taking full advantage of the culture's rich colloquialisms and betraying his love of the subject. Chang deftly manages to portray himself as a passionate fan while still maintaining the objectivity of an outside observer.

"SIPPLE OUT DEH" FROM *CAN'T STOP WON'T STOP*

Jamaica's Roots Generation and the Culture Turn

You know how a thing and the shadow of that thing could be in almost the same place together? You know the way a shadow is a dark version of the real thing, the dub side?

—Nalo Hopkinson

IN JAMAICA, YOU DRIVE from the wrong side of the car on the wrong side of the road. Rounding the hill down into Montego Bay, you hug the curves on two-lane roads. Even at rush hour, you slow for cows and goats chewing grass along the gutter side, because apparently all the animals in Jamaica are free-range.

It's dusk on Thursday, a school night, but the youths have taken over Mobay's narrow streets. Traffic is backed up along all of the roads into and out of the seaside town. Even transactions at the turnaround in Sam Sharpe Square—where unmetered taxis swoop in to drop off and pick up customers in a bewildering free-for-all—are slowed by the weight of teenage bodies.

They stream through the streets like tributaries toward the ocean, where, in a waterfront spit of dirt called Urban Development Park, ten-foot high columns of speakers rise in a half-circle around a small stage. The pouting, Tupac-shirted boys and the spandexed, braided girls ripple through the 6:30 P.M. commute—concrete, mixers, oil trucks, and family vans caught bumper to bumper on the Bottom Road—and in through a small gap in a low barbed-wire fence. On the field, they pass dice games played by kerosene lamp, higglers selling Red Stripe and Ting. The air smells faintly of ash from mountain fires. Smoke from dozens of portable roast-peanut and jerk-chicken carts hazes the half moon rising.

The rest of the countryside follows. Uniformed schoolchildren swinging their book bogs, young denim-skirted mothers with toddlers on arm, the barmaids and working boys stride off their shift and into the dance. The elder locksmen and the gray-haired grannys sway to the music. In the front of an earbleed-inducing bassbin tower, a turbaned Boboshanti gives an inscrutable grin, his fingers touching finger-to-finger, thumb-to-thumb in the sign of the Trinity.

Through modern Jamaican history, much more than musical vibes could be at stake in settings like these. In the dance, political fortunes might rise or fall, society made or undone. If political parties controlled jobs and turf, wealth and despair, they rarely exerted much control here. This was the people's space, an autonomous zone presided over by music men and women, a shelter of collective memory.

Tonight, while the band sets up onstage for a star-studded bill of twenty-first-century dancehall stars, the sound-system operators, housed in a series of special tents that enclose the circle of speakers, drink up and play music. Candle Sound System, the local "foundation sound," is spinning the classics. An old Bob Marley song, "Chances Are," inspires a resounding wheel-up and cries of "Big tune!" It is a thirty-year-old ballad, not danceable, but something more—a sweet echo of the post-independence years, before Marley was an international star, when his was a voice of a young nation bursting with hope and pride. Everyone, no matter their age, seems to know all the words. They sing, "Though my days are filled with sorrow, I see it-a bright tomorrow."

From his turntables, Candle's selector shifts time forward, cueing a Dennis Brown bassline. Another roar of recognition goes up, and a blast of approving airhorns. This time, hundreds of lighters raise, flickering lights over a black sea. As Brown sings the opening lines—"Do you know what it takes to have, a, revolution?"—the country youths release their aerosol cans into the butane. At the start of a new century, they recreate an elemental, biblical sight. Against the purple sunset, bolts of flames shoot up, tongues of fire licking up the night sky like history and prophecy.

The blues had Mississippi, jazz had New Orleans. Hip-hop has Jamaica. Pioneer DJ Kool Herc spent his earliest childhood years in the same Second Street yard that had produced Bob Marley. "Them said nothing good ever come outta Trenchtown," Herc says. "Well, hip-hop came out of Trenchtown!"

Reggae, it has often been said, is rap music's elder kin. Yet the story runs much deeper than just music. During the 1970s, Marley and the roots generation—the first to come of age after the island nation received independence from Great Britain in 1962—reacted to Jamaica's national crisis, global restructuring and imperialist posturing, and intensified street violence. Seeing politics exhausted, they channeled their energies into culture, and let it flow around the world. They pulled global popular culture into the Third World. Their story is the prelude to the hip-hop generation, felt as a portentous shudder from the dub side. "Some are leaves, some are branches," Bob Marley had sung. "I and I a di roots."

SO LONG RASTAFARI CALL YOU

When the 1970s opened in Jamaica, national pride was surging.

A song contest had played a major role. In 1966, Edward Seaga, a ranking conservative in the leading Jamaican Labour Party (JLP), who had been one of the first music executives to record indigenous music, instituted the annual Jamaica Festival Song Competition. The contest supported the young island industry and fostered national identity by introducing and making stars of *patwa*-singing, ghetto-identifying artists like Toots and the Maytals and Eric Donaldson. Long before many of his contemporaries, Seaga understood that Jamaica was the kind of place where it was hard to tell where the politics ended and the music began.

But the economy, still dependent on the former colonial arrangements, sputtered. Banana farming needed price supports and protection. The bauxite and tourist industries—the kind of businesses that extracted more than they put in—were growing, but had little effect on an island where more than one in three was unemployed. Here was where the optimism of official nationalism broke down.

The gospel of Rastafari offered faith, history, prophecy and redemption, a people's nationalism that countered the official nationalism. Rastafarians followed in the tradition of the Black nationalist Marcus Mosiah Garvey. Born in 1887 in the northern town of St. Ann's Bay, Garvey's mother had wanted to name him Moses. His followers in the Black diaspora of the Caribbean, North and Central America, and Africa—which, at the peak of his powers, likely numbered in the millions—called him the Black Moses.

Inspired by Booker T. Washington's *Up From Slavery*, and moved by the debased condition of Black farmers and canal workers he met on a visit to Panama, Garvey returned to the streets of Kingston to preach Black redemption and repatriation to a united Africa. He founded the United Negro Improvement Association in 1914 to formally spread the message. "Wake up Ethiopia! Wake up Africa!" he told his followers. "Let us work towards the one glorious end of a free, redeemed, and mighty nation. Let Africa be a bright star among the constellation of nations."

Two years later, Garvey left for Harlem after followers discovered he had used organization funds to pay for his living expenses. In the United States, Garvey's fiscal weaknesses were further exploited when he became the political target of a young Justice Department official named J. Edgar Hoover. But while his reputation had been sullied, his words remained the stuff of prophecy. He had said "We Negroes believe in the God of Ethiopia, the everlasting God—God the Son, God the Holy Ghost, the one God of all ages." And by the mid-1930s, former Garveyites found that God in the figure of Ethiopia's newly crowned emperor born Ras Tafari—"Ras" meaning "Duke" in Amharic and "Tafari" the surname of the royal family—and renamed Haile Selassie, "The Might of The Trinity."

To the followers of Rastafari, Selassie was god made flesh, the King of Kings, the conquering lion of Judah, the redeemer and the deliverer of the Black masses who had come in accordance with Garvey's prophecy. Rastafarianism was an indigenous fusion of messianism and millenarianism, anticolonialism and Black nationalism, and it gave the cause of "Black supremacy" spiritual, political, and social dimensions. The religion found a fast following in the impoverished western Kingston ghettos, especially in the yard called Back-O-Wall, where Rastas constructed a camp of wood and tin. Through the mid-1960s, amidst frequent and constant run-ins with the colonial authorities, their influence over the tenement yards grew.

Under a musician named Count Ossie, Rastafarians learned Burru drumming, an African art that had survived from the days of slavery and had come to the Kingston ghettos after slavery was abolished. Burru centered on the interplay of three drums—the bass drum, the alto *fundeh*, and the repeater. The repeater was reserved for the best drummer, who imbued it, in the scholar Verena Reckford's words, with color and tension, protest and defiance.[1] DJs, the Jamaican term for rappers, would later mimic the play of the Burru repeaters over reggae instrumentals, echoes across time.

Count Ossie gave the Rastas a medium for their message, and the drumming spread with Rastafarianism across Kingston from camp to camp. Ossie would receive and mentor many of the most important Jamaican ska, rock steady, and reggae musicians at his haven on Wareika Hill. Due in no small part to his efforts, Jamaican musicians began to blend the popular New Orleans rhythm-and-blues with elements of folk mento, jonkanoo, kumina, and Revival Zion styles into a new sound.

But while Rasta thought—first in coded forms, then gradually more explicitly spread through popular music, the authorities portrayed Rastas as bizarre cultists. Many of Jamaica's Black and brown strivers held the same opinion. As a child in Kingston, DJ Kool Herc recalls, he was told that anyone who had their hair twisted up was, in local parlance, a badman. In 1966, Rastas began to move from the margins to the mainstream of Jamaican society. On April 21, Haile Selassie came to Jamaica and was greeted by a gathering of more than a hundred thousand followers. As the plane landed, the rain stopped, which all gathered took for a sign.

"I remember watching it on TV," DJ Kool Herc recalls. "They took buses and trucks and bicycles and any type of means of transportation, going to the airport for this man who they looked upon as a god. That's when Jamaica really found out there was a force on the island.

"When that the plane came down, they stormed the tarmac," he continues. "Haile Selassie came out and looked at the people and went back on the plane and cried. He didn't know he was worshiped that strongly." The Rastas were exuberant, and their ranks swelled with new converts.

But three months later, history took another sharp turn. Seaga—then the Minister of Community Development and Welfare—was in need of a new political base. The JLP leader, former music exec, and cultural patron was an ambitious man with dangerous connections. He once faced down some hecklers at a political rally by saying, "If they think they are bad, I can bring the crowds of West Kingston. We can deal with you in any way at any time. It will be fire for fire, and blood for blood."[2]

Now Seaga fingered the Back-O-Wall ghetto, the west Kingston yard where the camps of the Boboshanti and two other Rasta sects thrived. It was an area that had voted for the opposing political party, the democratic socialist People's National Party (PNP), and Seaga wanted it cleared. So on the morning of July 12, armed police filled the air with tear gas, and dispersed the residents with batons and rifles. Bulldozers rolled in behind the police, flattening the shanties. "When the first raided camp was demolished," Leonard Barrett reported, "a blazing fire of unknown origin consumed what remained to ashes while the fire company stood by."[3]

On the site, Seaga built a housing project named Tivoli Gardens and moved in a voting constituency of JLP supporters. He recruited and armed young badmen to protect the area and expand the JLP turf, a gang that called itself, appropriately enough, the Phoenix.[4] The lines were now drawn for generations to come.

"And I can see it with my own eyes," Culture sang a decade later on "Two Sevens Clash." "It's only a housing scheme that divides." Politics, apocalypse—some reasoned—was it a coincidence the two words sounded so similar?

GLOBALIZING THE ROOTS REBEL

In 1973, Jamaica's record industry was on the verge of a major international breakthrough. Up until then, the island had produced occasional novelty hits, like Millie Small's "My Boy Lollipop," that crossed over from Britain's growing West Indian immigrant community to the Top of the Pops and the American top 40. But with the twin vehicles of film and music, the Third World roots rebel made his global debut.

Debuting in Jamaica in 1972, with wider global release the following year, Perry Henzell's movie *The Harder They Come* was a portrait of the Jamaica few yankees would ever trod. The movie opened with a country bus navigating a narrow northern road, the coconut trees of the stormy coastline eerily headless, their fronds and fruits sheered off by plague. Singer Jimmy Cliff played Ivan O. Martin, a peasant making the well-worn trip from rural parish to concrete jungle, the metaphoric journey of a newly freed nation into modernity. But this was not to be a narrative of progress.

Vincent "Ivanhoe" Martin was a real-life fifties Kingston outlaw who renamed himself Rhygin and summoned Jamaica's Maroon pride. *The Harder They Come* updated his story for a nation defining its postcolonial identity in and through its homegrown popular music. Cliffs Ivan was to be exploited by a greedy music producer, reviled by a Christian pastor, and eventually tortured and hunted by corrupt police. A country *bwai* innocent remade into the urban renegade Rhygin, he shoots down a cop and goes underground. A picture of him posing with two pistols hits the papers and his song controls the airwaves. "As sure as the sun will shine, I'm gonna get my share now, what's mine," he sings, "and then the harder they come, the harder they'll fall, one and all." The new legend of Rhygin would frame the island's turbulent seventies.

In another landmark 1973 film, *Enter the Dragon*, Jim Kelly's African-American activist character Williams had gazed at Bruce Lee's Hong Kong home from a sampan and said, "Ghettos are the same all *over* the world. They stink." Like Bruce Lee, the Third World reggae heroes seemed to First World audiences an intriguing mix of the familiar and fresh. The soundtrack to Henzell's film, and the debut album by Bob Marley and the Wailers positioned reggae as a quintessential rebel music, steeped in a different kind of urban Black authenticity.

The Wailers' album, *Catch a Fire,* would be a product of the sometimes giddy, sometimes halting dialogue between Third World roots and First World pop. When Bob Marley delivered the rough master tapes to the Island Records offices in London in the dead winter of 1972, a lot was riding on the getting the mix right.

Just months earlier, the Wailers had been stranded in Britain, abandoned by their manager after a European tour failed to materialize. Island Records head Chris Blackwell, a prominent financier of Henzell's film, bailed them out by signing them, advancing them £4,000, and sending them home to Kingston to record the album. They took their opportunity seriously—it was a chance for the boys from Trenchtown to bring the message of Jamaican sufferers to the world.

Blackwell, a wealthy white descendant of Jamaican rum traders now living in London, was beginning to have success in the rock market, and knew he might be on a fool's mission in trying to cross reggae over. But, emboldened by the success of *The Harder They Come*, and embittered by Jimmy Cliff's snubbing to sign a deal with EMI, he was eager to see how far reggae could be taken into the mainstream. He gave the Wailers fancy album packaging and put them on tour with rock and funk bands. Most importantly, he sent the music back for overdubs by rock session musicians, keyboardist—Rabbit Bundrick and guitarist Wayne Perkins.

The album's leadoff track, "Concrete Jungle," illustrated the perils and promise of translating Jamaican music for First World audiences. The opening notes drifted into a disorienting key, Robbie Shakespeare's bassline seemed to omit more notes than were played, Bunny Wailer and Peter Tosh's harmonies floated and attacked like rope-a-dope boxing. Marley's lyrics described the unrelenting bleakness of the west Kingston yard. "No chains around my feet," the Wailers sang, "but I'm not free." It was utterly brilliant, but the music, Blackwell decided, sounded far too Jamaican.

When he first played the music to Perkins, the Muscle Shoals guitarist couldn't understand the riptide of riddims. But as the song built to the break, Perkins cut loose with a bluesy torrent, culminating in a ringing sustain. Blackwell and engineer Tony Piatt hit the echo machine and the note fed back, soaring up two octaves. "It gave me goosebumps, it was one of those magical moments," Perkins says.[5] Marley, who had spent long, cold, destitute years in America pursuing his pop dream, thought so, too.

Their album would only sell 14,000 copies in its first year, but the Wailers had taken the first step in turning their local music into an international phenomenon. *Catch a Fire* was a landmark moment in the globalization of Third World culture. Fulfilling the destiny the elder Rastas in Trenchtown had long seen for him, Marley was on his way to becoming a worldwide icon of freedom struggle and Black liberation—the small axe becoming the first trumpet.

SOUNDS AND VERSIONS

The pop audience demanded heroes and icons, but reggae, perhaps more than any other music in the world, also privileged the invisible music men, the sonic architects—the studio producer and the sound system selector. Together, during the seventies, these two secretive orders emerged as sources of power in Jamaica.

One center, though it may not have seemed so at the time, was an odd backyard studio in the Kingston suburb of Washington Gardens. Lee "Scratch" Perry, its eccentric owner, was a diminutive man with a feverishly large imagination. Beginning in December of 1973, and continuing night and day for five years, Perry recorded an unceasing parade of harmony groups, singers, and DJs in the tiny, stuffy, concrete structure that he called the Black Ark. The music emerging from the Ark—including Junior Murvin's "Police and Thieves," The Heptones' "Mr. President," and The Congos' "Children Crying"—was mesmerizing and shocking, and would soon reverberate across the globe.

It was a gloriously weird place, this Black Ark, another autonomous zone. Its exterior walls sported a blue, red, and white image of Emperor Haile Selassie and the Lion of Judah, surrounded by purple handprints and footprints like a child's finger paintings. The interior walls were painted red and green, and were crammed with Rasta imagery, Bruce Lee posters, Upsetters album jackets, Teac equipment brochures, Polaroid shots, record stampers, horseshoes, and other ephemera, all covered over by a dense layer of Perry's obscure, signifying graffiti.

Behind a cheap four-track mixing desk, which by the standards of the time was hopelessly outdated, Perry whirled and bopped and twiddled the knobs, imbuing the recordings with wild crashes of echo, gravity-defying phasing, and frequency-shredding equalization. Influenced by his work with Osborne "King Tubby" Ruddock, Perry used aging analog machines like the Echoplex to turn sounds over and back into themselves like Mobius loops. Melodies became fragments, fragments became signs, and the whole thing swirled like a hurricane.

Upon his arrival in Kingston from his native northern countryside in 1960, Perry had headed straight for the powerful sound systems to try to find work, eventually becoming a songwriter for Duke Reid, then moving on to become a scout and operator for Reid's competitor, Coxsone Dodd. According to dancehall historian Norman Stolzoff, sound system culture had evolved in Kingston after World War II when the ranks of live musicians dramatically thinned due to immigration to the United Kingdom and the United States and the rise of the North Coast tourist industry.[6] By the time Perry came to Kingston, sound systems had largely replaced live bands.

Outfitted with powerful amplifiers and blasting stacks of homemade speakers, one only needed a selector and records to transform any yard. The sound systems democratized pleasure and leisure by making dance entertainment available to the downtown sufferers and strivers. The sound systems championed the people's choice long before commercial radio, and as independence approached, they moved from playing mostly American rhythm-and-blues to homegrown ska, rock steady, and finally, reggae.

The fiercely competitive sound systems—including Duke Reid's Trojan, Coxsone Dodd's Downbeat the Ruler, Prince Buster's Voice of the People, King Edwards the Giant, and Tom the Great Sebastian—fought for audiences; some of them even sent thugs to shoot up their rivals' dances and destroy their equipment in fits of anger or desperation.[7] More usually, they distinguished themselves from each other with "specials," records that no other sound system had, songs that mashed up their competitors and drew away their audiences. They even sometimes "clashed" live in the same hall or yard, song for song, "dub fi dub."

Early on, selectors made frequent trips to America to secure obscure exclusives. As the Jamaican music industry expanded during the sixties, sound systems began to record local artists' songs onto exclusive acetates or "dubplates."[8] In 1967, a sound system head affiliated with Duke Reid named Ruddy Redwood stumbled onto Jamaican music's next great innovation.

One afternoon Redwood was cutting dubplates when engineer Byron Smith forgot to pan up the vocals on The Paragons' hit, "On the Beach." Redwood took the uncorrected acetate to the dance that night anyway, and mixing between the vocal and the dub, sent the crowd into a frenzy during his midnight set. Rather than apologize for his mistake the next day, Redwood emphasized to Reid that the vocal-less riddim could be used as a B-side on the commercial release of the singles. Reid, for his part, realized he could cut his costs by half or more. One studio session could now produce multiple "versions."[9] A single band session with a harmony trio could be recycled as a DJ version for a rapper to rock *patwa* rhymes over, and a dub version in which the mixing engineer himself became the central performer—experimenting with levels, equalization and effects to alter the feel of the riddim, and break free of the constraints of the standard song.

Dub's birth was accidental, its spread was fueled by economics, and it would become a diagram for hip-hop music. A space had been pried open for the break, for possibility. And, quickly, noise came up from the streets to fill the space-yard-centric toasts, sufferer moans, analog echoes— the sounds of people's histories, *dub histories,* versions not represented in the official version. As musical competition was overshadowed by violent political competition, dub became the sound of a rapidly fragmenting nation—troubling, strange, tragic, wise slow-motion portraits of social collapse.

ROOTS AND CULTURE

Every Jamaican politician knew what every Jamaican musician knew—the sound systems were crucial to their success. During the seventies, the fight for political dominance between the conservative Jamaica Labour Party (JLP) and leftist People's National Party (PNP) seemed inevitably to turn on the mood of the people in the dance. All any prime minister had to do to gauge the winds was to listen closely to the week's 45 rpm single releases; they were like political polls set to melody and riddim.

The message was becoming decidedly roots and radical. In the fall of 1968, the JLP-led government had banned Black-power literature and icons like the pan-Africanist leader Walter Rodney from the University of the West Indies campus, then violently crushed the political riots that ensued across the city. But this did not stop the electorate from moving hard left. Intellectuals high on Malcolm X, socialists stricken by Castro, middle-class strivers impatient for price stability, poor strugglers facing dim prospects, even Rastas traditionally reluctant to participate in what Peter Tosh called the Babylon *shitstem* all clamored for change. Sufferer anthems took over the sound systems. The resistance to roots reggae finally gave way on JBC radio, as listeners came home from the yard dances to demand that tunes like Delroy Wilson's "Better Must Come" and the Wailers' "Small Axe" (cut with Perry) be played during daytime hours. Burning Spear summed up the mood of the time: "The people know what it is they want, so they themselves go about getting it."[10]

Compared to Seaga, who had worked the nexus of culture and politics for years, Michael Manley, the democratic socialist PNP candidate, was a late-comer. But as Manley geared up for the 1972 elections, he began appearing at political rallies with his "rod of correction," a staff that he said had been handed to him by Haile Selassie, in explicit recognition of the influence Rastafarianism held among the poor. The rod, he said, would lead him to redressing injustice. Befitting his new image, he spoke of reggae as "the people's language," and selected Wilson's "Better Must Come" as his campaign theme. The following year, the PNP swept the JLP out of office. In Laurie Gunst's worlds, Jamaica in the '70s was "a fever-dream of raised consciousness and high hopes."[11]

But better never came. The twin down pressing forces of Cold War positioning and global economic pressures ripped Jamaica apart.

Manley's democratic socialist government pushed through key social reforms, including lowering the voting age to eighteen, making secondary and university education free, and establishing a national minimum wage. But when Manley moved to reestablish relations with Cuba and build solidarity with leftist leaders in the Caribbean and Africa, CIA surveillance sharply intensified, and First World leaders withdrew aid and investments. In 1971, Jamaica received $23 million in aid from the United States. By 1975, that amount was down to $4 million.[12]

The worldwide oil crisis-fueled recession hit the Jamaican dollar hard, unleashing economic chaos. Prices tripled while wages declined by half; a paycheck suddenly bought one-sixth of what it used to. Labor unions unleashed an unprecedented number of walkouts. Between 1972 and 1979, there were more than three hundred strikes.

North American banks refused to renew aid loans. Jamaica's debt doubled between 1975 and 1980 to $2 billion U.S., the equivalent of 90 percent of the country's gross domestic product.[13] After a bitter internal fight, the PNP reversed course and finally agreed to accept emergency loans for Jamaica from the International Monetary Fund (IMF), who imposed severe austerity measures that caused goods shortages and massive layoffs. The IMF's plan wreaked long-term havoc on the island's economy, wiping out entire industries. To pay off the skyrocketing debt, the PNP raised taxes, causing other businesses to flee the island.

In 1973, gun violence broke out between rival gangs in the Kingston yards. Manley first placed the island "under heavy manners," expanding police powers to search and raid, and stepping up joint police–military operations. He then established a special Gun Court, where gunmen and illegal firearms traffickers faced mandatory indefinite sentences for their crimes.

By the end of 1976, when Manley declared a State of Emergency—the Jamaican equivalent of martial law—it was becoming clear that much of the violence was politically motivated. In the Kingston yards, gangs had divided and mapped their turf. As Seaga had long understood, gang leaders were useful to party machinery—they delivered a yard's votes in election years, fought the ground war during the off years. In turn, politicians granted jobs, favors, and programs to the area dons, who organized the youths into work-groups or militias.

Bounty Killer, the dancehall DJ who grew up in the Riverton neighborhood during the 1970s and '80s, says, "We used to love politics. When time de MP (Member of Parliament) come an' say, '*Bwoy*, we a go gi' weh dis an we a go gi' weh dat'—we interested.

"A poor people—weh a look a likkle help an' a look a hope inna Jamaica—a listen when de Govament a talk," he added. "But no hope no deh deh. Dem haffi hold *oonu* (everyone) inna dat position so dem can get *oonu* attention."[14] In 1974, singer Little Roy went into the Black Ark to record an anguished plea for peace, "Tribal War," a tune whose cyclical revival over the next three decades spoke to the permanence of political gang violence.

While Seaga and the JLP officials turned up the rhetorical heat on the Manley government in Parliament, the JLP gangs lit up PNP yards with Molotov cocktails and gunfire. PNP gangs retaliated in kind, fire for fire, blood for blood. When firefighters arrived in Rema, a JLP community, in January 1976, they confronted youths tossing stones from behind roadblocks of blazing tires. The shanties were left to burn.[15] Manley felt he saw a design to the violence—a devil's bargain between the CIA and the pro-U.S. JLP, Washington bullets in the Kingston streets. He wrote in his memoirs, "I have no doubt that the CIA was active in Jamaica that year and was working through its own agents to destabilise us."[16]

With guns and money flowing to the opposition party, the tribal wars rose to a new pitch. Smoke thickened the heavy air in the zinc yards, and Rhygins in JLP green or PNP red raged through the ghetto. In May, the warfare peaked when gangsters surrounded a tenement yard in West Kingston at Orange Lane and set it ablaze, trapping five hundred residents inside. Gunmen blasted away at the police and firemen who arrived at the scene, and eleven perished in the conflagration. As debate raged in Parliament over which party was responsible for the carnage, and the elections neared, hundreds more were gunned down.

During the tribal wars of the mid-sixties, the Wailers had cut "Simmer Down," a tune encouraging rudies to "control your temper." Now Bob Marley met Lee "Scratch" Perry at the Black Ark to record another track that might cool down the ghetto, "Smile Jamaica," and agreed to do a free concert bearing the same name on December 5. Hearing this news, the PNP scheduled elections for December 20, and made a show of sending armed guards to watch Marley's uptown compound at 56 Hope Road. Marley was enraged. Like many Rastas, he had supported Manley and the PNP in 1972, but now he was disgusted with where *politricks* had led the country.

Two nights before the show, the armed guard mysteriously disappeared. Minutes later, six assassins entered the mansion. Rita Marley was shot in the head, and manager Don Taylor took five bullets destined for Bob, whose chest was grazed as the last bullet entered his left arm. But on the night of the show, Bob was wheeled into National Heroes Park, where a crowd of 80,000, including Manley and a large PNP entourage, had gathered. Marley played a triumphant concert, then left for the Bahamas in a self-imposed exile.

Rumors spread that the JLP, perhaps even the CIA, was behind the hit. The point had been made: violence was striking dangerously near the heart of the people.

THE DUB SIDE

And so they sang of clashes, of war. From imagining distant and free African skies in songs like The Abyssinians' "Satta Massa Gana," The Mighty Diamonds' "Africa," Junior Byles's "A Place Called

Africa," or Bunny Wailer's "Dreamland," they moved to plead for relief from the violence borne of "isms and schisms."

Leroy Smart's "Ballistic Affair" was a tragic dispatch from the fire-scarred danger zone of Seventh Street, the militarized border between Rema and Concrete Jungle, a PNP yard whose Junglist gang was thought to be behind much of the violence:

> We used to lick chalice, cook ital stew together
> Play football and cricket as one brother
> Now through you rest a Jungle
> A you might block a Rema
> You a go fight 'gainst your brother.

Max Romeo and Lee "Scratch" Perry captured the moment's treacherous flux. As Romeo told David Kafz: "I had this song 'War In A Babylon' where me say, 'It wicked out there, it dread out there.' I took it to [Perry], said, 'You like it?' He said 'Yeah!' with excitement, 'but no dread and no wicked, it *sipple* out deh!' So I said, 'Yeah that have a ring to it', because sipple mean slippery, it's slidey out there."[17] In his new chorus, Romeo asked "So wha fi do?" and the answer came, "Mek we *slide* out deh." As the song climaxed, Romeo retreated high up to the Rasta hills as Kingston exploded under the burning sun:

> I man satta on the mountaintop
> Watching Babylon burning red hot
> Red hot!

Here was *The Harder They Come's* Ivan, a reef fish battling the ocean current, a flash of color in the tidal surge, pursued by police and enemies, making a last run through the ghetto, leaving graffiti tags on the concrete walls that mocked, "I was here but I disapear (sic)"—laughing mightily, knowing that he'd already become indelible in the public imagination, that even politics could not erase him—and, like a premonitory smoke above the shanty roofs: "I AM EVERYWHERE." Celebrating survival itself was the point.

While singers and DJs offered words of mourning or escape for the sufferers, dub reggae—the mostly wordless music of dread—ran directly into the heart of the darkness. In Perry's "Revelation Dub," time was creakily kept by a distended, phasing hi-hat and Romeo's vocal was either reduced to the low hum of some distant street protest or chopped into sudden nonsensical stabs—"Warinnai" "Balwarin!"—as if all words, even warnings, could not be trusted. The riddim—which Marley would later version for "Three Little Birds," with its bright chorus, "Don't worry about a thing, 'cause every little thing's gonna be alright"—was swung off its moorings, the textual integrity and authority was undermined. Perry's sound was the epitome of *sipple*. Dub answered the question: what kind of mirror is it that reflects everything but the person looking into it?

Dub had a compelling circularity. It exploded in the dancehall at the moment the tenement yards exploded in violence. Dub was the "B-side" to the soaring visions of the democratic socialist dreamers or the apocalyptic warnings of the Rasta prophets. As reggae historian Steve Barrow says, "The music of dub represents literally and figuratively *'the other side.'* There's an up and a down, there's an A-side and a B-side. It's a dialectical world."

As the two sevens clashed, dub peaked with album sets from Perry (*Super Ape*), Keith Hudson (*Brand*), Niney the Observer (*Sledgehammer Dub*), the Mighty Two-Joe Gibbs and Errol Thompson (Prince Far I's *Under Heavy Manners,* Joe Gibbs' *State of Emergency, African Dub All-Mighty* series), Philip Smart (Tapper Zukie's *Tapper Zukie in Dub*), Harry Mudie (the Dub Conference series), and the most influential dubmaster of all, King Tubby.

Born Osborne Ruddock in 1941, Tubby had collaborated with Perry to demonstrate the possibilities of dub on the 1973 album, *Blackboard Jungle Dub*. With *King Tubbys Meets Rockers Uptown,* an album-length collection of sides with melodica player Augustus Pablo dating to the beginning of Manley's first term, musical innovation and political disintegration seemed to stoke each other.

On the title track, a version of Jacob Miller's "Baby I Love You So," Tubby left Pablo's melodica, Carly Barrett's drums, and Chinna Smith's guitar in shards. Miller had sung, "Night and day, I pray that love will come my way." But Tubby clipped his lines—"Baby I-I-I-I," "night and day," "that love," "And I-I-I-I"—transforming Miller's longing into a prison. On the original, Miller had scatted loosely, then chuckled, perhaps at having missed an essential cue. Tubby added a ghostly echo, leaving the laugh to hang like a haunting, the smoke of Rhygin's trail. At the end, Miller's cry dissolved in a barrage of oscillations, a plunge through a trapdoor.

The last track, inexplicably left unannounced on the original album sleeve and label, was a dub of the Abyssinians' 1969 single, "Satta Massa Gana," colloquially known as the Rastafarian national anthem. In mistranslated Amharic, its title meant to "give thanks and praise" to Haile Selassie, while its harmonies yearned for "a land far far away."[18] Tubby gutted the song to a bass pulse and drum accent. The song's basic chords were twisted out of shape and pitch. Drums dropped like thunderclaps. Tubby's mirror world was the sound of the dreamland alliance of Rastas and democratic socialists disintegrating, its Utopia looted by thugs and left to the whipping hurricane winds of global change.

It was music of the crossfire lifted out of the progression of time, politics, and meaning. Dub embraced contingency. Everything was up for grabs. Dub declaimed, distorted, or dropped out at the razor's edge of a moment. It gave a clipped, fragmented voice to horrors the nation could not yet adequately articulate.

ONE LOVE PEACE MUSIC

When 1978 arrived, another round of election-year violence seemed imminent. But then the unexpected happened. Somehow in early January, Bucky Marshall, a gunman from the PNP-backed Spanglers Posse, ended up in the same General Penitentiary cell as some JLP gangsters and they got to talking.

They spoke of the event that had ended 1977. Renegade soldiers from the Jamaican Defense Force had set up and ambushed an unarmed posse of JLP roughnecks, killing five. But five more got away, and they told the story of the extra-legal set-up to *The Gleaner.* The resulting scandal potentially incriminated both PNP and JLP politicians, and many felt that a coup or a civil war was imminent. Certainly, the rival gunmen in that jail-cell reasoned, no political affiliations could save anyone from the army if something that serious was afoot.

When Marshall stepped out of jail, he went to meet with Claudie Massop, Seaga's man in Tivoli Gardens, who had come up through The Phoenix and was now the area don. The next morning, at a spot straddling the border of JLP and PNP territories in central Kingston, they announced a peace treaty. Marshall and Massop took photos together, and spoke to the press. "This is not political," said Marshall. "This is from we who have felt the pangs of jail."[19] Massop added, "The youths have been fighting among themselves for too long and is only them get dead. Everybody I grow up with is dead."[20] Amidst the spreading truce, elated youths left their yards and began to gather in parks and dances that had formerly been in enemy territory.

With the help of the Rasta sect, the Twelve Tribes of Israel, Marshall, Massop, and the ranking PNP don from Concrete Jungle, "Red Tony" Welch, went to London to see the man who had first brought them together, Bob Marley. Welch and Massop had been frequent guests when Marley was holding court on Hope Road. Now they asked him to return to Jamaica and headline a "One Love Peace Concert." The benefit would raise money for the most suffering PNP and JLP ghettos, to be distributed by the newly formed Central Peace Council, but more importantly, it could curtail the possibility of civil war or a military coup. Marley agreed, and flew home. In the days leading to the concert, Marley toured through the yards to talk up the peace treaty. At the Black Ark, he and Perry recorded "Blackman Redemption" and "Rastaman Live Up" as Massop and Marshall vibed together in the listening room.[21]

On April 22, thousands packed Kingston's National Stadium to hear the island's top musicians, including Dennis Brown, Culture, the Mighty Diamonds, Big Youth, Beres Hammond, Ras Michael and the Sons of Negus, Dillinger, and Jacob Miller, who, with his band Inner Circle, had the most popular tune in the country in "Peace Treaty Special," a rockers-style tribute to Marshall, Massop and the tribes set to a version of the American Civil War-era song, "When Johnny Comes Marching Home Again."[22] "Man can walk the street again, hurrah-ah-e-ah hurrah," Miller sang joyously. "From Tivoli to Jungle, Lizard Town to Rema-hurrah!" Peter Tosh played a scorching set, laced with withering criticisms of the politicians in attendance. Then Marley took the stage, and the crowd swelled to a roar.

As the Wailers gave an inspired performance of "Jamming," Marley called the political leaders onstage. His long dreads cut arcs through the night air, and he danced as if possessed, singing, "Show the people that you love 'em right, show the people you gonna unite." Manley stood to the left of Marley, Seaga to the right, and they tentatively gave each other a handshake. Marley clasped their hands, put them in a power grip and lifted them over his head, holding them high for all to see. The crowd was stunned. "Love, prosperity be with us all," Marley said. "Jah Rastafari. Selassie I."

Through music, Marley had brought together a trinity of power, and restored unity to the young nation. Culture, it seemed, had transcended politics.

THE PRESSURE DROP

But there were other signs as well. Five days before the concert, army soldiers fired on a peaceful ghetto march for better sanitation, killing three demonstrators. The leader of the Central Peace Council, who had called for an end to police corruption, fled the island in fear for his life. Police stopped and searched a taxi Claudie Massop was riding in, then coldly executed him in a hail of fifty bullets.[23] The peace treaty was over. So was Manley's democratic socialist experiment. In 1980, Seaga and the JLP would be overwhelmingly victorious at the polls, stepping up just in time to be courted by the new Reagan administration in Washington. Almost nine hundred people would die in election-year violence.

The reggae industry, too, felt the pressure drop. During the heady independence years of the sixties, Coxsone Dodd's Studio One and Duke Reid's Treasure Isle had been built from local sound system profits. But the Black Ark studio had been financed by the globalization of the reggae industry. Perry's dubs had been partly an answer to the growing international demand for reggae. Reggae music was not only a socially stabilizing force, it had become an important commodity.

The pressures fell disproportionately on the slender shoulders of musicians. Uptown, Bob Marley's Hope Road residence had become a magnet for Twelve Tribes Rastas, a sect that openly and controversially courted the wealthy, whites, and browns. But many more displaced sufferers also frequented the Hope Road yard. Marley archivist Roger Steffens believes that by the late '70s, Marley was directly responsible for the economic fortunes of six thousand people. By 1979, the Marley camp had also become aware of CIA operatives tailing them. And yet, despite being diagnosed with cancer, Marley maintained a hectic touring schedule through the end of 1980, perhaps because of such obligations. "'It took its toll," Steffens says. "He really wanted out." On May 11, 1981, he was dead.

At the beginning of 1978, Perry's Black Ark had become a center for the Boboshanti, an orthodox Rasta sect led by Prince Emmanuel Edwards that adhered to the ideal of Black Supremacy. Perry biographer David Katz notes that the Bobos hoped Perry and his Ark could help disseminate their message, much the same way Marley did for the Twelve Tribes, and that hundreds of people materially depended upon Perry's riddim factory. By the end of the year, Perry had ejected the Bobos, shaved his budding dreads, and turned away Rasta groups and visitors. He began dismantling the studio. He covered the Ark with brown paint and graffiti tags, crossing out words and pictures with Xs. In the summer of 1983, the Black Ark burned to the ground. Perry said he did it himself.

Years later, Perry dictated an extraordinary statement to Katz, a peripatetic freestyle. He began, "The First World and the Second World live, but the Third World is finished because I, Lee 'Scratch' Perry, knows the head of the IMF—the IMF big boss, the Bank of England big boss, the Midland big boss, the International Giro Bank big boss—...

"The Third World drawn in," he continued. "The game blocked; the road block, the lane block, and the street block, so who can't see good better see them eye specialist and take a good look upon the road. The road blocked; all the roads are blocked ...

"Reggae music is a curse, the ultimate destruction," he said. "Logical Fox, solid-state logic."[24]

Fevered dreams of progress had brought fires to the Bronx and Kingston. The hip-hop generation, it might be said, was born in these fires.

NOTES

1. Verena Reckord, "From Burru Drums to Reggae Riddims," *Chanting Down Babylon*, ed. Nathaniel Samuel Murrell, William David Spencer and Adrian Anthony McFarlane (Philadelphia: Temple University Press, 1998), 245.
2. Laurie Gunst, *Born Fi Dead* (New York: Henry Holt, 1995), 84. Darrell Levi notes that the political violence lasted into 1967 and that for a time a state of emergency was imposed. He also cites a 1980 *Jamaica Gleaner* article by PNP Secretary D. K. Duncan that portrays Seaga as violent, saying, "It will be blood for blood, fire for fire, thunder for thunder." Darrell Levi,

Michael Manley: The Making of a Leader (Athens, Ga.: University of Georgia Press, 1989), 117–118, 221, 319n.

3. Leonard Barrett Sr., *The Rastafarians* (Boston: Beacon Press, 1988), 156.

4. Laurie Gunst, *Born Fi Dead,* 79–80.

5. *Classic Albums: Catch a Fire Documentary,* directed by Jeremy Marre (Rhino Video videotape, 2000).

6. Norman Stolzoff, *Wake the Town and Tell the People* (Durham: Duke University Press, 2000), 41–43.

7. David Katz, *People Funny Boy: The Genius* of Lee "Scratch" *Perry* (London: Payback Press, 2000), 11–24.

8. The best discussion of the development of the Jamaican sound system is to be found in Norman Stolzoff, *Wake the Town and Tell the People.*

9. This section relies on interviews with Steve Barrow. Steve Barrow and Peter Dalton, *Reggae: The Rough Guide* (London & New York: Rough Guides/Penguin, 1997).

10. Lloyd Bradley, *This Is Reggae Music: The Story of Jamaica's Music* (New York: Grove Press, 2000), 270.

11. Gunst, *Born Fi Dead,* xvii.

12. Evelyne Huber Stephens and John D. Stephens, *Democratic Socialism in Jamaica* (London: Macmillan, 1986), Table A-20, 397.

13. Omar Davies and Michael Witter, "The Development of the Jamaican Economy Since Independence," *Jamaica in Independence: Essays on the Early Years,* ed. Rex Nettleford (Kingston: Heinemann Caribbean, 1989), Table 4b, 85. Director Stephanie Black contrasts Michael Manley's views with those of IMF official Stanley Fischer while documenting the effects of IMF, Inter-American Development Bank and World Trade Organization policies on the island's dairy farming, beef, carrot, and banana industries. She also covers the disastrous "free trade zone" experiment, where sweatshops producing Tommy Hilfiger and Brooks Brothers clothes are closed after workers begin demanding better working conditions. *Life and Debt,* directed by Stephanie Black (Tuff Gong Pictures, 2001).

14. Melville Cooke, "A Killer Interview," *Jamaica Gleaner* (August 23, 2001).

15. Stephens and Stephens, *Democratic Socialism in Jamaica,* 132–135.

16. Michael Manley, *Struggle in the Periphery* (London: Third World Media Limited, 1982),140.

17. Katz, People *Funny Boy,* 246.

18. 18. Steve Barrow, liner notes from The Abyssinians and Friends, *Tree of Satta, Volume 1* (Blood and Fire Records compact disc BAFCD 045, January 2004).

19. Laurie Gunst, *Born Fi Dead,* 96–1 06.

20. Ibid., 105.

21. Katz, People Funny Boy, 305–307.

22. "When Johnny Comes Marching Home" was reportedly adapted by Union Army bandleader Patrick S. Gilmore from an African-American spiritual.

23. Gunst, *Born Fi Dead,* 106–108.

24. Katz, *People Funny Boy,* 411.

OBJECTIVE QUESTIONS

1. Who was Edward Seaga? How did he affect Jamaican music?
2. Rastafarians followed in the tradition of Black Nationalist _____. What did his followers call him?
3. What was the style of drumming taught to Rastafarians by musician Count Ossie?
4. On April 21st, 1966, he came to Jamaica and was greeted by a gathering of more that one hundred thousand followers, because they thought he was God.
5. What is meant by "patwa"? What is a diaspora?
6. The first Jamaican record to make the American top 40 was "My Boy Lollipop," by _____.
7. What was the name of Bob Marley's first LP?
8. Who played the lead role in the movie *The Harder They Come*?
9. Who was the founder/owner of Island records, and how did he alter Bob Marley's music to help it "cross over"?
10. What was the name of Lee "Scratch" Perry's studio in the Kingston suburb of Washington Gardens?
11. What is a "dubplate," who invented it, and how? Who becomes the central performer?
12. What is name of the Abyssinians 1969 single that became known colloquially as the Rastafarians' national anthem?
13. What year did Bob Marley die?

QUESTIONS FOR FURTHER THOUGHT, RESEARCH, AND DISCUSSION

1. Research the history and ideology of the Rastafarian religion.
2. Compare the gang strife of Jamaicans to that of the Bronx and/or L.A.
3. How did the U.S. react to the Jamaican government of Michael Manley?
4. Report on the "secret life" of J. Edgar Hoover and how that may have affected history.
5. How many elements or characteristics of Hip Hop can you trace to Jamaica?

African Jive

By David Toop

David Toop is a musician, author and music curator. *Rap Attack*, his first book, is now in its third edition. His latest work, *Exotica: Fabricated Soundscapes in a Real World*, was published in summer 1999. Since 1995, he has recorded five solo albums, including *Screen Ceremonies*, *Pink Noir*, and *Spirit World*. He lives in London.

English critics and music journalists often have a refreshingly different take on American popular music and culture than American writers. American writers and fans are plagued by our rigid categorization of the music business. In America, white, black, northern, southern, rural, and urban are narrowly defined styles and markets, and they are most often viewed as essentially incompatible. To the British press and fans, however, it's all just American music, and therefore somewhat exotic. Remember that it took English rock bands to introduce white teenagers of the sixties to the rhythm and blues heritage of their own country, and it was a British executive at Mercury records who convinced his boss that he could sell Kurtis Blow's "Christmas Rappin'" in England. Likewise, it was the Clash who tried to introduce Grandmaster Flash to an angry crowd of American punk rockers, and Blondie's "Rapture" that eventually won them over.

Now in its third edition, David Toop's *Rap Attack* was first published in London in 1984. That makes it one of Hip Hop's very first published histories, and still one of the most interesting. David Toop writes in an almost "stream of consciousness" style, but he also makes a lot of sense. The chapter included here is one of three in his book that traces Hip Hop's deep roots and tentacles. These three chapters effectively and convincingly connect Hip Hop to Cassius Clay, Cab Calloway, doo-wop, rent parties, funk, preachers and radio DJs, just to mention a few. This particular chapter focuses on the relationships between African American folk traditions and their inevitable commercialization as forms of popular entertainment. This chapter is short, but in the somewhat loosely structured narrative, Toop drops a plethora of names, almost all of which have important and fascinating stories of their own. The chapter ends with a reference to the "bragger *par excellence*," Bo Diddley.

"AFRICAN JIVE" FROM *RAP ATTACK 3*

I float like a butterfly, sting like a bee, There ain't no motherfucker than can rap like me
—'CC Crew Rap' by CC Crew
(Golden Flamingo Records)

IN 1964 THE WHITE world was finding it hard to understand a young black boxer named Cassius Clay. Bill McDonald, the promoter of his first crack at Sonny Liston's world heavyweight title, and trainer Angelo Dundee, were failing to appreciate his reasons for associating with Elijah Muhammad and Malcolm X. The Nation of Islam was bad news in the white-run fight game. Those less close to the Clay camp were mystified by his seemingly hysterical behaviour and his rap poetry, the infuriating rhymes which predicted the demise of his opponents: 'Sonny Liston is great/But he'll fall in eight.'

The unfortunate Liston had a better idea of what was going on. An ex-badman, he was well aware that Clay (at the time secretly known as Cassius X but later known to the world as Muhammad Ali), along with his personal shaman, Drew Bundini Fastblack Brown, was engaged in a campaign to shame him into defeat before the first bell. Ali was prepared to take the campaign to Liston's home and remind his well-heeled white neighbours of their new resident's background in the black ghetto. History records that Liston was humiliated twice by Ali. Fight fans with a white complexion would have been less puzzled by the young braggard whipping the awesome monster if they had known something of black street culture.

The Clay versus Liston scenario has a storyline reminiscent of the famous black narrative poem called 'Signifying Monkey'. The monkey is a trickster who taunts the lion, despite its size and strength, and outwits it with verbal skill:

> *There hadn't been no shift for quite a bit*
> *so the Monkey thought he'd start some of his signifying shit.*
> *It was one bright summer day*
> *the Monkey told the Lion, 'There's a big bad burly motherfucker livin' down your way.'*
> *He said, 'You know your mother that you love so dear?*
> *Said anybody can have her for a ten-cent glass a beer.'*

These kind of narrative poems are called toasts. They are rhyming stories, often lengthy, which are told mostly amongst men. Violent, scatological, obscene, misogynist, they have been used for decades to while away time in situations of enforced boredom, whether prison, armed service or streetcorner life. Bruce Jackson, who has made extensive studies of toasts and prison songs, has written:

> There is much time to kill in county jails and little to do with that time, and a great portion of the population in county jails is lower-class black (they are the people without money to pay a bondsman for freedom before trial or who must serve jail time because they lack money to pay a fine).

Toasts, like most oral folk traditions, have become absorbed into commercial entertainment, albeit in a censored form. 'Stackolee', a badman figure familiar from many blues and ballads performed by both black and white musicians, was resurrected by Lloyd Price in 1958 as 'Stagger Lee' for a chart-topping hit and was revived for another shoot-out by The Isley Brothers in 1963. A year later, Rufus Thomas, a remarkable man whose career stretched right back to the medicine-show era, released a tune called 'Jump Back' on Stax. Though the sound is typical of the bluesy soul of the time—uptempo and rough, with cutting saxophone and guitar breaks—the verses of the song date back at least as far as nineteenth-century minstrel shows; a children's line-game song, 'Mary Mack' quoted by Harold Courlander in his book *Negro Folk Music*, has almost identical words:

I went to the river, river, river,
And I couldn't get across, across, across,
And I paid five dollars, dollars, dollars,
For the old grey horse, horse, horse.

Thomas used another verse from 'Mary Mack' for his 'Walking the Dog', another revival, this time of a dance that was around in the early 1900s. Although parts of 'Jump Back' had also been collected as a work-song, they were first made famous by Thomas Rice, a white dancer who performed blackface and whose stage name was Daddy 'Jim Crow' Rice. The legend goes that Rice had the good fortune to see a black slave named after his owner, Jim Crow, doing a song and dance with a great potential for the stage. Rice stole the idea, added some verses and by the end of the 1820s had a craze going for himself, not only through America but also as far away as England and Ireland.

Rufus Thomas's appropriation of 'Jump Jim Crow' was poetic justice. Working as a tapdancer, scat singer and all-round entertainer with the Rabbit Foot Minstrels in the 1930s, he felt the effects of racism both on and off stage.

For 'Jody's Got Your Girl and Gone', Johnny Taylor (a singer who, like Rufus Thomas, recorded for Stax) revived Jody, a character also known in toasts as Joe the Grinder. Jody's exploits, sung or narrated in prison or the army, symbolised the fear that somebody might be stealing your lover back home. Although the spoken toast fell into decline, the song version of the story—often about G.I. Joe returning from the war and finding Jody in bed with his wife—was still being sung in army camps in the 1970s, and Johnny Taylor's reworking is a testament to the longevity of the story's potency.

The cross talk between popular entertainment drawn back into folklore and mists-of-time traditions facelifted for contemporary styles can make it impossible to pinpoint origins. A toast collected by Bruce Jackson on Wynne Prison Farm in Texas in 1966—'Ups On the Farm'—and said by Jackson to be 'the only toast I've heard that expressly deals with black/white problems' was, in fact, part of Butterbeans and Susie's repertoire. Butterbeans and Susie were a husband and wife comedy singing/dancing act whose recordings spanned 40 years, from 1922 to 1962, and they formed part of a venerable tradition of comedy teams whose popularity was established on the TOBA (Theater Owner's Booking Association) black vaudeville circuit. A later team, Moke and Poke, were said by Marshall and Jean Stearns in *Jazz Dance* to 'conduct their dialogue in hip rhymes. "We're Moke and Poke, it ain't no joke, that's all she wrote, the pencil broke." '

Jazz Dance also notes the way in which the comedy dance teams developed a razor-sharp satirical humour aimed at and for black audiences, making the point that:

One of its sources was probably the West African song of allusion (where the subject pays the singer *not* to sing about him), reinterpreted in the West Indies as the political calypso, in New Orleans as the 'signifying' song, and in the South generally as 'the dozens'.

Although at least some of the origins of this rich material could be traced to the Bible or British folk songs, it had clear roots in West Africa. Ruth Finnegan, in her book *Oral Literature in Africa*, describes how poetry and music could function as a social weapon:

> Lampoons are not only used between groups but can also be a means of communicating and expressing personal enmity between hostile individuals. We hear of Galla abusive poems, for instance, while among the Yoruba when two women have quarrelled they sometimes vent their enmity by singing at each other, especially in situations—like the laundry place—when other women will hear. Abusive songs against ordinary individuals are also sometimes directly used as a means of social pressure, enforcing the will of public opinion.

In the savannah belt of West Africa this social pressure is embodied by the caste of musicians known as griots. The griot is a professional singer, in the past often associated with a village but now an increasingly independent 'gun for hire', who combines the functions of living history book and newspaper with vocal and instrumental virtuosity. According to Paul Oliver in his book *Savannah Syncopators*,

> though he has to know many traditional songs without error, he must also have the ability to extemporise on current events, chance incidents and the passing scene. His wit can be devastating and his knowledge of local history formidable.

Although they are popularly known as praise singers, griots might combine appreciation of a rich employer with gossip and satire or turn their vocal expertise into an attack on the politically powerful or the financially stingy.

If the hip-hop message and protest rappers had an ancestry in the savannah griots, the Bronx braggers, boasters and verbal abusers are children of the black American word games known as signifying and the dozens. During the late 1950s and early '60s a folklore student named Roger D. Abrahams collected tape recordings of many toasts, jokes and verbal contests in the predominantly black area of Camingerly, Philadelphia, where he lived. In his book *Deep Down In the Jungle* he explains the importance of 'good talkers' in Afro-American society, and concentrates particularly on the crucial role of talking skills in male society:

> Verbal contest accounts for a large portion of the talk between members of this group. Proverbs, turns of phrases, jokes, almost any manner of discourse is used, not for purposes of discursive communication but as weapons in verbal battle. Any gathering of the men customarily turns into 'sounding', a teasing or boasting session.

Abrahams found this kind of teasing among children who used 'catches' to trick each other:

Say 'washing machine'. '
Washing machine.'
I'll bet you five dollars your drawers ain't clean.

As the participants got older so the contests got more serious—sounding or the dozens could lead to serious fights among adults. The dozens contests were generally between boys and men from the ages of 16 to 26—a semi-ritualised battle of words which batted insults back and forth between the players until one or the other found the going too heavy. The insults could be a direct personal attack but were more frequently aimed at the opponent's family and in particular his mother. According to linguist William Labov, who studied these verbal shoot-outs in Harlem in the 1960s, 'In New York, "the-dozens" seems to be even more specialised, referring to rhymed couplets of the form:

I don't play the dozens, the dozens ain't my game
But the way I fucked your mama is a god damn shame.'

Working with teenage clubs like the Jets and the Cobras, Labov came across poetic insults like, 'Your mother play dice with the midnight mice', and more elaborate exchanges which are like fully developed comedy routines:

Boot: Hey! I went up Money house and I walked in Money house, I say, I wanted to sit down, and then, you know a roach jumped up and said, 'Sorry, this seat is taken.'
Roger: I went in David house, I saw the roaches walking round in combat boots.

The distance between talking rough with the dozens on the streets and moving it inside a roots club like Disco Fever with some beats for dancing is very small. It leads to the contradictions of Melle Mel, lyricist for the Furious Five, onstage in his ultra-macho metal warrior outfit trying to preach convincingly for an end to machismo and a beginning to peaceful co-existence.

Out among the grown-ups the dozens thrive in the 'dirty party' genre with a host of little-known comedians. You can also find Johnny Otis with Snatch and the Poontangs, the very funny Redd Foxx, the very unfunny Rudy Ray Moore whose record covers scale the greatest heights of porno-kitsch, and the notorious Blowfly. Blowfly, the unacceptable face of rap, is the pseudonym of Miami singer/producer Clarence Reid (the man who co-wrote 'Clean Up Woman' with Little Beaver for Betty Wright and released it on the Alston label).

One of the clearest links between present-day rappers and the rich vein of tall tales, tricksters, boasts and insults is Bo Diddley. Describing the type of rapping he was doing when he started out, Mr Biggs of Soul Sonic Force recollects that, 'we used to call it a Bo Diddley syndrome when we used to brag amongst ourselves'. Bo is the bragger *par excellence*—his street-talk boasts were originally combined with a unique Afro-Latin sound of maraccas, floor tom toms played by drummer Frank Kirkland and his own customised and distinctly weird guitar. His first single, recorded in 1955 for Chess Records in Chicago, was a double-sided punch on the nose for modesty—on the A side the ultimate macho anthem 'I'm a Man' and on the B side Diddley's personal plaudit called, aptly enough, 'Bo Diddley'.

Many of his later songs used material from toasts and the dozens: 'Who Do You Love', the story of a satanic badman who wears a cobra snake for a necktie, is like a toast in itself, using lines almost identical to Stackolee's 'I'm a bad motherfucker, that's why I don't mind dying'. Other songs use familiar themes—'The Story of Bo Diddley' with its full-grown baby playing a gold guitar, 'Run Diddley Daddy' and its rumble-in-the-jungle tall tale and 'Say Man', a record which grew out of Bo and maracca player Jerome trading the dozens in the studio. Put down on tape with some judicious editing, it became one of Bo's biggest hits, striking back at the record company notion that too much black content keeps records out of the charts.

'Say Man' is the great-grandfather of the rap attack. The anonymous Ronnie Gee prepares the crowd for his 'Raptivity', a tall tale of microphone battles that run deep in the night leaving heart attacks in their wake: 'Warning—the surgeon general of chilltown New York has determined that the sounds you are about to hear can be devastating to your ear-ear-ear-ear-ear.'

OBJECTIVE QUESTIONS

1. Who was Thomas Dartmouth "Daddy Rice"? What was the song and character that made him famous?
2. What is Muhammad Ali's birth name?
3. In 1958, who had a chart-topping hit based on the legend of Stagger Lee?
4. In the savannah belt of West Africa, there is a caste of professional musicians, singers and storytellers known as _____.
5. What does TOBA stand for, and what was it?
6. What year did Bo Diddley record his first record and on what label?

QUESTIONS FOR FURTHER THOUGHT, RESEARCH, AND DISCUSSION

1. Research and report on the work and career of Rudy Rae Moore, who called himself the "godfather of rap."
2. How many versions of the "Stagger Lee" legend and the "Signifying Monkey" can you find? Do these legends have any basis in fact? Can you find other similar legends and trace how they have been absorbed as forms of entertainment or used by rap artists?
3. Can you find any other examples of how the British press and British music fans have helped Americans better understand their own music?
4. Search out and listen to as many of the recordings and artists mentioned in this chapter as possible.
5. Research and write about the life and musical influence of Bo Diddley.

Hip Hop

By Steven Hager

Steven Hager has been covering the counter culture for over 35 years. He founded *Whistle*, his first underground newspaper, in 1968, while still a high school student in Illinois. Twelve years later, he was the first reporter to travel to the South Bronx to document the history of Hip Hop. Hager became editor of *High Times* in 1988.

Steven Hager was supposedly hired to write the original screenplay for the movie *Beat Street*, although he claims that nothing he wrote actually made it into the movie. No other writer understands the history of Hip Hop better than Steve Hager. No other writer has been writing about it longer. In this chapter, he sets the stage by tracing the ethnic history of the South Bronx, its gang problems, "urban planning," and arson. Since graffiti is unquestionably the first of the "four elements" to appear, its history is dealt with first. Next comes an introduction to the "Three Kings"— Kool Herc, Afrika Bambaataa and Grandmaster Flash—and the invention of a whole new way to dance and party. On the surface, Hager's writing seems somewhat dispassionate and journalistic, but it's full of interesting detail and is quite engaging.

"HIP HOP" FROM *ADVENTURES IN THE COUNTERCULTURE*
The Bronx on Fire

I N 1955, IT SEEMED like everyone wanted to live in the Bronx. Second-generation immigrants from Manhattan's impoverished Lower East Side, blacks leaving the South, Puerto Ricans fresh from La Guardia airport, servicemen returning from overseas duty—they poured across the Harlem River in search of the American Dream, which would be lived out in an art deco apartment building overlooking the Grand Concourse, New York's finest boulevard and the Bronx equivalent of the Champs Elysees.

"The Bronx at that time was a paradise compared to [Harlem]," recalled Victor George Mair, who soon joined the migration northward. "Everything was so neat, so clean, so tidy, so orderly. I mean they were living in luxury."

Queens was dubbed "the borough of private houses," but the Bronx was known as "the borough of apartment buildings." Despite all the buildings, it wasn't easy to find a place to live. Rent controls enacted during World War II had kept the housing market tight and leases were usually kept in the family, handed down like priceless heirlooms. Most buildings, especially those on the Concourse, had long waiting lists.

It seemed impossible that within a few years this distinguished, orderly neighborhood could begin to suffer a precipitous decline that would not be slowed until more than 1,500 buildings were left abandoned. Lifelong Bronxites moved out in droves, entire neighborhoods were decimated by arson, and the once beautiful landscape of the South Bronx became so dominated by rubble-strewn lots that some visitors said it reminded them of Dresden after the war.

"It happened so slowly and to such an extent that I wasn't even aware, of change until one day I decided to take a walk around the block and discovered we had no block," Mair told a historian from the Bronx Museum of the Arts. "Then I decided to take a walk around the neighborhood and found that we had no neighborhood."

The beginning of the end came in 1959, when Parks Commissioner Robert Moses began building an expressway through the heart of the Bronx. It was apparent that Moses cared little for the small, tight-knit communities that stood in his way. "When you operate in an overbuilt metropolis, you have to hack your way through with a meat ax," said Moses.

Marshall Berman vividly recalled the effects of Moses' ax in his book *All That Is Solid Melts Into Air*. "My friends and I would stand on the parapet of the Grand Concourse, where 174th Street had been, and survey the work's progress—the immense steam shovels and bulldozers and timber and steel beams, the hundreds of workers in the variously colored hard hats, the giant cranes reaching far above the Bronx's tallest roofs, the dynamite blasts and tremors, the wild, jagged crags of rock newly torn, the vistas of devastation stretching for miles to the east and west as far as the eye could see—and marvel to see our ordinary nice neighborhood transformed into sublime, spectacular ruins."

The middle-class Italian, German, Irish and Jewish neighborhoods disappeared overnight. Impoverished black and Hispanic families, who dominated the southern end of the borough, drifted north. Businesses and factories relocated. The open-air market on Bathgate Avenue was destroyed.

Along with the poor came their perennial problems: crime, drug addiction, unemployment. They also brought a smoldering sense of injustice, which exploded in nearby Harlem with a wave of "'race riots" in 1965. Although there were no riots in the Bronx, it wasn't long before a Black Panther Information Center opened on Boston Road.

In 1968, Robert Moses completed his second grand project for the Bronx, a 15,382-unit co-op apartment complex, located on the northern edge of the borough and conveniently serviced by one of his expressways. Vacating their comfortable apartments, the Bronx middle class poured into Co-op City so fast one might have thought the hounds of hell were chasing them. With vacancy rates skyrocketing, reputable landlords panicked and quickly sold out to professional slumlords, who began buying, selling and trading buildings at a furious rate.

Coincidentally, 1968 marked another important development in the Bronx's history. During that summer a group of seven teenage boys began terrorizing the vicinity around the Bronxdale Project on Bruckner Boulevard in the Southeast Bronx. In itself, this might not seem significant but it was the presence of this group that laid the groundwork for a surge of streetgang activity that overwhelmed the Bronx for the next six years.

At first, the group called itself the Savage Seven and were known primarily for beating up bus drivers and generally wreaking havoc near the Bronxdale Community Center. However, it wasn't long before other boys wanted to hang out with the Seven. The ranks swelled to several dozen and the name had to be changed. They chose "The Black Spades," which worked out nicely because they could take the spade emblem from a deck of cards, sew it on the back of a jean jacket and wear colors, just like the Hell's Angels. It wasn't long before a spray-painted Black Spade emblem began to appear in every hallway in the Bronxdale Project.

The Black Spades may have started out as kids aged 12 to 15, but collectively they assumed a power far beyond their age, a power that struck instant fear in the hearts of their elders. You couldn't pick a fight with one Spade without picking a fight with all of them. Together, they were invincible. They could swagger into any project in the Bronx and bully anybody.

The boys who lived in the Castle Hill Project in the North Bronx always hated the boys in the Bronxdale Project. It was one of those feuds that started shortly after the projects were built and never went away. Realizing it was time to get organized, the Castle Hill Project created a group called "Power," whose primary activity was getting into fights with members of the Black Spades. Wanting to do the Spades one better, they began creating divisions of Power in other projects.

Almost overnight, streetgangs appeared on every corner of the Bronx. Realizing they had a significant problem on their hands, the New York Police Department created the Bronx Youth Gang Task Force, a 92-member squad commanded by Deputy Inspector William Lakeman, who spent his first year on the job compiling dossiers on suspected gang leaders. By 1970, estimates of gang membership ran as high as 11,000. Reported assaults in the Bronx, had risen from 998 in 1960 to 4,256 in 1969. Burglaries during the same period had increased from 1,765 to 29,276.

It wasn't long before the media became interested in the streetgangs, and, strangely enough, most of the early articles were somewhat positive, focusing on the gangs' attempts to wipe out heroin addiction in their neighborhoods. Howard Blum wrote in the *Amsterdam News*:

There are no junkies on Hoe Avenue in the South Bronx. The Royal Charmers ordered all junkies and dealers to leave their turf. Most left quickly. Those who stayed were beaten or killed. The Royal Charmers were brutal, but effective: there are no junkies on their turf.

On an August afternoon last summer a bedsheet was tied to two corner lampposts and stretched high across 173rd Street and Hoe Avenue in the Bronx like a campaign banner. The message on the sheet, written in large, childlike black letters, was direct: "No junkies allowed after 10 o'clock." The message was signed "R.C."

This message began a two-month period of vigilantism by the Royal Charmers. It was a campaign in which one dealer was pushed off a roof, his dead body found weeks later in an alley garbage can, two others were murdered, junkies were whipped through South Bronx streets, and one Royal Charmer was blinded, the victim of a shotgun blast in the face from a vengeful drug dealer.

Contrary to the myth created by this and other articles, streetgangs did not appear in the Bronx solely to rid the streets of junkies. Junkies just happened to be the first convenient target of newly formed gangs that wanted to flex a little muscle: They were easy to identify, they had no potential as gang members and they could be beaten up without arousing a cry of anguish from the community. Gang leaders were also smart enough to realize that heroin was one of the major reasons why the Bronx remained pacified throughout the '60s.

As the gang culture spread through the city, several hundred new gangs were formed. Most were dominated by four members: the president, the vice-president, the warlord (who attended pow-wows with rival gangs and declared war if necessary) and the masher, the best street fighter. The gangs had clubhouses where weekly meetings were held, and ritualistic initiation rites, the most common of which was called "Running the Mill," a rite of passage that required new members to run between two rows of members wielding chains, pipes and studded belts. Every gang had the same uniform: Levi jackets with insignias on the back, Lee jeans, Garrison belts and engineer boots. Lists of rules and regulations were drawn up and severely adhered to. It was easy to join and hard to quit.

The number of gangs in the Bronx kept growing through the summer of 1971, but this development went largely unnoticed until Adlai E. Stevenson High School reopened its doors in September. Located in the North Bronx, Stevenson was a new school in a predominately white neighborhood. During its second year the school started receiving busloads of blacks and Hispanics from the South Bronx, as well as a sizeable contingent of whites from middle-class neighborhoods in Throgs Neck and Pelham Bay.

Afrika Bambaataa, who would later become a leader of the largest gang in the city, was in the eighth grade when he was bused to Stevenson. He recalled the first two weeks of school in a theme he wrote for English class titled "Street Gangs Beware":

> *For the first week things seemed to go okay. There were no sign of a gang or gang activities in the school, not until a couple of Black Spades and Savage Nomads started flying colors in the second week. Then other gang members from a variety of streetgangs started wearing their colors. Suddenly, Stevenson officials found out that at least a member from every streetgang in the Bronx and parts of Manhattan went to Stevenson High School. Tension arose between the black and Hispanic against the whites. There was all kinds of trouble happening. A couple of white teenagers had a fight with a black who happened to be in the Black Spades. After school was over, the Black Spades led an army of students to the Korvettes Shopping Center where the white teenagers catch the #5 bus to Throgs Neck/Pelham Bay area. A rumble broke out … A white got thrown through a window and other whites and blacks and Hispanics got stabbed and stomped. After that day Stevenson was never the same peaceful high school again.*

Several predominantly white gangs had been formed in the North Bronx, including the Aliens, the Golden Guineas and the War Pigs, but after the fight at Stevenson they merged into a single gang called Ministers Bronx. Violence in the school became an everyday occurrence. Many students refused to eat lunch in the cafeteria, where fights were likely to break out. All but a few of the bathrooms had to be locked permanently; those which remained open had guards posted at the doors.

Bambaataa joined the Black Spades in 1969, shortly after a division was founded at the Bronx River Project, where he lived with his mother. Although he became a devoted member, Bambaataa was far from a typical one. While the others were out playing basketball or hanging around street corners, Bambaataa was scouring record bins for obscure rhythm & blues recordings. Just as unusual was the name he chose for himself, inspired by the release of a feature film about the Zulus, a fierce warrior tribe in Africa. The original Bambaataa was a Zulu chief at the turn of the century. Translated into English, the word means "affectionate leader."

"Bam was never interested in sports. As long as I've known him, he's always been the music man," said Jay McGluery, who grew up at Bronx River with Bambaataa. "His mother was a nurse and she was constantly on the go, so we always went to his house to party. He had every record you could want to hear, including a lot of rock albums, James Brown and Sly and the Family Stone were his favorites."

In many snapshots from the period, Bambaataa looks young, lean and angry, his eyebrows fused in a permanent scowl of disapproval—just the sort of look designed to intimidate whitey. Despite the angry look, he tended to be quiet and philosophical, his guarded, reserved air frequently shattered by a laugh so friendly it infected everyone around him.

He was also more attuned to politics than many of his fellow gang members, some of whom understood only three basic concepts: "crush, kill and destroy." When he was 12, he had already begun hanging out at the Black Panther Information Center. His political leanings were encouraged by the appearance of "Say it Loud, I'm Black and I'm Proud" by James Brown and "Stand" by Sly and the Family Stone.

However, like many gang members, Bambaataa had a reckless, unpredictable streak. One time he and McGluery were playing war games and McGluery took refuge in one of the project's apartment buildings. Bambaataa poured gasoline on the sidewalk in front of the building, lit it, and announced he was holding everyone hostage. That same summer, he convinced his friends to buy bows and arrows so they could hunt rabbits on the banks of the Bronx River. "Bam was always a leader," said McGluery "He was always full of crazy ideas."

During the early '70s, life at Bronx River changed dramatically. Since it was a stronghold for gang activity, the project was under constant police surveillance. Any teenager wearing engineer boots was likely to be stopped for a grilling, which usually started with the question, "Are you a Spade or a Skull?" (the two largest gangs in the area). It was not unusual for fistfights to break out between gang members and the police. Since the police were almost entirely white at the time, charges of police racism were rampant. Considering newspaper stories from the period indicate white gang members were seldom arrested, the charges may have had some foundation.

Although several rumbles were arranged between the Black Spades and the Ministers, they were usually aborted. The Spades couldn't board a bus headed uptown without it being surrounded by squad cars before it reached the Ministers' turf. Typically, the windows of the bus would fly open and a shower of chains, knives, bats and zip guns would hit the pavement. On June 27, 1973, a brief battle was broken up by police in front of P.S. 127 on Castle Hill Avenue, resulting in the arrest of 18 Black Spades.

Gang activity tended to quiet down during the winter only to resurface with even greater intensity each summer. Every year the gangs seemed to fall under the control of older, more demented individuals, many of whom were returning from stints in prison. By 1972, Running the Mill was being replaced by gang rape.

* * *

Violence between gangs intensified as well. One feud between the Black Spades and the Seven Crowns lasted for 92 days, during which time the Bronx River Project was constantly peppered with gunfire from passing cars. Shootouts became so common that the residents started calling it "Lil' Vietnam."

"I was into streetgang violence," admitted Bambaataa. "That was all part of growing up in the Southeast Bronx." However, that's about all he'll say on the subject "I don't really be speaking on that stuff because it's negative," he explained. "The Black Spades was also helping out in the community, raising money for sickle cell anemia and getting people to register to vote."

"He was not what I would call gung-ho," added McGluery, who became warlord of the Bronx River division before quitting to join the Marines. "Bam was more like a supervisor. There were so many different gangs and he knew at least five members in every one. Any time there was a conflict, he would try and straighten it out. He was into communications."

Gang activity probably peaked in 1973, when there were an estimated 315 gangs in the city, claiming 19,503 members. The Black Spades were by far the largest and most feared, with a division in almost every precinct. However, by 1974, the Black Spades began to disintegrate.

"Some gangs got into drugs," said Bambaataa. "Other gangs got wiped out by other gangs. Others got so big that members didn't want to be involved no more. Girls got tired of it first. They wanted to have children. Plus times was changin'. The seventies was coming more into music and dancing and going to clubs. The lifestyle was changing."

After many of the original Black Spades were killed, jailed or dropped out of the gang, Bambaataa took on an increasingly influential role. His affiliation continued until January 10, 1975, when his best friend, Soulski, was shot and killed by two policemen on Pelham Parkway. Bambaataa insisted that the shooting was nothing short of an assassination carried out during a police crackdown on gang activity. A copy of his friend's death certificate hangs in his bedroom. "He got shot in about nine different places," said Bambaataa. "The back, the stomach, the face. At first, I wanted to go to war with the police, but we couldn't really win. The *Amsterdam News* calmed everybody down and told us to fight through the system. It went to trial, but the cops never got convicted."

For over five years the Bronx had lived in constant terror of street-gangs. Then, in the summer of 1976, they unexpectedly failed to appear. Something better had come along to replace the gangs.

THE WAR OF WORDS

You know what it evolved from? The toughest guy on the block always had his name the biggest in the street. It told everybody it was his area, that he had the juice to do what he wanted and nobody could mess with him.

Tracy 168

To tell the truth, nobody really knows how graffiti evolved—we just know it's been around for a long time. During World War II, a welding inspector at the Bethlehem Steel shipyard in Quincy,

Massachusetts named James J. Kilroy began writing "Kilroy was here" in crayon inside ships that were being built for the war. Many servicemen saw the markings and began spreading the message throughout Europe and the United States. Eventually the phrase was combined with a cartoon of a long-nosed face peering over a wall.

In the '50s, streetgangs used graffiti for self-promotion and marking territorial boundaries. Gang graffiti had other uses, such as intimidation. When rival gangs walked into a new area and saw "Savage Skulls" written a hundred times—each with a different name underneath—it told them the Skulls were a powerful force to be reckoned with.

But then something changed. Around 1969, graffiti became more than a gang-related activity or thoughtless moment of vandalism. For hundreds of New York City teenagers it became a way of life with its own codes of behavior, secret gathering places, slang and aesthetic standards. No one knows who started it. We only know who made it famous: TAKI 183.

His real name was Demetrius and he came to New York from Greece. His family moved to Washington Heights, a working-class neighborhood at the northern edge of Manhattan. Demetrius was 15 when an older boy in the neighborhood told him about the gangs from the '50s. "They had an initiation where they would hang a new member by his ankles off the side of a bridge," said Demetrius. "While hanging upside down, the guy would paint his name on a pillar. I never saw it done, but the idea interested me."

Graffiti writing got a big technological boost in the '60s with the invention of the magic marker, which was easy to conceal and, like spray paint, left an indelible mark on just about any surface. In 1967, Demetrius noticed the name "JULIO 204" written on the street around his house. Julio, who lived a couple of blocks away on 204th Street, like to write his name and street number wherever he went. Demetrius lived on 183rd Street and his nickname was Taki. So he started writing TAKI 183.

He put his first "tag" on the side of an ice-cream truck during the summer of 1970. "I didn't have a job. I did it to pass time," he said later. Meanwhile, Julio was arrested for vandalism and forced into early retirement. When Taki returned to school, he got a part-time job as a messenger. While making deliveries, he found an art supply store on 53rd Street that sold extra-wide markers. "I think I was the first one to find that wide marker," he said, "My name got noticed because it was wider than everyone else's. But even more important, I was writing in a different area than most people. My name could have been on every street corner in Brooklyn and I wouldn't have gotten the exposure I got from writing on the East Side. A writer might come out of his office, see my name, and—maybe because it was a boring day—he would decide to write a story about me."

Taki graduated from high school and began working full time until he saved enough money to attend college. He continued writing, only now the interiors of subway cars had become his primary target. People have nothing to do in subway trains except read the advertising posters, he reasoned, so why not give them a little something extra to look at?

Unknowingly, Taki created a major controversy. "Pretty soon people were wondering, what is the squad of Taki-commandos?" wrote Richard Goldstein in *New York* magazine. "Rumors began: Is it the surveying crew for a new subway line, or is it a madman quoting stock averages, or is it a streetgang so obscure not even Leonard Bernstein knows them, or else is it some kind of arcane religious rite, like when I was a kid and people went around writing 'Beware of 1960' on the roofs?" The controversy was finally settled in July 1971, when an enterprising reporter from the *New York Times* tracked Taki down. The first newspaper article on graffiti appeared a few days later.

"TAKI 183" SPAWNS PEN PALS

Taki is a Manhattan teenager who writes his name and his street number everywhere he goes. He says it is something he just has to do.

His TAKI 183 appears in subway stations and inside subway cars all over the city, on walls along Broadway, at Kennedy International Airport, in New Jersey, Connecticut, upstate New York and other places.

He has spawned hundreds of imitators, including JOE 136, BARBARA 62, EEL 159, YANQUI 135 and LEO 136.

To remove such words, plus the obscenities and other graffiti in subway stations, it cost 80,000 man-hours, or about $300,000, in the last year, the Transit Authority estimates.

"I work, I pay taxes too and it doesn't harm anybody," Taki said in an interview, when told the cost of removing the graffiti.

And he asked: "Why do they go after the little guy? Why not the campaign organizations that put stickers all over the subways at election time?"

It was apparent that Taki had gained considerable status in his community for the graffiti. "He's the king," said one neighborhood youth. "He's got everybody doing it," said another. After the article appeared, Taki's status was no longer confined to his block, but stretched to every borough in the city, including the Bronx.

Actually, the Bronx had been writing similar graffiti long before the article on Taki appeared. However, it wasn't until the spring of 1971 that the fad began taking off. In March, two writers appeared on 163rd Street, SLY II and LEE 163rd. Lee drew immediate attention for his unusual tag, which stacked and fused the letters in his name into a corporate-style logo.

In October, Lee's cousin, Lonny Wood, began writing. "The previous year we'd given this party," said Lonny "We were getting ready to give another one and I said, 'We'll call it Phase Two.' I don't know why, but I was stuck on the name. It had meaning for me. I started writing 'Phase 2.'" By this time, the unspoken graffiti code was already well established. Writers were supposed to be mysterious figures who never revealed their identities to outsiders (especially parents). They had to be light-fingered enough to steal markers and spray paint, and courageous enough to "run the train tracks" and participate in other daredevil stunts.

"We were like moles," said Tracy 168, one of the first writers to appear in the Bronx. "If anyone chased us, we ran into the nearest subway station and we'd be gone. Nobody would follow us down there." It took considerable nerve to jump off a subway platform and take off running down a dark, forbidding tunnel. The third rail, pulsing with 625 deadly volts, was just a stumble away Somewhere behind the writer, moving at 40 miles an hour or faster, was a subway train, while perhaps a thousand feet in front was an abandoned station or lay-up track, where the writer could leave a tag, like a flag driven into a mountain peak. It was criminal, dangerous behavior, but the thrill was undeniable.

Phase 2 joined a large number of writers at DeWitt Clinton High School. One advantage to attending Clinton was the proximity of a Transit Authority storage yard across the street, where parked trains could be found any time of day or night. It wasn't unusual for Phase and the other writers to spend their lunch hour in the yard marking up trains. After school the writers would gather in a nearby coffee shop. Whenever a bus pulled up outside, dozens of writers came pouring out of the coffee shop waving markers. By the time the bus pulled away, it would be drenched in freshly scrawled signatures.

At first there were only a handful of writers in each neighborhood, and it didn't matter what a tag looked like. But after hundreds of writers appeared on the scene, it was necessary to embellish the tags to make them stand out. Two female writers, Barbara and Eva 62, enlarged their signatures and made them more colorful. Cay 161 drew a crown over his tag. Stay High 149 drew a stick figure with a halo lifted from *The Saint*, a popular television show. Stay High incorporated two smoking marijuana joints into his tag and became one of the most respected of the early writers by placing tags in extremely hard-to-reach places. He was also the first to master tags created with dual-color markers.

Graffiti began to draw the scrutiny of outsiders, most of whom assumed it was done out of anger and frustration, "It is part of the widespread vandalism, the mood to destroy, the brutalism that is everywhere," said Dr. Fredric Wertham. Mayor John Lindsay denounced the writers as "insecure cowards" and launched an all-out campaign to remove graffiti from public property.

Although the writers continued to hit buses, handball courts, schoolyards and other locations, the subway system was the primary target. "One thing that kept me writing on trains was seeing my name again," said Tracy. "You thought your tag would just disappear because there were so many trains. But then it would come back the next day, and you'd see somebody else's tag right next to yours. That was part of the communication thing. The train would shoot over to Brooklyn and somebody over there would see your style. But there was also more adventure on the trains. Daredevil stunts like jumping from trains to platforms would really get your adrenaline going. Competition was important too."

The writers soon moved from marking the insides of trains to marking the exteriors. It was decided the best place to have a tag was on the front of the train, where it would be the first thing seen as the train entered the station. But in 1972, Super Kool completely changed graffiti by spray-painting his name in super-wide pink and yellow letters. It took him about five times longer than a normal tag, and used almost an entire can of paint, but the results were worth it. His thick, colorful letters over-powered every other signature on the train. At first, the other writers couldn't figure out how Super Kool had gotten his letters so thick. It didn't seem possible with a regular can of spray paint, and, in fact, it wasn't. Super Kool had replaced the narrow-dispersion cap on his spray-paint can with a "fat cap," a wider-spraying cap from a can of oven cleaner.

"'Everyone was damn negative about it at first," said Phase. "It took a whole can of paint for one signature! But then everybody picked up on it. I remember seeing some big block letters by Sentry. That's when I came out with my softie letters. People started calling it the bubble style."

The giant signatures became known as "masterpieces" and it suddenly became necessary to steal a lot of paint to execute them.

"Super Kool and his girlfriend were the first to rack up huge quantities," said Phase. "He always dressed very dapper and didn't look the part. Stealing went along with the graffiti style. I didn't get into it, but a lot of guys did. Not just paint, but leather coats, stereos. One time I led about twenty guys into a store. We went straight to the paint. Something came over me and I slapped all the cans off the shelf. It was crazy. There was so much confusion. The salesman tried to keep us in the store and guys had to throw blows to get out. The mounted police came. We ran around the corner and found we had four cans of paint between twenty guys. That wasn't the way to do it."

Like most writers in the Bronx, Phase was black. He was tall, skinny and almost always wore a hat jauntily perched on one side of his head—a French cap made by Flechet was his favorite. He projected an almost explosive sense of urgency, his occasional stuttering heightening the impression that his physical being was struggling to keep pace with a hyperactive imagination. While talking, he frequently twisted and clenched his fingers, as if creating patterns for some bizarre new lettering style.

Style became the most important aspect of graffiti. It was still possible to gain respect and recognition merely by "getting one's name around" in large quantities, but it was more prestigious to create original lettering styles which were imitated by lesser writers, who were known as "toys." One had to be artistically competent to execute huge murals on the sides of trains. The less talented writers were forced out of the limelight. Meanwhile, the Transit Authority continued cracking down on graffiti and it became progressively more difficult and dangerous to enter the train yards. However, the danger only increased the writers' sense of satisfaction.

A writer named Topcat moved to New York from Philadelphia, where a separate graffiti subculture was flourishing. Topcat painted thin, elongated letters on platforms. He called it the "Philadelphia style," but after the letters were imitated by most of the writers on the Upper West Side, they were renamed "Broadway elegant."

Although most writers tended to be fairly independent, it wasn't long before they began gathering in loose-knit groups, which were closer to professional associations than gangs. Meetings were held at various "writers' corners" around the city, the two most prominent of which were located at a subway station at 149th Street and Grand Concourse in the Bronx, and on the corner of 188th and Audubon Avenue in Manhattan. Wherever they gathered, writers compared notes on various lettering styles and discussed methods for thwarting the Transit Police.

The Ex-Vandals, one of the earliest and most revered of the writing organizations, was founded at Erasmus High School in Brooklyn by president Dino Nod, whose tag could be found in every borough of the city. The name was short for "Experienced Vandals." In imitation of the street-gangs, the Ex-Vandals wore jean jackets with their name on the back. They were not a fighting gang, however. They preferred to spend their time developing highly elaborate, script-like tags. It was the beginning of the Brooklyn style, which eventually became so complex most people found it indecipherable.

Phase became president of the Bronx chapter of the Ex-Vandals until he helped found a separate group called "The Independent Writers," whose membership included prominent writers such as Super Kool and Stay High. The Independent Writers indicated their affiliation by writing "INDS" after their signatures.

Wanted, another important writing group, was founded by Tracy 168 in 1972. Tracy was a gutsy, streetwise white kid, tough enough to hang out with the Black Spades in his neighborhood. Unlike many of the other groups, Wanted had a permanent clubhouse, in the basement of an apartment complex on the corner of 166th Street and Woodycrest Avenue in the Bronx. In the mid-'70s, Wanted became one of the largest groups, with more than 70 members.

"The best year for graffiti was 1973," said Tracy "Styles were coming out. We got into this thing with colors. First it was two colors, then three colors, then four. Then it was the biggest piece, the widest. Then it was top-to-bottom, whole car, whole train. We worked on clouds and flames. We got into lettering. Everybody was trying to develop their own techniques. When I would go into a yard, the first thing I'd do is look around and see who was good. That would be my objective. To burn the best writer in the yard. And I wouldn't leave until I did something better than him. I put a Yosemite Sam with two guns on a piece. That was the first cartoon character."

Although Phase wasn't painting as many trains as some other writers, he was inventing new styles on paper and handing them out to his friends. Many of his ideas found their way to the trains through Riff 170, who was considered a master colorist. "Riff revolutionized graffiti with a half-car, top-to-bottom," said Aaron 155, interviewed by Craig Castleman in *Getting Up*.

"It was a yellow 'Riff' with red, bloody drips coming down. And it had cracks painted on it. It took everybody out all over New York."

Other important writing groups included Magic Inc., Three Yard Boys, Vanguards, Ebony Dukes, Writers Corner 188, The Bad Artists, the Mad Bombers, the Death Squad, Mission Graffiti, the Rebels, Wild Style, Six Yard Boys and the Crazy 5. Many writers belonged to two or three at the same time.

* * *

HERCULORDS AT THE HEVALO

Since Clive Campbell's impressions of the United States had been formed watching *Dennis the Menace* and *Bewitched* on his next-door neighbor's television set in Kingston, Jamaica, it was easy to understand why he thought the country was so clean, without a trace of garbage anywhere. So it came as something of a shock when, at age 12, Clive landed at Kennedy airport and took the bus to his mother's apartment on 168th Street in the Bronx. It was 1967. Rather than clean suburban lawns, he found a ghetto similar to the one in Kingston—only bigger.

Clive had a lot of trouble adjusting to the Bronx. His accent made him sound like a hick and his favorite sports in Jamaica—soccer and bicycle racing—weren't at all popular. Instead, everyone was playing basketball The first day Clive tried the sport, he got kicked by an angry teammate. "I knew how to kick," he said, "so I kicked him right back. A fight started. Two members of the Five Percenters [a Black Muslim youth group] came to my rescue. They weren't gonna let anybody dog me. I hung out with them and started picking up the slang. Pretty soon, I was Americanized."

In 1970, Clive entered Alfred E. Smith High School, a trade school for auto mechanics. He began lifting weights and running on the track team. A friend nicknamed him Hercules for his well-developed body. "I resented the name," he said. "I broke it down to Herc. That sounded rare, so I kept it." That same year, Herc started hanging out at a disco called the Plaza Tunnel, which was located in the basement of the Plaza Hotel on 161st Street and the Grand Concourse. The deejay, John Brown, was the first to play records like "Give It Up or Turn It Loose" by James Brown and "Get Ready" by Rare Earth. Unfortunately, the Black Spades liked to drop by unexpectedly to steal girlfriends, rough up rival gang members and generally intimidate the crowd. When they arrived, Brown tried to pacify them by playing "Soul Power" by James Brown. They loved chanting "Spade Power! Spade Power!" along with the record.

"I was known as a graffiti writer," said Herc. "I wrote 'KOOL HERC.' I also ran the 880 relay on the track team, dressed well and danced. 'Get Ready' was my favorite song. But then the music stopped. I think the gangs stopped it. It got too dangerous for people to go to discos."

In 1973 Herc's sister Cindy celebrated her birthday by throwing a party in the recreation room of a housing project on Sedgwick Avenue. "She asked me to provide the music," said Herc, "so I went out and bought all the fresh, up-to-date records. I rigged a little hookup with two turntables. All our friends came to the party along with a lot of people from the neighborhood. I played songs like 'Give It Up or Turn It Loose.' People would walk for miles just to hear that record—because nobody could find it." The party was such a success that Herc continued deejaying at house parties and community centers. He collected a trunk full of dance 45s and invested in better equipment, including a mike with an echo chamber and strobe light. Later that year, he began charging a 25-cent entrance fee.

"I was twelve the first time I went to Herc's party," said Kevin, who became one of the original b-boys. "My brother Keith and I used to hang out with some girls around 165th Street and University Avenue and they kept saying: 'Y'all should come to Herc's! It's a party and he's jamming every week!' One night we decided to check it out. The thing I mostly remember was how loud the music was. The sound overtook you. The place was packed—a real sweatbox. Herc was on the mike. He'd say things like 'Rock the house' and call out the names of people at the party.

Wallace Dee, Johnny Cool, Chubby, the Amazing Bobo, James Bond, Sasa, Clark Kent, Trixie—those were the names you heard. Trixie had a big afro and he used to shake his head. It used to make him look so good! Wallace Dee had a move called the slingshot, which was a basic drop to the floor except he came up like he was shooting a slingshot. After that first time, we didn't want to go anywhere else. It was Kool Herc's, Kool Herc's, Kool Herc's. Every weekend. There was no such thing as b-boys when we arrived, but Herc gave us that tag. Just like he named his sound system the Herculords and he called me and my brother the Nigger Twins. He called his dancers the b-boys."

Despite their age, Keith and Kevin soon established themselves as the premier performers at Herc's parties. "When we danced, we always had a crowd around us," said Keith. "'We wore Pro-Keds, double-knit pants, windbreakers and hats we called 'crushers.' One of us would always have the hat on backwards and we both had straws in our mouth." During the week, the twins spent hours working on new routines, inventing steps that would amaze the crowd. "James Brown had a lot to do with it," explained Kevin, "because he used to do splits and slide across the floor."

In 1975, Herc moved into a club on 180th and Jerome Avenue. Formerly known as Soulsville, it had just been renamed the Hevalo. With the gang situation cooling off, discos were just starting to reopen. Everybody wanted to get into dancing again. But while most deejays played the same disco hits one heard on the radio, the music at the Hevalo was harder, funkier. Herc knew how to bring the crowd up to a frenzied peak and hold them there for hours. During these times, he seldom played an entire song. Instead, he played the hottest segment of the song, which was often just a 30-second "break" section—when the drums, bass and rhythm guitar stripped the beat to its barest essence. Herc played break after break to create an endless peak of dance beats.

It wasn't long before the dancers at the Hevalo were known as "break" dancers. Rather than doing the Hustle or other disco steps, which required a male and female partner, break dancers performed solo. The dance was usually a competition between males to establish who had the suavest, most graceful moves. "Before we called it 'breaking,' it was known as 'going off' or 'burning,'" said Phase. "When we were kids we did dances like the Washing Machine, the Popcorn and the Mod Squad. The Busstop came out in 1974. Burning came put before the Busstop. It was all about taking a guy out, burning him. The big phrase was 'I'm gonna turn this party out.' I used to do shit with my feet that people didn't understand. I danced with three guys, Stak, Timbo and Sweet Duke. I think we brought a lot of shit out. This girl asked us: 'Where y'all learn to dance? You don't dance like nobody else.' Hand movements were really important, especially in a dance called the Salute. But I have to give credit to the Nigger Twins. Those boys were bad."

The freelance deejay, an independent entrepreneur armed with a portable sound system and extensive record collection, emerged as the new cultural hero in the Bronx around 1975. Previously, anyone wishing to gain notoriety either became a graffiti writer or an incomparable break dancer. However, by 1976, the most powerful, most revered figures were the deejays. Herc remained in a class by himself, primarily because of his McIntosh amplifier and twin Shure speaker columns, the combination he called "The Herculords." The awesome power of the Herculords was most evident whenever Herc played the parks. Even outdoors, the system was surprisingly clean, free of distortion and ear-shatteringly loud.

Herc also had the best records. While most other deejays played disco (Donna Summer and the Bee Gees were popular), Herc played hard-core funk with stripped-down drum beats. No record better epitomizes his style than "Apache," a song recorded by the Ventures in the early '60s and redone by The Incredible Bongo Band in 1974. "Apache" combined a melodramatic, Spaghetti-Western, melody with wild bongo solos. The result was a bit corny, but it created a theatrical atmosphere perfect for a showdown between two break dancers. Since it was recorded by an obscure record company, "Apache" was not an easy record to find. To make matters even more difficult, Herc jealously guarded the names of the more obscure break records, even to the point of soaking them in his bathtub to remove the labels.

Other deejays began following Herc's style. At Stevenson High, Afrika Bambaataa formed a small group called the Zulus, who became an extension of the b-boy style, a gang into music and dance instead of violence. It wasn't long before the Zulus became a powerful force at Stevenson, so powerful, in fact, that the principal had Bambaataa transferred to a different school. On November 12, 1976, Bambaataa gave his first official party as a deejay at the Bronx Community Center.

At the time there were three main deejays playing "b-beat" music in the Bronx: Bambaataa in the southeast, Herc in the west, and, in the middle, an ambitious young deejay named Grandmaster Flash However, there, were also dozens of lesser-known deejays, all vying, for recognition. The easiest and quickest way to establish a reputation as a deejay was to "battle" a known deejay. These battles were usually held in parks or community centers. Both deejays played at the same time. Whoever collected the most dancers around his system was declared the winner. However, with both systems cranked to maximum volume, the winner was often the deejay with the loudest sound. "There was a lot of confusion going on at the time," laughed Bambaataa. "If you outblasted the other deejay, he'd get mad, cut off his system and leave."

During one legendary battle against Disco King Mario, Bambaataa opened his show with the theme song from the *Andy Griffith Show*, taped off his television set. He mixed the ditty with a rocking drum beat, followed it with the *Munsters*' theme song and quickly changed gears with "I Got the Feeling" by James Brown. His knack for coming up with unexpected cuts and "bugging out" the audience earned him the title "Master of Records."

During the summer of 1976, young b-boys cruised through the Bronx on bicycles, looking for block parties. "Where they jamming?" they'd ask anyone in the street. "Flash is jamming at Twenty-Three Park!" would come the reply, and before long several hundred kids, many of them stoned on angel dust, marijuana or beer, would come pouring into the park where Joseph Sadler and Gene Livingston had their system wired to the base of a streetlight. The audience knew the two deejays only by their stage names: Grandmaster Flash and Mean Gene.

Flash, an electronics wizard from Samuel Gompers Vocational High School, had been deejaying house parties for two years. In 1976, he began attracting widespread attention for his outdoor parties, which were usually held in a park at 169th Street and Boston Road.

"You had to be entertaining to throw block parties," said Flash. "It was always a rough crowd and there was never any security. If the crowd wasn't entertained, the situation could get very dangerous. I would go to the Hevalo sometimes to check Herc out, but Herc used to embarrass me quite a bit. He'd say 'Grandmaster Flash in the house,' over the mike, and then he'd cut off the highs and lows on his system and just play the midrange. 'Flash,' he'd say, 'in order to be a qualified disc jockey, there is one thing you must have … highs.' Then Herc would crank up his highs and the high hat would be sizzling. 'And most of all, Flash,' he'd say, 'you must have … bass.' Well, when Herc's bass came in the whole place would be shaking. I'd get so embarrassed that I'd have to leave. My system couldn't compare."

However, if Flash couldn't compete with Herc's system, he was determined to find another way to establish himself as the premier deejay in the Bronx. He began visiting Manhattan discos, where deejays like Pete Jones were playing music for an older, more sophisticated audience. Although he disliked the music, Flash noticed that Jones knew more about mixing records than Herc. "It wasn't no hit-or-miss thing, said Flash. "Herc would drop the needle and cut the record in and hope he was in the right spot, but Pete knew how to pre-cue his records."

One night Jones relented and let Flash temporarily take over the controls of his system. "Once I put on the headphones, I knew the secret," said Flash. "A simple toggle switch let me hear what was on each turntable. At school, we called it a SPDT—single pole, double throw—switch. I didn't have one on my mixer, so I took some Crazy Glue and glued one on. I ran wires to my turntables and to a small amp, just powerful enough to drive a set of headphones. When Gene came back I told him: 'Gene, I got something here! I found a way to lock these beats up and keep the shit going!'"

Although Herc was the first deejay to buy two copies of the same record so he could keep repeating the same break indefinitely, it was Flash who devised the method for repeating break sections while keeping a steady beat. Rather than find the section by chance, Flash began pre-cueing through headphones. He spent hours sitting in his room practicing his mixing technique. By playing short, rapid-fire cuts from a variety of records, he invented the art of musical collage. "Mean Gene never seemed to get the hang of it," said Flash, "but his baby brother, Theodore, used to skip school and hang out with me. That's when I discovered the clock theory and Theodore caught on to it right away." In order to make a mix using five or six different records, Flash had to be able to locate precise moments on each record in a matter of seconds. The problem was that every groove looked pretty much the same. How could you find the right spot fast enough? The solution, Flash discovered, was to "read" the record like a clock, using the record label as the dial.

Ray Chandler, an independent concert promoter, approached Flash in 1976 and tried to convince him to open a regular night spot. Because most of his fans were junior-high-school age, Flash was dubious. Why pay to see him when lots of other deejays were playing the parks for free? However, after Chandler found a tiny club on Boston Road, Flash agreed to give it a try. The club didn't have a name, but the front door was painted black, so they called it The Black Door.

"It had two rooms with a long hallway between them," said Flash. "Each room was about the size of a living room. First thing we did was have a lot of flyers made up. Phase and Buddy Esquire were the main flyer makers. Those guys were great. Chandler hired a crew to pass the flyers out at schools. We'd open at eleven o'clock and by midnight, the place was so packed you couldn't buy your way in. The doors wouldn't open back up until six or seven in the morning."

By this time, Flash had converted several members of his crew into "emcees," who were supposed to keep the crowd dancing by talking over a microphone. Most of the attention, however, was still centered on the dancers. "Everybody was doing the Freak," said Flash. "That was a dance that made it permissible for the male to damn near have sexual intercourse with the female. It was a fast dance and you would bounce around with the girl jammed against you. And she'd be doing it right back to you. With some girls, it was even permissible to have a guy in the front and one in back, like a sandwich! If you weren't on the dance floor when that shit was jumping off, you missed out. It got super frantic. I would blow my tweeters and they'd sound like gunshots. You think that would disturb the dancers? Hell no. I had to program a calm hour after the frantic hour just to bring the crowd back to a normal state of mind. Lots of stick-up kids were coming to the club and they were the type to go up to somebody and demand his gold chain. If you weren't ready to fight, you'd have to hand it over. There was this one record—'Listen to Me' by Baby Huey. Something happened every time I played it. We called it 'the trouble record.' The stick-up kids would start looking for somebody the minute they heard it. We were having problems until Chandler hired a former division of the Black Spades to act as security. They had changed their names to the Casanova Crew and we didn't have any more problems after the Casanovas started taking care of security."

Within a few months, Flash's popularity was soaring and he had to move to a bigger club. Despite his success, he continued improving and updating his technique. In 1977 he invented back-spinning, which allowed him to repeat phrases and beats from a record by rapidly spinning it backwards. For example, he would take a phrase like "Let's dance" and repeat it seven or eight times—without losing the beat. "We conquered quite a bit of territory," said Flash. "High-school kids were getting into the music and we knocked off all the high schools. But the pinnacle of our dream was to play the Audubon Ballroom."

Meanwhile, Theodore and his brother Gene had formed their own deejay crew with "Grand Wizard" Theodore as the star. Although only 13 at the time, Theodore was one of the few deejays who could compete with Flash. While Flash was perfecting the back-spin, Theodore was working on a technical innovation of his own, which he debuted at the Third Avenue Ballroom in 1978.

While practicing at home, Theodore noticed he could create sound effects by spinning the record back and forth while keeping the needle in the groove. It wasn't always a pleasant sound—in fact, it could be highly irritating—but if controlled properly, it could also be explosively percussive. Many deejays were already familiar with the sound because they heard it in their headphones every time they pre-cued a record. Theodore wanted to try the sound in public, but he wasn't sure how the audience would react. "The Third Avenue Ballroom was packed," said Theodore, "and I figured I might as well give it a try. So, I put on two copies of 'Sex Machine' and started scratching up one. The crowd loved it … they went wild."

"Scratching" was soon imitated and improved by other deejays, including Flash, Breakout, A.J., Jazzy Jay and Charlie Chase. In a few years, Whiz Kid and Grandmaster DST would use the technique to create unbelievably smooth, synthesizer-like effects. However, in 1978, the focus began shifting away from the deejays and onto their emcees, who were busy creating a new, aggressive style of talking on the mike, which would soon be known around the world as "rapping." Before long, few kids wanted to be deejays anymore. Instead, they all wanted to be rappers.

A NEW RAP LANGUAGE

It was a hot, sweltering night in the Bronx, but waves of thunderclouds were gathering over Westchester County and it looked as though rain might be arriving to cool off the city. Although the rain never came, a lightning storm did, and at 8:30 P.M. several bolts struck the power transmission lines at the Indian Point nuclear power plant, causing a short circuit. Like falling dominoes, relay circuits stretching south into the city began shutting off. Lights went blank, elevators stopped, subway cars rolled to a halt. Within 20 minutes it became the worst New York City blackout since November, 1965.

Unlike the previous blackout, however, which had been remarkably trouble-free, the blackout of July 14, 1977, was almost immediately marred by reports of looting, arson and robbery, most of which came from the ghetto areas of Bedford-Stuyvesant, Brownsville, Harlem and the South Bronx. By 10 P.M. gangs of youths were congregating in front of the major stores. "Let's do it, let's do it," they'd say, trying to work up the nerve to break a window. A steel door guarding the Ace Pontiac Showroom on Jerome Avenue was smashed and 50 cars were driven off the lot. When police answered an emergency call from a supermarket on 138th Street, they were bombarded by bricks and bottles. "They couldn't understand why we were arresting them," said Officer Gary Parlefsky of the 30th Precinct to a *New York Times* reporter. "They were angry with us. They said: 'I'm on welfare. I'm taking what I need. Why are you bothering me?'" Fires, many undoubtedly set by arsonists, illuminated the streets, which were lined with looters carrying TV sets, stereos, groceries, clothing and anything else they could cart away. Within 24 hours, more than 3,000 people were arrested and 100 policemen were injured. The state troopers were rushed in to restore order. "The blackout just totaled the whole damn neighborhood," said Phase 2. "The businesses never came up out of it."

Until the blackout, few people realized the extent of the anger and frustration in the South Bronx, emotions that had been subdued but not eliminated by social programs like welfare, methadone treatment and food stamps. It is not surprising that these hostile feelings were also reflected in the new style of rapping formulated that same summer. Although it is difficult to trace the origins of rap, the genre is firmly embedded in black American culture and stretches back farther than even most rappers realize.

In 1976, Dennis Wepman, Ronald Newman and Murray Binderman published a landmark study on black prison culture entitled *The Life: The Lore and Folk Poetry of the Black Hustler*. The book documented "toasting," a form of poetic storytelling prevalent in prisons throughout the '50s and '60s. "Toasts are a form of poetry recited by certain blacks—really a performance medium," wrote the authors. "They are like jokes: no one knows who creates them, and everyone has his own versions. ... Most recitation sessions are somewhat structured: a reciter performs to a silent, appreciative audience. Good tellers may be highly valued and much in demand. ... In Attica, Doe Eye, a young burglar from Harlem, could characterize the people of the toasts so exactly that, when he was speaking from his cell, one might have thought he had a group in there with him."

Probably the oldest and most famous toast, "The Signifying Monkey," had hundreds of different versions by 1976. Other famous toasts included "Duriella du Fontaine" and "King Heroin," a version of which was recorded by James Brown in 1972. Some toasts were moralistic fables, others related how a man in prison had been betrayed by a girlfriend. Almost all attempted to glorify the life of the petty criminal. The toast which follows was probably composed in 1964.

The Hustler
The name of the game is beat the lame
Take a woman and make her live in shame.

It makes no difference how she scream or holler,
'Cause dope is my heaven and my God the almighty dollar

I, the Hustler, swear by God
I would kill Pope Paul if pressed too hard.

I would squash out Bobby and do Jackie harm
And for one goddamn dollar would break her arm.

I, the Hustler, kick ass morning, noon and night.
I would challenge Cassius and Liston to a fight.

I would climb in the ring with nothing but two P-38s.
And send either one that moved through the pearly gates.

I, the Hustler, can make Astaire dance and Sinatra croon,
And I would make the Supreme Court eat shit from a spoon.

During the '50s, black radio jocks entertained and amused audiences with prison-style raps. In 1955, the most popular of these radio personalities was Douglas "Jocko" Henderson, whose "1280 Rocket" show on WOV anticipated a hip hop fascination with themes from outer space. Jocko often opened his show with lines like: "From way up here in the stratosphere, we gotta holler mighty loud and clear, ee-tiddy-o and a ho, and I'm back on the scene with the record machine, saying oo-pap-doo and how do you do!" His witty, bantering style was updated and refined by New York club deejays like Frankie Crocker, who later became a radio jock on WBLS.

It is worth noting that Jamaican music also has a history of toasting: poems written in Jamaican slang were spoken to the beat of reggae records by deejays with enormous portable sound systems. Because of this, many critics have drawn parallels between the development of rap and reggae, a connection that is denied by Kool Herc. "Jamaican toasting?" said Herc. "Naw, naw. No connection there. I couldn't play reggae in the Bronx. People wouldn't accept it. The inspiration for rap is James Brown and the album *Hustler's Convention*."

Released in 1973, *Hustler's Convention* was written and performed by Jalal Uridin, leader of a group of black militant ex-cons known as the Last Poets. The group was discovered in the late '60s by record producer Alan Douglas, who saw them on a local television show. "I called the station, found out who it was and through some sources I made a contact. I went to 138th Street and Lenox Avenue one afternoon and they recited for me on the street corner," said Douglas. "I made a deal with them. The deal was, they would come to the recording studio, put this on tape, and if we all like each other when it was over, I'd put the record out. And if they didn't, they could take the master home with them."

The group's first record, which contained such raps as "Run Nigger," "Niggers Are Scared of Revolution" and "When the Revolution Comes," reportedly sold more than 800,000 copies despite its aggressively radical overtones, which annihilated any hope of radio play. Under the pseudonym "Lightnin' Rod," Jalal went on to record *Hustler's Convention*, a solo album also produced by Douglas. It consisted of 12 prison toasts (with raps like "Four Bitches is What I Got," "Coppin' Some Fronts for the Set" and "Sentenced to the Chair") recited to musical compositions by Brother Gene Dinwiddie and Kool & The Gang, Although the record did not sell as well as the Last Poets' initial effort, it had enormous popularity in the Bronx.

With *Hustler's Convention* as inspiration, Kool Herc began composing prison-style rhymes using expressions like "my mellow" and "it's the joint." Herc discovered an echo chamber could provide dramatic flourishes at just the right moments, "Yes, yes, y'all," Herc would say. "It's the serious, serio-so jointski. You're listening to the sound system. The Herculords … culords … lords. And I just want to say to all my b-boys … boys … oys. Rock on. Time to get down to the A.M. But please remember—respect my system and I'll respect you and yours. As I scan the place, I see the very familiar face … of my mellow. Wallace Dee in the house. Wallace Dee, freak for me."

"I first went to the Hevalo when I was thirteen," said Sisco Kid. "This dude around my block said, 'Hang with me,' and he took me. Everybody was lined up around the block. They had a gangster look and were older than me. I said, 'Oh shit, this is crazy.' It was very dark inside, but there was an excitement in the air, like anything could jump off. You'd see some dude dancing and he'd be wearing alligator shoes. You'd say, 'Check out this dude!' Then Herc came on the mike and he was so tough. You'd get transfixed by his shit. He had this def voice that almost sounded like a, southern drawl. You thought, 'This is cool, I want to be like this.'"

"People got ideas from *Hustler's Convention*," said Theodore. "But it was hard to get on the mike and say a rhyme. Nobody really had any rhymes. Mostly it was 'You're listening to the sound of so-and-so deejay and next week we'll be at such-and-such park.' Then Flash wrote this rhyme. 'You dip, dive and socialize. We're trying to make you realize. That we are qualified to rectify that burning … desire … to boogie.' At this point he didn't have any emcees. He asked Melle Mel, 'Will you say this rhyme?' Mel said, 'No, let Cowboy say it.' Cowboy said, 'No, let Mel say it.' It went back and forth like that. Flash wanted that rhyme said so bad he finally grabbed the mike and said, 'I'll say it.' And that's how it happened."

"Vocal entertainment became necessary to keep the crowd under control," said Flash. "When people first came to the park, they'd start dancing. But then everyone would gather around and watch the deejay. A block party could turn into a seminar. That was dangerous. You needed vocal entertainment to keep everyone dancing. I tried so many people. I used to leave the mike on the other side of the table so anybody who wanted could pick it up. A lot of people failed the test. The first to pass was Cowboy. Then Mel. Then Mel's brother Creole."

Since Cowboy had a deep voice similar to that of a radio disk jockey, his early rapping style more closely emulated disco deejays like Hollywood, a Manhattan-based deejay who employed a slick, radio-jock sound. Mel and Creole, on the other hand, created a more percussive style of rap similar to the staccato exhortations used by James Brown on such hip hop classics as "Give It Up or Turn It Loose," a song in which key phrases were shouted to the beat. "Clap your hands!" screamed Brown.

"Stomp your feet! In the jungle, brother! Clap! Clap! Ain't it funky now? Need to feel it!" Although Brown's vocals could not really be called rap, they provided the perfect accompaniment for dance records: They encouraged the audience to participate more fully in the music, they emphasized rhythm and raw emotion over melody, and each syllable was spoken directly on the beat—something that had not been attempted with toasting, which put its emphasis on vocal ingenuity and lyrical content rather than rhythm. (Douglas attributes the difference to a change in musical styles. "The Last Poets were jazz-heads," he explained, "while today's rappers are into disco, rock and rhythm and blues. The words fall differently and you get a different feeling. The Poets didn't care if one could dance to the rap. The point was a story was going down that was memorable.")

Relying on an inventive use of slang, the percussive effect of short words and unexpected internal rhymes, Mel and Creole began composing elaborate rap routines, intricately weaving their voices through a musical track mixed by Flash. They would trade solos, chant and sing harmony. The result was dazzling. It was a vocal style that effectively merged the aggressive rhythms of James Brown with the language and imagery of *Hustler's Convention*. They were immediately imitated by every other emcee in the Bronx.

> *To the hip hop, hip hop, don't stop.*
> *Don't stop that body rock*
>
> *Just get with the beat, get ready to clap.*
> *'Cause Melle Mel, is starting to rap*
>
> *Ever since the time of the very first party,*
> *I felt I could make myself some money.*
>
> *It was up in my heart from the very start.*
> *I could super sell, at the top of the charts.*
>
> *Rappin' on the mike, makin' cold cold cash.*
> *With a jock spinnin' for me called Deejay Flash.*

To complement the new rap routines, Flash experimented with a recently invented electronic drum machine. The shock value alone made the machine a useful theatrical device. The turntables would be empty, Flash would step back from his set, and yet somehow the beats would continue with mechanical precision. "It bugged them out," said Flash, laughing. "Then we started featuring ourselves as Grandmaster Flash and the Three Emcees … with THE BEAT BOX. People would show up at the party just to see what the beat box was."

Failing to keep up with recent developments in hip hop, Kool Herc was having trouble maintaining his position, and, in fact, was undergoing a rapid decline in popularity, a development he attributed to his being stabbed at one of his own parties. "The party hadn't even started," said Herc. "Three guys came to the door and my people wouldn't let them in. They said they was looking for the owner. A discrepancy started. By this time, I'm finished dressing and I walk over and say, 'What's happening?' Boom, boom, boom. I got stabbed three times, once in the hand and twice in the side. The guy with the knife was drunk. Somebody stabbed him up but I'm sorry to say he lived. I took a piece of ice, put it on my side, and walked to the hospital. After that, the door was open for Flash. How do you think people feel about coming to a party when the host gets stabbed? Then my place burned down. Papa couldn't find no good ranch, so his herd scattered."

For over two years rap had developed in almost complete isolation from the rest of the world. Until 1980, hip hop music and rap were transmitted primarily through live cassette recordings which were noisily displayed via ghetto blasters, portable tape players carried by every self-respecting hip hopper. Tapes were circulated around New York, in prisons, in nearby states, and could even be found on army bases overseas. However, the first rap record using the South Bronx style was made not by a local group but by the Fatback Band, who recorded "King Tim II" in 1979. Several months later, Sylvia Robinson, a singer who recorded "Pillow Talk" and "Love is Strange" in the '70s, decided to make a rap record. One day she walked into a pizza shop near her home in New Jersey and heard a live tape being played by a man named Hank, who was the doorman at a rap club in the Bronx. The tape featured Grandmaster Caz and the Mighty Force Emcees.

"The way rap evolved is from people trying to outdo each other," said Grandmaster Caz. "You'd go to Herc's party and hear him say something. Then you'd go home and change it around to where it was your saying. I knew the entire *Hustler's Convention by* heart. That was rap, but we didn't know it at the time. Then everybody started saying nursery rhymes. Then Flash started the whole thing of having real groups. Then people started coming to parties just to see the emcees. I used to go to this club called the Sparkle and I told Hank about my group. I told him we needed a manager. So he went to work for us, helping us out on the financial end and stuff. He was also working at the pizza shop and that's where he met Sylvia. She heard him playing one of our tapes. So he told me about it. Later, I asked him, 'Whatsup?' and he said, 'Sylvia already has two rappers and she wants one more. And she asked me to do it.' So I said, 'Well, okay, I understand that.' If it was me, I would have done the same thing. And he said, 'Well, I want to use some of your rhymes.' I threw my rhyme book on the table and said, 'Take what you want.'"

Before long Robinson created the Sugarhill Gang, a group composed of Hank, Wonder Mike and Master Gee. Their first record, "Rapper's Delight," unexpectedly sold two million copies, launched a new independent record company and created a vast audience for rap music around the country. It also unleashed a mad scramble of emcee groups, looking for record contracts. The song's success was due more to its novelty and its musical track, which was lifted from Chic's "Good Times," than to its rapping, which was weak and unimaginative by Bronx standards.

OBJECTIVE QUESTIONS

1. The beginning of the end came in 1959, when Parks Commissioner _____ began building an expressway through the heart of the Bronx.
2. What year did the "Black Spades," originally called the Savage Seven, start? What did Robert Moses do that same year?
3. Every gang had the same uniform. Describe it.
4. Contrary to the myth created by this and other articles, street gangs did not appear in the Bronx solely _____.
5. What year did gang activity peak?
6. What gang did Afrika Bambaataa come from, and why does he think the gangs died out?
7. During WWII, a welding inspector at the Bethlehem Steel shipyard in Quincy Massachusetts began writing _____ in crayon inside ships that were being built for war.
8. No one really knows who started graffiti, but we all know who made it famous, _____.
9. Who was Phase 2 and how did he get his name?
10. How did Super Kool get his letters so thick?
11. After Topcat brought the "Philadelphia style" to New York, writers from the Upper West Side imitated it and called it _____.
12. According to Tracy 168, the best year for graffiti was____.
13. How old was Clive Campbell when he arrived in the United States?
14. Who coined the term "b-boys"?
15. Before 1975, anyone wanting to gain notoriety in the Bronx either became a graffiti artist or an incomparable break dancer. However, by 1976, the most powerful and revered figures were_____.
16. When did Bambaataa give his first official party as a DJ at the Bronx Community Center?
17. What was the name of Ray Chandler's little cub on Boston Road where Grandmaster Flash played in the late 70s?
18. What did Theodore "Grand Wizard" Livingston invent?
19. What did Kool Herc say about the influence of Jamaican toasting and rap? What does he say is the inspiration for rap?
20. According to Grandmaster Flash, "vocal entertainment became necessary to_____."
21. To what did Kool Herc attribute his rapid decline in popularity?
22. Up until 1980, how were Hip Hop and rap mainly disseminated?
23. Where did "Big Bank Hank" get his rhymes?

QUESTIONS FOR FURTHER THOUGHT, RESEARCH, AND DISCUSSION

1. Why do you think graffiti artists were particularly attracted to trains?

2. The personality and iconic persona of Afrika Bambaataa are larger then life. Can you describe him and the effect of his personality? Do some research on Zulu Nation. Go to www.zulunation.com.

3. What is the psychology of a graffiti artist? Where do we draw the line between expression and vandalism? Has Hip Hop culture condoned and even glorified other kinds of illegal or outlaw behavior? Research and report on criminologist James Q. Wilson and his "broken windows" theory.

4. Create your own rhymes over James Brown's "Give It Up Or Turn It Loose," "Get Ready" by Rare Earth, or The Incredible Bongo Band's "Apache."

5. Listen to The Hustler's Convention and compare it to more contemporary rap records. Can you find any direct influence on modern artists?

6. Read the Wepman, Newman, and Binderman book, The Life: The Lore and Folk Poetry of the Black Hustler and report on its influence on Hip Hop culture.

7. Compare and contrast the personalities and accomplishments of each of the "Three Kings:" Herc, Flash, and Bam.

Post Soul

By Nelson George

Nelson George was one of the very first music journalists to take notice of the new emerging Hip Hop culture and write about it. Of course, he literally grew up around it. *Rolling Stone* has called him "the most knowledgeable Hip Hop writer on the planet." Besides *Hip Hop America*, George has also written *Post Soul Nation* and *The Death of Rhythm and Blues*. Historically, Nelson George was instrumental in bringing together Russell Simmons, J.B. Moore and Robert Ford, the trio that produced Kurtis Blow"s "Christmas Rappin,'" which narrowly missed being the first Hip Hop recording by just a few months.

Steve Hager's story is a regional one that brings Hip Hop out of the culturally and economically isolated South Bronx. Nelson George, on the other hand, describes the landscape that spawned Hip Hop in a much broader context. He outlines the national politics, style, fashion, and music business ideas of the 70s from which Hip Hop emerged. Of all of the Hip Hop journalists, Nelson George probably has the best understanding of how the insides of the music business really work, and that is well demonstrated here. His other great strength is the way he deftly compares Hip Hop to movies, fashion, advertising and sports.

Also in this chapter is a continuation of the story of graffiti's break-out into the art world and a brief history of "breaking" and its two phases. The chapter ends as George reminisces about his 1992 interview with the "Three Kings."

"POST-SOUL" FROM *HIP HOP AMERICA*

I got so much trouble on my mind
(On my mind)
I refuse to lose
Here's your ticket
Hear the drummer get wicked

—Chuck D, "Welcome to the Terrordome"

T HIS STORY BEGINS as another is ending. The first story is full of optimism and exalted ideas about humanity's ability to change through political action and moral argument. The next story, the plot we're living right now, is defined by cynicism, sarcasm, and self-involvement raised to art. The turning point was the early '70s. Dashikis, platform shoes, and Richard Nixon were still in vogue. The phase of the civil rights movement led by Dr. King, with its philosophy of nonviolence, its marchers in starched white shirts and narrow ties, was already literally long dead. The succeeding phase of angry, burn-baby-burn rhetoric was itself receding as heroin's vicious grip, the mercenary diligence of FBI informants, and a philosophy of benign neglect replaced liberal guilt as the engine of our government's policy toward the poor. Street agitation for social change was over. Now African-Americans could sit at the front of the bus and downstairs at movie theaters. Now we could vote all over these United States. Now black politicians set their sights on controlling City Hall in big cities and small towns. Now ambitious black graduates of white colleges began slipping into corporate America's awkward, monied embrace. Dr. Martin Luther King's dream of civil rights as a way to open doors of opportunity was working—for some. The '70s would spawn the first graduating class of affirmative action babies. They weren't called buppies (black urban professionals) yet—there weren't even yuppies yet—but these pioneers blazed trails for them. They walked through doors cracked open by dog-bitten marchers in the South and radical nationalists in the North. They were not smarter or more worthy than their parents; they were just better trained in the ways of white mainstream protocol, proud of their new clout and poised for frustrations more nuanced than African-Americans had ever confronted.

Starting in the '70s, the new black professionals had an opportunity to pursue their ambitions with a freedom previously unknown to African-Americans. But they were faced with a new conflict between maintaining loyalty to their generally white employers—protect that job!—and espousing a problack agenda that could endanger their jobs. Just because you're in doesn't mean you *fit* in. It's no wonder that the business magazine *Black Enterprise*'s July 1974 issue focused on hypertension, noting that six of the nation's twenty-three million victims were black, making it the number-one health risk for African-Americans.

This new black middle class—products of tokenism, affirmative action, and their own hard work—lived as most middle class Americans of the '70s. They moved to the suburbs, often to predominantly black enclaves like Teaneck, New Jersey; Baldwin Hills, California; and Silver Spring, Maryland. They dabbled in cocaine, seeking the slick rush and status its ingestion implied.

The Cadillac, historic symbol of big money among African-Americans, slowly gave way to less ostentatious European luxury cars.

Corporations were, at last, looking at the black community with an eye to more than narrow recruitment. Along with the growth of black professionals came an acknowledgment by America's CEOs that there was money to be made in catering directly to the black masses. So the '70s saw the proliferation of "special markets" (i.e., black), divisions aimed at tapping the once ignored black consumer. In *Black Enterprise* during the '70s, one encounters the special markets euphemism used for hawking goods by General Foods, Johnson & Johnson, and sundry other American manufacturers. For the first wave of black corporate employees, special markets were often a velvet trap that guaranteed its employees the perks of mainstream American life (suburban living, credit cards, ski weekends) yet kept them segregated from their businesses' major profit centers and from any real shot at company-wide power. Becoming a vice president of special markets usually meant you had limited opportunity to shift to areas of distribution or production central to the core of whatever business or product you were hawking. The black executives too often found their most prominent role was to be trotted out in front of stockholders and noted in Equal Employment Opportunity Commission compliance reports.

Until the '70s, the recording industry wasn't really viewed as part of corporate America. During the rebellious '60s it had opened its doors to dopehead guitarists and bands advocating free love and left-wing ideology, which scared the mainstream to death. Ironically, the profits from the rock revolution music, and the expanded market it created, made small labels bigger and led to a consolidation of power within the business. Fueled by revenue generated by the Doors, the Rolling Stones, Jimi Hendrix, and sundry other counterculture musicians, the record industry became fat with cash and had to grow to keep up with demand, particularly in the areas of merchandising and distribution. The merger joining Warner-Reprise, Elektra-Asylum, and Atlantic in 1970 to form the WEA distribution system was symptomatic of the time.

The '60s rock stars imagined a better world to go along with the rhetoric, yet like most other aspects of our public life in the '70s, they lost their utopian vision and became fragmented into subgenres that lent themselves to highly targeted marketing. However, black music—which independent labels like Motown, Stax, and Chess had dominated since World War II—seemed an area of untapped growth for the corporate labels. What had been proven in the '60s, particularly by Motown, was that R&B-based music by black singers could easily be sold in massive quantities to white teens, creating a lucrative commercial-cultural crossover.

Just like General Motors and General Foods, CBS Records in 1971 (followed by Warner Bros., Polydor, RCA, ABC-Dunhill, and the other significant American record labels) opened special markets divisions. A few even had the guts to call themselves R&B divisions or, more boldly, "black music" divisions. In essence they were established to employ African-Americans to sell black popular music within their community and identify performers with "crossover" appeal. In terms of employment opportunities, salaries, and advances paid to artists, this was an important development worth celebrating. Black vice presidents abounded.

Lavish parties ensued. Soul singers, traditionally underpaid by the feisty labels that had nurtured R&B since World War II, enjoyed increases in contracts, recording budgets, and royalty rates. In the overall schemes of CBS, WEA, or RCA, these black music divisions were the farm teams, from which crossover stars, such as the O'Jays, Earth, Wind & Fire, and Michael Jackson, would be developed.

Of course this transition wasn't always smooth or without complications. Many older established soul stars couldn't adapt to the demands of the black music divisions, since the desire to reach pop consumers was always ever present. Many performers who had thrived in the old environment (including Tyrone Davis, Bobby Womack, and Candi Staton) floundered within these larger systems.

In addition, the black executives at these departments, like their counterparts at General Motors and Johnson & Johnson, were not given latitude to work on selling the "product" (as records are called in the industry) when it crossed over. With rare exceptions, any ambitious black executive soon slammed into the high, thick ceiling that cut off his or her ability to grow and gain power. While the music wasn't as boxed in by race, the staff developing the music absolutely was.

The sad irony of these divisions was that they were on their way to becoming corporate fixtures at exactly the same moment that one of African-American pop music's least creative periods began—roughly between 1976 and 1981. Two factors contributed mightily to this malaise. The first was that, hoping for crossover, producers artificially reshaped and usually diluted the sound of the records recorded and released. In many instances, singles were released only with potential crossover paramount in the label's mind. The arc of a performer's career, the taste of black consumers, and the record's quality were often secondary. While the records were initially marketed by black music departments, their long-range success was decided by the white executives who worked the record at pop (i.e., white) radio. Often the artist got lost in the translation. The second factor was the rise of disco. Not that the disco movement was, per say, bad for black music—it was not. What hurt was the perception of disco inside record companies and the subsequent attitudes of many white music fans.

DISCO TO GO

For those too young to remember, there were once vinyl records. New. Unscratched. Smooth. You tore open the plastic wrapping, pulled it out of the white paper inner sleeve and the sturdy cardboard jacket cover and in your hand was a black vinyl circle with a hole in the middle. Around the hole was paper with a design and words printed upon it. You placed it on your turntable and through stereo speakers the music played just like a CD. Forgive my nostalgia—I still love vinyl.

Discotheque is a French word coined in the '50s to describe clubs where people went to enjoy recorded, not live, music. In America, people had always danced at bars and malt shops to music from jukeboxes. But paying a cover charge for this privilege was rare. At the dawn of rock 'n' roll popularity, radio disc jockeys like Alan Freed and Murray the K hosted "teeny bopper" parties where kids paid to see the jock, see an act lip-synch to their hit, and dance to records. TV stations then began recruiting local DJs to host televised versions of their parties, which is how Dick Clark's *American Bandstand* got started in Philly before its two-decade-long national run. In the following decade, dance crazes (the Twist, the Frug, the Mashed Potato, the Hully Gully) established dancing to records at clubs—then often referred to as "go-gos"—as regular features of big city nightlife. Still, outside the New York–Los Angeles axis most bars and clubs featured live "cover" bands that played faithful renditions of current hits and oldies.

Up until this point technology was simple—recorded music in clubs came from either 7-inch singles played at 45 revolutions per minute or 12-inch albums played at 33 rpm on a single turntable. But the transitional decade of the '70s brought a change here too.

What happened was that a small bit of technology labeled a "mixer" was developed. The mixer allowed club DJs to shift the sound fluidly from one turntable to another, so that the party continued in a seamless flow of sound. The entire American disco experience, which flowered underground before its mainstream discovery circa 1976, was predicated on this simple technological breakthrough.

The ripple effect was profound. The continuous-sound environment created an atmosphere that was more conducive to dancing, drinking, and generally expanding the aural horizons of the customers. Live bands lost work, which meant less experience and exposure for them, which led to fewer live bands in dance music, which, along with the synthesizer, would ultimately change the nature of dance music from the arrangement of musical instruments to the manipulation of synthetic or prerecorded sound.

The advent of the mixer also inaugurated the cult of the club DJ. The record spinners behind the mixes became increasingly creative and idiosyncratic in their use of music. The more ambitious jocks began asking record labels for longer versions of their favorite cuts. Salsoul, West End, Wing & a Prayer, and other small dance-oriented independent companies began catering to DJs and their audiences by manufacturing extended 12-inch singles with vocal and instrumental versions for club use only. As certain DJs and their approach to mixing records at their clubs became known, the dance labels (and later the majors) began recording their mixes and selling them. A Larry Levan, Tom Moulton, or other star disco DJ enhanced the appeal of a record in the way a Puff Daddy mix does in the '90s, but for a smaller, more select audience.

By 1974, the phrase "disco" had become accepted as an overall description for both the clubs and the music they popularized. In New York City, discos were defined by money, sex, and race: There were gay discos in the West Village; Studio 54, Zenon, and other glitzy midtown spots for the monied; black discos for middle-class blacks, including Leviticus and Othello's; grittier black spots such as Harlem's Charles's Gallery; and white working class clubs dominated by Italian DJs in Brooklyn, Queens, and New Jersey. By 1975, *Rolling Stone* estimated that 2,000 discos were operating in America, with 200 to 300 in the New York area. On any given weekend in the Big Apple, 200,000 people were said to be partying at discos.

Very significant, but little appreciated outside New York's Caribbean community at the time, was the introduction of the Jamaican "sound system" style to the city's party-going mix. Using their own versions of mixing boards, since the '60s DJs around Jamaica had given "back-a-yard" parties where the bass and drum pounded like jackhammers. The "dub" style of these mobile DJs stripped away melody to give reggae's deep, dark grooves throbbing prominence. In ganja-filled gatherings, pioneering sound-system DJs such as King Tubby, Prince Buster, and Duke Reid created massive, rumbling sounds that elevated them to a star status rivaling the club DJs in the States.

If the bass beat orientation wasn't enough of a signature, over time DJs began to "toast" or talk about their prowess as lovers or DJs on microphones during their performances. One toasting DJ, U Roy, enjoyed large sales in Jamaica and even enjoyed a number-one hit on the island with "Wear You to the Ball" However, at the time the magic art of mixing smoothly—which drove disco—and the subterranean assault of the reggae sound system were not viewed in the same light. Disco was a pop culture phenomenon. Dub was an ethnic music lauded outside its community by rock critics and few others. Yet a synergy between disco mixing, dub sounds, and toasting would ultimately provide the techniques and sensibilities that allowed the birth of "hip hop."

DISCO SUCKS

The road that disco traveled—from underground style to regional scene to national and international trend—is a cultural migration pattern at the heart of popular culture. How the cultural artifact itself is transformed by the journey can not be predicted. In the case of disco, from 1973 to 1976, the music identified with the clubs would morph into a distinct and, depending on the taste of the club DJ, rigid formula of rhythms and instrumentation. Initially, music played in discos was dominated by high-quality black dance music, with Kenny Gamble and Leon Huff's elegantly funky Philly Sound productions and the lush sounds surrounding Barry White's bass voice the artistic benchmarks. Unfortunately, the most distinctive elements of the Philly Sound and White's hits gave way to a redundant blend of hi-hat drum patterns, swirling string arrangements, Latin percussion breaks, and moronic lyrics that crystallized negatively in the public consciousness as "disco."

Mainstream culture discovered this music around 1975 with the sudden appearance of disco records on the pop charts. Seeing how this music was escaping—or crossing over from—the dance underground ignited a feeding frenzy among the major labels. Black artists, most of whom were to some degree dance-floor friendly, were either pushed toward disco by producers and label executives or went on their own in pursuit of the disco dollar. This resulted in some major hits (Johnnie Taylor's "Disco Lady," Peaches & Herb's "Shake Your Groove Thing," Diana Ross's "Love Hangover"). More typical were records in which great voices and bands were sublimated to big, unwieldy orchestra arrangements and lousy rhythms. Among the disco era's noteworthy abominations were Aretha Franklin's awful "La Diva"; the Ohio Players' equally putrid "Everybody Up," produced by disco star Van McCoy, showing an exciting funk band pitifully selling out; and the Spinners' goofy "Dancin' and Lovin'," supervised by hack disco producer Michael Zager. Aside from wasting precious vinyl, these kinds of records (and other equally worthless novelties such as Meco's "Theme from *Star Wars*" and the Ritchie Family's "Brazil") sparked an antidisco backlash that tainted all black pop.

All this horrible music inspired the phrase "Disco sucks" and, sadly, it was often used in ignorant attacks against black artists in general. Despite optimistic talk inside the recording industry that disco would help black performers reach broader audiences and more lucrative careers, a glance at the charts from the period reveals just the opposite.

The willingness of pop radio to play black artists, and in the process reach a wider audience, actually decreased during disco's peak years. Look at the number of recordings by black artists to make *Billboard*'s list of top 10 singles from 1973 to 1978: In 1973, thirty-six records moved from the black singles chart to the top 100 on the year-end pop chart. In the next two years, as disco began to enter the popular consciousness and crossover thinking gripped the music business, the numbers fell to twenty-seven in 1974 and twenty-eight in 1975. The bicentennial year saw a rise up to thirty, which suggested the pendulum was swinging back. But in 1977, which can be considered disco's peak year, the crossover number was a disastrous twenty-three, including a few black radio-driven disco cuts.

Another reflection of the criminal disrespect then granted black pop was the outcome of the R&B song category in the 1977 Grammy Awards. Of the five slots for nominations two each went to the nondisco compositions of two great African-American bands: Earth, Wind & Fire and the Commodores. Yet all four of their songs were passed over in favor of white Englishman Leo Sayer's lightweight disco ditty, "You make Me Feel Like Dancing." In the uninformed minds of

Grammy voters, who at the time were almost uniformly white record industry employees, disco and R&B had become interchangeable. The corporate crossover agenda and the confusion over disco's impact on black music led to a profound musical identity crisis that—with notable exceptions like George Clinton's Parliament-Funkadelic, Marvin Gaye, and Stevie Wonder—very few African-American stars could avoid.

Calculated crossover, the obsession with disco, and the increasing corporate control of American music spoke to its insularity and narrow-mindedness. This corporate reality was mirrored by simple geography. In the mid-'70s, most of the major labels were clustered together in Manhattan on Sixth Avenue or a block or two east or west. All were in walking distance from each other and from the decade's posh discos—Regine's, Zenon, and the immortal Studio 54. The city's hippest black disco, Leviticus, was farther down Sixth, just off Herald Square and two blocks from Madison Square Garden. It was a place where suits were required, cognac was the favored drink, and all the newly minted special market executives of corporate America did the hustle while trying not to sweat.

The group mindset that grew out of this concentration of record companies, and the tendency of its executives to make professional judgments while doing blow in restroom stalls, is one reason the most important musical-cultural phenomenon of the last twenty years took so long to go mainstream. And, in retrospect, that was very fortunate.

THE BOOGIE DOWN

You gotta go out and paint and be called an outlaw at the same time.

—Lee quinones, graffiti artist,
In the film *Wild Style*

In 1976, after two hundred years of American history, the country gave itself a big party. Even neurotic New York, then in the depths of a frightening economic crisis, was laced with patriotic bunting and speeches full of high-minded boilerplate about democracy. In the great harbor, vintage tall ships sailed in tribute to a warm, loving America that existed only in a history that ignored Native American genocide, black lynchings, and the hypocrisy that begins with the words "All men are created equal."

America's dark side is comprised of those who don't fit neatly into the official history—unneeded workers and uneducated youth whose contact with American government is usually limited to mean-spirited policing, their filthy, abandoned neighborhoods covered up by graffiti. The suburban revolution, the one supported by the government and celebrated by major industry (auto, oil, rubber, real estate), along with prejudice against blacks and Hispanics, had left large chunks of our big cities economic dead zones that mocked the bicentennial's celebration of America as the promised land.

In the mid-'70s, when we did allow for some brief flickers of retrospection followed by judgmental finger-pointing, no place in America was held up more consistently as a symbol of our pitiful urban priorities than the Bronx, particularly its southernmost section. Despite the presence of the newly renovated Yankee Stadium and a pennant-winning team, images of burned-out buildings that left scores of blocks lifeless dominated the media. On *The Tonight Show* Johnny Carson and countless comedians, whenever in need of a cheap laugh, invoked the borough's name for sad isn't-New-York-pathetic chuckles. The borough had a gang problem, a heroin problem, and, like the other outlying boroughs, no industrial base on which to rebuild.

Hollywood capitalized on the South-Bronx-as-hell image in a number of exploitive films: *The Warriors* played the area as home base for highly stylized gang warfare and in *Fort Apache: The Bronx* Paul Newman revived his sagging career by playing a cop with a heart of gold languishing in the savage South Bronx. A few years later in his best-seller *Bonfire of the Vanities* Tom Wolfe caricatured and wallowed in white New York's worst fear—getting lost in the Bronx.

Yet, in 1976, the real Bronx was far from a cultural wasteland. Behind the decay and neglect the place was a cauldron of vibrant, unnoticed, and quite visionary creativity born of its racial mix and its relative isolation. It was within its boundaries that the expressions we associate with hip hop—graffiti art, break dancing, MCing, and mixing—all have roots.

TAGS

Graffiti has been around since man encountered his first stone wall. Much of what we know of the world's early history comes from pictures and symbols scrawled centuries ago. As humans grew more sophisticated and paper became the primary tool of communication, walls became sacrosanct and defiling them with words was viewed as a throwback to primitive times, which *is* surely why what we call graffiti has endured. As a way to pass on unconventional views, mark turf, or just make a brightly colored mess, graffiti will never disappear. It's too useful and way too much fun.

After World War II, when the country was putting a squeaky clean face on its history and architecture, contemporary graffiti began its career as a formal civic nuisance, yet it remained a modest urban irritant until a Bronx-inspired explosion in the '70s allowed graffitists to refine themselves as artists. Early in the decade, a community of graffiti artists began gathering in and around Dewitt Clinton High in the Bronx. Clinton is located just blocks from a Transit Authority yard where out-of-service subway cars are stored. Scribbling obscenities and doggerel on and inside subway cars has always been a pastime of the young and idle, but armed with Krylon, Rustoleum, Red Devil spray paint, Flowmaster Ink—and a relatively new bit of technology, the felt-tipped pen—Clinton students and their peers used the tools of the painter, art student and teacher, not to defile but to create guerilla art.

Since this activity was as illegal as it was fun, these teens gave themselves flamboyant new names, called "tags," that protected them from discovery and gave their work an air of mystery. Phase 2, the tag of Clinton student Lonny Wood, became one of the first to gain citywide renown as it appeared on subway cars up and down the IRT line. The lanky, light brown Wood is African-American but many of the key early graffiti writers were Puerto Rican and white. The display of a distinctive personal approach quickly outstripped racial background as a delineator of style. Not that the racial identity of graffiti's makers mattered to the average New Yorker. Most presumed it was the work of idle, and likely dangerous, youths. In fact, for many residents the surge of graffiti in the city's public life crystallized their fears about New York's decline. It made them feel things were out of control and proved to be a very strong argument for moving to Jersey, Florida, and elsewhere.

As the decade continued, the Big Apple's subway cars and stations became as much canvases as transportation. With creativity and a total contempt for the peace of mind of their fellow citizens, graffiti artists from every borough marked, defaced, and tagged (their preferred verb) public transports with large, elaborate murals that splashed the writer's slang name in colorful, cartoony letters across the length of a car. During graffiti's heyday there didn't seem to be a single car in the system that went unscathed.

To those young or observant enough to see beyond the nuisance caused to travelers, graffiti was the voice of kids using spray paint and Magic Markers to scream for attention and make art. For Mayors John Lindsay and Abe Beame, graffiti was a public policy nightmare. For those looking for manifestations of rebellion, for some last grasp for public defiance before the '60s spirit completely died, graffiti fit the bill—which was why by 1973 a gallery exhibit of twenty giant canvases won tremendous media attention, though many of the reviews were condescending and some downright contemptuous of claims that graffiti was art.

Interest in graffiti as "high" art quickly burned out. A 1975 gallery exhibit in SoHo, with prices ranging from $1,000 to $3,000, was deemed a disappointment and the trend spotters, once hot on turning this public nuisance into a saleable commodity, turned their appraising eye elsewhere.

Hip hop is nothing, however, if not resilient. While snubbed by highbrow critics, graffiti art found new followers in cutting-edge circles. This was partly the doing of several art-savvy promoters, including a young entrepreneur-artist born Fred Braithwaite, but better known to the world as Freddie Love and eventually as Fab Five Freddie, who started organizing graffiti artists and promoting them on the downtown art scene then blossoming in tandem with the punk rock club scene. His point was that this living, aggressive art was a perfect fit with the same antiestablishment attitudes that ruled at punk landmarks like CBGBs. If punk was rebel music, this was just as truly rebel art.

This revival of interest owed much to several charismatic personalities, the most prominent of which was Samo, a thin, curiously dreaded Brooklyn renegade who became the art world's primitive savant under his real name, Jean-Michel Basquiat. Sort of Jimi Hendrix with a paint can, Basquiat lived an intense twenty-seven years in which he moved from aerosol cans to canvas to three-dimensional forms. No matter his materials, Basquiat retained the passion of his Brooklyn background, a color palate that suggested his family's Haitian roots, and an offkilter perspective that was pure bohemian.

Sadly, his career, a trajectory of rise and fall worthy a pop star and later mythologized in a film, not only mirrored Hendrix's embrace by London's rock scene in the '60s but foreshadowed the suffocating success rappers would later experience when they were loved too well by those their art was intended to make uncomfortable. Basquiat died of a heroin overdose in 1988. Eight years later a wonderfully comprehensive retrospective at New York's Whitney Museum confirmed his status as an enduring artist.

At the dawn of the '80s, writers and hipsters in Greenwich Village, SoHo, and lower Manhattan began making the connection between the visuals produced by graffiti artists such as Phase 2, Dondi White, and Lee Quinones and the music and dance styles filtering through New York's streets. In 1982, a young white underground filmmaker named Charlie Ahearn scraped together the money to shoot *Wild Style*, a vibrant little film that used Quinones, Braithwaite, and other street artists to connect the dots between Bronx street culture and the downtown folks who embraced it as rebel art. Because of its uptown-downtown synergy *Wild Style* remains one of the best feature-length film documents of hip hop.

We know now that graffiti's spray can aesthetics and street roots combined to have an impact on artists worldwide. As a sales tool, early hip hop party promoters always used graffiti artists to design their flyers and posters. Later, as the music soared into the public consciousness, there was a period in the '80s when nothing related to selling the culture or, often more precisely, pimping hip hop didn't use some clichéd version of graffiti art. It still influences protest art wherever Magic Markers and spray paint are handy—for example, the angry scrawls of revolutionaries in Mexico and the bored paint jobs of restless teens in rich Zurich. In the gang-ridden cities of America today, warnings about turf and threats of violence are communicated via graffiti.

Unfortunately, in this country the overuse of graffiti style in advertising has drained the expression of its immediacy. Graffiti's wonderful subway-car-long pieces can now look as dated as unlaced Adidas. Yet there is a youthful integrity and humor to them that reminds us in the jaded '90s that hip hop didn't start as a career move but as a way of announcing one's existence to the world.

BREAKING

In 1997, the GhettOriginals, an all-star break-dancing crew that included the seminal b-boys K-Swift (Kenny Gabbert) and Crazy Legs (Richie Colon), did an international tour sponsored by Calvin Klein. Whether appearing on concert stages, in malls near the C.K. section, or at schools, these very adult men (and a few women) amazed audiences with moves they'd developed in the bygone era of shell-toed Adidas and straight-legged Lee riders.

I saw them at P.S. 122 in the East Village. I saw them at City College in Harlem. I saw them in Los Angeles at the Beverly Center mall. And every time they performed I relived that time when breakers moon walked for quarters in Times Square and no club was cool if it didn't have some kid in the corner spinning on his head. Breaking's story, however, is not one that fits easily into anyone's nostalgic memory.

This is because breakers are both hip hop's truest believers and its bitterest commentators. Their expression was spawned, celebrated, exploited, and spit out by the pop culture trend machine in a few overheated years. Breaking was not the only way to dance to hip hop in the '80s. You could turn out a party doing the Freak, the Smurf, the Patty Duke, or even the Wop. They were all fun, relatively simple social dances. Breaking, in contrast, was spectacular, dangerous, and, in its heart, grounded in a commitment to competition. While rappers with record deals verbalize their dedication to hip hop, there are dancers who have been spinning on their heads and groovin' to "It's Just Begun" for twenty years earning only infrequent clothing deals, scant exposure, and small compensation.

Breaking, like graffiti, has two different phases to its history. The first came in the early '70s and coincided with the disco era. What came to be labeled "breaking" was actually a medley of moves adapting a number of sources—the shuffling, sliding steps of James Brown; the dynamic, platformed dancers on Don Cornelius's syndicated *Soul Train* television show; Michael Jackson's robotic moves that accompanied the 1974 hit "Dancin Machine"; the athletic leg whips and spins of kung fu movies—all of which were funneled through the imagination of black New Yorkers.

The first break dancers were, according to old schoolers (I'll explain about the old and new schools of rap historians later), street gang members who danced upright, had names like El Dorado, Sasa, Mr. Rock, and Nigger Twins, and were overwhelmingly African-American. For them, breaking was just a way to dance at the time, not a lifestyle expression.

Within the African-American community it came and went. Perhaps breaking would have been forgotten altogether if it hadn't been for the almost religious zeal of Puerto Rican teenagers.

Trac 2 of the seminal breaking crew Starchild La Rock remembered breaking's two lives this way in *Rap Pages*:

"See, the jams back then were still close to 90 percent Afro-American, as were most of the earliest B-boys, but they took breaking more like a phase, a fad. I say this because I had to see the reactions on their faces when we started doing it. They were like 'Yo, breaking is played out' whenever the Hispanics would do it. For them, the 'Fad' was over by the mid-'70s and most of them got into something else—writing, graffiti, DJing. But we were still pulling crowds regardless. Hispanic kids were always in the circles dancing. When [Puerto Rican] Charles Chase came out DJing, it was a big boost for us 'cause now we had a Latino representing. It didn't matter what the black kids would say—we had a Puerto Rican DJ and we were gonna dance our Puerto Rican way."

Hispanics made breaking competitive. Breaking crews, in the long tradition of urban gang culture, challenged other dancers to meet them at a specific playground, street corner, or subway platform. Armed with large pieces of cardboard or linoleum, not guns or knives, they formed a circle where, two at a time, breakers dueled each other, move matching move, until one of the crews was acknowledged victorious. Like basketball, it was a team sport but it relied on the skill of individuals within each crew. It was a highly stylized form of combat that echoed the kung fu moves of Bruce Lee and the rituals of martial arts. The hat-to-the-back look, while practical for spinning dancers, also suggested a confrontational attitude that still flows through the culture. Grandmaster Flash once recalled, "When dancers actually started making contact, like doing jump kicks and kicking people on the floor, that's when the hat started going sideways. It was like, 'I ain't dancing with you, I'm gonna try to hurt you.'"

The fascination with breaking crested in 1984 with a PBS documentary, *Style Wars*, and three quickie Hollywood flicks: *Beat Street*, *Breakin'*, and *Breakin' 2: Electric Boogaloo*. In addition, breakers turned up in sundry music videos of the period, ranging from R&B diva Gladys Knight's "Save the Overtime (For Me)" and the arty funk band Talking Heads' "Once in a Lifetime."

The durable contribution of breaking, however, is how primarily Hispanic dancers made an impact on hip hop's musical development. Records such as Jimmy Castor's "It's Just Begun," the Incredible Bongo Band's "Apache," and Herman Kelly's "Dance to the Drummer's Beat" didn't become hip hop classics in a vacuum. DJs played them, and often unearthed them, but it was the dancers who certified them. It was their taste, their affirmation of certain tracks as good for breaking, and their demand to hear them at parties that influenced the DJ's and MCs who pioneered hip hop's early sound.

MAKING MUSIC

In the fall of 1992, I sat down with Afrika Bambaataa (Afrika Bambaataa Aasim), Kool Herc (Clive Campbell), and Grandmaster Flash (Joseph Saddler) for a *Source* cover story. Bambaataa came to the interview with a small posse of Zulu Nation disciples, some of whom came to provide moral support, others to interrupt the interview and irritate the hell out of me. Bambaataa is a large man with a brooding, authoritative presence; he rarely smiled during the interview and gave up very little personal detail on or off the record. Bambaataa is so guarded on these matters that his birth name is as hard to uncover as the digits on a Swiss bank account. Yet on subjects he cared about (break beat records, the Zulu Nation, world peace), Bambaataa waxed eloquent.

Kool Herc came with his sister, who'd convinced the reluctant DJ to participate. Here is more a myth than a man for even the truest hip hop fan. Tapes of his performances are rare and, since the '80s, he has performed only sporadically. Up until that 1992 *Source* interview, Herc's last major public exposure had been limited to a small role in the 1984 movie *Beat Street* and some speaking on Terminator X's 1994 solo album. If Bambaataa was selectively guarded, Herc spoke freely about "back-in-the-day" but didn't say much about the contemporary scene other than communicate his dismay with gangsta rap.

Grandmaster Flash came alone and was the most open and affable of the trio, perhaps because he's had the most successful career. Occasionally Herc and Bambaataa ganged up on him. For example, the question of who created "scratching" caused a bit of tension at the table. Though many initially credited Flash with its invention, it is now generally acknowledged that Grand Wizard Theodore (for a time Flash's helper) was the first to scratch but that Flash refined and popularized it. As the three legends got more comfortable, whatever tension that existed between them subsided and the conversation flowed. The hard edge of personality differences softened because this trio had so much in common. Sometime during the administrations of Gerald Ford and Jimmy Carter, Herc, Bambaataa, and Flash had created hip hop's sonic side.

Born in Jamaica and familiar with his native land's sound systems, Kool Herc is the man who, instead of just playing hits in parks and discos, sought out obscure records and played the instrumental breaks, extending them until they sounded like new records. Instead of disco spinning, Herc was doing what he called "break" spinning. Playing at the Bronx's Club Hevalo and Executive Playhouse clubs or in parks, Herc used the breaks and bridges from the Incredible Bongo Band's "Apache" and "Bongo Rock," Jimmy Castor's "It's Just Begun," James Brown's "Sex Machine" and "Give It Up or Turn It Loose," Baby Huey and the Babysitters' "Listen to Me," Mandrill's "Fencewalk," the Average White Band's "Pick Up the Pieces," and other records to create hip hop's original sound and build his rep.

It was equally important that Herc enhanced his presentation by employing a pal named Coke La Rock as his master of ceremonies (or MC) to introduce and comment on the selection. La Rock didn't rap as we'd recognize it now but was more in the style of the Jamaican sound system toasters or black radio announcers hyping a record. Still, several of his pet party motivating slogans ("Ya rock and ya don't stop!" "Rock on my mellow!" "To the beat y'all!") would become rap staples. Some old schoolers assert that La Rock was the first hip hop rapper. I'm not sure, but certainly La Rock's claim is as strong as anyone's.

While Herc's contributions were essentially musical, Bambaataa's most important contribution to developing hip hop may have been sociological. As a teenage record collector, Bambaataa attended some of Herc's parties and realized he owned many of the same records. Though he started from the same musical base as Herc, Bambaataa would range wider and include bits of African, Caribbean, soca, and D.C go-go music in his mixes, giving his work an electric, multiethnic quality. As a result, Bambaataa was labeled "the master of records" by his many acolytes. Ralph McDonald's "Jam on the Groove" and "Calypso Breakdown," Herman Kelly's "Dance to the Drummer's Beat," the Mohawks' "Champ," and Kraftwerk's "Trans-Europe Express" are among the cuts he discovered, featured, and added to the hip hop canon.

Bambaataa is as important for the myth he embodies as for his eclectic taste. Growing up in the Bronx River Projects, Bambaataa became a member of one of the city's biggest youth gangs, the Black Spades. The standard issue story is that in the mid-'70s gangs like the Black Spades faded out (which did happen) and that the various hip hop expressions (graffiti, breaking, Djing, rapping) filled the gap, effectively killing the gang culture of New York. But when asked if he thought hip hop killed New York's gangs, Bambaataa didn't subscribe to that theory: "The women got tired of the gang shit," he replied. "So brothers eventually started sliding out of that 'cause they had people that got killed." From a '90s perspective there is something almost quaint about the idea that gangs could be ended in a major city by the love of the members' women.

In 1974, Bambaataa founded the Zulu Nation, a collective of DJs, breakers, graffiti artists, and homeboys that filled the fraternal role gangs play in urban culture while deemphasizing crime and fighting. Many crucial figures of the period were early members of the Zulu Nation (the Rock Steady Crew, DJ-producer Afrika Islam); twenty-five plus years later, the organization survives, serving as an anchor for its members and a safety valve for the culture. Over the years many hip hop beefs have been squashed after Bambaataa and the Zulu Nation came in to mediate.

Grandmaster Flash is now best known as a recording artist, but there are several purely technical DJ breakthroughs that owe their existence to his hand-and-eye coordination. As I noted earlier, Grand Wizard Theodore may have introduced scratching but Flash is certainly the man who made it matter. "Punch phrasing"—playing a quick burst from a record on one turntable while it continues on the other—and "break spinning"—alternately spinning both records backward to repeat the same phrase over and over—are credited to Flash. Moreover, Flash was a showman. Unlike Herc, who primarily hovered over his turntables and didn't say much to the crowd, Flash mixed and entertained. Crowd-pleasing tricks associated with hip hop, such as spinning with his back to the turntables and using his feet to mix, first flowed from Flash's imagination.

Flash, who at one point trained to be an electrician, was always exploring and refining his equipment. Out of his curiosity came the "clock theory" of mixing where Flash was able to "read" records by using the spinning logo to find the break. He converted a Vox drum machine into what he labeled the "beat box," a device that allowed him to add additional percussion to a musical mix and anticipated the use of drum machines in making rap records.

Just as Herc had Coke La Rock as MC, Flash had an on and off relationship with a group of young MCs who would come to be known as the Furious Five. Between 1976 and 1980, in the years before they began recording, Flash often performed alongside some combination of Cowboy (Keith Wiggins), Melle Mel (Melvin Glover), Kidd Creole (Nathanial Glover), Rahiem (Guy Williams), and Mr. Ness aka Scorpio (Ed Morris). Because money was short for playing at a gig at 116th Street's Harlem World Disco or Times Square's Diplomat Hotel, there were often disputes over money and professionalism: sometimes all five MCs showed, sometimes none. At other times, another young MC, Kurtis Blow (Curtis Walker), worked the mike with Flash.

With Flash and without him, the members of what would become the Furious Five came up with some of the culture's benchmark phrases. "Cowboy came up with a lot of phrases," Flash recalled, "and had a powerful voice that just commanded attention." Cowboy is credited with inaugurating "Throw your hands in the air and wave them like you just don't care!" and "Clap your hands to the beat!" and "Somebody scream!"—three essential clichés of hip hop performance.

Kidd Creole and his brother Melle Mel were, according to Flash, "the first rhyme technicians. They were the first to toss a sentence back and forth. Kidd would say 'I,' Mel would say 'was,' Kidd would say 'walking,' Mel would say 'down.' They just tossed sentences like that all day. It was incredible to watch, it was incredible to hear."

I've mentioned that we now think of "old" and "new" schools of rappers and rap enthusiasts. What today is called "the old school" are the founding fathers, so to speak—a loose community of energetic, creative, and rather naive young people from the Bronx and upper Manhattan who reached adolescence in the '70s. Naive is the key and perhaps unexpected adjective in describing this crew, yet I think it is essential. I'm not simply saying they were naive about money. That's a trait they shared with nearly every young musician I've ever met (and no amount of much touted "street knowledge" ever protects them from rip-offs).

By naive, I mean the spirit of openhearted innocence that created hip hop culture. The idea of parties in parks and community centers, which is celebrated nostalgically as the true essence of hip hop, means that money was not a goal. None of the three original DJs—Herc, Flash, Bambaataa—expected anything from the music but local fame, respect in the neighborhood, and the modest fees from the parties given at uptown clubs or the odd midtown ballroom. They may have pocketed a couple hundred bucks here or there but none thought these gigs would make them millionaires. Like the graffiti writers and the break dancers, the old-school DJs, and those that quickly followed their lead, did it because it felt good and because they could.

For the graffiti artists, tagging walls wasn't about mimicking art school technique or being self-consciously postmodern. For the Hispanic breakers, it wasn't about simply departing from the traditions of Latin social dancing with its rigorous turns and upright posture. For DJs, break spinning wasn't some departure from the norms of soul music. For all these old schoolers it was an accidental, offhand discovery of a way to distinguish themselves in a very direct, self-contained, and totally controllable way. They needed simple tools to make their art and they made their own decisions about what made it good. Hip Hop was not a mass market concept. It was not a career move.

No one from the old school knew where hip hop would go and all were surprised, pleasantly and otherwise, by how it evolved. When I first experienced hip hop I was living out in a drug-scarred, working-class part of Brooklyn and, believe me, I had no idea I'd still care about it decades later.

OBJECTIVE QUESTIONS

1. The 70s spawned the first graduating class of affirmative action babies. They would eventually be called _____.
2. What was the euphemism used by corporations and record labels to describe their "black" or African-American divisions?
3. What two factors contributed to the years 1976–1984 being one of the least creative periods in African-American pop music?
4. What was the effect of disco on live bands?
5. What is the difference between disco and "dub"?

6. Hollywood capitalized on the South-Bronx-as-hell in a number of exploitive films: _____, _____, and _____.

7. Who is Fredrick Braithwaite, and what did he do for Hip Hop history?

8. In 1982, a young white underground filmmaker named Charlie Ahearn scraped together enough money to shoot _____, a film that included Fredrick Braithwaite and Lee Quinones.

9. While rappers with record deals verbalize their dedication to Hip Hop, there are dancers who have been spinning on their heads and groovin' to "_____" for twenty years, earning only infrequent clothing deals, scant exposure, and small compensation.

10. Perhaps "breaking" would have been forgotten altogether if it hadn't been for the almost religious zeal of _____.

11. What was the name of Herc's MC?

12. Who were the members of the Furious Five?

13. When Afrika Bambaataa was asked if he thought Hip Hop had killed New York's gangs, he said he didn't subscribe to that theory. He said the reason the gangs died out was _____.

14. According to the author, what is the key and perhaps unexpected adjective used to describe the "old school"?

QUESTIONS FOR FURTHER THOUGHT, RESEARCH, AND DISCUSSION

1. Describe the politics, fashion, business and social climate of the early 70s in America.

2. How were black executives absorbed into the corporate and business world?

3. How did the success of 60s rock affect the record industry?

4. Report on the tragic life and career of Jean-Michel Basquiat and his relationship to graffiti art. Is the comparison to Jimi Hendrix fair and accurate?

5. Discuss the importance of Puerto Ricans and Latin music in the early development of Hip Hop, particularly their importance in "breaking" and graffiti.

6. The author identifies the influences of break dancing as James Brown, *Soul Train,* Michael Jackson, and *kung fu* movies. Are there others? Compare "breaking" to other African-American dance crazes like the jitterbug, the twist, or even tap dancing.

PART THREE

Hip Hop Blows Up

Rapper's Delight:
Hip Hop Goes Commercial

By Jim Fricke and Charlie Ahearn

Jim Fricke is a cultural historian. He started filming a video record of interviews with Hip Hop's pioneers at the turn of the century for the Experience Music Project's Hip Hop National Exhibit.

Charlie Ahearn has been documenting Hip Hop history on film since the late 70s. His first movie, *The Deadly Art of Survival,* was a Super 8 documentary about martial arts and Kung Fu. His more famous movie, *Wild Style,* is the first dramatic movie about Hip Hop and turned several of its mythical characters, like Lee Quinones, Freddie Braithwaite, and Lady Pink into movie stars. Ahearn said that when Fredrick Braithwaite would introduce him to MCs and DJs from the Bronx, everyone would assume he was a cop.

First person histories are always the most revealing, if not always the most accurate. This volume gives everyone involved in Hip Hop's early history an opportunity to speak and express their own opinion. The chapter presented here is about "Rapper's Delight" and Sugar Hill Records. The story of Hip Hop's first commercial recording is a controversial and somewhat ironic one. It's told here, however, by the people who were involved. Everyone always seems to have a vivid memory of where they were the first time they heard "Rapper's Delight" and what went through their mind. The recurring theme of this chapter is probably the innocence and naiveté of everyone involved, especially the artists. The visual image of "Big Bank" Hank auditioning for Joey Robison in his Oldsmobile 98 in the parking lot of a pizza parlor couldn't be more dramatically effective if it had been made up by a Hollywood screenwriter.

"RAPPER'S DELIGHT: HIP HOP GOES COMMERCIAL"
FROM *YES, YES, Y'ALL*

THE RULES CHANGE

GRANDMASTER FLASH: Prior to the year 1979, we had DJ crews like DJ Breakout and the Funky 4 with a sound system, Kool Herc with a sound system, the L Brothers with a sound system, Kool DJ AJ with a sound system, Grandmaster Flash and the Furious 5 with a sound system, Afrika Bambaataa, with a sound system. ... But right around that time, DJ Hollywood changed the whole game of how DJs played a party. Hollywood would book himself in five spots in one night, and you would wonder how in the hell he could be in five places at one time. He would be at this party for a certain amount of time, but he would jump over to the next party at a certain time, and then jump over to the next party and the next party and the next party. ...

That became the way promoters hired DJs. This made the sound system a dinosaur. Everybody started putting their stuff away because you could be at two or three parties in one night and make triple the money, you know?

DISCO FEVER

SAL ABBATIELLO: My father opened his first bar in 1969 in the Bronx. As time went on, he partnered with a Black bar owner, and they branched out, opened other spots. 1976 rolled around, disco's starting to explode, and my father decides to open up an adult, classy R&B nightclub. John Travolta had just come out with the movie *Saturday Night Fever,* and we're watching the commercial, and my mom goes, "Hey, why don't we call it Disco Fever?" So that's how it became Disco Fever.

My father put in a white Spanish trendy DJ from uptown in the North Bronx. He used to play at one of our other clubs, but he just wasn't cutting it for the South Bronx. At about 4 o'clock he would leave, and this Black DJ would come on. His name was Sweet G. Four o'clock in the morning was the legal hour to close, but in the South Bronx it was kind of lenient—if you weren't having trouble you could get away with staying open. When Sweet G comes on he's playing all these hot R&B records, and he's talking over the music. He would be saying nursery rhymes and asking the crowd to repeat things, "Throw your hands in the air. ..." The energy of the crowd would change.

I'm leaning on the wall, observing the crowd, how the people who weren't dancing were involved with the music as much as the people who were dancing. It was bringing people together: people were talking to strangers, smiling across the bar at somebody, all doing the same thing. And I said, "Wow, this is some gimmick to maybe do a night with."

Sweet G starts telling me about hip-hop music and bringing me places to hear the music. I keep hearing this name Grandmaster Flash coming up, so I tell my father I want to get one of these street DJs to do a night, and I go meet Grandmaster Flash. I say to Flash, "I wanna do a Tuesday night, and I want you to DJ. What do you take?" He gives me these crazy prices. I say, "Look, this is a nightclub that's gonna be open every week. You can't charge me a one-nighter price. It's only a little club. I'm trying it out. I'll start you out with $50." He's laughing. He says, "I'll call you back."

Two or three weeks later he calls me back and says, "Look, I'm interested in doing it." I say, "I think you'll get discovered here, maybe you'll get on the radio. You know, DJ for the radio or something." We didn't think about records or anything. So he comes in. I handed out flyers for like three, four days, and 600 people show up the first night. We're overwhelmed. When the night finally ended, I knew this was something big. And we did it the next week. And the next week. …

After about three weeks Flash started bringing in the Furious 5. They were rapping, and now the night's kicking—now it's spreading all over the high schools and the colleges, about this one night at the Fever. So instead of having this one night, I went and found another rapper, Love Bug Starski, put him on Monday. I found Eddie Cheba, put him on Sunday. Reggie Wells—Thursday. And then finally June Bug left 371, came over to our club, and I gave him Thursday, Friday, Saturday, with Sweet G as the MC. So every night you came to the Fever, every night was a different MC, a different style of DJ.

Now the club's starting to blow up. We added another floor, we're adding rooms in the back. The older crowd started drifting out, and the younger crowd started coming in. Now every kid knows that they could come and hear their sound, their school sound, their street sound, in this club, and it's a major club with a great sound system, being run properly. A major operation, right in the middle of the South Bronx.

By now it's 1979. Things are really going good in the Fever. I'm in my office one morning, and it's only like 11 o'clock, 11:30, and I hear somebody rap. I'm like, "Who the hell's here so early rapping on the mic?" I go out to see who it is, and I don't see nobody there. I'm like, "What the hell? What is this?" Somebody said, "Somebody made a record."

RAPPER'S DELIGHT: THE BEGINNING AND THE END

LOVE BUG STARSKI: Sylvia Robinson will tell you: I was "Rapper's Delight." She got the idea off of me. I did her birthday party at Harlem World, and that's where she got the idea. She said, "I've got to have him." She'll tell you that. But I wasn't interested in doing no record back in them days, 'cause I was getting so much money for just DJ-ing.

JOEY ROBINSON: I said, "Mom, I've got somebody really great that I know, that can really, really rap, and he has a great sound." So she said, "Go find that guy." I went and found him; his name was Casper, and he used to rap with Sound on Sound, the same group where Wonder Mike used to rap.

I let my mom hear a tape of what he did, and she loved it! So my mother said, "Give us a couple of days." They were going to go in the studio and record a useful track, because back then we'd never heard of sampling. Our company at the time was called All-Platinum Records. It was a big R&B/soul company, and we were known for putting violins, strings, trumpets, bass, the whole nine yards on our tracks. She wanted to cut a track that was like "Good Times"—that one little part of "Good Times" that was really great, the bass line. And then we came up with another part, and we put them both together, and she went into the studio and cut the songs with her musicians.

The next day I went looking for Casper, the rapper, and all of a sudden I didn't hear from him for like two or three days. I finally found him, and I said, "Casper, we cut the track. We're ready to go," and he was like, "Listen, my father advised me not to do it." His father was a DJ, and at that time my parents' company was in a big litigation with Polygram Records overseas. That was public knowledge. They were trying to take over our company. And Casper's father told him not to do the record with us.

Later I was with a friend named Warren Moore, and he said, "We know some other people that rap, don't worry about that. ... Get in the car, and we'll take you somewhere to let you hear somebody."

So we left our studio in my Oldsmobile 98 and went to Palisades Avenue, which was about five minutes away. My friend Warren knew of Henry Jackson—I didn't know Hank, didn't know he could rap. Warren went in the pizza parlor, and said, "Listen, Mrs. Robinson is auditioning rappers. ..."

BIG BANK HANK: I grew up with people like Kool Herc; he lived two buildings down from me. We're going back to like '74, '73. Coke La Rook, Kool DJ Herc, we all went to high school together. We all lived within one minute of each other, and every party we was always together. We always hung out at night. Then I hooked up with a person by the name of Caz.

GRANDMASTER CAZ: I met Big Bank Hank at the Sparkle. He worked the door, and I'd kick it with him. He had a genuine interest in hip-hop and seemed to have his head on straight. He was a little older than most of the guys I was around, and I felt like he could help us. I thought he'd be good as our manager. We had the records but lacked a good sound system—a set. Hip-hop was still at a time where it was about the DJ and your sound system. You had to have a big sound system to be competitive with the Kool Hercs and the Bambaataas and the Flashes, the Breakouts, so that's what we went about doing.

Hank went to his parents—his father was a superintendent of a building behind University Avenue where he lived. They gave him a loan so he could buy us some equipment. He had this Jamaican guy build us four speakers the size of refrigerators. This was before the Cold Crush—the group was the Mighty Force. We got a big power amp. We thought we was ready! Four Dynaco 700 power amps, four big double-15" speakers!

But money was coming in too slow. We was only charging $2 to get into our parties back then. In order to pay back the loan, Hank got a job at a pizza shop in Jersey. I used to make practice tapes at my house, saying my rhymes and DJ-ing my beats. Hank took the tapes to work with him. One day Sylvia Robinson's son came into the pizza shop. They heard Hank rhyming along to the tape, and they asked him if he wanted to become part of this group they was forming called the Sugar Hill Gang.

HANK: My friend owned a pizza shop, and I was on summer break. I'm making pizza, and Joey and his mother walk in. I don't know these people at all, right? It's like somebody walking up to you and saying, "I want you to make a record for me." I'm looking around going, "Did I miss something here? It's a joke, right?" No, no, no—they were serious! Picture this: I'm full of pizza dough, and I'm like, "Okay, they want me to come outside and audition in the car?" I'm like, "Ooookkkkaaaayy. ..."

JOEY: So people was eating at the pizza parlor, and all of a sudden he's kicking everybody out the pizza parlor. "Take your food and leave, you gotta go!" Then he's got all this dough on him, and an apron. He gets in the back of my Oldsmobile car, and my car goes like [makes car groaning noise].

HANK: Okay, I am a big guy. That's where the Big Hank came from. I'm a football player.

JOEY: So he gets in the car, and I play the musical track on the tape deck, and he starts rappin'. And all this commotion starts going on around my car, people started singin'. … I was like, "Wow! He's rockin'!" Then, with all the commotion going on, another friend of mine happened to be walking by with someone else, and he heard all this stuff going on. I rolled my window down, and he says, "Joey. Hank … he's nice, but listen to my man. He's even nicer than him!" And that was Guy O'Brien, Master Gee. So then Guy gets in the car, and he starts rappin', so now the two of them are battlin'.

HANK: I did my thing, not thinking of the immensity of what could happen. I mean who could have even dreamed of something like that? When Guy came and we started battling, it gave me a little bit more enthusiasm, you know?

JOEY: So then Wonder Mike happened to be playing a guitar across the street, and he says, "I can rap, too." So I have all this commotion going on, all these people hearin' this stuff, the crowd's getting bigger and bigger. … He jumps in my car, and we go to my mom's house. That night my mother's listening to Guy—Master Gee—and Hank, and she says, "That's it! That's it! I just came up with a new record company called Sugarhill Records, and you all are the first group on Sugarhill Records. We'll name you the Sugar Hill Gang." Then Wonder Mike, who has asthma, says, "Mrs. Robinson you didn't hear me. …"

WONDER MIKE: I was sittin' there, and Guy and Hank were going back and forth—this is in Ms. Robinson's living room, it's about midnight—and they're, "Yeah, yeah, that sounds good!" I'm thinking to myself, "Look, speak up. This could be your chance." So I said, "Mrs. Robinson, you know, I can rhyme, too."
JOEY: She wasn't really interested in hearing Mike because she already heard these two guys here really rap. But she says, "Okay, let me hear you rap."

MIKE: So I start, "The hip … hop … the hibbit, the hibby dibby hibby hibba … ," and I kept going, incorporating everything I saw in the room, from the dog to the statue to the library books. …That was how it started. Our voices and styles blended so well that she said, "We're going to use all three of you guys."

CAZ: Hank came over to my house and said, "Yo. These people want me to make a record." "You? You ain't no MC! You tell them about me?" Hank said, "Yeah, but they wanted me." Personally, I was shocked because Hank is not an MC, you know? He was the manager, so I would figure that he would say, "Well, I'm not an MC, but I manage these guys that are on this tape." But whatever. … So he came to me, and he told me about it, and I figured if somethin' comes out of it I guess we're next. I guess if you get anything from it, it can only help us.

MIKE: The audition was on a Friday night. She said, "Come in Monday, and we'll cut a record." It took one day to make "Rapper's Delight." A few hours to do the music, and the raps were done in one take, except we stopped one time; the rest of it just went straight through.

We gleaned the lyrics from our own repertoire and just improvised from there what we were going to use. But I didn't want to just open "Rapper's Delight" by going into rhymes. I thought, "There has to be a little phrase where I'm explaining what's going on, because this is like new to the world." So I said: "Now what you hear is not a test, I'm rappin' to the beat. ..." And I kinda explained it right then, and it went on from there. In fact the only thing written for "Rapper's Delight" was the intro; all those other rhymes throughout the whole fifteen-minute song was already in our repertoire. But I said, "We have to start this thing out right."

RAPPER'S DELIGHT HITS THE AIRWAVES

HANK: I'm in the pizza shop making pizza. The shop is jam-packed with people. There's a radio station by the name of KTU that's on, and I hear, "We have a new record by the Sugar Hill Gang." I'm like, "Whoa man! Turn this up! This is me!" They play the record. Now you have to understand, this record is almost sixteen minutes long, right? They played it in its entirety. When they got maybe three minutes into the record, the DJ got on and said, "Our phone lines are locked. Please do not call this station anymore. We will play the record again." They had to play the record twice, back-to-back. That's thirty-two minutes!

JOEY: When we released the record, it was massive. I mean, people were waiting in the stores for weeks upon weeks. We couldn't sell the record fast enough; we couldn't press it fast enough. People were calling the radio station ... the radio would go on the air and say, "Stop calling, we're not going to play the record any more. We're going to play it at 7 o'clock, we're going to play it at 10 o'clock, we're going to play it at 12 o'clock." Just so that the phone lines would be free, because so many calls were coming in on this record.

BILL ADLER: I was working as the pop music critic at the Boston Herald in 1979 when "Rapper's Delight" became this phenomenon on radio there. I used to listen to the Black music radio station in Boston, and they played "Rapper's Delight." What was remarkable about it to me wasn't so much the fact that these guys were rapping, but that that particular song lasted fifteen minutes. It was fifteen minutes long. There was an edited version of it, but I never heard the edit because it was such a smash that people wanted to hear it at its full length. I mean this was a Black radio station, but it was a pop format—most of the songs were three minutes long—yet this song would play for five times that length every time you heard it. So that was remarkable to me. More remarkable than the fact that these guys weren't singing, because in terms of the music, the Sugar Hill Gang just sounded like the R&B of the day.

MIKE: We did our first show in a place called Club Paradisio in Newark. We did two shows there, and ohhh it was crazy! The first show was on a Friday night; the second show was a Saturday matinee show with younger kids. During that matinee show on Saturday, there were girls fainting, and they were passing them over the crowd. We didn't even get to finish the show. We had these big burly bodyguards standing in the front of the stage, and the crowd just pushed them aside, rushed the stage. We had to run off the stage through the crowd, through the back door, down the alley, and there were like 100, 150 kids chasing us. And we ran into the van and just got out of there. It was crazy.

HANK: I mean one minute you're walking down the street. The next minute you've got bodyguards and being chased down the street.

MIKE: I originally thought hip-hop was going to be big in the tri-state area—New York, New Jersey, and Connecticut. And when we got calls to do shows in South Carolina and Virginia, I said, "Wow this is really spreading fast!" And we'd get the Billboard magazine and see that we'd been added to play lists in San Diego, L.A., Texas. And then London and Italy, and I said, "Well, this is here to stay! This is not a fad."

CONTROVERSY

GRANDMASTER FLASH: I knew all the crews, what they were doing, when they were doing it, and where they were doing it. But strangely enough, in '79, there was this record that came on the radio: "to the hip hop the hibby dibby. …" I'm like, hold off. This is not AJ. It's not L Brothers. It's not Herc. It's not Bam. It's not Breakout. Who are these people? Turned out it was some crew from Jersey. I'm wondering why don't I know about them because I was real particular about who was doing what, at least the ones that was rocking, you know what I mean? This group consisted of three people. One person I knew to be a bouncer at the Godfather's Club, Kool Herc's place. And some of the rhymes that he was saying I knew from Grandmaster Caz. I'm saying, "Well, damn, I heard these rhymes said by Caz." But this guy, who was a bouncer at the club is saying these rhymes on the record. These other two guys, I didn't have a clue who they were.

CAZ: Hank was like, "Yo. I want to use some of your rhymes." I said, "Here. …" It wasn't like, "How much you gonna pay me?" or none of that. I just threw the book on the table and said, "Use whichever one you want." That turned out to be "I'm the C-A-S and the O-V-A and the rest is F-L-Y"—that's Casanova Fly, that's my name. He never changed it. He just took the rhymes like they were, and he didn't change it up. "I'm the Grandmaster with the three MCs," and all that. That's my stuff. The Superman rhyme about Lois Lane, flying through the air, panty hose? That was one of my earliest rhymes before I really developed as a writer, in 1977 or '78. It was one of the most popular rhymes on the street—everybody that knew hip-hop knew that rhyme.

WHIPPER WHIP: When you'd go around town you'd hear people say Caz's rhymes, 'cause Caz was a story writer. His first thing was this Superman rhyme, what Big Bank Hank did on the Sugarhill. He had the whole city saying his Superman rhyme. I mean we'd go places and hear other rappers saying his rhymes as if it was theirs, you know?

CAZ: I didn't see Hank for another month. When I saw him again, he came to my house with the acetate of "Rapper's Delight," and he played it for me. I fell asleep listening to it 'cause it was garbage. "That's not MC-ing. None o' you niggas is MCs. That ain't what we doing. That's some cornball shit."

At the time hip-hop was limited to a small group of people. Whatever you did, everybody knew what it was and who was doing it. Boom … every car that went by was playing "Rapper's Delight." People would be coming up to me, "Yo! I heard your record! Yo! I heard you on the radio! I heard your rhyme!" I was, "Nah, that ain't me. That's just my rhyme." "Yo! I know you're getting paid!"

RAHIEM: Big Bank Hank bit a portion of my rhyme in "Rapper's Delight"—the first rhyme that I had ever gotten any kind of notoriety for: "I said I'm hip, the dip, the women's pimp, the women fight for my delight. …" I don't remember how the rest of his rhyme went, but I do know that Hank was a bouncer, and he had access to all of the tapes of everybody who was doing shows at the time. So that's how he knew everybody's rhymes.

DISCO WIZ: Hank used to take Caz's practice tapes and sing along a little … but that's it! Like if you were to sing a Britney Spears joint, you know what I mean? There's no connection—you're just singing along to somebody else's stuff. Hank's not an MC! He was just hangin' on. Caz, being the way he was, trusted the guy, because Caz was looking for a shot, too. Hank used his rhyme, word for word, and Caz never saw a dime from that. It's funny, because "Rapper's Delight" skyrocketed hip-hop onto the map, but it's a farce. It's a total farce. You know what I mean?

MIKE: Yeah, people say they wrote our stuff. I remember everything I wrote and where I wrote it. That food rap, where I went over to a friend's house to eat, I wrote that in an alley next to a record store and a ladies dress shop. It just came to me, and I just stopped and I wrote it right there. But I think there's no denying there's a lot of shout-outs and phrases that were just like the common vocabulary at the time.

JOEY: I see different interviews where some of the rappers have a lot of animosity for the Gang because they say they wasn't from the streets, they wasn't from this, and they wasn't from that. But Hank was from the Bronx. He was from the streets. Master Gee was in the group called Phase 2. Wonder Mike was in a group called Sound on Sound. So these guys were all in rap groups at the time that my mother had the idea to do this. She happened to come up with it first. And whenever you come up with something first, people knock you for something, where truthfully it should be praised.

MIKE: You cannot deny the fact that Sugar Hill Gang was the first big rap group! And if we don't get respect from someone, screw 'em! We opened the doors for a lot of people. Ninety-nine percent of the hip-hop world respects us, and they show us mad love. But this pocket of people … instead of concentrating on their own careers and getting a record deal, their life consists of trying to belittle the Sugar Hill Gang. It's unfortunate.

CAZ: Hank never got back in touch with me. Not only did he not compensate me for my rhymes, we didn't even get to keep the equipment! Hank is still on the road, touring with that shit. By the time I caught up with him, Hank had two Cadillacs. He had rings on every finger. He was living!

WHIPPER WHIP: When "Rapper's Delight" first came out, I was really proud. I had no idea what the money was like, but just the fact that you got a record that's being played on every radio station everywhere you go, and you know it was written by your people, said by your people—this was a great thing. I had no idea what publishing meant, I had no idea what writers meant … 'cause a few of my lines are in there, too, you know? So it was good in a way, but then it turned out to be a nightmare for Caz, 'cause when you think about it, he'd be a millionaire right now. Literally, because that is the classic, and he never saw 10 cents from it. The record went and sold I don't know how many million copies, and to this day it's still getting played, and it'll be getting played forever because it was the first of its kind. So Sylvia Robinson knew what she was doing. Joey Robinson knew what they were doing. It's just that that's what happens when you don't know.

CHRISTMAS RAPPIN'

J. B. MOORE: Robert Ford and I got to know each other at *Billboard* magazine [the primary music trade journal]; Robert was there for eight years, and I was there for five. I started in '75. He was a Black guy from the middle of Hollis, Queens, and I was a white guy from the north shore of Long Island. As we got to know each other, we realized that our record collections were virtually identical—we had much of the same taste in music, especially jazz.

I was at Downstairs Records [in midtown Manhattan] one day, asking John—one of the owners—what's new, and he said, "B-boys and b-beats." Kids from the Bronx had been coming down and requesting some record that had the lyrics "sex machine" but was not James Brown. They were desperate for this record, and John finally tracked it down. He had ten guys come in, and they asked him the same question. I thought … there must be something going on here.

I came back to the office and talked to Robert, who then had the Rhythm and Blues column, and said, "Robert, this is interesting. You should go talk to him. There's something happening here." Because it had the aroma, to me, of doo-wop, which was something that came from the street up rather than from the top down.

ROBERT FORD: Thanks to J.B., I went up to Taft High School in the Bronx with Nelson George, and we met DJ Kool Herc, who was really sort of the father of a lot of the rapping and cutting DJs up in the Bronx. That was the start for me; I did stories on DJ Kool Herc, DJ Hollywood, Eddie Cheba, DJ Starski. My early stories ran as far back as '77.

At one point I was on the bus, and I saw a kid putting up these stickers for Rush Productions. The kid turned out to be Russell Simmons's brother; he went on to become Run [of Run-D.M.C.]. I became friends with Russell. He was always at my house, at my office, and he was, to a certain degree, my ambassador to rap music. Russell introduced me to a lot of people and was directly responsible for the series of interviews I did with Starski, Hollywood, Cheba.

Russell had this bright idea to make a record with this guy called Kurtis Blow. Now … for me, Russell was more important than Kurt was himself, only because Russell understood the business end that I couldn't understand. I was already thirty years old, and I felt that I was a little long in the tooth for this art form.

Around that time, Nelson and I went to Harlem to the Apollo to see the Ohio Players, Kool and the Gang, and DJ Hollywood. At that point in the history of the world, the Ohio Players and Kool and the Gang were the two biggest acts in Black music, and yet, by the end of the Ohio Players set, people were yelling to bring back Hollywood, 'cause Hollywood was so talented—he had so much charisma. He wasn't the matinee idol-looking type of person, but he could do everything.

He talked, he rapped, he sang … he did almost everything you could want anybody to do. He, to me, may have been the most talented rapper I ever saw. If DJ Hollywood was available, there's no question, I would have made records with Hollywood. Or for that matter, Eddie Cheba who is also very talented and had a lot going for him. But they weren't available. Hollywood was apparently well connected with some very well connected people in Harlem, and they were the sort of people who were not necessarily conducive to a long, healthy, happy career.

I discovered I was gonna become a father in 1979, so I needed money. So Russell's idea about making a record with Kurtis Blow suddenly made a lot more sense to me. One of my mentors at *Billboard* was Mickey Addy. He was the person who taught me about music publishing. Mickey always had nice little checks from writing old Christmas songs for Perry Como, so I said, "I'm gonna write a Christmas record." I had this idea to write a record and use Kurtis. Russell just, basically, wanted to get over. … He wanted to be a part of it and obviously wanted Kurtis to be a part of it. I had no idea how to write it or anything like that. Then one day, J.B., who I talked about everything with, called me up with 90 percent of the "Christmas Rap."

J. B.: We both had quit Billboard in September of '79 for different reasons, but we were still both writing. We ran into each other in the office in September, and Robert said he had the idea for a "Christmas Rap." I went home that night and did a parody, basically, of "The Night Before Christmas," done in rap. Robert and I got together the next day. I had a studio that I liked in New York, which was called Big Apple, and an engineer that I liked, Roddy Hui, who's since done quite a few rap records. I knew a couple of musicians, and Robert knew some musicians, and we all got together and wrote that song—Robert and I, Kurtis, Denzil Miller, who's a well-known keyboard player, and Larry Smith. We assembled everyone down at the studio and made this record in a big fat hurry.

I had been saving money for five years to leave *Billboard* to write a book. I had about $10,000 saved, and that got invested in making "Christmas Rappin'." The record went to twenty-two or twenty-three different labels—all of whom turned it down.

ROBERT: This is before any other rap record, with the exception of the Fatback Band's "King Tim," which really was the first charted rap record. Nothing else had been out at the time we started doing it, so I kind of expected all of the majors to just turn us down. You have to remember the fact that rock 'n' roll, in its very early days, was rejected by a lot of labels. But I also knew that it was a record that was going to sell, if it ever got to the light of day. Rap was something that any idiot had to know was at some point going to be big, so I fully expected other people were working on it. Then "Rapper's Delight" came out in October. All of a sudden, it was the biggest-selling record ever, you know. I mean … it was selling 100,000 copies a week in New York City alone. So we knew that this was going to sell. Unfortunately, corporations generally are fairly slow to understand.

J. B.: When we finally got the deal at Mercury, it was because it was releasable in England. The record was discovered by a newly arrived English A&R man in Los Angeles as a tape on his desk. His name was John Stains, and he called up Chicago, which was where Mercury headquarters was then, and said, "I can recoup this out of London." So they picked it up for $6,000 and did, in fact, recoup it out of England. The record broke the Top 30 over there.

Our idea was to make an acceptable-to-major-label record on the first four minutes of it and make a rap record on the back four minutes, which was exactly what we did. And it was the back-end lyrics that made the difference on the record. The record was basically a great funk record with a rap on top of it.

ROBERT: The record sold about 100,000 records before Christmas and about 300,000 after Christmas. Russell was still somewhat green, and I was enlisted as Kurtis's road manager. We were on the road, working in markets like North Carolina, South Carolina, Detroit. … Cleveland was very big for us, Baltimore was very big for us. Mercury ended up releasing the flip side as something called, "Rappin' Blow." That was Kurtis's free-form rap, his contribution to the record; he did a lot of the stuff that he was doing live.

One of the great advantages with Kurtis Blow was that he could travel light. It was me, Davy D—who was his original DJ, Kurtis, and a garment bag, which they carried turntables in. So we were able to do shows at the drop of a hat, things that other acts couldn't do. If somebody called us on Thursday and said, "We got a date for you on Saturday," we could be there. We could fly, which is something that very few live acts could do, so we could go anywhere.

One of the interesting things about the early days of rap was that nobody involved knew what they were doing. I knew most of the old standard record-business clichés: go to the town, meet the promotion man, go do the radio station interviews, that sort of thing. I learned from working at Billboard that I had to do that. That was another reason I became Kurtis's road manager, 'cause I could maximize things early on, which Russell took a while to pick up on. Mercury stayed out of our way, which kind of was nice.

J. B.: Our deal with Mercury was a so-called "step deal." You make the first 12", we give you "x" number of dollars; if we feel like maybe you could make another one, we give you the next 12", and thereafter you finally give an album. They asked us for "The Breaks" in March or April 1980. "Christmas Rappin'" had been the winter of 1979. And we began in late April, early May of 1980 to make "The Breaks," which was the biggest dance record of the summer of 1980.

POST-RAPPER'S DELIGHT: THE FALLOUT

MIKE: It's a strange feeling. When "Rapper's Delight" came out, the world heard my voice first. Sometimes when I'm alone, I think, "Wow! Out of all the people that have done hip-hop records and gone to the concerts and bought the clothes, and practiced and wished and dreamed and failed and succeeded in this world, no matter what anybody says, they heard the Sugar Hill Gang first, heard my voice first!"

JOEY: You can't take away the history. You can't take away the reality that it was Sugarhill that had the idea to take this kind of music, take a chance, and put it out on wax—record it. But if people say, "Did you invent rap?" No, we never said we invented rap. But we made it mainstream, took it to another level. So many people try to knock what we came with, but the reality is, if we didn't come with "Rapper's Delight" and it wasn't as big a record as it was … you never know. …

RICHARD SISCO: Not takin' anything away from Sugar Hill Gang or nothin', but Caz's style was one of the best in rap. He really had the stories down pat, with his rhymes, the story line. … He was a master, not just some guy who could do it or a wanna-be. If he was the one recording, it would've been a different thing. You would've had a leader, and everybody would've followed him, but the way it happened, there wasn't a real leader out there. If the leaders of the street thing that we was doin' had got to do the record first, it would definitely have been something different. But, you know … that's neither here nor there.

ART ARMSTRONG: The beginning of the end really started when rap started being recorded. A lot of artists from the first period didn't understand a change was coming, so I don't think they took recording seriously enough. Rap was becoming more sophisticated, and I don't think that a lot of the old-school rappers really understood that.

It was like when Jackie Robinson made the major leagues. They had the Negro League during that period, so what happened was, Black people started going to the majors, and that signaled the end of the Negro League. That was what happened when rap started being recorded. Of the rap artists who were very popular before recorded music, only a few started recording, and everything started focusing on who was putting out records.

GRANDMASTER FLASH: The game of hip-hop changed. "Rapper's Delight" just set the goal to whole 'nother level. It wasn't rule the Bronx or rule Manhattan, or rule whatever. It was now how soon can you make a record.

REGGIE REG: Guys was going crazy over this "Rapper's Delight" thing. It was a very good record, and seeing how good that record was doing, the attention that record got, we knew we had to make a record.

SAL ABBATIELLO: When "Rapper's Delight" came out all the kids started becoming recording artists. Each week we had a new kid becoming a recording artist, so it was a very fun time and exciting, except we were still in a very poor neighborhood. The people making records was still poor 'cause they weren't getting advances or anything. They was just like, "Oh god, I got a record out." This went on for a few years before they even started thinking about money, you know? This was just so exciting, coming back to their neighborhood with a record.

AFRIKA BAMBAATAA: When we started seeing the recordings, a lot of us in the Zulu Nation stayed away from that at first because people thought once it got into vinyl it was going to kill the culture. We waited on the line just to see where everybody was going because we started hearing that a lot of people was getting robbed; they wasn't getting paid for this and that, and certain record companies would keep you away from knowing about how many records you were selling. They didn't teach you about your mechanical rights or your royalties or your publishing. The same thing that happened with a lot of the groups in the '50s and the '60s, they was doing it again to the groups in the '70s and the early '80s.

DJ BARON: We pioneered the rappin' in the street. We had our stint between 1977 and 1980, but it really never happened for us. You have to do your homework before you get into this game, 'cause if you don't do your homework, you'll be lost in the sauce. And that's a fact. People just sign on the dotted line; that first check, oh … they're all happy with that. And then, as time goes by, they say, "Well, where's the money at?" Record company's got all the money.

SHA-ROCK: Putting it on vinyl did change things a lot, and I think it changed it for the best. What recording did was open it up. A lot of people that didn't have the opportunities to listen to it in New York when it first started could now see that it was something good. This is a part of history. So I think that it was for the best.

OBJECTIVE QUESTIONS

1. Who was Sylvia Robinson, and what was her background?
2. Who was the owner of Enjoy Records?
3. What was the first rap record to go "gold"?
4. Who was the owner of Disco Fever?
5. According to Lovebug Starski, what gave Sylvia Robinson the idea to record a rap record?
6. Who are the original members of the Sugar Hill Gang?
7. What was "Big Bank" Hank's role with the Cold Crush Brothers?
8. What was Bill Adler's reaction to "Rapper's Delight"?
9. Who wrote most of the rhymes on "Rapper's Delight"?
10. Where did Robert Ford and J.B. Moore meet?
11. How did Robert Ford meet Russell Simmons?
12. Who did Robert Ford say may have been the most talented rapper he had ever seen?

QUESTIONS FOR FURTHER THOUGHT, RESEARCH, AND DISCUSSION

1. Compare the first rap record to the first jazz record by the Original Dixieland Jazz Band.
2. Why was the recording business establishment so slow to react to the success of "Rapper's Delight"?
3. Examine the historical relationship between major labels and the small independents.
4. When Afrika Bambaataa said, "The same thing that happened with a lot of the groups in the 50s and 60s, they was doing it again to the groups in the 70s and early 80s." What did he mean?
5. Art Armstrong compares the impact of "Rapper's Delight" to Jackie Robinson joining the Brooklyn Dodgers. What does he mean?
6. Does Grandmaster Caz deserve a more prominent place in Hip Hop's history?
7. In what ways did the recording industry change Hip Hop culture?

"The Force" and
"Making Records"

By Russell Simmons with Nelson George

Russell Simmons of course needs no introduction. He is Hip Hop's most successful entrepreneur and the cofounder of Def Jam records and Rush Management. His credits and contributions would easily fill this entire page. We have heard from **Nelson George** already. Another chapter from his *Hip Hop America* will appear later in this collection as well. Notice that George, the professional journalist, takes care to preserve the tone, style and personality of his subject Russell Simmons, as he transcribes what was probably recorded on a tape recorder.

Life and Def is intended to be the "best-selling" autobiography of Hip Hop mogul Russell Simmons. The two chapters printed here describe Simmons' more formative years and what inspired him to become a concert promoter and record producer. His early adventures in the world of Hip Hop clubs and concerts are entertaining if not always inspiring. What is most valuable here is the insight into the man and his business philosophy, as well as an accounting of the frustrating and often dishonest aspects of the record business. Pay attention to the strategy Simmons used to get Kurtis Blow signed to Mercury records. There is also a short discussion of the offshoot of the Nation of Islam called the Five Percent Nation of Gods and Earths and their influence in rap.

"THE FORCE" FROM *LIFE AND DEF*

THE NEW YORK CITY that created hip-hop wasn't the one we live in today. The Big Apple back in the mid-'70s wasn't the strictly policed, prosperous, typified place it is today. Middle-class people were leaving in droves. Johnny Carson was on every night cracking

Central Park mugging jokes. There were transit strikes, teacher's strikes and a crazy night all the lights went out. Landlords were torching the South Bronx, and Harlem was best known as the home turf of the city's "Mr. Untouchable," dope kingpin Nicky Barnes.

Even the school I started attending in 1975, City College of New York, in Harlem, was viewed as a symbol of what was wrong with New York. City College had open enrollment, which guaranteed every student in the city a shot at college. This flooded the school with black, Latino and immigrant kids, something resented by the old alumni. Within all this negativity the most influential pop culture of the last part of the twentieth century was born. I must admit my entry into this culture didn't come in the most wholesome manner.

It started in the last semester of my senior year in high school, when my friend Robert Middleton and I would take LSD every Friday. Usually we'd do it after school; we'd drop acid, and suddenly Mickey Mouse would be chasing us down Jamaica Avenue. Compared to taking heroin and nodding out, acid was like taking a trip, like going to the Village from Hollis. We'd take that stuff and trip all weekend.

One morning Robert and I were just coming down from an acid trip when my man Bud, a tall, lean guy who was a charter member of the Hollis Crew, came over with this new drug that was hot uptown. It was called angel dust, and the bag was stamped Red Devil. Though I didn't know it yet, angel dust would become my drug of choice. In the fall of 1975, when I entered City College, Harlem, like most ghettos then, was full of dust, so school gave me many chances to increase my appreciation. For you students of urban history, angel dust, or PCP, was the big recreational drug of the late '70s and early '80s. It wasn't a cool rush like cocaine or trippy like acid, but it did something to your head that was unique to each person. Personally, I loved getting "dusty." It made me happy. For real, however, it could have dangerously unpredictable consequences. Angel dust was so powerful that people would smoke it and get crazy enough to jump off a building or take on twelve cops and not feel the blows.

Dust was everywhere uptown, and there were many competing brands. When dust made you violent, the police didn't just arrest you. They'd take you to Harlem Hospital and shoot you up with Thorazine. All the Thorazine was supposed to do was calm you down. But the combination of PCP and Thorazine would fry your brain and have a lingering effect. People who got shot with the Thorazine treatment would talk slow and have a seemingly permanent lethargic look about them. The police used to have teams out there looking for dust heads like we were zombies in some bugged-out urban horror flick. When you were high off Red Devil you did your best to avoid the cops and Harlem Hospital. While attending City College, I maintained my angel dust ritual, but instead of going home to Queens, I'd hang out in the student lounge at City College until eleven or twelve at night and then roll over to Charles' Gallery on 125th Street, a club in the late '70s that was one of the first to cater to young people and the emerging new music scene.

It was in the CCNY student lounge that I met Rudy Toppin, aka Rudy Spli, one of the most influential people in my life. It was Rudy who nicknamed me Rush and got me into promoting shows, so he played a big part in shaping my identity. Rudy was attending City College and received BEOG, a form of financial aid where you got a check for $600 or so every semester. Back then $600 for a college student was a lot of cash. People would get the check, think they were rich and stop going to classes. Aside from collecting his BEOG checks, Rudy's main interest was working as a promoter at Charles' Gallery. Calling him a promoter may be overstating his original involvement, since basically all Rudy did was give out flyers. Still, it allowed him to get into the club for free, which made his gig attractive to me.

Rudy was a slick Harlem nigga who'd hang in the student lounge and then spend hours snapping on anybody who walked by. Rudy and his crew were slick in a different way than the Hollis Crew. They weren't into the Blye knits and A.J. Lester slacks that took up most of my money but they had an organic Harlem cool that a Queens guy like me aspired to. No matter how much fly gear I bought or how much cool I tried to project, I was from Queens and Rudy was from Harlem, the spiritual home of urban culture. I could aspire to having the aura of a Harlemite, but for Rudy it came natural and smooth.

Hanging out with Rudy at Charles' Gallery is what led me to my first hip-hop experience. As I said, Charles' Gallery catered to a young crowd by using young DJs, unlike a lot of spots uptown that either had jazz or R&B bands or aspired to be low-rent Studio 54s. On this particular night it was Easy G on the ones and twos, cutting up the kinds of records kids were into uptown. But the real revelation was the "world-famous" Eddie Cheeba rhyming to get the crowd excited. I don't know about the crowd, but shit, it got me excited.

Most of what he performed were simple rhymes to get people to dance and make noise ("Somebody, anybody, everybody scream!") plus lines about how fly he was. Most of the crowd had heard Cheeba before, so they chanted along or responded with their bodies, moving harder to the beat because the MC said so. It wasn't a sophisticated rhyme flow by current standards. But hearing Cheeba in '77 made me feel I'd just witnessed the invention of the wheel.

Just as shooting at Red and missing let me know, happily, that I had no future in real crime, watching and hearing Cheeba had an equally powerful effect. I was standing there in a room full of peers—black and Hispanic college kids, partying and drinking—and it hit me: I wanted to be in this business. Just like that I saw how I could turn my life in another, better way. All the street entrepreneurship I'd learned selling herb, hawking fake cocaine and staying out of jail, I decided to put into promoting music. It seemed a lot less dangerous, more fun and more prestigious. Just like that, I decided I no longer would be involved in something like drug dealing that risked my life.

With Rudy as my partner, I started investing my hard-earned money into renting venues and negotiating with acts. I was still taking drugs—that wouldn't be curtailed until years later—but I was no longer selling them, which surely helped the quality of my life. It was amazing to realize how much the long hours on the streets and the harassment by police and stickup kids had affected my demeanor. Once out of that game, I felt better about myself and related to the world differently. I was more relaxed, happier and not as edgy. No matter how intense a negotiation was with an MC or his manager, it never felt as dangerous as standing in an alley trying to convince a stranger to buy fake cocaine.

Starting to promote was great for my spirit, though it had a terrible, ultimately fatal effect on my schoolwork. I actually did more schoolwork while selling drugs. Maybe I started fucking up in school because I felt I'd already found my life's work. What was the point of chemistry when I knew my job was to sell tickets?

Eventually I left City College in my senior year, just four or five credits short of a sociology degree. This really upset my father, who thought I was a fool. Over and over he lectured me that the only way for a black man to make it was to get a degree and a job. For a while there I felt like I was a failure in my father's eyes, which hurt a lot, but promoting felt right in my gut I knew that to be a man I had to follow my heart. My mother was always more open to Danny, Joey and me pursuing a more nontraditional, entrepreneurial way.

Early in my promoting career I lost all the money I'd saved putting on a show in Harlem no one came to. I came out to Hollis and no one would help me. My father just wanted me to go back to school and told me so. What could I say? I had no money. Then my mother went back in the house and came out with $2,000 in crisp $100 bills from her personal savings. It was that money that kept me afloat until Kurtis Blow broke and I entered the record business. That act of love and faith, which is what kept me in business at a key time, is my favorite memory of her.

HOLLYWOOD

In the world of promoting rap shows for black teenagers in the late '70s there was a real hierarchy. There was Eddie Cheeba, Luvbug Starski and others at that level. But they were all beneath DJ Hollywood. A lot of people say a lot of things about who started what in hip-hop and who played at this park or that. But the bottom line is that to me Hollywood was the biggest figure in that era of hip-hop, because he was the man people would pay to see.

Hollywood could play Club 371 in the Bronx. He could play at the Diplomat Hotel in Times Square. He could play at a party at Jones Beach before five thousand people. In the days before hip-hop records were being made, Hollywood expanded the market in New York for MCing and break beats. Anywhere in the five boroughs Hollywood played, he could entertain and move the crowd. Hollywood's name always went at the top of the flyer whenever a show was being promoted. Just because he played inside clubs and giant halls for paying customers didn't make what he did any less creative, rebellious, hip or hot than the DJs and MCs who played in the park. It just made him bigger.

Hollywood was a chunky, jolly guy who'd been in vocal groups until he went solo as an MC. His voice was deep, rich and joyous. And he communicated that inner vibrancy like no one before or since. Whatever was fun, fresh and dynamic about this new scene, Hollywood epitomized it. Like most MCs of the day, Hollywood could DJ as well as rap. But he was at his very best with a DJ like Starski working with him, freeing him to do nothing but talk. Of all the party rockers, Hollywood was the best entertainer, but all the DJs and MCs knew that what they were doing uptown in the Bronx and Harlem was radically different from what was going on in suit-and-tie black downtown clubs like Leviticus.

It's so appropriate that Chic's "Good Times" was used by the Sugarhill Gang on "Rapper's Delight," the first recorded rap hit. Chic had become well known by doing disco records, but "Good Times" reflected the new aesthetic even if Chic's Nile Rodgers and Bernard Edwards didn't know it when they made the track. It had simple melody, a memorable hook and an incredible bass, guitar and drum arrangement that b-boys could instantly relate to. Not only was it a great single, but it spawned many other records (Vaughn Mason's "Bounce, Rock, Skate, Roll," Kurtis Blow's "Christmas Rappin'," Queen's "Another One Bites the Dust," Kool & the Gang's "Ladies' Night") that were used by DJs and MCs to spread the aesthetic.

Whether you were in a park in the Bronx or a club on Lenox Avenue, there was a certain sensibility Hollywood and all the other young MCs and DJs shared. If you were playing for this teenage, uptown crowd, you didn't put on dance records by the Village People or Cerrone. You'd play the first eight bars of Bob James's "Take Me to the Mardi Gras" or James Brown's "Funky

President" or do a mix of Eddie Kendricks's "Girl, You Need a Change of Mind" or the Incredible Bongo Band's "Apache." These parties were built around records that either weren't on the radio in New York, were from a different era or style (jazz, rock, or funky '60s James Brown) or were being mixed and cut up in ways Frankie Crocker, the city's number one radio DJ on the urban contemporary station WBLS, and the other radio people simply couldn't understand.

KNOWLEDGE ME

Just like Hollywood has not been given his due in the history of hip-hop, I feel another smaller but important influence has been overlooked—the Five Percent Nation of Gods and Earths. The Five Percenters are members of a religion that developed in jail among black inmates from the New York area. In fact, let me put it this way—if the Nation of Islam is a religion that finds converts in prison, Five Percenters find their converts *under* the prison. That's how street it is. It began as an offshoot of the Nation of Islam, but it never had the discipline or strong organizational structure of the NOI. Based around the idea that the black man was God and that only 5 percent of us had true knowledge of self, it's been very influential over the years in the young black community because it was very much a religion about talking.

Slick, smooth-talking, crafty niggas gravitated to it because the Five Percent religion's membership was built on the ability of its members to articulate their devotion to a strict set of beliefs with as much flair as possible. A true Five Percenter could sit on a stoop or stand on a street corner and explain the tenets of the sect for hours on end—and be totally entertaining! The Five Percent religion elevates black men, telling them they're all gods here on earth but only 5 percent are true believers. A Five Percenter will says some fly shit like "I've got seven moons, three suns and two earths." It sounds mystical, but he's really talking about all his women, with his two earths being his closest girls. Not only was their rap hot, but phrases like "knowledge me," "true mathematics," "360 degrees of knowledge," and "droppin' science" are just some of the linguistic contributions the Five Percent religion made to hip-hop. Street names like True God, U-God, Wise Allah and Divine Intelligence emerged because of how Five Percenters labeled themselves.

Listen to rappers from Brooklyn or the Queensbridge projects, like Nas, and you hear Five Percent speak all in their rhymes. Rakim's poetry is immersed in it. A lot of the poetic images in hip-hop are informed by them, from "Eric B. Is President" (in his three references to seven MCs, which relates to Five Percenter beliefs) up to Erykah Badu's "On and On." The Nation of Islam is more visible and respectable in terms of its presentation, and is clearly more powerful than the Five Percenters as an organization. However, during the period when the gangs I hung with in the '70s gave way to '80s hip-hop culture, it was the street language, style and consciousness of the Five Percent Nation that served as a bridge.

THE TRACK

As I started to grow my business, I watched how other promoters were handling their operations. Jerry Roebuck is now best known for promoting the huge Black Expos that have been institutions in the African-American community for almost two decades, but back in the day Jerry was a party promoter. He would give out flyers to his events with headlines that read, "Jerry Roebuck in association with Harold Maynard [another promoter] and Reggie Wells [a top DJ]." So I started headlining my flyers "Rush Productions in Association with Rudy Toppin and Kurtis Blow." I became Rush, "the force in college parties," which gave my shows an identity. Guess it was an early example of branding.

Kurtis Blow, aka Curtis Walker, who went to City College with me, was the first artist I managed and would also be the first rapper signed to a major label. He was a smooth, handsome Harlem native with a booming low tenor voice and real charisma. He was first known as Kool DJ Kurt, but I gave him the name "Blow" because long after everyone else had stopped, Kurtis was still selling coca leaf incense as cocaine. By then stores no longer had it under the counter. Now it was on top of the counter. Everybody and their mother knew about the scam. But Kurtis still sold it, right up until he made records. Calling him "Blow" was also a bite on Eddie Cheeba's handle; something Eddie never liked, and it's one reason he was never enthusiastic about doing shows I promoted.

By 1977 our club promotions started blossoming, and we were working in a lot of venues. One of the hottest was Small's Paradise, the old Harlem jazz club off 135th Street that Wilt Chamberlain once owned, where we promoted a night called Terrible Tuesdays. Competition uptown grew fierce around '77 because rapping DJs got really popular and started to challenge traditional DJs and bands for gigs. This was the disco era, so people "were already used to going to clubs not to see a band, but to see a DJ. Now hip-hop added a charismatic MC, someone who kept the party going. That added more value for your dollar. Club owners started to notice that an MC and a DJ drew bigger crowds than just a local band or a DJ, especially when they were trying to attract a younger black crowd.

A "track" developed of places you could work in Manhattan—City College, Small's Paradise, Hunter College, Charles' Gallery, the Renaissance Ballroom, Club 371 and Broadway International. And the audiences on this track didn't get bored, because even though there was an MC on the mike, you were under no obligation to stand and watch him. It was still a party. You could dance, drink, get busy or all of the above.

This was a whole different world from the downtown disco world of progressive clubs like the Paradise Garage and the Loft or midtown black bourgie clubs like Leviticus or Justine's. Those were the venues the uptown b-boys were—in their choice of clothes, music and attitude—rebelling against. In New York at this time, uptown and downtown were two different worlds. The black club scene downtown was about aping white disco and crossing over to white taste. Our scene uptown was about being our ghetto selves. I was learning important lessons—that being on the edge was where the excitement and creativity were, and that to be successful, you had to be true to your audience. Simple, but not obvious if you weren't paying attention.

The only people who knew or cared about the hip-hop track were the b-boys. There was no press coverage. No TV. No radio. No one outside of this community paid any attention to what was going on until after "Rapper's Delight" came out. So word of mouth was important, but you still needed to promote to make a real impression. The more flyers you were on, the more stickers and posters you could have stuck on walls or street lamps, the more popular you became as a promoter. Because the competition in Manhattan was so thick, Rush Productions began doing shows in Queens. We billed Kurtis as "Queens' #1 rapper," though he was a Harlem native and at the time didn't know Jamaica from Flushing. Early on we learned the value of hype and creating mystique. A Harlem MC working in Queens in '77 was the equivalent of a New York MC in LA in '83. It was a must-see for any hip-hop fan.

At that time Kurtis was a soloist, spinning and rapping at the same time. Obviously it was difficult to mix, keep the beat and rap at the same time, so he favored records that had longer instrumental sections or breaks. MFSB's "Love Is the Message" has a great three-minute break that Kurtis would just rap over. One reason that record became a hip-hop classic was because every young DJ who wanted to rhyme but didn't have great mixing skills would drop that on and only have to change it twice in six minutes.

Hollywood, Cheeba, Starski and Reggie Wells were all MCs who were way ahead of Kurtis in terms of celebrity. Kurtis really didn't get ghetto famous until he hooked up with Grandmaster Flash in late '77. When I started booking Grandmaster Flash, he would bring some, but not all, of his Furious Five MCs to Queens from the Bronx, where he was already a legend. Eventually Kurtis Blow became Flash's unofficial sixth MC. That was very important to Kurt, who gained some credibility in the Bronx through this association. In my eyes the great Grandmaster was the DJ from the park youth scene who was most ready to grow to adult ballroom status. Kool Herc, Bambaataa, Grand Wizard Theodore and many others were great creative stars, but they played in a different world from the one I aspired to promote in. They were the b-boys who played the high school gyms, where there was more angel dust (which I liked), more fighting and less money (which I didn't). I'm the first to admit that I am not an authority on their influence, but these stars were more DJs than MCs. They were also younger and less profitable than a Hollywood or Cheeba was.

Flash's main indoor venue up until then was a Bronx place called the Sparkle, where Big Bank Hank, later to be part of the Sugarhill Gang, was a bouncer. So we said, "Get down with us. You bring your Bronx fans. Kurtis brings his Queens fans. We then promote with all that clientele in our pocket." We did two shows back to back—one in Queens, one in Manhattan—and got out fifteen thousand flyers in the streets and a couple of thousand stickers in the subways. I remember Kurtis walking from 155th Street to 110th Street on Broadway just giving out flyers. I did a similar stroll through Queens. Way before street teams started putting up snipes (aka posters) on walls around the city, the people who worked for Rush Productions were walking the streets to sell our promotions.

The first show was Flash's first appearance in Queens. It was at the Fantasia, a tough spot near a housing development known as the 40 Projects in Jamaica. The 40 Projects would produce some of the city's legendary black gangsters—like Fat Cat Nicholas and "Pappy" Mason. These guys were the drug kingpins for our generation. While Nicky Barnes was a king in Harlem—he got so big Jimmy Carter ordered him taken down after reading about him in the *New York Times*—these guys were new gangsters, steeped in the new street culture. They had Kangols and big jewelry and looked as hip-hop as Kurtis or Flash. So the crowd that night was rough, but they loved hip-hop and formed a mob outside the Fantasia. Flash was that much of a legend in the streets. And remember, this was four years before he made a record.

We'd work a lot in the Fantasia after that. The Kurtis Blow–Flash combination really was hot in Queens. Then in '78 we had a problem. We'd done well at the box office and were leaving the Fantasia late one night. When we stepped into the street, bullets started flying—stickup kids were trying to rip us off for the gate. I remember ducking under a car and holding on to the money as guys ran by looking for us. That was my last show at the Fantasia.

The next night we were at the Hotel Diplomat in Times Square, and that was wild, too! The Diplomat was a run-down spot on 43rd Street between Sixth and Seventh that was clearly on its last legs, since they were letting a bunch of black teenagers do shows there. Down the block on the same side of the street was Xenon, which was the number two glam disco of the time, right behind Studio 54. Xenon was the place you went to do coke if you couldn't crash 54. It had a velvet rope, limos lined up, a picky doorman, the whole nine. Across the street was Town Hall, a nice sedate concert venue where folk singers and jazz musicians performed.

Suddenly 43rd Street was jammed with b-boys, pouring in from Times Square on the Seventh Avenue end and off the D train from uptown at Sixth Avenue. The result was a mini-riot. You had people getting robbed, mugged, stomped, trampled. Outside the Diplomat you had a clash between all these different groups of party people on the street and people desperately trying to get into the Diplomat. It was a mess outside, but as always, the show still went on. At the Diplomat they had bulletproof box offices, so Kurtis and I escaped there that night. Not surprisingly, we had a lot of trouble getting security companies to work with us. We'd get a company for one promotion, and that was it. The next company would do one show and then they'd quit, too. Eventually Kurtis hired my little brother, Joey, who we called "DJ Run his disco son," to work the turntables for him. At that point Run was 13 years old. After a year and a half working with Kurtis, Run broke his arm, and Kurtis found a new DJ, Davey D, a kid from Queens with twelve crates of records, which was a serious accomplishment at the time. Flash had seventeen crates and Afrika Bambaataa had twenty, so twelve made Davey D a contender. Davey wasn't just a DJ, but a real musician who played guitar and other instruments. Not only did he become Kurtis Blow's first DJ, but he'd later play on and produce a lot of influential records, including his solo hit "One for the Treble." But the time we spent working with Flash was crucial to building Kurtis's, and Rush Productions', credibility in the growing scene.

"MAKING RECORDS" FROM *LIFE AND DEF*

MY FIRST CONTACTS WITH the world of the adult music business weren't too fruitful. All the black people in the business in the late '70s were true R&B people. They thought R&B was all commercial black music was or could ever be. Plus they were all in their late twenties and older, and treated us young hip-hop promoters as kids who were just playing at being in the business. Even before hip-hop was really a force on vinyl, you could see a real generation gap between the black adult world and the young black culture that spawned hip-hop.

My first experience with this attitude came with a guy who went by the name of Saint Saint James (he named his son Saint Saint Saint James), who was the booker at Club Hollywood and a consultant for Club 371. Saint was one of the many black gatekeepers hip-hop had to go through to grow. And, unfortunately like a lot of those people, he just saw us as kids off the street. We wouldn't be around for long, they thought, so why treat us with respect?

Once I gave Saint $1,900 for a show I wanted to promote at Club Hollywood with Evelyn "Champagne" King and Hollywood, and he straight up stole it. Just took my $1,900 and disappeared.

The irony of that story is that years later Saint James ended up working for me at Rush Management and Def Jam, doing independent promotion and getting my records played on stations along the East Coast. I had no bitterness toward him. I needed Saint's contacts, and by then he needed a check. Holding a grudge against him would have been easy. But the fact that Saint knew me early on actually made him work aggressively for me later. There may have been some guilt involved, but there was also a certain pride there, too. He knew how far I'd come and now respected me for hanging in there. I never trusted him completely, but I felt now he was gonna use his tricks for me. I try very hard not to hold grudges—the guy you hate today could easily be working for you tomorrow. If you stick around long enough in this business, everything comes full circle.

My first positive encounter with the recording industry turned out to be my most important. Robert "Rocky" Ford worked in *Billboard* magazine's production department, but he was very visible in the R&B music scene because he also contributed articles and reviews on black music to *Billboard,* the industry's number one trade publication. Rocky lived, with his mother in St. Albans, the Queens neighborhood right next to Hollis, which is why Rocky was walking down Jamaica Avenue one afternoon in 1978 and saw my brother Joey hanging up posters for one of my parties in Queens. Rocky asked Joey about Rush Productions and gave him his card. I called Rocky and we hooked up. Turned out he was doing a story on what were called "b-beats," or break beats, and rapping DJs. Through his contacts in retail, Rocky had noticed other flyers and heard about DJs looking for beats in obscure records. Rocky's story in *Billboard* would be the first national coverage of hip-hop.

But Rocky wasn't just a writer. He'd worked in advertising before he got with *Billboard* and had a good eye for a strong idea. Behind his glasses and his unruly curly Afro, there was a keen mind. Way before most adults, Rocky saw potential in this emerging scene. So after hanging out at some of our promotions and seeing how the scene was developing, Rocky got the idea to make a rap record. The only problem was that he was stuck on recording Eddie Cheeba. Rocky was always talking Eddie Cheeba this, Eddie Cheeba that. Of course, he'd heard of Cheeba more often than he had of Kurtis. That all changed when he saw Kurtis at the Diplomat on August 31, 1979. Kurtis was on fire that night. His rhymes were flowing. His Afro was tight. He just looked and sounded like a star. It didn't hurt that he was performing with Grandmaster Flash. After seeing Kurtis that night, Rocky decided he wanted to use him instead of Cheeba for his record.

Rocky also influenced Kurtis to let me manage his recording career. Kurtis was my man, but I was just a party promoter with no experience outside that field. Not surprisingly, Kurtis felt that Rocky, because of his age and *Billboard* background, should have been handling him in this new area. But that really wasn't Rocky's thing.

Yes, he would aid in guiding Kurtis, and he often used his contacts to help us, but he convinced Kurtis that my energy and commitment were what he needed on a day-to-day basis. Rocky's confidence in me at that moment really helped me grow and expand my reach. "A few years later Rocky would, like Saint James, come work for me at Rush Management. Both men were mentors—one introduced me to the dark side, the other to the light—and both proved useful to me later. I believe all experiences, good and bad, have the capacity to mold you and make you stronger. You learn from all of it.

Rocky and J. B. Moore, an advertising salesman at *Billboard* who wanted to produce, got the idea for Kurtis to cut a single called "Christmas Rappin'," figuring the novelty of Santa Claus in

Harlem would help overcome resistance to its being a rap record. Rocky and J.B. wrote most of the lyrics for the first half of the song, laying down the concept of the record, and then Kurtis came in to put in the call-and-response rhymes he'd been using uptown, and some that Joey had been using when he performed as the "son of Kurtis Blow."

Looking back, it's a funny thing how naive I was. I trusted Rocky and J.B. completely. I had so little knowledge about contracts and the business that they could have totally ripped us off. We signed contracts with them without consulting a lawyer because we believed they were honest. It was a mistake, one that young people make all the time in this business. We were just lucky that we got in with two honest guys. It didn't have to be that way.

It was sad what happened to most of the old school. As early as 1984, when Kurtis had made a couple of albums, most other original rappers had only cut some 12-inches; it was clear those guys were making no money and were going to make no money. None of these guys had professional managers. Their business was being handled by relatives, friends or small-time gangsters with big-time talk but no knowledge. Unlike Kurtis, who was on a major label, all of them were on small labels that, at best, gave a modest advance and paid little or no royalties. These other rappers would come up to Kurtis's apartment in the Bronx and act like he was living in a mansion, since most of them were still living in the projects or with their moms. Of the old-school originators, I believe Kurtis, between his record sales and the tours we'd get him on, was the only one making a real good living from hip-hop. And the fact that Kurtis did so well is why Rush Management would later grow so large. But first we had to get our record made—and that wasn't easy.

"WE'RE STILL GONNA GO TO THE MOON"

I'll never forget this: It was fall 1979 and there was a show at the Armory in Queens. There were probably four thousand kids there. Hollywood was there, as were most of the performers now known as the old school—Flash, the Furious Five, Cheeba and others. A DJ played "Rapper's Delight" by the Sugarhill Gang. It was the first time most of us had heard the record, and we were just stunned. Someone had taken our rhymes, our attitude and our culture and made a record. And not one of us in the community had anything to do with it! I remember after the record played, DJ Starski got on the mike and said, "Y'all know we started this shit. Don't worry. We're still gonna go to the moon."

All of us—MCs, DJs, promoters—resented it. I personally was wrecked. I had so much animosity toward the Sugarhill Gang. They sure weren't known where the real MCs hung out. At a place like the Disco Fever, a hip-hop hangout in the Bronx, I felt they'd get booed just walking in the door. A few people thought, "Well, that's it. The one rap record that's ever going to be on the radio is out, and none of us made it." Rocky, J.B. and I had been having no luck getting anyone interested in financing or releasing a Kurtis Blow record. So hearing "Rapper's Delight" was deeply disappointing. You see, at first we thought that record had shut the door, when in reality that door was about to swing wide open.

After the Sugarhill Gang record came out, Rocky, J.B. and I focused on getting "Christmas Rappin'" finished and sold. Through Rocky and J.B. I fell in with a group of musicians from Queens, real jazzy types who'd work with us for the next few years—Denzel Miller, a keyboardist, guitarist Eddie Martinez (who later played on "Rock Box"), drummer Trevor Gale and a bass player named Larry Smith, who'd become my producing partner. Most of these guys were jazz players turned R&B heads, and you can hear their influence in all the early Kurtis Blow records.

We recorded at Greene Street studio with an engineer named Rodney Hui, who would be behind the board for many early rap hits. Working on "Christmas Rappin'" was my first time in the studio, but I was never passive. I had suggestions about how the beat should feel and on the melody and the rhymes. But Rocky and J.B. ran the sessions and took Kurtis in a more R&B direction, with strong hooks and choruses that made "Christmas Rappin'" and later "The Breaks" very radio-friendly. They were great records, but I knew they didn't truly reflect the hard-core b-boy attitude in the street.

Once we'd finished "Christmas Rappin,'" we began shopping it around town. There was interest, but no one was biting. The industry's attitude was that "Rapper's Delight," despite its U.S. sales and international appeal (it went top ten all over the world), was an unrepeatable fluke. We identified PolyGram, which had a great roster of funk and R&B acts (Kool & the Gang, the Gap Band, Parliament), as the best place for Kurtis, so we made up a gang of test pressings and took them to clubs all over the city. Response in the street from DJs and club goers was great. So to hype up PolyGram we placed fake orders for the record in their system by telling retailers and wholesalers to order the 12-inch through PolyGram. PolyGram didn't own it yet, but we created an appetite for "Christmas Rappin'" that led them to buy it.

Significantly the 12-inch wasn't picked up by the black music department. A white English A&R guy made the deal. The black music executives reluctantly promoted it as a novelty record, nothing more. That a white man would give hip-hop a chance and black adults established in the business were skeptical was typical of rap's ongoing struggle for credibility with black industry executives.

So in the fall of 1979 Kurtis Blow signed with Mercury Records, a division of PolyGram, making him the first rapper on a major label. Christmas Eve 1979 was the first time I heard "Christmas Rappin'" on the radio; I was upstairs at my family's house. Frankie Crocker, the biggest radio DJ in New York, played it on WBLS. I ran downstairs. I told my mother. I told my father. I sat looking at the speakers. A record I made was on the radio. It was an unbelievable moment.

Unfortunately that was one of the only times 'BLS played the record. Like I said, most people saw it as a novelty. But the limited airplay "Christmas Rappin'" received at 'BLS and other urban stations at the end of '79 was the crack we needed. Over the course of the next seven months Kurtis and I traveled all over the country, as well as overseas, based on that one record. Though it was a holiday record, "Christmas Rappin'" played on black radio stations and in clubs around the country well into the summer of '80. We went down to places like South Carolina to work gigs in July and August because "Christmas Rappin'" was just breaking in many markets.

That was an amazing time for me. Everything was new, and it was the first time I had ever really felt successful. I remember in early 1980 I'd been sniffing coke all night when Kurt and I got a call at nine o'clock in the morning. It was Rocky. "You're going to Amsterdam," he said. I'd only been on one plane in my life—a short trip to Philly when I was a kid. Now I was so large I needed a passport because I was going to Europe.

We got to Amsterdam, and immediately the local record company rep took us to a weed house. The whole time we were just waiting to be raided. Then we came out of the weed house paranoid, expecting to be arrested. Then we thought we were being followed back to the hotel. After a while we realized that nothing was going to happen. Not only was weed legal in Amsterdam, but in fact everyone in town seemed happy we were there. So, of course, once we realized that, we went back to the weed house. Here we were, two students from City College, being flown to another country for Kurtis to perform a hit record. I felt rich. That shit felt amazing!

SUGAR HILL

The first institution in hip-hop was Sugar Hill Records, a black-owned label out of Englewood, New Jersey. Sylvia Robinson had been a minor R&B star in the '70s ("Pillow Talk"), and she and her husband, Joe, had run a really ghetto R&B label called All Platinum that went bankrupt. Their most popular act had been a falsetto-lead vocal group, the Moments, who had a string of hits ("Love on a Two-Way Street" was the biggest) and later changed their name to Ray, Goodman & Brown. They jumped on hip-hop to get back in business, and they were the first people to make any real money in the game.

Soon after they put out "Rapper's Delight" they signed up real MCs like Spoonie Gee, Busy Bee, the Treacherous Three (Kool Moe Dee was a member) and, most important, Grandmaster Flash & the Furious Five, who'd become the first successful old-school group to blow up nationally. In fact, Flash & the Five would, with "The Message" and "The Adventures of Grandmaster Flash on the Wheels of Steel," make hip-hop's first artistically important records.

Sylvia Robinson was like everybody's mother. You'd often see her in an uptown club sitting at the bar, looking like royalty. She was always very nice to me, and her son Joey was always cool to me. I wasn't really a competitor, because they were making a lot of money and at the time I was just some young guy managing some acts. To this day I never felt any threat or negativity from them. The only difference between me and Sugar Hill is that I got my artists paid more than Sugar Hill would pay.

As a manager, I never handled a Sugar Hill act. I never even went in their building out in Englewood. It was never like, "Oh, I'm Flash's manager. How come he didn't get a royalty check?" So I guess that's why they never bothered me. It just happened to work out that way. I loved Flash—that's my man forever and ever—but he and his crew never had a manager once they started making records. In fact, I don't think anybody at Sugar Hill had a manager once they started making records there. I don't think Busy Bee or the Treacherous Three or Spoonie Gee or any of them had a manager. Sugar Hill should have been as successful and enduring a label as Def Jam, but they weren't able to build on that early monopoly position. As more labels moved into the rap game, Sugar Hill's deals looked less attractive, and the newer talent signed on elsewhere. You have to stay competitive. The basic truth about the record business is this: You get ripped off, and then you learn to rip the next person off. That's how I've seen it work. Now, I was never jerked by the people who first brought me into the record game. Rocky and J.B. didn't jerk me, so I don't jerk people. I know that sounds simplistic, but then the truth is always very simple. It's lying that's tricky. So treating people fairly is one reason I'm still here and so many of my former competitors are not.

I did a radio interview a couple of years ago in Los Angeles along with Snoop Dogg and the Dogg Pound. I told the interviewer that I'd given Kurtis Blow ten points on his records, and Snoop Dogg almost fell out of his seat. Royalty points are the cream in a recording act's coffee. The more points you have, the more money you make on record sales. Out of a universe of a hundred points, most artists get less than ten points on average. We'd given Kurtis ten points, which was what we could afford back then, and Snoop was shocked. My impression was that his early deals weren't very generous.

But to be fair to Sugar Hill, it's hard to be really generous with points and payments as an independent label. If you have less, you generally give less. Your pockets aren't as deep as Sony's or BMG's. Often you survive from record to record. But if you start doing well and come to dominate the market, as Sugar Hill did in the early '80s, then you should share the wealth. If you expand the market, as Sugar Hill did, you encourage others to enter the business, which is what began to happen. Once that happens, paying the market rate is the only way to hold on to your artists and stay competitive.

MAKING CONVERTS

In 1981 I was 24 years old and feeling a lot of pressure. Here I was with Kurtis Blow, an act that had two gold singles. ("Christmas. Rappin'" and "The Breaks") and who was getting booked on major tours. In the wake of that success my management company was signing new clients every week, as more rappers were recording and needed representation. At that time there were no other managers who knew or cared about hip-hop with any credibility in that community. And on top of that, I was producing records, too.

Yet I didn't really know how to do some of the things I had to. Everything was new, and there was no textbook. I was learning how to be a manager with every meeting, with every phone call. Often it was just a matter of learning to command respect, which comes with the confidence that you know what you're talking about.

The biggest challenge was dealing with concert promoters. In 1982, following on the success of Kurtis Blow's "The Breaks," we were booked by the major urban promoters of the time—Al Hayman and Quenton Perry. Because we were hot and simple to book (just a DJ, an MC and a road manager), that year Kurtis Blow opened a tour for the Commodores, who were a huge act before Lionel Richie went solo. From that tour we got great exposure and were well paid. In contrast, when we booked Kurtis as a solo act, we dealt with low-level promoters who wouldn't pay you until after the show—if you could find them after the gig. When we were on tour with the Commodores, we had to promote our album on the club circuit. Kurtis and I would roll into a town and he would do radio and in-store appearances to create excitement. We were playing small places and dealing with small-time promoters with short money. Often we'd get beat. We'd be in the dressing room before the show when the promoters would walk in. Either they'd say the gate wasn't as big as they'd hoped or we hadn't done enough promotion or some other bullshit in an attempt to pay us less than we'd contracted for. So we'd be stuck: There'd be a roomful of fans waiting on us—people we needed to go buy the album—and we weren't going to be paid what we'd been promised. Kurtis could have refused go on, but disappointed fans don't buy albums.

A lot of the promoters felt comfortable jerking us because they were sure we were gonna disappear. They just knew Kurtis and I were never gonna come back to their town, so fuck us. Moreover, there was a lot of resentment from traditional promoters and acts about how we performed and the financial advantages it gave us. This was the early '80s. Big bands with horn sections and background singers were the norm in black music. Guys were on the road with seven or eight pieces, plus the roadies and a road manager. They'd all walk away with $10 per gig, while Kurtis, with a DJ and a road manager, was making less but pocketing more. There was no big nightly nut to crack for a rap act. We were revolutionizing the concert business by playing major venues without a band. People acted like we were stealing money so they treated us like thieves.

Because Kurtis's act was so simple production-wise, we could do incredible things. For example, there was one day that Kurtis played in three different fifteen-thousand-seat arenas in three cities. First we were in Birmingham, Alabama, with Graham Central Station and the Bar-Kays. Then we flew to Greensboro, North Carolina, and opened for the Commodores, Patti LaBelle, and Stephanie Mills. Then we hopped another plane to Augusta, Georgia, where we closed for Con Funk Shun and Cameo. Cameo was a hell of an act to come behind, especially at that stage of their career. Those guys were a loud, flashy funk band that really put on a show. But Davey D would just go out there and tear shit up on the turntables, and then Kurtis would come on and rock the house. You gotta remember that in a lot of these markets this was the first time people were seeing hip-hop. We'd be up there setting up turntables on the stage and people in the crowd would mutter, "We paid money to see a band." But night after night people would be up dancing on their seats by the end of the set.

I remember our booking agent, a real character named Norby Walters, who worked with us for years and still didn't understand what we did. Norby was a real old-school hustler who had specialized in lounge acts until disco came in. When disco came in, he got his lounge singers to tour as disco acts. From that he got into black music and for a long time had the biggest booking agency in the game. But his company had been booking us for a while before he actually saw what we did. So when he came to San Diego one time to see our show, he just stood there with his mouth open as the crowd went crazy. Norby had seen a lot of things, but never two turntables and a microphone wreck a packed arena. As Flavor Flav said later, "We got some nonbelievers out here tonight." But everywhere we went we made converts.

OBJECTIVE QUESTIONS

1. What did the police give to kids who were arrested under the influence of angel dust?
2. Who was Russell Simmons' original partner in Rush Management? Where was he from?
3. Who was the DJ that Simmons' saw at Charles' Gallery that made him feel like he'd just witnessed the invention of the wheel?
4. "All the street entrepreneurship I'd learned selling herb, hawking fake cocaine and staying out of jail, I decided to put_____."
5. According to Simmons, who was the greatest of the DJs of the late 70s?
6. Where was Kurtis Blow from? How was he billed?
7. How did Kurtis Blow get "ghetto famous"?
8. What happened at Kurtis's last show at the Fantasia?
9. Who replaced DJ Run as Kurtis's DJ?
10. His story in *Billboard* would be the first national coverage of Hip Hop: _____.
11. According to Russell Simmons, who was "Rocky" Ford's first choice of artists to record a rap record?

12. Of the old school originators, _____ was the only one making a real good living from Hip Hop.

13. Name the musicians who worked on "Christmas Rappin" with J.B., "Rocky" and Russell Simmons.

14. According to Simmons, what are Hip Hop's first artistically important records?

15. The basic truth about the record business is this: _____.

QUESTIONS FOR FURTHER THOUGHT, RESEARCH AND DISCUSSION

1. Why do you think that Def Jam became an important label and Sugar Hill didn't survive?

2. Summarize the reactions of Russell Simmons and the people in the Hip Hop community to "Rapper's Delight."

3. "Love is the Message" by MFSB has a great 3 minute break that made it a Hip Hop classic. Who are MFSB and what else did they record?

4. What is it about the Five Percenter's beliefs that make them so adaptable to Hip Hop?

5. Summarize some of Russell Simmons' business philosophy.

6. Many people have compared Russell Simmons to Berry Gordy. In what ways are they similar and in what ways are they dissimilar?

Uptown-Downtown: Hip Hop Music in Downtown Manhattan in the Early 1980s

By Jonathan Toubin

Jonathan Toubin has completed an M.A. in Liberal Studies with a concentration in American Studies at the CUNY Graduate Center and is currently working on a Ph.D. in History. He has recorded with numerous groups as a guitarist, bassist, and keyboardist.

At about the same time that Hip Hop was overtaking the burned-out Bronx, white teenagers were embracing punk rock in the drugged-out East Village. At first glance, it appeared that the two styles and cultures were at odds and couldn't have been more different. But after closer examination, it turned out they both had a great deal in common—more in common than either one initially realized. Both Hip Hop and punk rock were reactions against the commercialized sentimentality of disco and the other music the record industry promoted, both white and black. Both Hip Hop and punk rock come from an urban wasteland, express a kind of hopelessness about the future, and appropriate discarded and recycled icons of pop culture with which to make their art. This very scholarly article describes the movement of Hip Hop from the isolation of the Bronx to the nightclub scene in Harlem, and eventually to the trendy art scene of the East Village and its conflation with English punk. This is the most academic of any of the writing in this anthology, and it is included here, to some extent, just because it's such a great example of academic writing. This article is as tightly structured as a Mozart Sonata. Notice how meticulously everything is notated and documented, how logically all of the information is organized, and how the author's own opinions and personality remain very closely guarded.

The irony here is that even though Toubin gives us all of the important names, dates and places, he doesn't really give us an inkling into how much fun, excitement and drama were really going on. It's like a novel with all of the "good parts" expurgated. The parties at the Ritz, the Roxy and the Negril were wild and exemplify the power of music to bring people of different backgrounds together in the cause of a good party. The vivid description of the parties and their aftermath is sadly missing from this narrative. Likewise, there is no description of the unusual and eccentric personalities of people like Lady Blue, Afrika Bambaataa, Henry Chalfant, Deborah Harry, Fredrick Braithwaite, Charlie Ahearn, and the others that came together in the early 80s to make Hip Hop into a phenomenon that would circle the globe. Toubin will argue that it was largely because of the influence of these diverse patrons of Hip Hop and their connections to more established arts that Hip Hop emerged and spread as global pop culture.

"UPTOWN–DOWNTOWN: HIP HOP MUSIC IN DOWNTOWN MANHATTAN IN THE EARLY 1980s" FROM *CRITICAL MINDED*

No matter black white or brown in our own way we can all get down.
—Grandmaster Flash and The Furious Five, "Freedom"

DURING THE MOST segregated period of pop radio since the 1940s, the early 1980s,[1] a number of rap, punk, and new wave songs deliberately crossed racial and cultural boundaries. Blondie's "Rapture" and the Clash's "The Magnificent Seven," both from 1980, are two of the first recorded examples of punk and new wave acts incorporating hip hop elements into their songs. Conversely, Grandmaster Flash and the Furious Five's "Its Nasty" and Dr. Jeckyll and Mr. Hyde's "Genius Rap," both from 1981, are based on samples from new wave band Tom Tom Club's 1981 track "Genius of Love." The Clash's "Overwhelmed by Funk" from 1982 features a rap by uptown graffiti writer/rapper Futura 2000. DJ Afrika Bambaataa and punk vocalist Johnny Lydon performed a duet on their 1983 apocalyptic dance-floor hit "World Destruction." 1982's "Planet Rock" is the product of Bambaataa and MCs Soul Sonic Force with white dance music producers Arthur Baker and Tommy Silverman and keyboardist John Robie. The most popular breaking hit of the era, jazz legend Herbie Hancock's "Rockit" from 1983, was born out of Hancock's interracial, intercultural collaboration with DJ Grandmixer D.St. and producer/bassist Bill Laswell.

Each of these examples sprouted directly out of alliances formed in lower Manhattan's art and club scenes. After years of relatively isolated development in the Bronx and Harlem in the 1970s, hip hop rapidly became a downtown fixture in the early 1980s. Along with breaking and graffiti, the music not only served as a bridge between two polar geographic regions of New York, but also between people of different races, ethnicities, classes, subcultures, and musical tastes.[2] MCs and DJs appeared on stages and on bills with new wave, experimental, and punk bands. Breaking crews were the star attractions at large nightclubs, art galleries and public festivals. The work of graffiti writers shared museum and gallery walls with canvases by popular neo-expressionist artists.

Uptown residents were going downtown and, to a lesser extent, downtown residents were going uptown, to witness the new spectacles. Afrika Bambaataa recalls his first experience with the new diverse audience:

> When I got down there, and I started playing all that funky music, you seen them punk people start going crazy! Slam-banging, jumping crazy, with the hip-hop people looking at them like, "What's this?" Then you see the hip-hoppers trying to do that punk dance and that thing where they're going side to side, and then the punks trying to do the rap steps and all this sort of stuff. (Fricke and Ahearn 2002: 309)

While graffiti, breaking, DJing, and MCing left a stamp on lower Manhattan's art and club scenes, the four elements of hip hop[3] were also affected by downtown culture. In addition to the artistic benefits of new outside influences, the uptown/downtown nexus was also mutually profitable economically. In what DJ Jazzy Jay refers to as "the Great Hip Hop Drought," when hip hop's Bronx audience was shrinking as members got too old for parties at high school gyms, parks, and community centers, going downtown provided graffiti artists, break dancers, rappers, and MCs with a new expanded market for their art.[4] Downtown galleries, clubs, and artists financially and culturally profited from their association with the new trends. The press had something new to write about. The underground art, dance, music and film scenes of lower Manhattan were also hip hop culture's points of contact with the mainstream art, dance, music, and film industries.

Hip hop's journey downtown can be told as a story of the removal of geographical and cultural barriers between groups of people. Here I explore these formative years between hip hop's initial isolation in the Bronx and its later explosion around the world. I will argue that hip hop's voyage downtown and into the mainstream was brought about by the persistent efforts of a few people. These protagonists were a small, loosely knit group of artists, performers, gallery owners, promoters, and journalists. This study will be limited to the period that begins with the Funky 4+1's first show at the Kitchen in Soho in 1980 (Fricke and Ahearn 2002: 216) and ends with the formation of Def Jam Records in 1984. While uptown and downtown artists certainly interacted before 1980, particularly in the realm of graffiti, the Kitchen show is the first documented live hip hop performance downtown. The founding of Def Jam provides a perfect bookend for the era because it marks the point where the concepts of uptown and downtown are no longer necessary in understanding the relationship between rappers and their audiences.

ESCAPE FROM THE BRONX

In the beginning, hip hop music existed primarily in the Bronx. Kool Herc's performance at his sister's birthday party in 1973 marks the point at which most publications date the beginning of hip hop music (Fricke and Ahearn 2002: 23–43; Keyes 2002: 55–57; Light 1999: 14–15). Herc's primary contribution was his discovery of the "breakbeat," in which the DJ extends the drum break by alternating back and forth between two copies of the same record. His second important contribution was his MC crew, the Herculords. Herc's work with breakbeats and MCs was further articulated by followers such as Afrika Bambaataa and Grandmaster Flash. The Bronx's DJs, MCs, breakdancers, and graffiti writers helped create what had become a substantial subculture in the South and West Bronx by the late 1970s. By this point Harlem disco DJs such as Eddie Cheeba and DJ Hollywood began incorporating Bronx hip hop music styles into their acts ("Rap Records" 1980). A young Russell Simmons, after his introduction to hip hop via a performance by Cheeba and Easy G at Charles' Gallery in Harlem in 1977, started RUSH productions and began booking hip hop acts into high school gyms, fraternity houses, neighborhood community centers, and nightclubs in Harlem and Queens, and, soon, lower Manhattan (Simmons 2001: 34). By 1979, Kurtis Blow, already under the management of Simmons, brought hip hop performance outside of the New York metropolitan area and into major east coast cities (George et al. 1985: xii).

While social and geographic isolation kept live hip hop music from being heard outside of black and Puerto Rican communities, an absence of commercial recordings kept the music off of the air and out of the stores. Over the six-year period from 1973, when Kool Herc began DJing at block parties, to 1979, the year Fatback Band's "King Tim III (Personality Jock)" was released, not one commercial rap recording appeared on vinyl.[5] Homemade audiocassettes were hip hop's primary release medium during the genre's formative years. Home recordings and live tapes were sold on the streets and at performances. These cassettes and their pirated duplicates not only reached other parts of the city, but also other parts of the country. The tapes were heard in New York's parks, streets, and subways through large portable radios, or "ghetto blasters," that were fashionable among urban youth (Keyes 2002:67).

Sylvia Robinson of Sugar Hill Records got the idea of releasing rap on vinyl after noticing how popular the homemade tapes were with her nieces in New Jersey. These cassettes indirectly led to Sugar Hill's first release, a song that reached #4 on the R&B charts and broke into the Top 40, Sugarhill Gang's "Rappers Delight" from 1979.[6] Also in 1979, the first major label rap release—Kurtis Blow's "Christmas Rapping" on Mercury—sold 600,000 copies and made the R&B charts. Local independent labels such as Enjoy and Winley began releasing the first recordings of artists such as Grandmaster Flash and the Furious Five, Afrika Bambaataa and Soul Sonic Force, the Funky 4+1, the Treacherous Three, and Spoonie Gee.[7] Because all of the artists except for Kurtis Blow had releases on independent labels, rap's early recordings were often difficult for potential customers to find (Keller 2004). The first hip hop radio show did not appear until "Mr. Magic's Rap Attack" appeared on Newark's WHBI in 1979 (Keyes 2002: 72–73).

Despite the Bronx's isolation, homemade tapes, ghetto blasters, a handful of vinyl releases, a smattering of radio play, occasional rotation at discos, and word of mouth randomly transmitted the areas music across the geographic, social, and economic boundaries of New York. Afrika Bambaataa recalls meeting East Village residents who were familiar with his music through mixtapes when he debuted downtown in 1981.[8] Mike D of the Beastie Boys heard hip hop music for the first time from a mix tape at his high school (Keller 2004). Producer Arthur Baker witnessed live DJs and MCs at a park in Harlem in the late 1970s ("Archive Interviews: Arthur Baker" 2004). In an email interview conducted 1 October 2004, Bad Seeds percussionist Jim Sclavunos informed me that he witnessed a Rock Steady Crew subway performance long before he appeared in the Kitchen Tour with them in 1982. While downtown did not see a live performance until 1980, a number of downtowners found hip hop before it found them.

THE ART SCENE

Visual art, music, and dance were so deeply intertwined in hip hop music's introduction to the downtown club scene that the genre's southern migration cannot be understood outside of the context of graffiti and breaking. The Mudd Club, Club 57, Danceteria, and other clubs that began popping up in the late 1970s were unlike many of their predecessors in that "people didn't just dance and do drugs and hob nob." Jean-Michel Basquiat's biographer Phoebe Hoban explains that "they were venues for performance art, underground films, New Wave music. ... Artists were mixing up their media; music, film, painting, and fashion were recombining in innovative ways" (Hoban 1998:9). This is the context in which hip hop music downtown must be viewed. Before it came into its own downtown, the music functioned as a soundtrack for the more popular elements of graffiti and breaking. Not only did the early success of graffiti and breaking downtown help create a market for the music, but at the Kitchen, the Mudd Club, Negril, and later at Danceteria and the Roxy, MCing and DJing were often presented as part of a spectacle that involved all four elements.

While a number of downtowners were aware of uptown graffiti, breaking, and hip hop music, an exponentially broader recognition of the movement was created by the physical placement of graffiti artists, b-boys, DJs, and MCs in downtown venues. Members of downtown's art scene, such as Fred "Fab 5 Freddy" Braithwaite, Henry Chalfant, Patti Astor, Charlie Ahearn, and Michael Holman, played a more important role than figures from the music community in hip hop's downtown migration. Graffiti had appeared sporadically in art galleries since the United Graffiti Artists (UGA) exhibit at the Razor Gallery in 1973 (Austin 2001: 72). By traveling daily across hundreds of miles of subway tracks, graffiti, of the four elements, was witnessed by the greatest diversity of people. With a heterogeneous assortment of practitioners, graffiti's ability to cross racial, geographical, and gender lines enabled it to connect geographically and culturally separated people.

The downtown galleries' direct predecessor in commingling the emerging uptown and downtown art scenes was the Bronx art gallery Fashion Moda. Downtowner Stefan Eins opened the space in a South Bronx storefront in 1978 as "a means of communication beyond ideology" that connected "the street ... with the international art world" (Webster 1996). Along with a number of Bronx graffiti writers and downtown artists, punk rockers Charlie Ahearn and his brother John both exhibited at Fashion Moda in 1979. Charlie Ahearn, who later went on to direct the 1982 hip hop movie *Wild Style*, exhibited his 1979 film *The Deadly Art of Survival* and John Ahearn created an installation of plaster casts of Bronx residents in "South Bronx Hall of Fame." A performance by graffiti writer Phase II's Bronx rap crew the Wicked Wizards in 1979 was perhaps the first hip hop music performance in an art gallery. Also, in a reversal of the later trend at the Kitchen and the Mudd Club, downtowners the Relentless Blues Band commuted uptown to perform (Webster 1996). In October 1980, nineteen year-old graffiti writer Crash curated the exhibit "Graffiti Art Success for America" featuring his friends Lady Pink, Futura, Ali, Zephyr and Fab 5 Freddy ("Guide to the Fashion Moda Archive" 2003). Collaborative Projects, or Colab, a downtown socio-political art collective founded in 1977, co-curated, in conjunction with Fashion Moda, the "Times Square Show" in June of 1980. Located in an abandoned massage parlor in Times Square, the exhibit included a mix of uptown and downtown artists (Frank and McKinzie 1987: 28; Hager 1986: 111). Fashion Moda's intermingling of the uptown and downtown was a catalyst for later downtown Manhattan activity.

FAB 5 FREDDY AND FRIENDS AND MORE FRIENDS

If there is a common thread in the narratives of the fusion of hip hop and downtown art, it is Fab 5 Freddy. A point of origin or a point of intersection for almost every important early downtown hip hop alliance can be located within his New York crisscrossings. Grandmaster Flash explains Fab 5's role in bringing hip hop downtown:

> Fab was like one of the town criers. He would come into the hood where whites wouldn't come and then go downtown to where whites would go, and say, "Listen, there's some music these cats is playing, man. It's hot shit, you gotta book these guys. So I got my first taste of playing for an audience that wasn't typically black, you know, which broadened my horizons musically." (Chang 2004)

A graffiti writer from Brooklyn, Fab 5 Freddy became notorious for his 1980 subway homage to Warhol—Campbell's soup cans painted across the 5 Train (Hoban 1998: 36). Braithwaite wanted to make inroads into both the Bronx graffiti and lower Manhattan art scenes and consequently sought out acquaintances such as Blondie, Charlie Ahearn, and *Interview* editor/Mudd Club curator Glenn O'Brien downtown, and Lady Pink, Grandmaster Flash, and the Rock Steady Crew uptown. He was quick to recognize the parallels between the hip hop and punk scenes:

> Both were reactions against disco, both had affectations for S&M leather gear, both had musical styles derived from late-sixties records, both were youth movements despised by middle class. In fact, CBGB had a parallel club in the South Bronx called The Black Door. Even more remarkable—the two scenes knew next to nothing about each other. (Hager 1986: 107)

Braithwaite's vision for fusing hip hop elements ran parallel to that of the multimedia aesthetic of the emerging downtown clubs.[9] The downtown scene not only often mixed various media, but also different styles. This combination of stylistic eclecticism and formal variety is perhaps best illustrated by the lists of names that appeared along side one another at downtown events. The advertised bill for the 1981 "Kitchen Birthday Party" includes not only Fab 5 Freddy and Friends, but also performances by contemporary composers Steve Reich and Glenn Branca, rock bands Devo and DNA, dance troupes Douglass Dunn Dancers and the Bebe Miller Dancers, comedians Dan Ackroyd and Eric Bogosian, writer Terry Southern, and roughly a dozen more acts ("Kitchen Birthday Party" advertisement 1981). The Mudd Club combined its upstairs art gallery and downstairs performance space for similar results. Advertised as "the best in hip-hop rap music produced by Fab 5 Freddy featuring the top turntable technologists and rap vocalists on the South Bronx scene," Braithwaite's "Rapper Night" took place in the performance room of the Mudd Club in 1981 (Mudd Club advertisement 1981). "Beyond Words," billed as an "Art Show of All Major Graffiti Artists," co-curated by Keith Haring, Braithwaite, and Futura 2000, opened in the Mudd Club's upstairs gallery on the same night. In addition to exhibiting the top names in graffiti, "Beyond Words" included works by artists from other styles and media including Iggy Pop, Alan Vega, Martha Cooper, and Charlie Ahearn. True to the diverse spirit of the Mudd Club, "Rapper Night" and "Beyond Words" were scheduled between Glenn O'Brien's "Heavy Metal Night" and a performance by Sun Records rockabilly legend Sleepy LaBeef. The downtown aesthetic of eclecticism that reigned in the early 1980s found in hip hop yet another genre to throw into the mix. While a number of patrons had trouble getting past the ropes outside the Mudd Club, these new uptown art, music, and dance forms had no problem gaining admittance.[10]

BLONDIE: SPREADING THE RAP(TURE)

In addition to bringing uptown acts downtown, Fab 5 Freddy also brought a number of down-towners uptown. After Glenn O'Brien introduced him to Blondie members Deborah Harry and Chris Stein, Braithwaite arranged to take the trio uptown for a hip hop event at the Police Athletic League in the Bronx. Stein and Harry were taken by the new sound and incorporated some of its elements into a track on their new record, *Autoamerican* (1980) (Fricke and Ahearn 2002: 283). "Rapture" topped both the American and British charts (Light 1999:48). At a time when only a handful of hip hop singles had hit the market, Harry's rhymes became many listeners' first exposure to rap. In addition to helping popularize the genre, the song's references to Grandmaster Flash and Fab 5 Freddy aroused the general public's curiosity—establishing the two as the most prominent names in hip hop.

In 1980, Blondie was at the peak of its popularity and one of the most famous bands in the world. Its celebrity and influence made the group hip hop's most powerful ally in these formative years. The band's role in the growth of the genre did not end with "Rapture." After witnessing the Funky 4+1 at the Kitchen, Harry invited the young quintet to make a guest appearance in an upcoming broadcast of "Saturday Night Live." The 14 February 1981 broadcast was the first rap performance in television history ("Saturday Night" n.d.; Light 1999:178; Fricke and Ahearn 2002: 216). Additionally, Fab 5 Freddy became a frequent guest performer at Blondie's arena concerts and Kurtis Blow was awarded the support slot in Blondie's 1980 British tour (Light 1999: 46). Blondie was thus not only responsible for bringing rap into mainstream consciousness at the top of the pop radio charts, but also for introducing live hip hop music on national television, the arena stage, and overseas.

LEGITIMACY: GALLERIES, PERFORMANCE SPACES, AND DOCUMENTARIES

Sculptor/photographer Henry Chalfant, an acquaintance of Braithwaite, began obsessively photo-graphing graffiti as early as 1976 (Fricke and Ahearn 2002: 299). Originally displayed at OK Harris gallery under the exhibit title "Graffiti in New York" in 1980, Chalfant's graffiti photography also appears in the pages of the seminal 1984 book *Subway Art* (Chalfant and Cooper 1984). Finding his Soho studio transformed into "a salon for graffiti artists" Chalfant soon branched out into the world of dance when he asked graffiti writer Take 1 "if he'd ever heard of breaking" (Fricke and Ahearn 2002: 299). The next day Take 1 returned with Crazy Legs and Frosty Freeze of the Rock Steady Crew in tow. Chalfant organized a breaking event at the Common Ground performance space in Soho featuring Rock Steady Crew, Fab 5 Freddy, and Rammellzee. The promotion for the Common Ground show resulted in a *Village Voice* cover story titled "Breaking is Hard to Do" by Chalfant's friend dance critic Sally Banes (Banes 1981). Though the Common Ground show was cancelled at the last minute, it not only inspired the first breaking cover story in a major publica-tion, but its preparation created stronger links between the breaking, graffiti, and downtown art communities (Fricke and Ahearn 2002: 299–306).

Later in 1981 Chalfant organized a breaking contest between the Rock Steady Crew and the Dynamic Rockers at Lincoln Center's Out of Doors festival. The prestige of the event not only helped legitimize breaking, but also introduced it to new segments of New York's population (Fricke and Ahearn 2002: 299–306). Chalfant's greatest contribution to the transmission of hip hop was his work with Tony Silver in creating the first hip hop documentary, *Style Wars*. Initially filming as an independent production in 1981, the program was picked up by Public Broadcasting System and aired nationally in January 1984 (Fricke and Ahearn 2002: 300; Light 1999: 40, 56). The soundtrack is peppered with songs by crews such as Grandmaster Flash and the Furious Five, the Treacherous Three, and the Fearless Four. In addition to providing the general public with a glimpse into hip hop culture, Chalfant's efforts to legitimize graffiti and breaking also helped promote the accompanying music.

Independent film star Patti Astor also played an important role in introducing hip hop culture downtown through the art world. Along with Bill Stelling, Astor opened the Fun Gallery on East 10th Street in 1981. The site of important early solo shows for Kenny Scharf and Jean-Michel Basquiat, Fun featured one-man shows by graffiti writers. The idea for Fun grew out of Astor's ex-hibition of a mural in her apartment by Futura 2000. Tracing the origin of Fun, Astor states, "The beginning of the Fun was when I met Fab 5 Freddy" ("Patti Astor Interview" 2002). Becoming what journalist Steve Hager labeled "the most influential gallery in New York" (Hager 1986: 110), Fun not only curated one-man shows for Fab 5 Freddy, Dondi, Lee Quiñones, Zephyr and dozens of other graffiti writers, but also became a favorite downtown hangout for DJs, MCs, and breakers.

WILD STYLE: UNITING THE ELEMENTS, UNITING NEW YORK

Another important connection to Fab 5 Freddy was Charlie Ahearn. Through Fashion Moda and Colab, Ahearn, like Braithwaite, had been participating in both the uptown and downtown art scenes. Fab 5 Freddy met Ahearn at the screening of his kung fu movie *The Deadly Art of Survival*:

> He said, "I've been looking for you, but I thought you were black" and he wanted to get together with me and make a movie. So he learned that I was really interested in Lee. He said, "I work with Lee, I'm good friends with Lee. I'll bring him tomorrow." And I said, "If you come here with Lee tomorrow, I'll give you $50 and you can put a big graffiti mural out." Which they did. And when they came, we were like okay let's make a movie together. That was June of 1980. ("Archive Interviews: Charlie Ahearn" 2001)

The movie that Braithwaite suggested became *Wild Style*. While the graffiti and murals of Lee Quiñones were well known and respected in the streets of New York, he was at this point unknown in the art scene ("Archive Interviews: Charlie Ahearn" 2001). Within a few weeks of the encounter, Fab 5 Freddy had introduced Ahearn to the Bronx hip hop scene (Fricke and Ahearn 2002: 290). Consequently, Grandmaster Flash, Cold Crush Brothers, Busy Bee, Fantastic Freaks, Double Trouble (KK Rockwell and Lil' Rodney Cee from Funky 4+1), Rammellzee, Lady Pink, and Rock Steady Crew all make appearances in *Wild Style*.

Resulting from a collaboration between uptowners and downtowners, *Wild Style* also contains an uptown/downtown theme. The plot leads the protagonist, Zoro, a Bronx graffiti writer played by Quiñones, through the Bronx hip hop world and downtown art scene. In one sequence, Virginia, played by Patti Astor, drives uptown to see the work of Zoro on a tip from Fab 5 Freddy. She brings Busy Bee, Freddy, and Zoro back downtown to a gallery opening with her and introduces them to the patrons. Virginia commissions Zoro to paint the East River Amphitheater in Manhattan's Lower East Side. Despite name changes, the actors reenact their own personal roles in the uptown/

downtown story. Ties to Blondie are highlighted by the band's music pumping out of Virginia's car speakers on her way uptown and Chris Stein's soundtrack work with Fab 5 Freddy. The movie culminates with an event at the amphitheater in which rappers and breakdancers perform in front of Zoro's new downtown mural.

The process of Ahearn and Braithwaite's creation of *Wild Style* between 1980 and 1982 strengthened the ties between hip hop's elements and solidified the scene. More importantly, as his introduction of Blondie to hip hop resulted in pop radio, television, and arena audience's first exposure to rap, Braithwaite's bringing together of Ahearn, Quiñones, and the Bronx hip hop scene culminated in hip hop's first appearance in front of an international cinema audience.

WHEELS OF STEEL: HIP HOP RULES THE NIGHT

Two figures associated with the Rock Steady Crew—Michael Holman and Kool Lady Blue—played an important role in the creation of a downtown hip hop market. After Michael Holman brought Malcolm McLaren to the Bronx River Projects to witness a Zulu Nation jam in 1981, the punk impresario asked Holman to coordinate a hip hop performance to open for Bow Wow Wow at the Ritz (Brewster and Broughton 2000: 248). After witnessing Holman's spectacle featuring the Zulu Nation DJs and MCs with the Rock Steady Crew, Kool Lady Blue, a former associate of McLaren and Vivien Westwood, asked Holman to help her coordinate a hip hop event (Brewster and Broughton 2000: 250). While Patti Astor began arranging hip hop performances in the East Village at the Fun Gallery, Holman and Blue began promoting a Thursday hip hop night around the corner at the small basement reggae club on Second Avenue named Negril that came to be known as "Wheels of Steel." While the weekly featured attraction was the Rock Steady Crew, Afrika Bambaataa, Grandmixer D.St., and other Bronx DJs began developing a downtown following at Negril (Fricke and Ahearn 2002: 302, 309). Combining live graffiti writing, breaking, MCing, and DJing, the event developed into New York's most important regular hip hop event.

Outgrowing Negril in 1982, the party relocated to the more spacious Danceteria on West 21st Street. After only a few short months of existence, the event found its final home at the Roxy, a cavernous former roller rink on West 18th Street. By this point three-to four-thousand patrons, a heterogeneous mix of uptown and downtown audiences, were attending Blue and Holman's spectacle.[11] Inflated by celebrity visitors and a barrage of media coverage, the "Wheels of Steel" nights propelled hip hop into the mainstream. Out of the large and diverse crowd, unlikely alliances were forged—for example, between uptowner Grandmaster D.St. and downtowner Bill Laswell, two of the forces behind Herbie Hancock's "Rockit" (Prasad 1999; Quan 2004). The high level of direct exposure to powerful forces in the art, entertainment, and media industries resulted in new opportunities such as Rock Steady Crew's appearance in the blockbuster film *Flashdance* (Fricke and Ahearn 2002: 302).

HIP HOP A LA CARTE: MUSIC VENUES AND THE PRESS

In addition to art galleries and nightclubs, hip hop was also appearing in live music venues. The first such concert was Sugar Hill Records' "Ritz Rap Party" at the Ritz on East 11th Street in 1981. The show featured a cross-section of the New Jersey label's stable of talent: Sugarhill Gang, Grandmaster Flash and the Furious Five, Spoonie Gee, Funky 4+1, and The Sequence ("Ritz Rap

Party" advertisement 1981). The presentation of hip hop music at a live music venue instead of a dance club or gallery drew another audience altogether. The "predominantly white, enthusiastic crowd" (Palmer 1981a) included journalists Robert Palmer, Robert Christgau, and Vince Aletti, all of whom wrote about the show (Christgau 1981; Aletti 1981). While critical praise of the event in the *New York Times* and the *Village Voice* helped validate the genre, the sold-out attendance proved that there was a significant market for hip hop performance downtown. After the Ritz event, the more popular uptown acts such as Kurtis Blow, Grandmaster Flash and the Furious Five, and the Funky 4+1 began performing primarily at large Manhattan live music venues. A step up from entertaining clubbers at general hip hop spectacles, these acts eventually received headline billing and drew crowds on their own merits.

As illustrated by the coverage of the Ritz Rap Party, the new downtown location brought hip hop performance into direct contact with some of the world's most important music journalists. These writers played a significant role in the dissemination of hip hop downtown and around the United States. Before the Ritz Rap Party, few words about rap music had appeared in major New York publications. Christgau began reviewing twelve-inch singles for the first time in his "Consumer Guide" in the 25–31 March 1981 issue of the *Village Voice*. Since there were still no hip hop LPs at this point, sans Kurtis Blow's debut, the exclusion of twelve-inch singles also meant the absence of hip hop recordings from his column. Christgau, after explaining his decision to expand his criteria for reviewing material, made good on his claim that he "had a lot of catching up to do" by reviewing Afrika Bambaataa, Kurtis Blow, Funky 4+1, Grandmaster Flash and the Furious Five, and the Treacherous Three in the same issue (Christgau 1981). Christgau at the *Voice* and Palmer at the *New York Times* regularly reviewed and recommended hip hop recordings and performances throughout the years of the uptown–downtown nexus. The tireless efforts of New York music writers created interest in and lent legitimacy to hip hop when its popularity and validity as an art form had not yet been solidified.

"TRICKED INTO YELLING 'HO!'": THE ROCK AUDIENCE

The advocacy of rock musicians was another important factor in the rise of hip hop in lower Manhattan. In the spirit of Blondie's patronage of Fab 5 Freddy and Funky 4+1, the Clash, Malcolm McLaren, and other punks and new wavers exposed hip hop to new audiences. Delivering the keynote address at the 1982 New Music Seminar, McLaren devoted the majority of his speech to hip hop music. Familiar with the concepts and language of the industry, McLaren declared hip hop "the most rootsy folk music around" and "the only music that's coming out of New York City which tapped and directly related to the guy in the streets." He concluded that, "if Elvis Presley was that in the '50s, then Afrika Bambaataa is that for the '80s" (Hager 1982). While McLaren's rhetoric helped initiate the dialogue about hip hop as urban American folk culture, his bold comparison to Elvis Presley no doubt left dollar signs in the eyes of the record industry. He himself attempted to capitalize on the phenomenon, releasing his own rap hit, "Buffalo Gals," in 1982.

After hearing "Rapper's Delight" and other early rap singles while visiting New York, the Clash included a rap in "The Magnificent Seven" on their *Sandinista!* album. Futura 2000 designed their stage sets, painted live backdrops at their concerts, designed their *Combat Rock* album cover, and rapped on "Overpowered by Funk" and "The Escapades of Futura 2000." While the Clash's fans accepted graffiti as a stage backdrop and an occasional rap in a song, it remained unclear as to how they would react to a live hip hop act.

This marriage of punk and rap in a live setting was tested at the Clash's 1981 infamous eighteen-night stand at Bond's International Casino in Times Square. Each night the band invited their favorite acts to play unbilled support slots. Opening the show on the first night of the engagement, Grandmaster Flash and the Furious Five—despite being adorned to the hilt in flamboyant stage attire—failed to win over the rock audience with their good-time anthems and choreographed dance moves. The band was shouted down and driven off-stage by a "hail of paper cups." Hoping to inspire a better reception from the dressed-down crowd, Flash and the Five appeared the next night in low-key street attire. Despite the wardrobe modification, the group was again driven offstage by shouts and paper cups (Hill 1981).

While the fate of the Grandmaster Flash shows suggested that rap might never catch on with rock audiences, five days later the Treacherous Three's opening slot performance proved that punks could accept hip hop if it was presented differently. Punk rock DJ Pearl Harbor, who also was the "unofficial emcee" of the shows, "reminded the audience that all support acts were 'friends of the Clash.'" She helped create an atmosphere for the music by playing familiar Motown singles. The Treacherous Three then took the stage rapping about the Clash and began to engage the crowd in audience participation. In the words of *Village Voice* journalist Michael Hill, "the audience didn't have time to get mad … because they had been tricked into yelling, 'Ho!'" (Hill 1981).

This anecdote illustrates how hip hop's crossover success required more than merely placing the acts in front of white rock audiences—the young genre needed to be effectively placed in the right context. The Treacherous Three also altered the content of their performance to win the crowd's acceptance. Rapping about the Clash seemed to have succeeded more than Grandmaster Flash's change of attire. Both bands' attempts to modify their presentation are evidence that hip hop modified its practices to adapt to the new environments and audiences. Recorded at the request of Sylvia Robinson, "The Message," Grandmaster Flash and the Furious Five's first sociopolitical song, appeared less than a year after their engagement with the politically conscious Clash. The Furious Five, like the Clash, were now talking about social issues instead of astrological signs and birthdays. The arrival of "The Message" resulted in a number of feature articles by white writers praising the Fives new social consciousness.[12]

BAMBAATAA: BEYOND THE RAP MAP

A Bronx native and one of the founding fathers of hip hop, Afrika Bambaataa had been placing rock records in a context that hip hop audiences could appreciate since the 1970s. Bambaataa, "the Master of Records," also had both the knowledge and the vinyl to appeal to a downtown audience. His experiments with the fusion of rap, rock, funk, electronic music, and other genres had appeal across cultural lines, creating a soundtrack that served as a force that united downtown's increasingly diverse audiences under one groove on a weekly basis. A 1982 *Village Voice* feature recounts the story of Bambaataa's first appearance downtown:

> Bambaataa was greatly impressed, not only by the enthusiasm and energy of the crowd,
> but by their appreciative response to "Zulu Nation Throwdown" … What Bambaataa

did was to go into the studio and immediately begin work on a new record, one that would appeal to the new wave crowd as well as the hip-hoppers. (Hager 1982)

The record, Afrika Bambaataa and Soul Sonic Force's "Planet Rock," illustrates the potential of cultural hybridity to birth unique forms. Much more than the material realization of Fab 5 Freddy's shuttling back and forth between the north and south poles of New York, "Planet Rock" was the next step forward. While "Rapture" or Tom Tom Club's "Wordy Rappinghood" are excellent illustrations of hip hop's early influence on downtown music, and "Genius Rap" and "It's Nasty" show downtown's influence on the uptown sound, none of these examples sufficiently departs from its initial genre to create something entirely new. The stark distinction between "Planet Rock" and its predecessors not only establishes the recording as the ultimate sonic relic of the uptown–downtown nexus, but also marks it as the climax of this narrative.

More than a rap record attempting to appeal to a rock audience or a rock record attempting to appeal to a rap audience, "Planet Rock" is its own animal. While the recording contains hip hop elements such as MCing and DJing, the vocoder singing, synthesizers, and drum machines place the song somewhere between the futuristic 1970s rock and funk music of Kraftwerk and Parliament. Here the Soul Sonic Force debuts their new "MC popping" technique in which the rappers cut phrases with abrupt pauses and overlaps. In an era in which most rap records featured funk bands instead of DJs, Bambaataa provides a soundscape comprised exclusively of electronic instruments and turntables. Additionally, the primary sample in the song, from Kraftwerk's "Trans Europe Express," is also completely synthetic.

"Planet Rock" is also unique in its creative employment of cutting-edge sound technologies. The beat, emanating from the just-released Roland TR-808 drum machine, has a highly artificial tone with an ultra-low bottom and a bright, thin snare sound. After "Planet Rock," the device immediately became a standard in rap, freestyle, and dance-pop in general. John Robie's artful programming and layering of synthesizer sounds also contributes to the piece's futuristic feel. When Tom Silverman requested "a polyphonic orchestral hit on the studio's Fairlight keyboard," Robie obliged, resulting in what David Toop describes as an effect that "combined the qualities of a Grandmaster Flash scratch, amplified to monstrous bandwidth, with the science-fiction suggestion of ten orchestras, all playing in perfect synchronization" (Toop 2000: 99). Imitations of this sound can also be found on countless club hits of various genres in the years that immediately followed.

UPTOWN AND DOWNTOWN: RANDOM POINTS IN AN EXPANDING UNIVERSE

After the climax of "Planet Rock" in early 1982, hip hop, originating in the Bronx and making a stop in lower Manhattan, had enveloped the globe by 1983. The successful European "Roxy Tour," a package featuring Bambaataa, Rock Steady Crew, Fab 5 Freddy, and the McDonald's Double Dutch Girls, spread hip hop to new international and corporate levels in November 1982 (Light 1999: 49–50). During the tour, the Rock Steady Crew accepted Queen Elizabeth's invitation to dance for her at the Royal Variety Performance (Backspin Productions 2004). In addition to breaking's introduction to a mass audience in *Flashdance* and hip hop's film debut in *Wild Style*, and the impending PBS broadcast of *Style Wars*, *Beat Street*, the first in a number of major studio hip hop films, was already in production. Most importantly, 1983 saw the release of Run DMC's first single "It's Like That" backed with "Sucker MCs" and the Beastie Boys' hip hop-informed "Cooky Puss."

By 1983, hip hop, no longer a grassroots movement, was developing an infrastructure for what would become a multibillion dollar industry.

Springboarding their careers from the Roxy, the Danceteria, and other downtown venues, Run DMC, the Beastie Boys, and LL Cool J were among the new generation of rap artists whose sounds developed while hip hop's home base was Manhattan. All were managed by Queen's concert promoter/manager Russell Simmons' Rush Productions. Run DMC, signed to Profile Records, was the first to streamline hip hop sound, fashion, and performance aesthetics. Replacing disco beats with hard rock beats, flamboyant stage attire with basic street attire, and dance routines with a static "b-boy stance," Run DMC became the biggest hip hop act of their time. Simmons and downtown punk rock producer/musician Rick Rubin met in 1984 and became partners in Rubin's Def Jam label (Light 1999: 156). Rather than "produced by Rick Rubin," LL Cool J's 1985 debut album, *Radio,* contained the credit "reduced by Rick Rubin." Further articulating the stripped down rock-based sound being developed by Run DMC, *Radio,* followed in 1986 by the Beastie Boys' *License to Ill,* cemented new standards for the hip hop sound. While Rush's artists had driven rap deep into the pop and R&B charts by 1986, in the process they also displaced Grandmaster Flash and the Furious Five, Afrika Bambaataa and Soul Sonic Force, and the other original Bronx DJs and MCs at the forefront of the hip hop movement. Similarly, as new wave and punk styles exemplified by now-defunct bands such as Blondie and the Clash disappeared from the popular music charts, hip hop entered the Top 40 not only via Def Jam, but also through dance pop and other styles influenced by the genre.[13]

The final step in the integration of uptown and downtown aesthetics, the Run DMC/Def Jam aesthetic left no need for an uptown–downtown alliance, largely through the efforts of artists such as Bambaataa to create a hybrid sound that would appeal to both audiences. By 1985, hip hop music, its producers, its stars, and its audiences were from all parts of New York. None of Rush's major acts were Bronx-based.[14] The Bronx and Harlem were now only two of many hip hop locations. Just as uptown was no longer equated with hip hop, downtown was no longer associated with its new crossover audience. Hip hop was now becoming a part of multiracial life from the suburbs to the inner cities, from coast to coast, and across oceans. The music was now a national phenomenon, no longer tied to Manhattan.

As for how hip hop became mass culture, downtown was clearly a pivotal point in the genre's voyage to the stratosphere. While Fab 5 Freddy and other members of downtown's art and music scenes gave rap a new cultural context and geographic location, the skill and creativity of the practitioners of the powerful new musical genre were ultimately responsible for its success. The story of hip hop's journey downtown illustrates music's ability to transcend boundaries of geography, race, ethnicity, class, and culture. The uptown–downtown nexus also exhibits the way in which a few individuals can bring previously isolated groups of people together and, in the process, permanently change the world.

NOTES

1. The death of disco had an important effect on the pop scene—especially in radio, where backpedaling programmers were shying away from black records of any kind in an effort to stay as far from the "disco" tag as possible. By the time "Rapper's Delight" was released in 1979, these programmers were deep into the process of segregating the airwaves to a degree

not seen since the pre-rock era. While in a typical week in the first half of 1979 nearly fifty percent of the records on *Billboard's* pop singles chart could also be found on the R&B chart, by the first half of 1980 that number had dropped to twenty-one percent, and by the end of 1982 the crossover percentage was at a rock-era low of seventeen percent. In the extreme, October 1982 saw a three-week period during which not one record by an African American could be found in the Top 20 on *Billboard's* pop singles or albums charts—a polarization that had not occurred since the 1940s (Light 1999: 26–27).

2. It is important to note that both the uptown hip hop and the downtown art scenes were not homogeneous in terms of race, ethnicity, gender, or class. But when hip hop went downtown, it broadened the variety of people and the cultural influences that they brought along with them.

3. "Comprised of disc jockeys (DJs/turntablists), emcees (MCs), breakdancers (b-boys and b-girls), and graffiti writers (aerosol artists)—commonly referred to as its four elements—hip-hop further encompasses what its adherents describe as an attitude rendered in the form of stylized dress, language, and gestures associated with urban street culture" (Keyes 2002: 1).

4. "In like the very late '70s and early '80s. Everything died down in Hip-Hop and we [Afrika Bambaataa and the Jazzy Five] went from playing in front of thousands of people at the parties—we found ourselves now playing for like 25 people! It happened for about a year and a half" (Ivory and Paul S. 2004). "Then our audience was getting older. I was wondering where my core audience was going. They wanted to move on and wear a dress or a suit" (Chang 2004).

5. "King Tim III (Personality Jock)" and "Rapper's Delight," which contain rhyming over funk jams, are typically considered the first two rap records (Keyes 2002: 70; Light 1999: 26; Fricke and Ahearn 2002: 177). As this paper is not concerned with the debate about what constitutes rap, I'll agree with the experts for the moment.

6. "Rapper's Delight," reaching #4 on the R&B chart and #36 on the Pop chart, sold over two million copies.

7. It is also important to note that, unlike the homemade cassettes, raps initial recordings featured live bands instead of turntablists behind the rappers. Accordingly, those who heard these songs on the radio were not necessarily prepared for live hip hop music.

8. "Cassette tapes used to be our albums before anybody recorded what they called rap records. People started hearing all this rapping coming out of boxes. When they heard the tapes down in the Village they wanted to know, 'Who's this black DJ who's playing all this rock and new wave up in the Bronx'" (Toop 2000: 132).

9. Fab 5 Freddy: "At that time people weren't seeing all these different elements as one thing, you know? It was like people doing graffiti were just doing graffiti. Rapping people were rapping. The break-dance scene would go on at hip-hop parties, but it was pretty much like a Latin thing, so there were Latin clubs that would happen where break-dancing would go on. So I had this idea to bring these things together" (Fricke and Ahearn 2002: 290).

10. A parody of Studio 54, the Mudd Club initially had a velvet rope and selected patrons based on their physical appearance. Patrons pulling up in limousines were often forced to wait as poor downtown artists were admitted.

11. Afrika Bambaataa: "I ended up in Negril with Michael Holman and Lady Blue. Thursday nights down there became one of the biggest nights downtown. Then it got too big for

Negril. One time the fire marshals closed the whole place down so we moved it to Danceteria. Finally, we made home at The Roxy. It started slow building at The Roxy, and now Friday nights it's always 3000, 4000. Then it became a big commercial thing." (Toop 2000: 133).

12. Not only did the *Village Voice* praise "The Message" (Aletti 1982) but also both Robert Palmer and John Rockwell in completely separate articles wrote pieces in the *New York Times* about the song. Palmer wrote, "'The Message' has radically expanded the horizons of rap" (Palmer 1981b: 20). Rockwell concluded that "sometimes tension sparks creativity, too, and with 'The Message' that seems to have happened to Grandmaster Flash and the Furious Five" (Rockwell 1982).

13. The new hip hop-influenced style of dance pop is best exemplified by Bronx-born DJ Jellybean Benitez's production on Madonna's multi-platinum self-titled debut album. The beats for this style of music relied heavily on the feature of early hip hop that Def Jam left on the cutting room floor—the disco beat. The electronic instrumentation places it in the post-"Planet Rock" category. On a final note, Madonna herself was a regular at the Roxy's "Wheels of Steel" and took the Beastie Boys on her first arena tour.

14. Run DMC (not on Def Jam) and LL Cool J were from Queens. The Beastie Boys and the Fat Boys were from Brooklyn.

REFERENCES

Aletti, Vince. 1981. "Golden Voices and Hearts of Steel." *Village Voice,* 18–24 March: 57.

——. 1982. "Furious." *Village Voice,* 20–26 July: 63.

"Archive Interviews: Arthur Baker." 1999. *Djhistory.com.* http://www.djhistory.com/books/archiveInterviewDisplay.php?interview_id=8 (accessed 4 October 2004)."Archive Interviews: Charlie Ahearn." 2001. *Djhistory.com.* http://www.djhistory.com/books/archiveInterviewDisplay. php?interview_id= 13 (accessed 4 October 2004).

Austin, Joe. 2001. *Taking the Train: How Graffiti Art Became an Urban Crisis in New York City.* New York: Columbia University Press.Banes, Sally. 1981. "Breaking is Hard to Do." *Village Voice,* 22–28 April: 31–33.Backspin Productions. 2004. "The Legendary Rock Steady Crew: Biography" http://rocksteadycrew.com (accessed 4 October 2004).

Brewster, Bill, and Frank Broughton. 2000. *Last Night a DJ Saved My Life: The History of the Disc Jockey.* New York: Grove Press.Chalfant, Henry, and Martha Cooper. 1984. *Subway Art.* New York: Holt, Rinehart and Winston.

Chang, Jeff. 2004. "1982: The Year the Planet Rocked." http://www.kingtubbis.com/ex2/herc.html (accessed 4 October 2004).Christgau, Robert. 1981. "Christgau's Consumer Guide." *Village Voice,* 25–31 March: 90.

Frank, Peter, and Michael McKinzie. 1987. *New, Used & Improved.* New York: Abeville Press.

Fricke, Jim, and Charlie Ahearn. 2002. *Yes Yes Y'all: The Experience Music Project Oral History of Hip-Hop's First Decade.* New York: Da Capo Press.

George, Nelson, Sally Banes, Susan Flinker, and Patty Romanowski. 1985. *Fresh: Hip Hop Don't Stop.* New York: Random House.

"Guide to the Fashion Moda Archive 1978–1993." 2003. Fales Library and Special Collections, New York University. http://dlib.nyu.edu:8083/falesead/servlet/SaxonServlet?source=/fashion. xml&style=/saxon01f2002.xsl&part=body (accessed 4 October 2004).

Hager, Steve. 1982. "Afrika Bambaataa's Hip Hop." *Village Voice,* 21–27 September: 69–73.

———. 1986. *Art After Midnight: The East Village Scene.* New York: St. Martin's Press.

Hill, Michael. 1981. "The Clash at the Clampdown." *Village Voice,* 10–16 September: 74.

Hoban, Phoebe. 1998. *Basquiat: A Quick Killing In Art.* New York: Viking.

Ivory and Paul S. (The P Brothers). n.d. "Interviews: Jazzy-Jazzy-Jay-Jay-Jay." *The Heavy Bronx Experience.* http://www.heavybronx.com/interviews/jazzyj.htm (accessed 4 October 2004).

Keller, Travis. 2004. "An Interview with Michael Diamond." *Buddyhead.* http://buddyhead.com/music/miked/ (accessed 4 October 2004). Keyes, Cheryl L. 2002. *Rap Music and Street Consciousness.* Urbana: University of Illinois Press.

"Kitchen Birthday Party" advertisement. 1981. *Village Voice,* 27 May–2 June: 70.Light, Alan, ed. 1999. *The Vibe History of Hip Hop.* New York: Three Rivers Press.

Mudd Club advertisement. 1981. *Village Voice,* 8–14 April: 109.

Palmer, Robert. 1981a. "Pop: The Sugar Hill Gang." *New York Times,* 13 March: C23.———. 1981b. "Pop/Jazz: 'The Message' Is That 'Rap' is Now King in Rock Clubs." *New York Times,* 3 September: C4.

"Patti Astor Interview." 2002. *@149th New York Cyber Bench.* http://www.at149st.com/astor.html (accessed 4 October 2004).

Quan, Jay. 2004. "Interview With Grandmixer DXT." *The Foundation: The Original School, 1975–1982,* 11 January. http://www.jayquan.com/dst.htm (accessed 4 October 2004).

Prasad, Anil. 1999. "Bill Laswell: Extending Energy and Experimentation." *Music Without Borders Innerviews,* 27 April. http://www.innerviews.org/inner/laswell.html (accessed 4 October 2004).

"Rap Records: Are They a Fad or Permanent?" 1980. *Billboard,* 16 February: 57–59.

"Ritz Rap Party" Advertisement. 1981. *Village Voice,* 4–10 March.

Rockwell, John. 1982. "Rap: The Furious Five." *New York Times,* 12 September: 84."Saturday Night Live Guests by Season." n.d. *Saturday-Night-Live.com.* http://www.saturday-night-live.com/snl/guestsbyseason.html (accessed 4 October 2004).

Simmons, Russell, with Nelson George. 2001. *Life and Def.* New York: Crown Publishers.

Toop, David. 2000. "Iron Needles of Death and a Piece of Wax." In *Modulations: A History of Electronic Music: Throbbing Words on Sound,* edited by Peter Shapiro, 88–107. New York: Caipirinha Productions, Inc.

Webster, Sally. 1996. "Fashion Moda: A Bronx Experience." http://ca80.lehman.cuny.edu/gallery/talkback/fmwebster.html (accessed 4 October 2004).

DISCOGRAPHY/FILMOGRAPHY

Afrika Bambaataa and Soul Sonic Force. 1980. "Zulu Nation Throwdown" (12" single). Paul Winley Records 12x33-9.

———. 1982. "Planet Rock" (12" single). Tommy Boy 823.

Ahearn, Charlie, dir. 1979. *The Deadly Art of Survival.* CineFile Video.

———. 1982. *Wild Style.* Rhino Home Video.

Beastie Boys. 1983. "Cooky Puss" (12" single). Rat Cage Records MOTR 26.

Blondie. 1980. "Rapture." On *Autoamerican.* Chrysalis 1290.

Blow, Kurtis. "Christmas Rappin" (12" single). Mercury BLOW 1312.

Chalfant, Henry, and Tony Silver, producers. 1983. *Style Wars*. Reissued in 2003 on DVD by Plexifilm.

The Clash. 1980. "Magnificent Seven." On *Sandinista!* Epic E3X-37037.

———. 1982. "Overpowered by Funk." On *Combat Rock*. Epic 37689.

———, with Futura 2000.1983. "The Escapades of Futura 2000" (12" single). Celluloid 104.

Dr. Jeckyll and Mr. Hyde. 1981. "Genius Rap" (12" single). Profile Records 7004.

Fatback Band. "King Tim III (Personality Jock)." On *XII*. IMS 16723.

Funky 4+1 More. 1979. "Rappin' And Rocking The House" (12" single). Enjoy Records 6000.

Grandmaster Flash and the Furious Five. 1981. "It's Nasty" (12" single). Sugar Hill 569.

Hancock, Herbie. 1983. "Rockit." On *Future Shock*. Columbia Records 38814.

McLaren, Malcolm, and the World Famous Supreme Team. 1982. "Buffalo Gals" (12" single). Charisma MALC 1–12.

Run DMC. 1983. "It's Like That" / "Sucker MCs" (12" single). Profile Records 7019A.

Spoonie Gee. 1979. "Spoonin Rap" (12" single). Sound Of New York 708.

Sugarhill Gang. 1979. "Rappers Delight" (12" single). Sugar Hill Records 542.

Tom Tom Club. 1981. "Genius of Love" and "Wordy Rappinghood." On *Tom Tom Club*. Sire SRK/XM5S 3628.

OBJECTIVE QUESTIONS

1. What was the most segregated period in pop radio since the 1940s?

2. Grandmaster Flash and the Furious Five's "Its Nasty" and Dr. Jeckyll and Mr. Hyde's "Genius Rap," both from 1981, are both based on a track called "Genius of Love" by_____.

3. Who is the DJ on Herbie Hancock's hit "Rockit"?

4. What was the first live Hip Hop performance "downtown"?

5. What was the first hip hop radio show?

6. Before it came into its own downtown, Hip Hop music served as a soundtrack for the more popular_____.

7. A point of origin, or a point of intersection for almost every early downtown Hip Hop alliance, can be located within his New York criss-crossings.

8. The downtown aesthetic of _____ that reigned in the early 1980s found in Hip Hop yet another genre to throw into the mix.

9. It topped the American and British charts at a time when only a handful of Hip Hop singles had hit the market. Its rhymes became many listeners' first exposure to rap.

10. After witnessing them at the Kitchen, Deborah Harry invited them to make a guest appearance on *Saturday Night Live*. The February 14th, 1981, broadcast was the first rap performance in television history.

11. What is the story behind the first cover story on break dancing in a major publication?

12. In the movie *Wild Style*, who plays the role of Zoro?

13. What is the significance of the "Ritz Rap Party" of 1981 in the popularization of Hip Hop?

14. In 1982, at a New Music Seminar, he declared Hip Hop "the most rootsy folk music around" and compared Afrika Bambaataa to _____.

15. They included a rap in "The Magnificent Seven" on their album *Sandinista!* and invited Grandmaster Flash to open their show at the Bond International Casino in Times Square.

16. What is the primary sample in Bambaataa's "Planet Rock"?

17. The European "Roxy Tour" spread Hip Hop to new international and corporate levels in November_____.

18. What label did Run DMC record for?

19. The story of Hip Hop's journey downtown illustrates music's ability to _____.

QUESTIONS FOR FURTHER THOUGHT, RESEARCH, AND DISCUSSION

1. Write a short biography of Henry Chalfant, Martha Cooper, Fredrick Braithwaite, Charlie Ahearn, or Patti Astor.

2. Research the life and storied career of Malcolm McLaren.

3. Compare and contrast the emergence of Hip Hop and punk rock.

4. What were the reasons for Grandmaster Flash's reception at the Bond International Casino?

5. Discuss the importance of "The Message."

6. Discuss the importance of "Planet Rock" and how it differs?ed from its predecessors.

7. Why did the Run DMC/Def Jam aesthetic leave no need for an uptown–downtown alliance?

PART FOUR

Hip Hop Grows Up

What We Got to Say

By Jeff Chang

Chang describes this period of hip hop history in a broad loop that starts out with the early influence of Def Jam and its roster and continues with racial housing patterns in the New York boroughs in the 60s and 70s, all of which sets the stage for Public Enemy to emerge from Long Island. There are many who would vote for Public Enemy as the most important Hip Hop group in its history and a sizable number who would consider *It Takes a Nation of Millions to Hold Us Back* the greatest Lp. Public Enemy certainly took Hip Hop to a whole new level of seriousness and maturity. They called themselves the "black panthers of rap," but they were often referred to as the "Bob Dylan" of rap. Both Dylan and Public Enemy were to some extent children of middle-class privilege who took it upon themselves to speak up against the hypocrisy and inequities they saw crippling their generation. And in both cases, their image became a metaphor for their message. Besides the background of the individual members of Public Enemy, this chapter also includes a discussion of Marley Marl (Hip Hop's first important producer), the famous Bridge Wars, and a Five Percenter from Long Island who called himself Rakim Allah.

WHAT WE GOT TO SAY: BLACK SUBURBIA, SEGREGATION AND UTOPIA IN THE LATE 1980s FROM *CAN'T STOP WON'T STOP*

Ay uh we didn't get our forty acres and a mule but we did get you, C.C.
—George Clinton

Long Island, where I got 'em wild and
That's the reason they're claiming that I'm violent

—Chuck D

"DEF JAM IS the ultimate suburban record label," wrote music critic Frank Owen in one of the earliest articles on Public Enemy. He argued that Russell Simmons and Rick Rubin were creating "the first Black music that hasn't had to dress itself up in showbiz glamour and upwardly mobile mores in order to succeed." They were leading the battle "against the gentrification of black music."[1] Significantly, Simmons, Run DMC and LL Cool J were from home-owning Queens, and Rubin, Original Concept and Public Enemy were from "the well-to-do beach communities of Long Island."

Owen quoted Public Enemy's lead rapper, Chuck D, an intimidatingly articulate guy whose eyes always seemed hidden beneath the brim of his baseball cap. "Raps from the suburbs are a little more broad," Chuck said. "They don't have the closed-in focus like inner-city raps. In the suburbs you can rap about regular everyday life like going to the park and taking a swim. The rest of America can relate to that."

But Public Enemy's art would always belie easy sociology. Public Enemy's second single, "You're Gonna Get Yours," was Chuck's ode to his 98 Olds, "the ultimate homeboy car!"—a theme as American as The Beach Boys' "Little Deuce Coupe." Yet the song was also about facing down racial profiling with Black posse power, an act of defiance set within the historical context of Robert Moses's expressway-fueled segregation and Levittown's racial covenants. Chuck himself would never rap about going to the park or taking a swim. The suburbs that birthed Def Jam's cultural vanguard were no white-bread New Frontier futurama.

THE BLACK BELT AND THE RESEGREGATION OF LONG ISLAND

After World War II, African Americans began moving to the suburbs of Queens. Soon what would become known as "the Black Belt" spilled past Queens's eastern borders into Long Island's Nassau and Suffolk Counties. By the 1970s, it stretched from Merrick and Freeport through Roosevelt to Hempstead.

"Long Island represented an outpost for many New Yorkers trying to escape what had become the ravages of urban America in the '60s," says Bill Stephney. "White ethnics—Italians, European Jews, Irish—were all moving out from their various sectors of New York City to escape Blacks and Latinos. The thing is the working-to middle-class Black generation living in the Bed-Stuys and the Parkchesters, the Bronx and Harlem, also wanted the same thing. Raise their kids with backyards and birds. The quote unquote American dream."

The core of what would become Public Enemy—Carlton "Chuck D" Ridenhour, Bill Stephney, Hank "Shocklee" Boxley, William "Flavor Flav" Drayton, Richard "Professor Griff" Griffin and Harry "Allen" McGregor—were all born between 1958 to 1961, and had moved to the Black Belt by the early '70s. 1980 census data showed that over 40 percent of white New Yorkers lived in the suburbs, but only 8 percent of Black New Yorkers did.[2] In other words, they were part of the race's "talented tenth," the very embodiment of the brightest hopes of integrationists.

Bill's father, Ted Stephney, had been a Jackie Robinson of sorts, joining the staff of *Sports Illustrated* magazine in 1954 and eventually rising to become the magazine's first Black editor. In

1965, he moved his family from Harlem to Hempstead. The Stephneys were pioneers on their block, one of three Black families among about forty whites. More Black families moved in, but in practice, integration never worked the way that civil rights activists had hoped.

In 1966, integration orders were issued by New York State education officials for Freeport, Glen Cove, Roosevelt and Amityville. These communities suddenly looked more attractive to Black homebuyers. White real-estate agents descended on white homeowners to encourage them to sell their homes and "upgrade" to new developments to the north and east. By skillfully exploiting fears, real-estate agents could double their sales in a practice known as "block-busting." For all practical purposes, racism and the market ensured that these neighborhoods were "integrated" only in passing.

When Chuck's family moved from the Queensbridge projects to Roosevelt in 1969, buying their piece of the dream for the relatively affordable price of $20,000, the number of Blacks in the neighborhood had long passed the tipping point—that unspoken ratio somewhere between 10 and 20 percent that triggered white flight. "Two years prior it was about maybe 90 percent white. When we moved in it was about 50 percent. Two years later, about 90 percent Black," he says. The oldest of three children, Chuck grew up in virtually an all-Black suburb.

Although the 1968 Fair Housing Act had banned discrimination in selling and renting homes, Stephney says, "Black folks were shown Hempstead and Roosevelt and parts of Freeport, also New Cassel." Other Long Island towns, like Wyandanch, Brentwood and Amityville—homes to the rappers Rakim Allah, EPMD and De La Soul, respectively—also became largely Black. In between, places like East Meadow, Baldwin, Rockville Centre, the fading *über*burb of Levittown and the sparkling "edge cities" or exurbs encircling the Black Belt to the north and east remained mostly white.

By the early 1970s, Long Island's Black Belt was firmly established. Two decades later, *Newsday* would find that illegal steering practices were still commonplace and called Long Island housing patterns "apartheid-like."[3] While the victories of the civil rights and Black power movements had expanded the Black middle-class, that middle-class was now just as segregated as its "underclass" counterparts were.

ALWAYS BETWEEN: THE BLACK MIDDLE CLASS

So yes, they had made it to Long Island. But no, this wasn't the promised land. Black suburbia was a safe island in a sea of whiteness, and incontrovertible evidence of white resistance to King's dream.

Newsday found that while many of Long Island's white students attended some of the best schools in the country,

> [m]ore than half of the Island's 40,000 Black public school children attend 11 districts where academic programs and resources are measurably inferior to those in white schools: They are poorly equipped, their teachers are less experienced and underpaid. Test scores are low, the dropout rate is high, few students go on to college.[4]

In a *Newsday* poll, most Blacks rated race relations as "fair" or "poor."[5] Three-quarters wanted to live in integrated communities. By contrast, fully 55 percent of white Long Islanders preferred to live in mostly white neighborhoods, a rate high above the national average.

Some white youths apparently shared their parents' feelings. In 1985, a cineplex in Franklin Square, a white town edging against Hempstead, opened the Run DMC vehicle, *Krush Groove*, next to the Freddy Krueger bloody-white-picket-fence flick, *Nightmare on Elm Street*, and fights between Black and white youths broke out. One white teenager complained that *Krush Groove* was "attracting a Black crowd to a white town. That means trouble, especially because they come out of the movie all psyched up."[6] The movie was a comedy. Critics hated the movie, but no one else had ever accused it of being provocative.

White cops seemed to treat the Black suburbs as an advancing border. Although Blacks made up only 9 percent of Long Island's population, they made up over 30 percent of the arrests in Nassau and Suffolk counties, and 43 percent of suspects shot at by police. Only 2 percent of the police force was Black.[7] The poll found that Blacks were four times more likely than whites to distrust police.

Sociologists had begun calling places like the Black Belt "inner-ring suburbs." The housing stock was aging, housing values had leveled off, education and social services were declining and crack dealers were beginning to appear. These suburban Blacks were caught between Black poverty and white flight. They were buffers between inner-city ghettos of color and the *new* New Frontier of white wealth in the exurbs.

To neoconservative and neoliberal pundits, the end of integration meant it was time for the Black race's talented tenth to take responsibility to save the race. But as journalist Ellis Cose wrote in his book *The Rage of a Privileged Class*, "The irony in such arguments is that the 'decent Black people' who will save America from the underclass, those paragons of middle-class virtue who will rescue the ghetto from violence, are themselves in a state of either silent resentment or deeply repressed rage. Taken as a group, they are at least as disaffected and pessimistic as those struggling at society's periphery."[8]

Living in this borderland, where everything mixed and clashed, one might be freighted with a feeling of being in-between all the time—a Duboisian double-consciousness complicated by the burden of class. But being Black and middle class could also be liberating. The *Newsday* poll noted what it thought to be a conundrum: "[M]ost Blacks were optimistic about the future even while believing that segregation will stay the same or increase."[9]

A sacred tenet of the civil rights movement had been that allowing Black families into white neighborhoods or Black students into white classrooms would lift their expectations, eliminate their alleged pathologies, and brighten their life chances. Integration was presumed to be the economic and cultural ideal for Blacks, just as assimilation was for immigrants. But while most Long Island Blacks liked the idea of integration—indeed, much more than their white counterparts—they certainly did not feel that they needed integration to succeed.

To them, the Black Belt was also an idyll, the sort of place in which Marcus Garvey's son, a doctor named Julius, could open his heart surgery practice. Whites often came to Dr. Garvey's office, took one look at him, and never returned. But this Black-owned business was not suffering, nor were many others.[10]

The Black Belt was culturally rich. Chuck's mother, Judy Ridenhour, formed the Roosevelt Community Theater and ran it from 1971 to 1985, mentoring a number of young actors and actresses, such as Chuck's childhood buddy, Eddie Murphy. Chuck, Hank, Eddie and Richard Griffin, were sent to study blackness on white campuses. Between 1970 and 1972, they attended a summer program at Hofstra and Adelphi universities organized and taught by Black Panthers,

Black Muslims and university students, called "The Afro-American Experience," the local manifestation of the national movement for ethnic studies and Afro-American studies. The program proved instrumental in convincing Chuck and Hank to attend those still largely white universities years later.

And the Black Belt never felt far from the city. "Every weekend my family and most of our families would come back from Long Island and visit our grandparents, aunts, uncles, and cousins on the weekend in Harlem and in the Bronx," says Stephney. That's where the kids discovered the future culture.

"My grandmother lived in the projects in the northern Bronx where DJ Breakout basically was doing his thing in the Quadrangle," says Stephney. "I'm thirteen, fourteen. The noise that we heard my parents thought was *crime*," he laughs. Stephney was aware of the class gulf. These weekend trips offered a constant reminder of the way things *really* were, and even suggested an opportunity to be grabbed.

Stephney says, "We could sort of vicariously live out the life that our cousins were living. It was sort of like we were slumming. But then we could go back to Long Island and go to school and maybe get a couple of extra dollars from our parents to buy turntables, take some of the advantages that our cousins in Bronx River and Soundview Houses didn't have economic advantage to do."

They were products of the failure of the civil rights dream of integration, but the Black Belt youths also had access to different realities, and they had the time and space to think through and map out how to take their place in the new world.

THE BIG STREET BEAT COMES TO BLACK SUBURBIA

When Schoolly D's "P.S.K." hit the Black suburbs of Long Island, Harold McGregor and Hank Boxley were two clerks in dead-end entry-level jobs at a fading department store called TSS. They were bored, unhappy and underemployed. They stole time to discuss the hottest new rap single and dream of the future.

By night, Boxley was a famous DJ, the Afrika Bambaataa of Long Island. In 1974, he had started doing shows as a teenager at the Roosevelt Youth Center. Now his mobile DJ unit, Spectrum City, was the one of the best-known sound systems in the Black Belt. But he had doubts about how far it could all go.

At one point, Spectrum City had been in the right place at the right time. In the mid-1970s, the teenagers of Queens's Black middle-class were building the biggest sound systems yet seen in the boroughs, putting scads of funk cover bands out of work. Long Island DJ crews followed soon after. Spectrum City and its rivals, Pleasure, King Charles, and the Infinity Machine, rocked community centers, roller rinks, Elks Club and hotel ballrooms, and then moved to a bigger, more attractive base, the area's universities, including Adelphi, C.W. Post and Boxley's alma mater, Hofstra. Soon, folks came from as far away as the Queens neighborhoods of Jamaica and Hollis to check out the campus parties.

Carlton Ridenhour began writing rhymes after the blackout of 1977, inspired by cassettes he had encountered while working summer jobs in Manhattan. He and Hank both came of age just as the nascent Long Island scene hit a transition point in 1978 and 1979. While the hip-hop core in the city was growing up and moving away from the big street beat, a young Long Island hip-hop constituency was forming. Spectrum City was at the center of a new energy.

But their flyers were wack. Ridenhour was at Adelphi studying graphic design. He stepped up to Hank to offer to redesign their flyers. "Hank looked at me like I was crazy" he says, and nothing came of the request.

By September 1979, Boxley was convinced he needed a permanent MC to front Spectrum City. One night at the end of an open mic session at Adelphi's Thursday Night Throwdown, a booming voice turned Shocklee's head. Ridenhour, it seemed, had other talents.

In fact he had the kind of voice that cut through brick walls. He had patterned himself after DJ Hollywood, DJ Smalls and Eddie Cheeba, disco rap DJs whose greatest skill lay in moving their crowds. "To get the party crowd amped, to get them hyped?" says Stephney, "Chuck D was one of the greatest party MCs of all time."

"When they got to 'Love Is the Message' or especially when they got to 'Good Times,' you had people lining up on the mic trying to get down. And me, I would just get on the mic just to shut people up, because I just didn't want to hear nine million people on the mic," Ridenhour recalls. "And when he found it was me, the same guy with the flyers, he was like, 'What the fuck! You from Roosevelt! Why don't you get down with me?'"

As Ridenhour pondered the decision, "Rapper's Delight" came out. The decision was sealed. He took over flyer design duties and became the rapper "Chuckie D." He began wearing his Spectrum City jacket around campus. He landed a daily cartoon in the school paper and called the Pedro Bell-styled strip, "Tales of the Skind." In it, Spectrum City became a crew of superheroes who regularly saved the world from Reagan the "King of the 666," and a host of lesser villains.

Harold McGregor wasn't much of a party-goer. His Jamaican parents were strivers who had moved to Costa Rica, then Brooklyn, and finally to Freeport. He had grown up a devout Seventh-Day Adventist and gone to a boarding school in upper Pennsylvania. At Adelphi, he came upon his future by accident. On the first day in an animation class, he sat next to a guy who was doodling. Struck dumb, he leaned over to tell Chuck he was a big fan of his work. ("I still am," he chuckles.) They teamed up to do an animated video set to Malcolm McLaren's "She's Looking Like a Hobo." In a few years, McGregor would be calling himself Harry Allen, Hip-Hop Activist and Media Assassin.

Bill Stephney came to Adelphi on an Urban League-sponsored communications scholarship that he had won by writing an essay on why more Blacks were needed in the media industry. Stephney had gone to Spectrum City parties as a youngster and now had a Monday night hip-hop show at the campus radio station, WBAU. The small Garden City liberal arts college was a predominantly white commuter campus. Most of the 10 percent of the student body that was African-American came from outside the area. So when Stephney spotted Chuck D sporting his Spectrum City jacket in the school cafeteria, he couldn't believe it. Stephney soon asked Chuck and Hank to join his radio show.

Stephney's scholarship had included a coveted internship at the trend-setting rock station, WLIR-FM. Armed with a wealth of radio tricks from WLIR and the famous Spectrum City crew, he began transforming a 300-watt station into a contender for rap-hungry ears on Strong Island. He became program director in 1982, and gave Chuck and Hank a Saturday night rap show, the "Super Spectrum Mix Hour." Harry was a frequent visitor.

It was the beginning of a long, some say fated, friendship. They did not fit in with the Black fraternity and sorority scene, full of bougie wannabes who looked down their noses on hip-hop.

They mixed more easily with the white, mullet-haired Long Island freaks that hung around the radio station.

"We were the rebels," says Stephney, "and hip-hop was everything to us. Everything, all culture, all western civilization flowed through Bam, Herc, and Flash. We weren't trying to hear anything."

Many people remember their old homies by the adventures they shared. Chuck, Bill, Hank, and Harry talk about the intense debates they had. Every topic—the aesthetics of Schoolly D, the comparative emotional qualities of various basslines, the taste of White Castle cheeseburgers, the Mets and the Yankees and Jets and the Giants and the Knicks, Vanessa Williams's Miss America fiasco, Jesse Jackson's presidential campaign—was up for grabs.

To Allen, hanging with the crew was an advanced rap seminar. To Stephney, it was a salon reminiscent of the Harlem Renaissance. To the authorities, it was something else. One late night after a gig as they partied and argued in the parking lot of a White Castle, a police helicopter and a fleet of Nassau County cop cars swooped down and surrounded them. There were reports that a riot was going on.

HARDER INTELLECT

Rap crews popped up all over the area, and many found their way into the WBAU-Spectrum City nexus. Stephney added Adelphi classmate Andre "Dr. Dre" Brown and his man, T-Money, who had a crew called Original Concept, to the BAU roster. Dre later took over Stephney's show and his program director duties, and gave a show to a bizarre, classical piano-playing, jheri-curled, all black-wearing character from Freeport named William "Rico" Drayton who called himself the MC DJ Flavor.

A friend from Roosevelt, Richard Griffin, director of a martial arts school and a Nation of Islam devotee, came in to handle Spectrum City's security with a team he called Unity Force. Chuck's 98 Posse, a group of hard-rocks and hustlers from around the way, rolled to the parties in their tricked-out Oldsmobiles. The two crews—one representing form and discipline, the other street wildness—had that Zulu/Gestapo dynamic going on. They didn't always get along, but they came together under Spectrum City.

Chuck and Hank's radio drops topped WBAU's request lists. Run DMC came down from Hollis to do their first New York radio interview and left huge fans of the Spectrum City crew. Tapes of the shows spread into New York City, and they compared favorably with Mr. Magic's Rap Attack on WBLS, Eddie Cheeba's WFUV show and the World Famous Supreme Team's show on WHBI. The Spectrum City empire expanded to TV when Bill hooked up a UHF show. Hank, placing a bet on the future, rented out a space on 510 South Franklin Street in Hempstead and set up a recording studio.

They had the crew, they had the skills, they certainly had the desire. But could a hip-hop crew break out from Long Island? There was no road map. Then the rap-loving rebels found a mentor in a young African-American studies professor and jazz drummer named Andrei Strobert.

Born in 1950, Strobert grew up in Crown Heights and Bedford-Stuyvesant and became a drumming prodigy. By the time he was in his teens, Strobert was supporting himself with music gigs through Mayor Lindsay-funded youth programs like the Harlem Youth Opportunities Unlimited, "Har-You" for short, where he recorded his first record with fourteen other teens, the great Latin jazz album, *Har-You Percussion Group*. At eighteen, he left to tour North America. He later played with jazz mavericks Makanda Ken McIntyre and South African exile Abdullah "Dollar Brand" Ibrahim, and finally devoted himself to teaching.

The Black Arts movement had creatively and literally fed Strobert. But after the riot season of 1968, the network that sustained him began to dry up. Radio marginalized jazz. Clubs and theaters closed. Many school music programs and nonprofit youth organizations ended when government money dried up. Strobert recognized that hip-hop had come out of a traumatic break between generations, and he was now in a position to take the rap rebels back to their roots.

For two semesters, Strobert offered a class called "Black Music and Musicians." African music, he taught, was the source. It had come first; it was *first* world music, not *third* world music. Unlike many of his age, Strobert was respectful of rap music. Fats Waller, he told them, was a rapper. Louis Armstrong was a rapper. The only thing different with your rap, he told them, was that it went over a different rhythm. But even the beat wasn't new; it came from Ibo rhythms, through the pulse of the New Orleans second-line. Recognize the source, he said, return to the source. Bill, Harry, Andre, and Chuck—usually back-of-the-class kind of guys—were in the front row for all of Strobert's lectures.

After class, they peppered him with questions. Strobert gave them impromptu seminars. Control your image by developing your theme, he said. All the great artists—Mahalia Jackson, Dizzy Gillespie, James Brown—had a theme, and when the theme was over, they moved to a new one. Tell a story, he said. A rap means nothing if it tells no story. The students worried that critics were calling rap a passing fad and record companies might lose interest. Strobert laughed sagely.

"Don't believe the hype," he told them. Strobert now says, "I did *not* think they were really listening to me. I really didn't."

Understanding how they fit into the historical continuum gave Chuck, Harry, and Bill confidence, and reinforced their impatience with the state of hip-hop. Crack had ushered in an era of conspicuous wealth and raw violence, and even the slang reflected the change. It was all about getting ill, cold getting dumb. Chuck complained, "It's like being content with being stupid."[11]

When the media excoriated Run DMC for the gang violence at the 1986 Long Beach concert, Chuck got really angry. "Shit, if they ever come to me with that bullshit," he said, "I'll have some shit to say that they won't want to fuck with. I'll give them the exact reasons that bullshit like that happens."[12]

The times indeed called for someone new to flip "It's Like That" and "Proud to Be Black" the way those records had flipped "The Message" and "Planet Rock." But even more, the times required a harder kind of intellect.

Bill Stephney challenged Chuck, "Why don't you be the one?" Chuck wasn't so sure. But then he was writing as if he already had the freedom to say what folks couldn't: "I'm a MC protector, US defector, South African government wrecker. Panther power—you can feel it in my arm. Look out y'all, cause I'm a timebomb tickin'!"

FALSE START

The tempos were slowing down, the style changing. Run DMC's "It's Like That" and "Sucker MCs" shifted the game again—harder beats with harder rhymes that gave no quarter to anyone not already down. Hollis, Queens, was in the house, and the Spectrum City crew hoped Long Island could be next.

Chuck and Hank had always wanted to make a record. When the World's Famous Supreme Team broke out of WHBI in 1982, they began thinking it was possible. Two years later, Chuck and Hank landed a single deal with the dance indie, Vanguard. Harry Allen says he was convinced that "as soon as the rest of the world heard this music, we were just gonna take over."

The Spectrum City single duplicated the split of "It's Like That"/"Sucker MCs." On the A-side, "Lies." Chuck and fellow Spectrum City rapper Butch Cassidy went topical. Opening with the notes of "Hail to the Chief," the song seemed to promise a vivid deconstruction of Reagan. Instead it was a generic dis record, delivered over a beat derived from Arthur Baker, James Brown, and Larry Smith. Chuck's voice thundered like Melle Mel's second coming, but lyrically this was no "Message."

Instead, the B-side won. "Check Out the Radio" was based on one of Chuck's famous radio drops. Hank and his brother Keith assembled a beat based on a b-boy perennial, Juicy's "Catch a Groove," and took a risk by pitching it down. If the trend was to decrease the tempo and pump up the bass, the Shocklees wanted it slower and lower. In a year, as if tipping their baseball caps to them, Def Jam would drop two more B-side trunk crushers—Original Concept's "Pump That Bass/Live (Get a Little Stupid … HO!)" and the Beastie Boys' "Slow and Low."

The track hinted at Chuck's talent for deep signifying. He introduced Hank Boxley as Hank Shocklee, a very smart dis of the early-twentieth-century physicist and eugenicist William Shockley. But the crew still had not harnessed its strengths—Chuck's wordplay and presence, Hank and Keith's experimentalist drive, the crew's restless, race-conscious, collective intelligence. In December of that year, they found the prototype in a buzzsaw radio drop set to a loop of the intro to The JB's "Blow Your Head" and called, after James Brown's anti-heroin lament, "Public Enemy #1." But by then the single had stiffed. Chastened by the experience, the crew retreated to lick their wounds.

So now in the break room in the bowels of a dying department store in the middle of Still Nowhere, Hip-Hop America, Hank and Harry talked Schoolly D's "P.S.K."—repping Philly—with a mix of awe, envy and discouragement. "I think there was a lot of disappointment," says Harry. "It was like, we could be doing this the rest of our lives—working at TSS, handing out our fliers, having people come to our club, nothing really happening. And it would all just be a minor footnote somewhere."

Chuck graduated and helped land Flavor a job delivering furniture for his father's business. Then he moved on to work as a messenger for a photo company, scribbling raps on notepads on long drives into the city, letting WLIB's mix of Black-talk radio and booming beats fire his imagination.

The bills at their Spectrum City office in Hempstead were piling up. Their club and party audiences were maturing and moving on. The "Super Spectrum Mix Hour" was coming to an end.

In 1985, Original Concept signed to Def Jam. The label president Rick Rubin was calling Chuck's house to see if he would agree to be their rapper. "Mom!" Chuck would yell from his room, "Tell him I'm not home. Tell him I don't wanna make no stupid goddamn records!"[13] Once bitten, twice shy was the way he and Hank felt about record labels. They had already built a local empire by themselves. What next? At the end of long wearying days, they talked about starting their own indie record label.

Bill Stephney graduated and began working in the radio world, establishing a reputation in the record industry. Harry left for Brooklyn to finish his degree. Both of them were surrounded by the music, which seemed to be undergoing tectonic stylistic shifts every few weeks. The city seemed charged with importance—so many ideas, so much ferment. People were talking about things that mattered. Change was in the air. Something had to happen.

THE BIGGEST CROSSOVER

At Def Jam and Rush Artists Management, Russell Simmons and Rick Rubin's crew had big dreams.

Bill Adler was one of Russell's first hires. When he signed on to work at Rush Management and Def Jam in 1984 at thirty-two years of age, he was older than everyone on the tiny staff, twice as old as LL Cool J. A third-generation Jewish American from the Detroit suburb of Southfield, Adler had arrived at the University of Michigan in the feverish fall of 1969 and met a local hero, a self-described "cultural radical" named John Sinclair.

Sinclair was part of a generation of post-World War II whites, including Allen Ginsberg, Norman Mailer and Bob Dylan, who wanted to root themselves in what they thought was the special authenticity of African-American culture. To Sinclair, Black musicians like James Brown, John Coltrane, and Sun Ra offered a model of liberation for young whites. After Black Panther cofounder Bobby Seale told Sinclair whites could not do anything for Black people but to fix their square parents, he was inspired to form the White Panthers and draft their ten-point program. The first point was a full endorsement of the Black Panthers' program. The second read, "Total assault on the culture by any means necessary, including rock 'n' roll, dope and fucking in the streets." For Adler, who had spent his teen nights under the covers listening to blues, Motown, and "freedom jazz" on local radio, joining Sinclair's funkdafied guitar army of white radicals made perfect sense.

After Sinclair left Ann Arbor, so did Adler, moving first to Boston. Fired from his DJ job at WBCN for playing Joe Tex, bored with his pop music critic job at the *Boston Herald*, Adler left for New York City in 1980 with a box of brand new rap records under his arm. He met Russell Simmons while doing a story on rap for *People* magazine and they became fast friends. When Adler approached Simmons to try to sell him an anti-Reagan rap intended for Kurtis Blow, Simmons demurred but hired Adler to do publicity for his acts. Adler immediately understood what set Simmons apart from the Black-owned indie pioneers like Enjoy and Sugar Hill. "He was never gonna just be a guy who operated within the confines of Black cultural institutions," Adler says. "He was gonna take this Black culture and promote it everywhere."

Simmons was twenty-six, an extroverted, infectious son of civil rights activists, less concerned with political parties than with being the center of the party. Even during his brief stint as warlord of a Queens chapter of the Seven Immortals, his thing had been bumrushing school dances and concerts. No social crowd ever gathered that Simmons could not work his way into the middle of. He had a sixth sense for the popular.

When Simmons met Rick Rubin, a twenty-one-year-old, gnomic Jewish long-hair with Bambaataa-sized tastes in music and a Sinclairian talent for fomenting white teen cultural rebellion, he found the perfect partner. Rubin had grown up on Long Island playing metal and punk, and became a rap devotee through the WBAU shows and Mr. Magic. When he moved to Manhattan to attend New York University, regular trips to Blue's "Wheels of Steel" night at Negril and The Roxy sealed his love for hip-hop.

Rubin had a hardcore aesthetic. "I think Rick helped radicalize Russell's rhetoric," says Adler. "He used to say, 'We're gonna pull the mainstream in our direction simply on the basis of the integrity of the records themselves. We are going to win with no compromise.'"

Radio had long calcified into racialized formats—Album-Oriented Rock for whites, Urban Contemporary for Blacks. Rap was the most exciting new music to come along in years, but there was no room for it in either. MTV had burst onto the scene by championing rock and new wave, and all but excluding Black artists. Only after Columbia reportedly threatened to boycott the young network in 1983 did MTV begin airing Michael Jackson videos. Winning meant desegregating radio and music video.

Not long after the ink dried on Def Jam's contract with Columbia in 1985, Rubin hired Bill Stephney as the label's first full-time staffer. Rubin was a Spectrum City fan. But perhaps more important was the fact that Stephney played guitar, was from Long Island, and dug AC/DC the way Rubin did Schoolly D. After graduating from Adelphi, Bill Stephney had done a short, influential stint at the College Music Journal, launching its "Beat Box" urban chart and mapping what would become a powerful network of rap radio shows. Stephney had also maintained his old white rock radio contacts, which later proved crucial to Def Jam's success.

Russell was a Black executive able to bridge Black and white tastes like no one since Berry Gordy. He hired Adler. Rick was a Jewish music producer who understood how profoundly Herc, Bam, and Flash's insights could reshape all of pop music. He hired Stephney. The staff for Rush and Def Jam was uniquely suited and highly motivated to pull off a racial crossover of historic proportions.

Bill Stephney convinced his friends at rock radio to stay on Run DMC's cover of Aerosmith's "Walk This Way," even when the call-out research showed racist, "get the niggers off the air" feedback. He then succeeded in propelling the Beastie Boys onto rap radio, a feat no less difficult. By the end of 1986, their strategy had been perfectly executed. The Black group crossed over to white audiences with *Raising Hell*, then the white group crossed over to Black audiences with *Licensed to Ill*.

Forget busing, Adler thought. Hip-hop was offering a much more radical, much more successful voluntary desegregation plan. It was bleeding-edge music with vast social implications. "Rap reintegrated American culture," Adler declared. Not only was hip-hop *not* a passing novelty, the ex-Sinclairite told journalists, it was culturally monumental, and Run DMC and the Beastie Boys were the new revolutionaries. "Young, smart, fast, hard," he called them. "Lean and winning."

Def Jam's epochal feat of pop integration unleashed a rap signing blitz. Majors realized that rap music was not a fad, and they were far behind the curve. Their Black music departments had become calcified, geared toward promoting expensive R&B acts that appealed to an upwardly mobile audience quickly losing its trend-setting power. By the end of 1986, and continuing for the better part of a decade, majors moved in the other direction, trying to sign every rap act they could. It was one of those rare moments in pop music history where major-label disorientation left the door open for any visionary to walk through and do something radical.

At the same time, the teens weaned on Herc and Bam and Flash were growing up, and they felt they had something to say. They simply needed to figure out what that something was.

BECOMING THE ENEMY

When Stephney left CMJ, he had written in his last column that he hoped to develop a group that was equal parts Run DMC and The Clash. He wanted to be a part of making the rap *Sandinista!* Back in Hempstead, at 510 South Franklin, he, Hank, and Chuck were at a crossroads. If they were going to do something, Hank says, "We had to create our own myth for ourselves."

But while their homies from Hollis were taking over the world, Spectrum City had run out of steam. Chuck was about to turn twenty-six and had little intention of remaining a rapper. Rick Rubin was still pestering Chuck's mother with phone calls. Chuck was thinking, "Yo I need to make some radical moves. And that's not radical enough." He wanted to get a job as a commercial radio personality.

Rubin joked that if Stephney couldn't get his best friend signed to Def Jam, he would have to be fired. So Bill offered Chuck and Hank a meeting with Rubin. The two brought in a four-song demo which included "Public Enemy #1," "The Return of Public Enemy" (which would become "Miuzi Weighs a Ton"), "Sophisticated Bitch," and "You're Gonna Get Yours." Rubin immediately offered Chuck an album deal. "I was like, well I'm not going to go in there by myself," Chuck says. After he negotiated to include Flavor Flav and Hank, the deal was done, and he set about finding a place for the entire crew.

As he had done with "Tales of the Skind," he created alter-egos for each of them. Richard Griffin took the name "Professor Griff" and the title that Eldridge Cleaver had held in the Black Panthers, "Minister of Information." Unity Force, the Spectrum City's security team run by Griffin, were renamed the Security of the First World (S1Ws). Hank assembled the musical team, starting with his brother Keith, also known as "Wizard K-Jee." Army fatigue-wearing Eric "Vietnam" Sadler—like Stephney and Flavor Fiav—was a veteran of the Long Island funk cover-band scene and was learning to program drums and synthesizers. Spectrum City DJ Norman Rogers became "Terminator X." Paul Shabazz and the DJ for the Kings of Pressure, Johnny "Juice" Rosado, also made key contributions. Hank's team became known as the Bomb Squad.

Most important, Chuck, Hank and Bill had to come up with a concept for the crew. Spectrum City was done. But they had yet to come up with a new name and concept.

Bill's dream was for the group to make the cover of the *Rolling Stone*. "Let's make every track political," he said. "Statements, manifestoes, the whole nine." Hank worried that kind of approach might lose them credibility with their core audience. He says, "Everyone making Hip-Hop wasn't a thug, everybody wasn't about being stupid." But, he adds, "we found that people were really against the political aspects of the music. That wasn't a slam dunk."

Characteristically, Chuck was somewhere in between. He wanted to write rhymes that were more explicit, but he says, "It was impossible to put that type of shit in your rhymes. It was like, you better rock the fucking crowd. You could throw in one line or two, like 'Reagan is bullshit.' Motherfuckers be like, 'Yeah, okay.'"

Then there was the crazy DJ MC Flavor, whom Hank had renamed Flavor Flav. Both Hank and Chuck wanted Flav to round out the crew, be the MC yin to Chucks yang. Bill objected. "I wanted the group to be so serious, I didn't want Flavor in the group. Flavor was like a comic cut-up, so my thing was, 'Here we are trying to do some serious shit, how are we gonna fit this guy in?'" he says. "They were completely right. With Chuck being serious, with the stentorian tones, you needed a break, you needed someone to balance that or else it would have been too much."

One night while they were recording *Yo! Bum Rush the Show,* Bill returned from the Def Jam offices to 510 South Franklin. On a bulletin board, Hank had written the crew's new name: "Public Enemy." Stephney smiled. The name perfectly fit their underdog love and their developing politics. He recalls thinking, "Okay, I can spin this. We're all public enemies. Howard Beach. Bernhard Goetz. Michael Stewart. The Black man is definitely the public enemy."

REPRESENTING NEW BLACK MILITANCY

A generation after COINTELPRO, Black radicalism had gone underground. Chuck's striking logo for Public Enemy—a silhouette of a young black man in a gunsight—suggested exactly why. But Public Enemy and the other crew that most represented the bumrush aesthetic, Boogie Down Productions, used their album covers to depict the return of the black radical.

P.E.'s cover for *Yo! Bum Rush the Show* and B.D.P.'s cover for *Criminal Minded* depicted the crews in dim-palled basements, readying themselves to bring black militancy back into the high noon of the Reagan day. Scott La Rock and KRS-1 were bunkered down in the Bronx with handguns, ammo belt, grenade, and brick cell phone. Whether or not they intended to, they recalled southern revolutionary Robert F. Williams's bracing 1962 Black power manifesto, *Negroes with Guns.*

In 1959, Williams, an integrationist who supported armed self-defense, was thrown out of the NAACP. But his ideas helped theorize the shift from Civil Rights nonviolence to Black Power confrontation. In 1967, Huey Newton set Williams's concept in motion, using a California law that allowed individuals to carry loaded firearms in public. His Black Panther Party began brandishing rifles at rallies in the parks and streets of Oakland. When a white legislator tried to overturn the law, the Panthers stormed into the California State Capitol and national consciousness.

Those days had been long since eclipsed by counterrevolution and crack. But Public Enemy tapped back into that urgent theatricality when they called themselves "the Black Panthers of rap." On the shadowy basement shot for the cover of *Yo! Bum Rush the Show,* Chuck D was the rightstarter/"riot starter," the only one bathed in Muslim white. Professor Griff looked in from the right in a red beret. Flavor Flav leaned his hand forward as if out of DONDI's *Children of the Grave* burner to consecrate the wax. Another black hand reached down from the corner to press the turntable's Start button to begin the revolution. Across the bottom ran the punchline, perfectly pitched and in repetition: THE GOVERNMENT'S RESPONSIBLE ... THE GOVERNMENT'S RESPONSIBLE ... THE GOVERNMENT'S RESPONSIBLE ...

Old school rappers—and most of the new schoolers, for that matter—invited comparison with entertainers like Cab Calloway, Pigmeat Markham, Rufus Thomas, Slim Gaillard. But Public Enemy and Boogie Down Productions pointed back to the voices of Black radicalism, heard on the albums of the Watts Prophets, the Last Poets, H. Rap Brown, and Gil Scott-Heron. While the new political radicals were out in the streets and on the campuses fighting apartheid and racism, Public Enemy and Boogie Down Productions repped the new cultural radical vanguard. Preparing to emerge from the darkness, they demanded to be heard as the expression of a new generation's definition of blackness.

THE NEW VANGUARD

The key issue of the '80s was representation. The political radicals saw overwhelming whiteness in institutions of power and fought for multiculturalism and diversity. The cultural radicals saw an ocean of negative images and tried to reverse the tide with their own visions.

From Fort Greene, a filmmaker named Spike Lee crashed through the gates of the movie industry with independently produced box-office hits, *She's Gotta Have It* and *School Daze*, unapologetic slices of Black life that refused to cater to *Superfly* blaxploitation cliches or Eddie Murphy crossover expectations. During the '70s, after the success of Melvin Van Peebles's breakthrough, *Sweet Sweetback's Baadasssss Song*, Hollywood had co-opted and finally crushed Black indie filmmaking sensibilities. In the '80s, communities of color boycotted Hollywood for the "cultural insensitivity" of films like *Fort Apache: The Bronx* and *Year of the Dragon*. But with Lee's success, Black filmmakers—including Robert Townsend, Keenen Ivory Wayans, Charles Burnett, John Singleton, Warrington and Reginald Hudlin and Allen and Albert Hughes—again received cautious studio backing.

Like Spike Lee, Chuck and his crew were ready to storm the citadel. He says, "We were all gonna bumrush the business from a bunch of different angles, be it radio, journalism, records." Chuck and Harry Allen, who had begun writing for the *Brooklyn City Sun* and *The Village Voice*, regarded mass media as inherently hostile to Black people. Allen, the "media assassin," coined the term "hip-hop activism" to describe how they could turn their culture into a weapon of resistance.

For the hip-hop generation, popular culture became the new frontline of the struggle. While the political radicals fought a rear-guard defense against right-wing attacks on the victories of the Civil Rights and Black Power movements, the cultural radicals stormed the machines of mythmaking. Their intention was not only to take their message into the media, but take *over* the media with their message. Pop music, rap radio, indie film, cultural journalism—these could all be staging areas for guerilla strikes.

SUCKAS NEVER PLAY ME

After Public Enemy finished *Yo! Bum Rush the Show*, Chuck came down to reconnect with Harry. Chuck was angry that, while white critics were excoriating him for his pro-Black nationalism, Black radio had remained indifferent to Public Enemy's music and message.

Black radio was a medium that survived on a paradox: integration had made it both obsolete and more necessary than ever. Before the '60s, Black radio had been a crucial space for marginalized Black voices. As the 1970s proceeded, it began to reflect the desires of a professional class trying to make good in the white world. The reactionary 1980s demanded an outlet for a resurgent rage against racism that united the middle class and the so-called underclass. But, caught up in the crossover, black radio was now afraid of being "too black." Chuck found this state of affairs maddening.

He and Harry sat down to plot an attack. The result was an article in the February 1988 issue of *Black Radio Exclusive*, an industry magazine targeted at Black music executives. In the interview, Chuck unleashed his 2,000-pound Uzi on the Black bourgeoisie. He said, "R&B *teaches* you to shuffle your feet, be laid back, don't be offensive, don't make no waves because, *look at us! We're fitting in as well as we can!*"[14]

Picking up a copy of *BRE*, he read it aloud: *Favorite Car*: Mercedes Sports. *Favorite vacation spot*: Brazil … Look at them! They're going for Mercedes, Audis and BMWs … And this is what all these boot-lickin', handkerchief-head, materialistic niggers want!"

Harry, playing the straight man, protested, "But Chuck, *BRE* is a music trade journal, not a mass circulation newspaper or magazine."

"But even so, Black radio has its responsibilities. The question they ought to be answering is, 'How we gonna make our listeners, the Black nation, rise?'" Chuck said, alluding to a never-aired rap classic by Brother D and The Collective Effort. "The juggernaut of white media never stops. We have to build a system that consistently combats and purifies that info that Black America gets through the media. Instead, Black radio is pushing a format that promises 'More Music, Less Talk,' which is the worst thing.

"The point is that there's no hard information in any of these formats. Where's the news about our lives in this country? Whether or not radio plays us, millions of people listen to rap because rap is America's TV station. Rap gives you the news on all phases of life, good and bad, pretty and ugly: drugs, sex, education, love, money, war, peace—you name it."[15]

In time, this idea would harden into Chuck's most famous soundbite, that rap was Black America's CNN, an alternative, youth-controlled media network that could pull a race fragmented by integration back together again. Here was the meaning of the media bumrush: to force media—Black or white—inimical to the interests of young Blacks to expose itself, and to break open a space for these voiceless to represent themselves more truthfully.

At the end of the article, in bold, read this disclaimer: "The interview with Chuck D in no way reflects the views of Columbia Records."

NEVER WALK ALONE

And so the Trojan horse rolled through the gates. Bill Adler and indie publicist Leyla Turkkan pitched Chuck D to rock editors and writers as "the new Bob Dylan." In a year, Chuck D had probably done more interviews than any other rapper to that point. "Our interviews," Chuck says, "were better than most people's shows."

Chuck treated his mostly white interrogators as adversaries. He often maumaued them, as if to extract a toll for every patronizing indignity and every highway robbery ever suffered by an old-schooler. He had never forgotten how the media treated Run DMC, and this antagonistic stance remained a constant for Public Enemy's first decade. When Harry Allen later became the crew's publicist, he added the additional honorific of "Director of Enemy Relations."

The British tabloid music press found this package irresistible, and with a strange mixture of fanboy irony, Frankfurt School skepticism and thinly disguised racial fear, they began calling Public Enemy the world's most dangerous band. Their music was so good it was scary. Their idea that rap should advance the radicalism of the Black Panthers and the Black Muslims—and that the white media's role was simply to transmit these messages—was even scarier.

In fact, Public Enemy was still trying to figure out what it was about. Stephney watched from the Def Jam offices as Chuck went out on the road and had an epiphany. Chuck told a reporter, "When kids have no father image, who fulfills that role? The drug dealer in the neighborhood? Motherfucking Michael Jordan? Rappers come along and say, 'This is everything you want to be.

You want to be like me, I'm your peer, and I talk to you every day.' So the kid is being raised by LL Cool J, because LL Cool J is talking to the kid more directly than his parents ever did."[16]

Public Enemy's worldview began with a scathing generational critique of Black America. In a 1987 interview with Simon Reynolds, Chuck laid out his view of history:

> There was a complacency in the '70s after the civil rights victories of the '60s. Plus some of our leaders were killed off, others sold out or fled. There was propaganda by the state to make it seem like things had changed, a policy of tokenism elevating a few Blacks to positions of prominence, on TV shows and stuff, while the rest was held down. Blacks couldn't understand how they'd suddenly got these advantages, and so they forgot, they got lazy, they failed to teach their young what they had been taught in the sixties about our history and culture, about how *tight* we should be. And so there was a loss of *identity*—we began to think we were accepted as Americans, when in fact we *still* face a double-standard every minute of our lives.[17]

Public Enemy's theme was Black collectivity, the one thing that had been lost in the post-Civil Rights bourgeois individualist goldrush. Over the years, rap groups had shrunk down to duos, but Public Enemy brought the crew back. They rolled deep, because Black people always overcame through strength in numbers. The S1Ws epitomized the crew's values: strength, unity, self-defense and survival skills. They carried plastic Uzis as props to show that they were not slaves. They were in control because they were armed with knowledge. Violence became their primary, and most often misunderstood, metaphor.

Stephney says, "In dealing with the apparent day-to-day, minute-by-minute cultural power that Chuck saw Public Enemy wield, I think he truly and legitimately believed that you could create a generation of young people who had a drive and ambition to make serious change and reform within the community."

He adds, "Was it something that was mapped out by all of us at 510 South Franklin—a ten-point Panther-like plan on how we were going to take over the media? No." As the crew moved out into the world and encountered resistance from white journalists who took their symbolism on its face, they began freestyling their message. Stephney chuckles, "A good portion of Public Enemy was jazz improvisation."

DOING CONTRADICTION RIGHT

Like Bambaataa, Chuck had been raised within his mother's embrace of Black Panther-styled revolutionary nationalism and anticolonial Pan-Africanism. On his first presidential election ballot, he voted for Gus Hall and Angela Davis, the Communist Party ticket. In rhyme, he boasted that he was "rejected and accepted as a communist." He told a writer from the glossy teen zine *Right On!*: "We are talking about bringing back the Black Panther movement and Communism. That's dead serious. That's going a little too deep, but that's our edge."[18]

Yet he had also been raised on James Brown's "Say It Loud (I'm Black and I'm Proud)," and "I Don't Want Nobody to Give Me Nothing (Open the Door, I'll Get It Myself)," anthems that seemed not only to speak to the Black Panther's Sacramento takeover, but to the rise of the Booker T. Washington-like Black conservative movement that would push for economic self-sufficiency and the end of civil-rights programs like affirmative action. When Public Enemy was opening for the Beastie Boys, Professor Griff played cassettes of Farrakhan and Khallid Abdul Muhammad on the tour bus. Chuck listened closely. Here were the ultimate public enemies.

So Public Enemy's worldview did not adhere to traditional politics. Stephney, for instance, worked closely with civil rights organizations, and closely watched mainstream politics, but refused to join any political party. As Minister of Information, Griff told reporters Public Enemy was drawing on the thinking of Malcolm X, Mao Zedong, the Ayatollah Khomeini, Moammar Khaddafi, Winnie and Nelson Mandela and Minister Farrakhan.[19] As for Chuck, a self-declared communist captivated by Farrakhan, he says now, "I don't know what I was. I definitely wasn't a capitalist. And I definitely wasn't American."

In all of the crew's frequent discussions of politics, Stephney says, ideology had never come into question. Stephney admits, "In retrospect, I *wish* we had legitimate discourse about economic systems and what made sense and what didn't." In his autobiography, Chuck did not describe his core philosophy in terms of ideology but instead something close to fraternal responsibility.

> What Flavor believes and what Griff believes may be two different things, but they were both a part of Public Enemy. What Drew believes and what James Allen believes may be two different things. It's my job to bring it to a center point and say what's true for all of us. "We're Black, we fight for our people and we respect our fellow human beings." Once you start getting into tit-for-tat rhetoric, then you fall into a sea full of contradiction."[20]

Stephney says, "Chuck sees much of what he does through the lens of sports. Teams. Teamwork. Working together as much as you possibly can until it may become too difficult on certain issues." The concept of the public enemy brought together Huey Newton and Elijah Muhammad, Assata Shakur and Sister Ava Muhammad. Teamwork—an NBA-era take on Black collectivity—was a manifestation of Black love.

But white and Black critics alike began to bait Chuck and Griff, especially on questions of racial separatism, homosexuality and militarism. Griff and Chuck often responded with lines straight from Farrakhan's and Khallid Abdul Muhammad's speeches. It was agit-prop, theater, call and response. It got the desired rise out of journalists.

They read the crew's militaristic symbolism, Chuck's aggressive approach, Griff's sometimes bizarre pronouncements and Public Enemy's encompassing embrace of Black Marxism and Black Islam as revealing of undercurrents of violent fascism. After interviewing Chuck and Griff, Simon Reynolds wrote:

> Ahem. What *can* I say? Rectitude in the face of chaos. An admiration for Colonel Khadaffi ("Blacks in America didn't know who to side with"). Harmonious totality. No faggots. Uniform and drill. It all sounds quite logical and needed, the way they tell it. And it's all very very dodgy indeed.
>
> If there's one thing more scary than a survivalist, it's a whole bunch of survivalists organised into a regiment. ... Fortunately, Public Enemy and Security of The First World are sufficiently powerless ("52 and growing") to remain fascinating to us pop swots, rather than disturbing. ... Let's hope it stays that way.[21]

Despite abhorring the crew's politics, the British music press took Public Enemy seriously enough to declare *Yo! Bum Rush the Show* one of the best albums of the year. Back home it was another story.

One key critic, John Leland, who wrote for *SPIN* and *The Village Voice*, set the tone early, ducking the group's politics entirely when he confessed that he found Chuck boring. "I like a good time," he wrote, "and when Flavor Flav says he's got girls on his jock like ants on candy, or threatens to scatter suckers' brains from here to White Plains … yo that's when I'm hooked."[22]

Stung by the criticism, Chuck told a British reporter he had gone looking for Leland at an industry reception to "fuck him up bad."[23] Later Chuck wrote "Don't Believe the Hype" and "Bring the Noise," dumping his critics in the same wastebin as racist cops, corrupt conservatives and Black radio programmers. It was the first shot in what would become an increasingly vituperative relationship with the American press.

But the group also agreed to play a National Writer's Union benefit with Sonic Youth to support the freelancers' bitter fight for recognition against *The Village Voice's* management. "They do contradiction right," wrote *Voice* columnist R.J. Smith, "like publicly dissing music crits for what they've said about Public Enemy and then coming off by far the most militant in their solidarity with writers. Like quoting Malcolm X and saying Blacks deserve $250 billion in reparations *and* playing a benefit on the 18th for Jesse."[24]

THE NEW SCHOOL RISES

None of this press stuff would matter much if they didn't sell records. And at that point, the album had barely sold 100,000 copies. Against the Def Jam/Rush roster—with Run DMC, Whodini, LL Cool J and the Beastie Boys all pushing platinum-plus—it was a huge disappointment.

The record did decently in the south and the midwest, but New York City wasn't feeling the group. Melle Mel heckled the crew at their first show at the Latin Quarter. Mr. Magic played "Public Enemy #1" only once, making a point of saying that he hated it. And in Queens, Magic's DJ, Marlon "Marley Marl" Williams was making them look played-out with his sonic innovations.

Marley had been a studio apprentice to Arthur Baker, watching him struggle with the early, prohibitively expensive Fairlight sampler. In 1983, Marley launched his own producing career with a classic single, "Sucker DJs (I Will Survive)," featuring his smooth-rapping then-girlfriend, Dimples D. On his early dance records, like Aleem's 1984 club hit, "Release Yourself," he used a sampler to repeat and pitch up and down vocal snippets: "Release yourself! Re-re-rererere-rererere-release yourself! Yo-yo-yo-yourself!" While trying to sample a voice for another song on his affordable new E-mu Emulator, he caught a snare snap. Punching it a few times, he suddenly realized the machine's latent rhythmic capabilities.

On the 1986 hit "The Bridge" by MC Shan, he revealed the fruits of his discovery, with a booming loop of The Honeydrippers' "Impeach the President" drum break. No more tinny, programmed DMX or Linn drums, which stiffened the beat and reduced most rappers to sing-songy rhyming. On top, Marl kept his vocalists bathed in billowing Rubinesque arena echoes, but on the bottom, the groove suddenly felt slippery. Inevitably, his rappers responded with more intricate rhymes.

By contrast, Hank, Eric and Keith had made "Public Enemy #1" the old fashioned way—with Eric banging out the drums in real time, and a long two-inch tape loop of "Blow Your Head" that stretched across the room and around a microphone stand. Marl's sampler breakthrough forever altered rap production techniques. It wasn't clear Public Enemy could stay competitive.

The Black Belt had bred a new school, and these artists—Biz Markie, De La Soul, JVC Force, Craig Mack (then known as MC EZ) and EPMD, even their homies, Son of Bazerk, Serious Lee Fine, True Mathematics and Kings of Pressure—were breathing down P.E.'s necks. And then there was Marley Marl's roommate, a DJ from the Black 'burbs of Queens named Eric Barrier, and his rapper, a Five Percenter from Wyandanch, Long Island, named William Griffin, Jr. (no relation to Professor Griff) who called himself Rakim Allah.

Rakim was about to graduate from high school, where he was the star quarterback, when a mutual friend introduced him to Eric B. The two hit it off, and Barrier asked Marl about recording something in their studio. They headed into Marl's studio and cut Rakim's demo, "Check Out My Melody." MC Shan sat in.

Rakim obviously had lyrics, battle rhymes funneled through Five Percenter millenarian poetics. He didn't just slay MCs, he took them out in three sets of seven. "My unusual style will confuse you a while," he rhymed. "If I was water, I'd flow in the Nile."

Shan and Marl weren't sure they understood this guy. At the time Shan's excitable high-pitched style ruled New York City. But Rakim refused to raise his voice. "Me and Marley would look at each other like, 'What kind of rap style is that? That shit is wack,'" Shan recalled.[25] "More energy, man!" he yelled at Rakim.[26]

Figuring "My Melody" was too sluggish, they gave Rakim another beat that was almost ten beats-per-minute faster. Based on Fonda Rae's "Over Like a Fat Rat" and James Brown's "Funky President" and alluding to Marl's by-now famous jacking of "Impeach the President," the concept became "Eric B. Is President," Marl and Shan listened to Rakim's intro in amazement:

> I came in the door I said it before
> I never let the mic magnetize me no more

In the lyric, Rakim described the act of rhyming as if it were a pit bull on a long leash, an undertow pulling into a deep ocean of words—above all, a dangerous habit from which there was no return:

> But it's biting me, fighting me, inviting me to rhyme
> I can't hold it back
> I'm looking for the line

Rakim rocked a weird mix of braggadocio and self-consciousness, a metarhyme—encompassing the paralysis of stage-fright and the release of the moment of first utterance, all delivered with an uncanny sense of how to use silence and syncopation, lines spilling through bars, syllables catching off-beats, it made them believers. Rap had found its Coltrane.

Rakim came from a musical family. His mother was a jazz and opera singer. His aunt was R&B legend Ruth Brown. His brothers were session musicians who had worked on early rap records. He was a gifted saxophonist and had participated in statewide student competitions. He switched from tenor to baritone sax because he preferred the deeper tone.

The Griffins had left Brooklyn to come to Wyandanch, an unincorporated town of seven thousand, one of the oldest in the Black Belt and deteriorating into one of the most troubled. Blacks began moving there during the 1950s, expanding southward toward the wealthy white beach community of Babylon. By the end of the decade whites in Babylon rezoned its northern border from residential to industrial. From there, Wyandanch went downhill.

William was a smart student with a lean athleticism and a nose for trouble that kept him close to the streets. By his teens, he was a graffiti writer turned stick-up kid, getting high, staying paid, holding down corners in Wyandanch and spinning drunkenly out of the projects in Fort Greene, before he became righteous, took the name Ra King Islam Master Allah, recircled Strong Island and Brooklyn to build from cipher to cipher.

The graf burners on his bedroom wall were covered over by primer. Photos of Elijah Muhammad, Malcolm X and Minister Louis Farrakhan went up. He met Eric, Marl and Shan, cut the record, abandoned a football scholarship to the State University at Stony Brook, signed with Rush Management, and became a rap legend.

Rakim never smiled. Draped in African gold, inside Dapper-Dan customized *faux*-Gucci suits, he stood tall in a way that assured he was in supreme control of his body. He was, as he put it, "serious as cancer." He asked rhetorical questions like, "Who can keep the average dancer hyper as a heart attack?" Chuck D and Rakim had come from similar circumstances and had similar aspirations for themselves and the race, but they had different ways of seeking their utopias. As Greg Tate wrote, "Chuck D's forte is the overview, Rakim's is the innerview."

Rakim had joined the Nation of Gods and Earths, better known as the Five Percenters, in 1985, the year that Supreme Mathematics signified as: "*Build Power.*" Founded in Harlem (renamed Mecca) in 1963 by a charismatic former student minister of the Nation of Islam, Clarence 13X, their core belief was taken from Lost-Found Lesson Number 2. Eighty-five percent of the people were uncivilized, mentally deaf, dumb and blind slaves; 10 percent were bloodsuckers of the poor; and 5 percent were the poor righteous teachers with knowledge of self, enlightened teachers of freedom, justice and equality, destined to civilize the uncivilized.

Like Bambaataa, Rakim was now on a lifetime mission to lift the word from the street into the spiritual. Whether he could escape the social prisons represented by Fort Greene and Wyandanch was immaterial. Rakim told a journalist, "You're dealing with heaven while you're walking through hell. When I say heaven, I don't mean up in the clouds, because heaven is no higher than your head, and hell is no lower than your feet."[27]

"It's 120 degrees of lessons," he told Harry Allen, "and you gotta complete it by Knowledge, which is 120, Wisdom, another 120, and Understanding, which is 360 degrees. That's what I'm saying. 360 degrees I revolve. And 360 degrees is a complete circle—a cipher. So you must *complete* it."[28]

CLOSING THE CIRCLE

In rhyme, Chuck compared himself to Coltrane, but he had more in common with Miles Davis, whose earthy middle-class rage always boiled beneath the mask of blue minimalist cool. The streetwise mystic Rakim was closer to Coltrane, and "I Know You Got Soul" was Rakim's "Giant Steps," a marvel of rhythmic precision and indelible imagery, a masterful declaration of transcendent black identity and a certifiable crowd-pleaser.

Based on the Bobby Byrd song of the same name and featuring a monstrous Funkadelic drum-roll by Ben Powers, Jr., "Soul" began with unusual flattery to its audience—an apology for keeping them waiting. It described writing as a difficult sacrament, but a necessary rite to uplift the race. In the end, the performance of the words—like a triumphant Ali title bout—became an act of deliverance.

"I Know You Got Soul" dropped only weeks after *Yo! Bum Rush the Show*. When Chuck and Hank heard it, they realized that hip-hop's aesthetic and political development had suddenly accelerated. Envious and yet confident that the game had somehow shifted decidedly in their direction, they retreated to 510 South Franklin to close the circle that Eric B. & Rakim had begun.

"We knew we had to make something that was aggressive," Hank says. "Chuck's voice is so powerful and his tone is so rich that you can't put him on smooth, silky, melodic music. It's only fitting to put a hailstorm around him, a tornado behind him, so that when his vocals come across, the two complement each other."

Unlike Marley Marl's method—which flowed with the possibilities of the new technology, privileging sampling and mixing over arranging—the Bomb Squad mapped out the samples in the song's key and structure, piled them atop each other, then played them by hand as if they were a band. A Bomb Squad composition mounted tension against all-too-brief release.

Their musical method mirrored their worldview. "We were timing freaks," Hank says. "[W]e might push the drum sample to make it a little bit out of time, to make you feel uneasy. We're used to a perfect world, to seeing everything revolve in a circle. When that circle is off by a little bit, that's weird. ... It's not predictable."[29] Public Enemy was never about elevating to perfect mathematics or merging with sleek machines, it was about wrestling with the messy contradictions of truth. "It's *tightrope* music," Chuck said, "in confrontation with itself."[60]

Hank and Chuck pulled out James Brown's "Funky Drummer," the not-yet-famous Clyde Stubblefield break, and the JBs' 1970 single, "The Grunt, Part 1," which had an elemental, squawking intro reminiscent of "Blow Your Head." On his Ensoniq Mirage sampler, they grabbed two seconds of Catfish Collins's guitar, Bobby Byrd's piano and, most important, Robert McCollough's sax squeal, sampled it at a low rate to grit it up, and then pounded it into ambulance claustrophobia. Underneath, Flavor Flav made the Akai drum machine boom and stutter. The only release came in a break that layered a live go-go groove, funky guitar, a horn-section blast and the drums from Jefferson Starship's "Rock Music." When Terminator X transformed Chubb Rock's shout, "Rock and roll!", "Rebel" staked a claim to more than soul. The effect was hypnotic and relentless.

From an intro as memorable as Rakim's through an ending that declared it was "my time," Chuck brought pure boxing-ring drama, with Rakim as muse and opponent. Chuck offered props where they were due—"I got soul too"—but reserved for himself the title of "the voice of power." Rakim had rapped, "It ain't where you're from, it's where you're at," an epigram not at all unlike "Who feels it, knows it." Chuck flipped that into an explicit call for Black solidarity: "No matter what the name, we're all the same—pieces in one big chess game." His lines encapsulated P.E.'s game-face competitiveness, anti-authoritarian howl and gleefully punning, polycultural, signifying trashing of Standard English:

Impeach the president
Pulling out the raygun (Reagan)

Zap the next one
I could be ya shogun!

"Man, you got to slow down," Flavor yelled over the break. "Man, you're losing 'em!"

Titled "Rebel Without a Pause," it was the perfect balance to "I Know You Got Soul." "Soul" moved the crowd in divine, timeless ritual. "Rebel" was a Black riot. Stephney took the record to club DJs at the Latin Quarter and the Rooftop, places that had dissed P.E., and watched from the booths as the fader slid over to "Rebel" and the room hit the boiling point like a kettle. It was John Brown playing "Soul Power," Kool Herc spinning Mandrill's "Fencewalk" or Grandmaster Flash dropping Baby Huey's "Listen to Me" all over again. "Just to see kids go crazy," Stephney remembers. "In many instances, fights started."

"Rebel," and its follow-up, "Bring the Noise"—in which Chuck ripped crack-peddling, Black incarceration and the death penalty, and then compared critics' condemnation of his support for Farrakhan to being shot by cops, all in just the first verse—captured the tensions of the time and externalized them. The records stormed the airwaves, boomboxes and car stereos that summer and fall. They became unavoidable. Public Enemy sounded like the new definition of black power—smarter, harder, faster, leaner and winning.

OBJECTIVE QUESTIONS

1. What did music critic Frank Owen say about the music Russell Simmons and Rick Rubin were producing at Def Jam?
2. What was Hank Boxley's mobile DJ unit called?
3. How did Chuck D say raps from the suburbs differ from raps from the inner city?
4. Charlton Ridenhour originally approached Hank Boxley about_____.
5. What inspired Charlton Ridenhour to start writing rhymes?
6. Who coined the term "Hip Hop activist"?
7. Who did Rick Rubin hire as Def Jam's first full-time staffer?
8. At 32, he was at least a generation older than anyone else on the Def Jam stall and twice as old as L.L. Kool J.
9. In his last column for CMJ, Bill Stephney said he hoped to form a group that was equal parts _____ and _____.
10. What was Flavor Flav's role in Public Enemy?
11. What did Chuck D say about R&B in an interview in *Black Radio Exclusive* in 1988?
12. Chuck D said, "_____ were better than most people's shows."
13. Who did Marley Marl apprentice with?
14. What are the characteristics of Marley Marl's productions?
15. Who famously rapped, "It ain't where you're from its where you're at"?

16. According to the author, besides Public Enemy, the other group that represented the bumrush aesthetic was_____.

QUESTIONS FOR FURTHER THOUGHT, RESEARCH, AND DISCUSSION

1. Examine the question. Is integration necessary for African-Americans to succeed?
2. Public Enemy are from the first generation to grow up in the post civil rights era and are among the first to receive the benefits of affirmative action. How does that affect their message?
3. What are Chuck D's political beliefs?
4. Discuss the difference in personalities and the aesthetics of Russell Simmons and Rick Rubin. How did that mix affect the business?
5. What are the intended metaphors of the plastic Uzis and the revolutionary rhetoric?
6. Research in more detail the life of the self-described "cultural radical" John Sinclair.
7. Compare Public Enemy's purposeful confrontation with the media to the unfriendly media image of some other bands, like the Rolling Stones or the Sex Pistols.
8. Who was Ruth Brown? What were her hits?
9. The author compares Rakim Allah to John Coltrane and Chuck D to Miles Davis. Are those fair comparisons? Where do the analogies break down?
10. How did Michael Jackson succeed in integrating MTV in 1983?

KRS-One

By Charles Aaron

Charles Aaron is a prolific Hip Hop journalist who has written for VIBE magazine and is currently a senior editor at *Spin* magazine. He has written about Hip Hop and related music for many publications including *The Village Voice*, VIBE, and *Why Music Sucks*. The first rap record he ever purchased was *Roxanne's Revenge*.

Alan Light is the editor and chief of *Spin*. He was VIBE's founding music editor and served as the editor and chief from 1994 to 1997. He is the editor of the best-selling illustrated biography *Tupak Shakur*.

No rapper's life parallels the meteoric rise of Hip Hop and its inherent contradictions more than does the life of Lawrence Brown or KRS One. Where ever and whenever the discussion about Hip Hop gets heated, one invariably finds that KRS One has to voice his opinion. A homeless drop out who spent his adolescents in a public library, he is the self-proclaimed "Teacher" and sometimes lecturer at Yale and Harvard. Often considered the beginning of "conscious rap", his oft-quoted line "Its not about a salary / Its all about reality" is still the mantra of his many followers. This engaging article traces KRS One's history and his relationship with partner Scott La Rock. This article also contains another accounting of the famous "Bridge Wars" with Marley Marl and DJ Mr. Magic.

"KRS-ONE"
FROM *THE VIBE HISTORY OF HIP HOP*

THE NEWARK (N.J.) Collaboration Group's Unity Jam, held November 7, 1991, was the type of "positive" gathering of African-American youth that armchair politicians and op-ed columnists usually wet their pants over. Featuring panels that discussed teen parenthood, religion, AIDS, police brutality and the high homicide rate among young black and Latino males, the event was organized almost entirely by high school and college kids. And their choice for keynote speaker? None other than hip hop's stentorian mentor, KRS-One of Boogie Down Productions.

A homeless teenager who became an internationally successful rapper and a lecturer at Harvard and Yale, KRS-One boasts a bootstrap success story of mythological proportions. Self-educated and self-proclaimed as "The Teacher," he, along with Public Enemy's Chuck D, redefined hip hop as a culture not only of music, graffiti, and breakdancing, but of *big ideas*. His funk meant to free your mind; your wack ass could follow somebody else. And for hip hop fans of the late '80s who had grown tired of simply throwing their hands in the air like they just didn't care, he was virtually a messianic figure.

From 1987–1989, Boogie Down Productions recorded three legendary albums: their debut, *Criminal Minded,* brilliantly leavened Run-D.M.C.'s b-boy bravado with the broken-glass poetry of Melle Mel's "The Message," while DJ Scott La Rock (and engineer Ced Gee of Ultramagnetic MC's) tautly scratched up blasts of James Brown gone wicked inna dancehall; *By All Means Necessary* (written and produced by KRS-One after Scott La Rock's murder in 1987) offset its more politically explicit lyrics with even more infectiously playful tracks; and *Ghetto Music: The Blueprint of Hip Hop* was a stark broadside, like a sound system lashing out in all directions. Unlike punk rock, which laid waste to the lies of *right now!,* hip hop, at least in KRS-One's fevered dreams, rearranged the past to depict the present. But perhaps more important for kids like those who organized Unity Jam, KRS-One was a survivor of the ghetto's gauntlet. He was an older brother who knew the tricks of the trade.

"Why you wanna go to college?". bellowed Zizwe Mtafuta-Ukweli, director of African Student Programs at the University of California–Riverside, and director of KRS-One's multimedia "movement," HEAL (Human Education Against Lies). The audience responded, "To get our education!" Zizwe asked again, "For money?" ("No! Education!") After a pause, Zizwe narrowed his gaze. "Then you might be going to the wrong place. ... Let me tell you, I have a master's degree." (Cheers from the crowd.) "Now, that's dope, but I'm a slave with a master's degree. ... I can tell you that college is set up to wreck you and destroy your life, to turn you into a slave and a ho." Zizwe exhaled and introduced KRS-One, who indulged in 45 minutes of the exact same rhetoric. Finally, the floor was opened to questions.

"Do you think going to college is wrong?" inquired a bewildered female student. KRS-One quickly answered with a proverb: "For some of us to be revolutionaries, others of us have to be house niggers." Dead silence in the hall. "No university is built by black people for black people, therefore if you're going to the university, you're going to be taught your murderer's ignorance;

the education you get is dipped in bullshit. Your degree is not going to get you a job. You get jobs through family and friends."

"You gonna be my friend?" another young woman asked sarcastically, drawing scattered giggles.

Like a clueless parent, KRS-One had quickly managed to alienate most of the Unity Jam audience. These kids, who probably curled up and went to sleep with BDP's "My Philosophy" flowing through their Walkmans, trooped home confused and crestfallen. What's more, KRS-One exhibited a much different opinion when the student in question was a member of his own family. Six months later, in *The Source,* he demanded that his younger brother Kenny "go to college, one of us gotta go to college. Somebody gotta get some kind of education. … I don't care what the degree is in, just get something."

KRS-One has never failed to passionately contradict himself—footnotes, bibliography, and dope beats included. Both driven and trapped by an impoverished childhood, he has triumphed and blundered in blunt strokes. His aphoristic rhymes ("It's not about a salary / It's all about reality"; "We got to put our heads together and stop the violence / 'Cuz real bad boys move in silence") have become some of the culture's central myths and truths. In many ways, his life's story *is* the evolution of hip hop—the roots in poverty and gang culture; the calls for consciousness collapsing into violence; the pop spectacle of racial martyrdom. But above it all, he has always possessed the plainspoken, live-wire ability to say what few others had the smarts or nerve to think.

Born Lawrence Brown in Park Slope, Brooklyn, August 20, 1965, he was the eldest son of Jacqueline Jones, a real estate secretary, and Sheffield Brown, a Barbadian handyman (and illegal alien who was soon to be deported). In 1969, his mother remarried, to a United Nations security guard, John Parker, who moved the family to Harlem. Parker, who kept a large gun collection, began to abuse Jackie and the kids. "My mother was so caught up in wanting to be married, she sort of just allowed it to happen," KRS-One solemnly told *ego trip* in 1995. Parker left in 1972, the family returned to Brooklyn, "and that started our life of poverty" (Jackie's third marriage ended in 1975).

By the mid-'70s, Lawrence (known as Kris, short for his nickname Krisna, a reference to the Krishna religion) dreamed of MC'ing and doing graffiti—where he developed the tag KRS-ONE, for "Kris-Number One." But he clashed with his mother, who preached spirituality and African history to her sons, pushing them to excel in school. At 13, Kris started playing hooky, eventually leaving home in 1981 at age 16 to live on the streets (his mother didn't see him again until the fall of 1988). He slept in the parks (Prospect, Wingate, Central) and on the F train, taking odd jobs and obsessively reading at the Brooklyn Public Library: "I wore a size thirteen shoe, was a little over six feet, had pimples all over my face … I was nerd like a muthafucka!" he recalls. One day when he was 17, Kris walked over the Williamsburg Bridge to Manhattan, discovered a men's shelter on the Bowery, and before long, was placed in a group home. There he earned his high school general equivalency diploma and considered attending the School of Visual Arts.

But if there's one constant in KRS-One's life it's his distrust of institutions. So instead of enrolling in college, he ran with the United Artists graffiti crew, which included Fab 5 Freddy (who later directed a couple of Boogie Down Productions videos); the crew also had a loose affiliation with the Casanovas, a Bronx gang spun off from the Black Spades. After serving time for transporting marijuana from Upstate New York, Kris, 20, moved into the Bronx's Franklin Armory Men's Shelter, where his social worker was Scott Sterling, 22. "If I hadn't met Scott then we probably would have fought," Kris told *Soul Underground.* "He was with another gang, the La Rocks. Coke

La Rock, T. La Rock, Scott La Rock, all of them from the same project." Scott was also a weekend DJ at a club called Broadway International, and he and Kris (along with two other MCs) started recording as Scott La Rock and the Celebrity Three.

Their first single, 1984's "Advance," put stark, jittery beats behind Kris's already unique rhyme style, forcefully enunciating a nuclear alarm. The group soon broke up, and Scott and Kris (renamed 12:41) recorded "Success Is the Word," a song they didn't write, for Sleeping Bag Records; it got a token spin on WBLS by taste-making DJ Mr. Magic. But later, when the duo, now known as Boogie Down Productions, shopped a demo to Magic, he brushed them off. Kris returned to the shelter and wrote the legendary throwdown "South Bronx," an answer to MC Shan's "The Bridge," a Magic fave that big-upped Queens. Released on B-Boy Records in 1986, "South Bronx" was an underground rage, and another answer record, "The Bridge Is Over"—built on a jaunty Supercat piano riff and KRS-One's raggafied gunman lyrics—cemented BDP's rep as hardrocks who backed up their boasts.

The feud between Magic's Queens-based Juice Crew (Shan, Marley Marl, Biz Markie, Big Daddy Kane, Roxanne Shanté) and Bronx loyalists Boogie Down Productions (supported by Kiss-FM's DJ Red Alert, and Chuck Chillout, the Jungle Brothers, et al.) only intensified with the release of BDP's *Criminal Minded* in 1987. Marley Marl even made a persuasive case that his drum reel of trademark snare sounds, which had been swiped from Power Play Studios, was used by producer Ced Gee on the album.

Regardless, *Criminal Minded* transformed hip hop. Stressing the reality behind the music's posturing metaphors, BDP spoke the brutal slang of the street *and* promised revelation. KRS-One's name may have sounded like a "wack radio station" (per Roxanne Shanté), but his voice boomed like Radio Free Hip Hop. While Run-D.M.C. and L.L. Cool J were superheroes chillin' in their own worlds, and Public Enemy was a supergroup swooping down out of the suburban sky, BDP were kids striding up out of the subway. Holding pistols on the *Criminal Minded* front cover while thanking moms on the back, giving shout-outs to specific gangs (Casanovas, Cyprus Boys) while bemoaning violence, Scott and Kris were a funky-fresh brand of b-boy—they waved the culture's contradictions in your face like a dare. Hip hop's future seemed to be theirs; they even moved into their own apartments.

On August 25, 1987—after trying to peacemake between BDP side-kick Derek "D-Nice" Jones and a girlfriend's ex-boyfriend—Scott Sterling, 25, was shot in the head and neck while sitting in his Jeep outside a South Bronx housing project. "I couldn't go to the hospital," KRS-One later told *People*. "I always want to remember him alive." Eight days later, at Def Jam '87 in New York City's Madison Square Garden, "Blastmaster" KRS-One, 22 years old and still an underground enigma, stood on his tiny, allotted portion of the stage next to a wrinkled poster of Scott La Rock and tore through a remarkably controlled version of the single "Poetry" that left early-arriving L.L. Cool J fans gasping for breath, some wiping away tears. "You seem to be the type that only understands / The annihilation and destruction of the next man / That's not poetry, that is insanity / It's simply fantasy, far from reality," he rapped, his huge eyes aglow.

Ten years later, Sean "Puffy" Combs staged an MSG celebration for his murdered friend Christopher Wallace, a.k.a. The Notorious B.I.G., complete with video screens., dance routines, and exploding effects. Its savvy' production now makes KRS-One seem like a nappy-headed innocent; but in fact, after Scott La Rock's passing, KRS-One flashed Bad Boy–like ambition. Inspired by *The Autobiography of Malcolm X,* 1988's *By All Means Necessary* cleverly and obsessively exposed

American hypocrisy—government-sanctioned poverty, crooked cops, legalized abuse of alcohol and tobacco—but caught flack for ideological inconsistencies.

On the album cover, KRS-One posed with an Uzi, staring out a window as if under siege (a nod to Don Charles's famous photo of Malcolm X), then on "Stop the Violence," he righteously rhymed about ending gunplay in hip hop, as if every syllable held volumes of hopeful meaning. On "My Philosophy," he eloquently argued and won about 20 often-conflicting streetcorner debates. Then there were the witty non sequiturs and spiteful boasts—"Ya Slippin'," "I'm Still #1," "Part Time Suckers."

Such was the uneasy birth of "conscious" rap, a two-year phase in which artists such as the Jungle Brothers, Brand Nubian, Queen Latifah, and X-Clan made it cool to flaunt your Afrocentric knowledge. *By All Means Necessary* went gold and shouts of "How many intelligent people in the house?" replaced the suddenly tired "Everybody say ho!" And KRS-One now translated to "Knowledge Reigns Supreme Over Nearly Everyone."

The BDP crew expanded to include D-Nice, Kris's wife, Ramona "Ms. Melodie" Scott, her sister Pam (a.k.a. Harmony), Kris's brother DJ Kenny Parker, producer Ivan "Doc" Rodriguez, and dance-hall DJ Jamal-ski. But it was KRS-One, now billing himself as "The Teacher," who dominated the spotlight. He housed the Op-Ed page of the *New York Times;* went on a 40-city college lecture tour; started the Stop the Violence movement, which raised an estimated $400,000 for the National Urban League with the all-star single "Self Destruction" (featuring Chuck D, Kool Moe Dee, MC Lyte, and others); published a book, *Overcoming Self-Destruction;* and appeared at Earth Day in Washington, D.C., with Michael Stipe, his partner-in-rant on R.E.M.'s "Radio Song."

By the time of 1990's outrageously pedantic *Edutainment,* KRS-One was applying the cut-and-paste DJ aesthetic to his own sociopolitical ideas. He rapped that world history had been produced much like a hip hop record—Eurocentric historians sampled according to what moved the crowd. So KRS-One answered in kind, kicking ghetto linguistics about Egyptology, vegetarianism, and homelessness over tight, bumpy bass lines. But for all his grand pronouncements, at heart KRS-One could also be heartbreakingly boyish, an insecure kid who wouldn't let anyone get close to him. "Love's Gonna Get Cha (Material Love)," with its tick-tock bass line and light Roy Ayers-ish keyboard sample, was an unforgettable, if overheated, sermon against the evils of cheap material fulfillment. (love sadly included). It's not hard to imagine him shouting the song's enraged exit line, "Tell me, what the fuck am I supposed to do?" as he stormed out of his mother's house 10 years before.

For someone who exhorted that we should all think for ourselves, though, "The Teacher" soon became a rather oppressive presence; no hip hop conversation was complete until he dropped in his (extremely loud) two cents. He took breaks to produce Sly and Robbie's *Silent Assassin* album and a solo joint for Harmony; but the HEAL tract *Civilization vs. Technology* was an embarrassment, and the lively if disposable *Live Hardcore Worldwide* was basically ignored. After P.M. Dawn's Prince Be questioned The Teacher's lesson plan in a 1992 *Details* interview, KRS-One gave him a public beatdown, later saying that the incident was a "triumph for hip hop." His best-forgotten *Sex and Violence* album, released that same year as a belated shot at the gangsta rap plague he'd unwittingly helped spawn with the reality rhymes of *Criminal Minded,* swaggered through silly, vindictive cant about social engineering, sucker MCs (!), and statutory rape. In the liner notes, he harshly disowned D-Nice, Ms. Melodie (now the mother of his child), Harmony, and Jamal-ski. He even stopped reading, insisting that the library was where the "lies" were "buried."

After BDP finally dissolved in 1993, KRS-One regrouped and became more of a bottom-line icon, toning down his politics and counseling young artists. Three quality solo albums—*Return of the Boom Bap, KRS-One,* and *I Got Next,* a surprising commercial success—allowed a sense of humor to peek through (on "I Can't Wake Up," he dreamed that he was a blunt being smoked by an all-star cast), and offered hip hop realness, racial uplift, and top-shelf beats courtesy of DJ Premier and Showbiz. "A Friend," from *I Got Next,* was a rare, vulnerable plea for male companionship, rapped over a sample of the jazz standard "Round Midnight".

No longer burdened with starting or refuting trends, "The Teacher" became simply "The MC," a respected, still-skillful elder. Of course, there was the Nike commercial that perverted Gil Scott-Heron's "The Revolution Will Not Be Televised," the clumsy junglist chatting on Goldie's "Digital," and the inevitable Puffy remix ("Step into a World [Rapture's Delight]"). "I'm no Gandhi" he admitted to *USA Today.* "I'm still a black youth in the ghetto. I'm six-foot-four, 260 pounds; I'll stomp somebody if they come in my face."

> *In another room you hear yourself telling a black man that your real name is. … You see yourself scratch your woolly head trying to remember. Then you remember but it is too late. It was probably lost on him anyway.*
> —Cecil Brown, from *The Life and Loves of Mr. Jiveass Nigger*

KRS-One has taken to saying that he *is* hip hop, which is a pretty motherf#&*in' hip hop thing to say, when you think about it (and not because he's ego-trippin' again). While rapping has always been a joyfully desperate shout-out—naming yourself before the next fool does it and steals you blind—this was *some other shit,* as the critical theorists say round the Brooklyn quad. This was KRS-One going past all the woolly-headed identity gaming, the grandiose sobriquets, the Blastmaster This or Notorious That.

Years back, in the much lamented '80s, KRS-One proclaimed that he wanted to use hip hop as a "revolutionary tool for changing the structure of racist America" but he was going past that as well. After more than 10 years and nine albums, after testing hip hop culture's limits and possibilities, KRS-One was finally 'fessing up that hip hop wasn't a tool, a fad, or a political program. It's who he is, and what he cares about most deeply—the ever-evolving styles, the militantly thrilling beats, the undeniable voices, the specters of authenticity and death. An adult still playing a kid's game, KRS-One rolls on like a subway train bombed with cryptic masterpieces, throwing third-rail sparks, hurtling God knows where. Like it or not, by any reasonable definition, the man *is* hip hop.

DISCOGRAPHY

Boogie Down Productions

Criminal Minded (B Boy, 1987). *By All Means Necessary* (Jive/RCA, 1988). *Ghetto Music: The Blueprint of Hip Hop* (Jive/RCA, 1989). *Edutainment* (Jive/RCA, 1990). *Live Hardcore Worldwide* (Jive/RCA, 1991). *Sex and Violence* (Jive/RCA, 1992).

KRS-One

Return of the Boom Bap (Jive/RCA, 1993). *KRS-One* (Jive, 1995). *KRS-One vs. M.C. Shan: The Battle for Rap Supremacy* (Cold Chillin', 1996). *I Got Next* (Jive, 1997).

D-Nice

Call Me D-Nice (Jive/RCA, 1990). *To Tha Rescue* (Jive, 1991).

Harmony

Let There Be Harmony (Virgin, 1990).

HEAL

Civilization vs. Technology (Elektra, 1991).

Heather B.

Takin' Mine (EMI, 1996).

Ms. Melodie

Diva (Jive/RCA, 1989).

Stop the Violence Movement

Self Destruction [EP] (Jive/RCA, 1989).

OBJECTIVE QUESTIONS

1. What was Boogie Down Production's debut album?
2. How did Lawrence Brown get the nickname "Kris"?
3. What was the name of the graffiti crew that he ran with and who else were members?
4. How did he meet Scot Sterling?
5. What was Marley Marl's claim about *Criminal Minded?*
6. What does KRS One stand for?

QUESTIONS FOR FURTHER THOUGHT, RESEARCH, AND DISCUSSION

1. Does KRS One's somewhat tragic childhood give him a different perspective on the truth that a middle-class college educated Chuck D?
2. How does KRS One feel about colleges and college degrees?
3. Discuss the origins and importance of STOP the Violence.
4. KRS One is often described as having a unique style and "flow". Describe his style and what makes it unique and effective.
5. In the 1980s KRS One said that he wanted to use Hip Hop as "a revolutionary tool for changing the structure of racist America." Did he do that? Is that still true?

The Culture Assassins

By Jeff Chang

Chang's broad narrative about West Coast rap begins in 1988, but manages to trace the history of Watts and Compton back to the housing covenants of the 1920s and through the "zoot suit" riots in the 1940s and the race riots in the late 1960s. He also includes the histories and influence of the Black Panthers, the Watts Prophets, and eventually the evolution of the modern day Crips and the Bloods. The rap that came from the West Coast was obviously modeled on what came out of New York, and sometimes in an almost sarcastic and satiric way, but it immediately had its own identity nevertheless. Just like in the Bronx, West Coast Hip Hop started as a dance and sound system culture with its roots in disco and "house," but the dances on the West Coast were different: "locking" instead of "rocking," and the Latin culture mix was chicano instead of Puerto Rican. This not only affected the beats, but the graphics of the graffiti as well. Chang does a fantastic job of covering this subject from almost every angle and includes every pertinent detail and character. Besides the historical perspective, he also describes the culture, the music business, and the reaction to *Straight Outta Compton* from the African-American establishment and the Hip Hop community on the East Coast. After KRS One and Public Enemy had made Hip Hop globally serious, N.W.A. had suddenly made "serious salary" from making Hip Hop very local and exploiting its sensationalism.

"THE CULTURE ASSASSINS" FROM *CAN'T STOP, WON'T STOP*

GEOGRAPHY, GENERATION AND GANGSTA RAP

We *want "poems that kill."*
Assassin poems, Poems that shoot guns.

Poems that wrestle cops into alleys
and take their weapons leaving them dead
—Amiri Baraka

They shot bullets that brought streams of blood and death. Death.
From the age of seven on, Jonathan saw George only during prison visits.
He saw his brother living with the reality of death, every day, every hour, every moment.
—Angela Davis

WHEN NINETEEN-YEAR-OLD O'SHEA Jackson returned to South Central Los Angeles in the summer of 1988, he was hopeful. All he had ever wanted to do in life was rap, and now it looked like he might be able to make something of it. Arizona had been hell—hot, dry and boring. Still, his architectural drafting degree from the Phoenix Institute of Technology might get moms and pops off his back for a few months, and within that time perhaps he could write some rhymes, make some records, cash some checks and soon move out of his folks' house.

Just two years before, he had been a junior at Taft High School, bused from his home in South Central to the suburbs of San Fernando Valley, slipping out on the weekend to grab the microphone at Eve's After Dark nightclub in Compton as the rapper named Ice Cube. He and his partners Tony "Sir Jinx" Wheatob and Darrell "K-Dee" Johnson had a group named CIA (Criminals In Action). They dropped sex rhymes to shocked, delighted crowds over the hits of the day. It was a silly act—Dolemite karaoke over UTFO beats—but it was getting attention. Eve's was owned by Alonzo Williams, and because of Alonzo, Eve's was the place to be. A smooth-talking type who had secured a contract from CBS Records for his recording project, the World Class Wreckin Cru, Lonzo used the money to build a studio in back of the club to lure producing and rapping talent.

Eric Wright was in the crowd every weekend, prowling for talent. Wright had seen the South Central hip-hop scene mature around him in the early eighties. Now the diminutive twenty-three-year-old drug dealer hoped to make some quick cash on rap, a way to go legit after years of hustling. At Eve's, Wright would catch Antoine "DJ Yella" Carraby and Andre "Dr. Dre" Young spinning records. They were members of the Cru, had a mixtape side-hustle going and were learning to make beats in Lonzo's studio. They were also two of the first DJs on KDAY's AM hip-hop radio station to join the taste-making Mixmasters Crew. New tracks that they played on the weekends often became Monday's hottest sellers.

Dre, his cousin Tony and O'Shea had been neighbors in the South Central neighborhood near Washington High School, and Dre had taken a liking to the C.I.A. boys, especially Jackson, with whom he formed a side group called Stereo Crew. He got them a gig at Skateland where he was DJing. He told them how and what to rap—filthy, dirty-down X-rated rhymes. After they stole the show and got invited back, he helped them make mixtapes to get their name out, got them a shot a Eve's, and eventually, a deal to do a single for Lonzo's Kru-Cut Records.

Dre kicked in the bass for C.I.A.'s three cuts. "My Posse" and "Ill-Legal" were Beastie Boys' bites that replaced references to White Castle with lines about cruising down Crenshaw. On the third track, "Just 4 the Cash," Cube rapped, "It's all about making those dollars and cents." Now they were indemnified to Lonzo, who gave them all tiny weekly stipends instead of royalty checks.[1]

Wright had begun talking to Dre, Yella and Jackson individually. Wright told Jackson he would put them all together and form a South Central supergroup. Why not? Jackson figured. "Eazy had a partner named Ron-De-Vu, Dre was in the World Class Wreckin Cru, I was in C.I.A.," recalls Jackson. "We all kinda was committed to these groups so we figured we'd make an all-star group and just do dirty records on the side."

So one night early in 1987, Young and Wright were in Lonzo's studio with a stack of rhymes that Jackson had penned. Wright had bought some time for an East Coast duo called HBO that Dre had found. The idea was that the duo's slower New York-styled cadences and accents would be more marketable than the uptempo techno-pop rhymes that sold everywhere else—Seattle, San Francisco, Miami, Los Angeles. New York, after all, was supposed to represent the epitome of authenticity. But this notion would soon be obsolete.

DANCING TO BANGING

In the early 1980s, one prominent node on the Los Angeles hip-hop map was a downtown club called Radio. It was modele'd on the Roxy's "Wheels of Steel" night, and presided over by local rap kingpin Ice T and jet-setting Zulu Nation DJ Afrika Islam.

New York–style b-boying went off there, but West Coast styles dominated the dancefloor. There was locking, a funk style dance started by the Watts crew, the Campbellockers, in the early '70s; popping, a surging, stuttering elaboration of The Robot, pioneered by Fresno dancer Boogaloo Sam, that would later show up in New York as the Electric Boogaloo; and strutting, a style that had come down from San Francisco's African-American and Filipino 'hoods to take hold with L.A.'s Samoan gangs.[2]

Radio made the Roxy's diversity look like a Benetton ad. Kid Frost and his cholos rolled down to the club in their low-riders, sporting their Pendletons and khakis. There were slumming Hollywood whites and South Central Korean-American one-point-fivers escaping long hours at the family business. Everyone but the hardest brothers left the menacing Blue City Strutters—a Samoan Blood set from Carson that would become the Boo-Yaa Tribe—alone.

When Radio faded, live hip-hop parties spread through the efforts of a popular sound system called Uncle Jam's Army, led by Rodger "Uncle Jam" Clayton who had begun throwing house parties in 1973 in South Central. A decade later, the Army was regularly filling the Los Angeles Convention Center and the Sports Arena. At their wild dances, the Army showed up in army fatigues and bright Egyptian costumes. They stacked thirty-two booming Cerwin-Vega speakers in the shape of pyramids.

Then shit turned real bad real quick.

Dance crews like the Carson Freakateers, Group Sex and the Hot Coochie Mamaz gave way to the Rolling 60s Crips and the Grape Street Boys. Playlists featuring frenetic sensual funk like Prince's "Head" and the Army's own "Yes Yes Yes" slowed down for a new audience that wanted Roger's "So Ruff So Tuff" and George Clinton's "Atomic Dog." The Freak was replaced by the Crip Walk. American-made .22's were replaced by Israeli-made Uzis. Chains got snatched, folks got robbed. One night a woman pulled a gun out of her purse and shot a guy in the jaw.

THE NEW STYLE

Although they had come up in 111 Neighborhood Crip territory, Cube and Dre were not active gang members. Perhaps it was because Cube was being bused out of his 'hood or maybe it was because he was a jock. As far as Dre was concerned, banging didn't pay.[3]

But it wasn't hard for them to notice that the streets were changing. The effects of Reagan's southern hemisphere foreign policy were coming home, making millionaires of Contra entrepreneurs, illegal arms dealers, and Freeway Rick. There was a lot of firepower out there now. Since 1982, the number of gang homicides had doubled.[4] Forget knowing the ledge. Lots of these West Coast ghetto stars had already leapt screaming over it.

Yet the music on the West Coast wasn't changing. It was still about Prince-style expensive purple leather suits and slick drum machines. The World Class Wreckin Cru was a perfect example. Dre thought Lonzo was corny, but he owed him lots of money. Lonzo not only owned the studio Dre used, he had handed out loans to Dre, sometimes bailed him out of jail for not paying his parking tickets, and even let Dre take his old car.

While Lonzo was still paying off the note, the car got stolen and ended up impounded. At the same time, Dre landed himself in jail once again, just as Lonzo was coming up short and ready to cut him off anyway. Wright saw his chance, and offered the nine hundred dollars to bail him out.[5] But Dre had to agree to produce tracks for Wright's new record label, Ruthless.

What the hell, Dre figured. That's why he was now in Lonzo's studio on Wright's dime. He was working off the bond and the fees for getting the car back. Lonzo was out of a car and a DJ. Dre's mercenary willingness to sell his creativity in exchange for security would prove his downfall over and again.

One of the records in heavy rotation on KDAY was by Russ Parr's local comedy rap act Bobby Jimmy and the Critters, a track called "New York Rapper" in which Parr covered Run DMC, LL Cool J, the Beastie Boys, Eric B. & Rakim, UTFO, Roxanne Shante and Kurtis Blow in a goofy country accent. "New York rappers made the street-hard sounds. L.A. rappers? Buncha plagiarizing clowns," he rapped, with emphasis on the word "clowns." By 1987, that shit wasn't so funny anymore.

LA. rap had hit an artistic dead end; it could carry on its raunchy, cartoonish sound or imitate serious-as-cancer New York. Lonzo was milking a four-year-old cow that was going dry. Meanwhile, Dre working with HBO seemed like an admission of defeat. Cube was tired of being a follower. He had done sex rhymes, he'd done East Coast. Maybe he wanted to show these no-name New Yorkers what Los Angeles was really about. The rap he penned for them was packed with local detail, violent in the extreme.

On hearing the lyrics, HBO refused to do it, saying the track was "some West Coast shit," and walked out. Dre, Laylaw, and Wright looked at each other—now what? Dre suggested that Wright to take a turn with the track. Wright was reluctant. He was supposed to be a manager, not a rapper. Dre pressed, not wanting to see a great beat and precious studio time going to waste. When Wright reluctantly agreed, Eazy E was born, and they began recording "Boyz-N-The Hood."

The record hit the streets in September of 1 987, but Jackson had already left for Phoenix. The single he cut for Lonzo had not done anything. Who knew what this single would do? "The rap game wasn't looking too solid at that time, so I decided to go ahead and go to school," he says. "I went to a technical school just to make sure that I did what I wanted to do for a living, no matter what."

But now that Jackson was returning to Los Angeles, it was becoming clear that something had changed. While Jackson was working with T-squares, Wright's hustle and Dre and Yella's radio pull was getting the record off the ground. By the end of 1987, it was the most requested record on KDAY. Wright went from selling the record out of the trunk to swap meet vendors and retailers to a distribution deal with indie vanity label Macola. He had even paid Lonzo $750 to introduce him to a white Jewish manager in the Valley, a guy named Jerry Heller who had once promoted Creedence Clearwater Revival, Pink Floyd, Elton John and REO Speedwagon.[6] A year after they had cut "Boyz," the single was taking hold on the streets, selling thousands of copies every week.

A DUB HISTORY OF "BOYZ-N-THE HOOD"

Jackson was proud of his rhyme. In it, Eazy cruises through town, "bored as hell" and wanting "to get ill." First he spots his car-thief friend Kilo G cruising around looking for autos to jack. Then he catches his crackhead friend JD trying to steal his car stereo. After having words, JD walks off. When Eazy follows him to make peace, JD pulls his .22 automatic. In an instant, Eazy kills him.

Like nothing has happened, he decides to see his girl for a sexual interlude. But she pisses him off, so he "reach(es) back like a pimp and slap(s) the hoe," then does the same to her angry father. Later, he witnesses Kilo G getting arrested. Kilo won't be given bail, so he sets off a prison riot.

In "Boyz-N-The Hood," girls serviced the boys, fathers were suckers and crackheads were marks. It was a seemingly irredeemable sub-Donald Goines pulp world. But then there was the unexpected finale.

Kilo makes his trial appearance and there his girlfriend, Suzy, takes up guns against the state. In the gunfight, Suzy seems bulletproof. The deputies can't stop her. Instead she goes out on her feet, not on her knees, getting sent up for a bid just like her man, barbed-wire love. By introducing this twist, a sly interpolation of Jonathan Jackson's real-life drama, "Boyz-N-The Hood" rose to the level of generational myth.

Perhaps O'Shea had heard the story as a youngster of another seventeen-year-old brother named Jackson, killed by sheriffs and prison guards in a 1970 Marin County courthouse shootout.

As Angela Davis would later remind jurors in her own trial, Jonathan Jackson lost his brother, the writer George Jackson, to the prison system at the age of seven, serving a one-to-life sentence for second-degree robbery. In early 1970, some white and black prisoners at Soledad had a minor fistfight. White prison guard O. G. Miller swiftly ended the fight by firing at three black inmates—all of whom had been known as political activists. Two died almost instantly. Guards refused to allow medical aid, and the third was left in the yard to die. Later that winter, after an announcement that a grand jury investigation had cleared Miller, prisoners attacked another guard and threw him off a third-floor balcony. George and two others, Fleeta Drumgo and John Clutchette, the ones considered the political leaders of the prison, were framed for the murder. The crime could automatically bring George the death penalty.

George's letters to Jonathan, later collected in *Soledad Brother*, revealed the depth of their relationship. In the letters, he taught the younger sibling about communism, sex, resistance, being a man. But the letters remained much of what Jonathan would know of his brother, and words only hinted at the loss Jonathan was feeling. Davis wrote, "[B]ecause it had been cramped into prison visitors' cubicles, into two-page, censored letters, the whole relationship revolved around a single aim—how to get George out here, on this side of the walls." In turn, George noticed a change in his brother. In a letter to Angela Davis in May of 1970, he wrote of Jonathan, "[He] is at that dangerous age where confusion sets in and sends brothers either to the undertaker or to prison."

On August 3, in what many took to be an ominous sign, George was transferred from Soledad Prison to San Quentin Prison, in whose gas chamber he might be executed. Four days later, Jonathan strode into the Marin County Courthouse where a prisoner named John McClain was defending himself against charges he had stabbed a prison guard. Two other prisoners, Ruchell Magee and William Christmas, were also present to testify on McClain's behalf. Jackson marched into the trial chambers with an assault rifle and a cache of weapons, and sat down. When he rose, it was to calmly say, "All right, gentleman, I'm taking over now."

Jackson taped a gun to the judge's head, took several jurors and the district attorney as hostages, then walked with the three prisoners out to a van in the parking lot. Soon enough, a San Quentin guard shot at the van, and other guards and sheriffs joined in with a hail of gunfire. The bullets wounded the district attorney and a juror. The judge, Christmas, McClain and Jackson were killed.

Deputies immediately began a nationwide search for Angela Davis, who was accused of supplying Jackson with one of the guns. She was captured and sent to prison on trumped-up charges of murder, kidnapping and conspiracy. During Davis's trial, George was killed by prison guards in a deadly prison-break attempt. Davis, Drumgo and Clutchette were later acquitted of all charges.

Jonathan Jackson's rebellion had been fearless, inarticulate and fatal. George mourned his brother by writing, "I want people to wonder at what forces created him, terrible, vindictive, cold, calm man-child, courage in one hand, machine gun in the other, scourge of the unrighteous."[7] He considered Jonathan "a soldier of the people," an image that would find a different resonance in the Los Angeles street wars of the '80s.

Whether Cube had intended to or not, "Boyz-N-The Hood" recovered the painful memory. Tracking the lives of Compton hardrocks "knowing nothing in life but to be legit," "Boyz-N-The Hood" became an anthem for the fatherless, brotherless, state-assaulted, heavily armed West Coast urban youth, a generation of Jonathan Jacksons. The impact of "Boyz" had to do with its affirmation, its boast: "We're taking over now."

And even as these boys unloaded both barrels into their authority symbols, Eazy E revealed their vulnerability. He delivered the rap in a deadpan singsong, a voice perhaps as much a result of self-conscious nervousness as hardcore fronting. Dre mirrored Eazy's ambivalence in the jumpy robotic tics of the tiny drum machine bell. And as if to cover E's studio anxiety, Dre added a pounding set of bass drum kicks to help drive home the chorus:

> Now the boys in the hood are always hard
> You come talking that trash we'll pull your card
> Knowing nothing in life but to be legit
> Don't quote me boy, 'cause I ain't said shit

The kids knew Eazy's mask instantly. They might have quoted his lines in their own adrenalin-infused, heart-poundingly defiant stances against their parents, teachers, the principal, the police, the probation officer.

So Eazy E's mask stayed. The mercenary b-boys were suddenly a group, perhaps even the "supergroup" Wright had talked about. He named it Niggaz With Attitude, a ridiculous tag that set impossibly high stakes. Now they had an image to uphold.

LOS ANGELES BLACK

Gangsta rap and postindustrial gangs did not begin in Compton, but a short distance north in Watts. Just like the Bronx gangs, they rose out of, as the ex-Crip warrior Sanyika Shakur would put it, "the ashes and ruins of the sixties."[8]

Watts was a desolate, treeless area located in a gully of sand and mud, the flood catchment for all the other neighborhoods springing up around downtown. In the 1920s Blacks had nowhere else to go.

They had been present at the very first settling of Los Angeles in the late eighteenth century, and established their first community one hundred years later. Starting at First and Los Angeles streets in downtown, they spread east and south along San Pedro and Central Avenues, where they began developing businesses.[9]

While the UNIA and the Urban League had established offices in the city by the 1920s, Los Angeles's Blacks were different—less idealistic, more pragmatic, even a little mercenary. They joined together to break into all-white neighborhoods by sending a light-skinned buyer or a sympathetic white real estate agent to make the down payment. When Blacks moved in, whites moved out. In this way, they won blocks one by one. Sociologists had a term for this process of reverse block-busting: "Negro invasion."

One Black entrepreneur had even figured out how to hustle racial fear. He told the scholar J. Max Bond:

> One of my white friends would tip me off, and I would give him the money to buy a choice lot in a white community. The next day I would go out to look over my property. Whenever a white person seemed curious, I would inform him that I was planning to build soon. On the next day the whites would be after me to sell. I would buy the property sometimes for $200 and sell it for $800 or $900. The white people would pay any price to keep the colored folks out of their communities.[10]

But during the 1920s, the Ku Klux Klan burnt crosses at 109th Street and Central Avenue, and whites erected racial covenants and block restrictions that prevented blacks from moving into their neighborhoods under legal threat of eviction. Watts, literally the bottom, called "Mud Town" even by its own residents, was the only place left to go. Because so many Blacks were moving into the city, and a Black mayor was certain to be the result, Los Angeles hastened to annex Watts in the mid-1920s.

When World War II broke out, southern migrants poured into Los Angeles to fill the need for over half a million new workers in the shipyards, aircraft and rubber industries.[11] Now African-American neighborhoods, especially Watts—which had become the center of Black Los Angeles—were overwhelmed with demands for health care, schooling, transportation and most of all, housing. Racial discrimination kept rents artificially high, and led to overcrowding as slumlords exploited poor families, who often joined together to split a monthly bill. Historian Keith Collins writes, "Single-dwelling units suddenly became four-unit dwellings; four-unit dwellings became small apartment dwellings; garages and attics, heretofore neglected, were suddenly deemed fit for human habitation."[12]

These conditions were barely eased when racial covenants were ruled unconstitutional in 1948 and huge public housing projects—the largest of which were Nickerson Gardens, Jordan Downs,

Imperial Courts and Hacienda Village—began opening in the mid-1940s.[13] Watts soon had the highest concentration of public housing west of the Mississippi. But after the end of the World War II, a deep recession set in, and much of Black Los Angeles never recovered.

To the south, Compton looked like a promised land.[14] The bungalow houses were clean and pleasant; the lots had lawns and space to grow gardens. At one time, the Pacific Electric Railroad station had hung a sign: NEGROES! BE OUT OF COMPTON BY NIGHTFALL.[15] But after desegregation, Blacks filled the Central Avenue corridor from downtown all the way through Compton—the area that would come to be known as South Central.

Black Los Angeles now had a rough dividing line down Vermont Street, separating the striving "Westside" from the suffering "Eastside."[16] East of Watts, in towns like Southgate and Huntington Park, white gangs like the Spook Hunters enforced a border at Alameda Avenue.[17] And when whites began to leave the area in the 1950s, they were replaced by an aggressive, zero-tolerance police department under the leadership of Police Chief William Parker, a John Wayne-type character that made no secret of his racism.[18] Black youth clubs became protective gangs.

Los Angeles was a new kind of city, one in which most of the high-wage job growth would occur far from the inner-city outside a ring ten miles north and west of City Hall.[19] When these suburban communities proliferated after the war, people of color were effectively excluded from the job and housing bonanza. Indeed, from nearly the beginning of the city's history, Blacks and other people of color in Los Angeles had been confined to living in The Bottoms—the job-scarce, mass-transit deprived, densely populated urban core.

These were the conditions that underlined the city's first race riots, 1943's Zoot Suit riots, in which white sailors, marines and soldiers brutalized Chicanos and then Blacks from Venice Beach to East Los Angeles to Watts. And these conditions had only worsened by the time a late summer heatwave hit Watts in 1965.

REMEMBER WATTS

On the night of August 11, a routine drunk driving arrest on Avalon Boulevard and 116th Street escalated into a night of rioting. White police had stopped a pair of young Black brothers, Marquette and Ronald Frye, returning from a party only a few blocks from their home for driving erratically. As a crowd formed in the summer dusk and their mother, Rena Frye, came out to scold the boys, dozens of police units rumbled onto Avalon. In an instant, the scene began to deteriorate.

Marquette, perhaps embarrassed by the appearance of his mother, began resisting the officer's attempts to handcuff him. Soon the cops were beating him with a baton. Seeing this, Frye's brother and mother tussled with other cops and were arrested as well. Another woman, a hairdresser from down the street who had come to see what was going on, was beaten and arrested after spitting on a cop's shirt. Chanting "Burn, baby, burn!" the crowd erupted.

Over the next two nights, the police lost control of the streets. They were ambushed by rock-throwing youths. They were attacked by women who seized their guns. Their helicopters came under sniper fire. Systematic looting and burning began. Among the first things to go up in smoke were the files of credit records in the department stores.[20] Groceries, furniture stores and gun and surplus outlets were hit next. After these places were ransacked, they were set ablaze. One expert attributed the riot's blueprint to the local gangs—the Slausons, the Gladiators and the mainly Chicano set, Watts Gang V—who had temporarily dropped their rivalries.[21]

"This situation is very much like fighting the Viet Cong," Police Chief William Parker told the press on Friday the 13th. "We haven't the slightest idea when this can be brought under control."[22] Later he called the rioters "monkeys in a zoo."[23] By the evening, the LAPD and the Sheriff's Office had begun firing on looters and unarmed citizens, leaving at least six dead. Two angry whites reportedly drove into Jordan Downs and began shooting at Black residents.[24] Newspaper headlines read ANARCHY U.S.A.[25]

The National Guard arrived the next day. The death toll peaked sharply in the last two days of civil unrest. Rioting lasted five days and resulted in $40 million in damages and thirty-four dead. Until 1992, they were the worst urban riots ever recorded.

After the riots, Watts became a hotbed of political and cultural activity. Author Odie Hawkins wrote, "Watts, post outrage, was in a heavy state of fermentation. Everybody was a poet, a philosopher, an artist or simply something exotic. Even people who weren't any of those things thought they were."[26] It was a time of new beginnings: A week after the riots, the Nation of Islam's downtown mosque had been shot up and nearly destroyed by LAPD officers who claimed to be searching for a nonexistent cache of looted weapons. But the mosque survived and thrived. Soon the Nation would welcome Marquette Frye as its most prominent new member.

The gangs, as Mike Davis wrote, "joined the Revolution."[27] Maulana Ron Karenga put together the US Organization by recruiting the Gladiators and the Businessmen.[28] Members of the Slausons and the Orientals formed the Sons of Watts, another cultural nationalist organization. The powerful Slauson leader Alprentice "Bunchy" Carter led many more ex-Slausons and other gang members to reject Karenga and the cultural nationalists and affiliate with the revolutionary nationalist Black Panthers.[29]

On 103rd Street, the Black Panthers set up an office next to the Watts Happening Coffee House, which housed Mafundi, a cultural performance space. In 1966, the screenwriter and poet Bud Schulberg opened the Watts Writers Workshop there. It quickly became a cultural haven for some of the most promising artistic voices in the area, including Hawkins, author Quincy Troupe, poet Kamau Daa'ood, and three young poets that would call themselves the Watts Prophets.

Anthony "Amde" Hamilton, a Watts native, was an ex-convict and an activist when he found the Workshop through Hawkins. Soon he was working at Mafundi and serving as the Assistant Director of the Workshop. In 1969, Hawkins and Hamilton assembled a group of poets from the Workshop to record *The Black Voices: On the Streets in Watts.* In a bulldog voice—one that Eazy E would later evoke, and that would be sampled by dozens of gangsta rap producers—Hamilton growled, "The meek ain't gon' inherit *shit,* 'cause I'll take it!"

Through the happenings on 103rd Street, Hamilton met Richard Dedeaux, a Louisiana transplant, and Otis O'Solomon (then Otis Smith) from Alabama. They began performing poetry with a female pianist Dee Dee O'Neal, and conga accompaniment. In 1971, they recorded *Rapping Black in a White World,* a prophetic rap document. On the cover a child of the Revolution—a boy who would come of age in the eighties—wrapped himself in a soldier's oversized uniform and embraced a shotgun.

During the Watts riots, they had seen a racial apocalypse outlined in the "freedom flames" blackening the structures they did not own and could not control. Their poems were decidedly edgy, imbued with righteous rage, full of wordly pessimism. On "A Pimp," Otis O'Solomon rapped,

> Growing up in world of dog eat dog I learned
> the dirtiest dog got the bone
> meaning not the dog with the loudest bark
> but the coldest heart.

They chronicled tragic pimps, recounted drug-addled and bullet-riddled deaths, and called for the rise of ghetto warriors in the mold of Nat Turner. It was Black Art, as Baraka had called for, that drew blood. But this ferment could not last forever.

PANTHERS TO CRIPS

The Prophets were close to the young Bunchy Carter. Once a feared leader of the Slausons, as well as its roughneck inner-core army, the Slauson Renegades, he met Eldridge Cleaver while doing time for armed robbery, and was now the Southern California leader of the Black Panther Party. He was formidable—an organic intellectual, community organizer, corner rapper, and "street nigga" all at the same time—"considered," Elaine Brown wrote, "the most dangerous Black man in Los Angeles."[30] The Slausons had started at Fremont High in Watts, but Carter now commanded the love of Black teens of the high schools in South Central.[31] His bodyguard was a Vietnam veteran named Elmer Pratt, whom he renamed Geronimo ji Jaga. The two were enrolled at UCLA, where they studied and planned the Revolution.

The Panthers and Karenga's US Organization were fighting for control of UCLA's Black Studies department, as FBI and LAPD provocateurs secretly and systematically raised the personal and ideological tensions between the two. On the morning of January 17, 1969, a Black Student Union meeting ended with the organizations firing on each other in Campbell Hall. Carter and Panther John Huggins were shot dead. Coming after a year of bloody confrontations with authorities across the country that had left dozens of Party leaders dead, the Panthers called Carter's and Huggins's deaths assassinations.

A year later, after the beef between the two organizations had been squashed, LA. police arrested Pratt, the new Panther leader, on false charges, found an informant to pin a murder to him, and had him sent away for life. Even the Watts Writers Workshop was destroyed through the efforts of a FBI double agent who had been employed as the Workshop's publicist.

Filling the void of leadership was Raymond Washington, a charismatic teen at Watts's Fremont High School who had been a follower of Bunchy Carter. By the time Washington turned fifteen, the Slausons and the Panthers had both died with Bunchy. In 1969, Washington formed the Baby Avenues, carrying on the legacy of a fading local gang, the Avenues.[32] Over the next two years, he walked across the eastside with a gangsta limp and an intimidating walking cane, kicked his rap to impressed youths, and built the gang.

The Baby Avenues wore black leather jackets in a display of solidarity with the Panthers' style and credo of self-defense. But somewhere along the line, the goal changed to simply beating down other Black youths for their jackets.[33] Godfather Jimel Barnes, who had joined in the early days when Washington came to the Avalon Gardens projects, says Washington had summed up his vision in this way: "Chitty chitty bang bang, nothing but a Crip thang, Eastside Cuz. This is going to be the most notorious gang in the world. It's going to go from generation to generation."[34]

The origins of the name are now shrouded in legend. It may have been a corruption of "Cribs" or "Crypts." It may have stood for "C-RIP," all words that represented the gang's emerging "cradle to grave" gang-banging credo. Or it may have come from an Asian-American victim's description of her attacker, a "'crip' with a stick."[35] In any case, as O. G. Crip Danifu told L.A. gang historian Alejandro Alonso, "'Crippin' meant robbing and stealing, and then it developed into a way of life."[36]

For years, Mexican pachuco gangs had been the most organized and most feared in town. Now the Crips would transform young Black Los Angeles. Spreading through the Black corridor south to Compton and west to South Central, the Crips became, in Davis's words, "a hybrid of teen cult and proto-Mafia" and "the power source of last resort for thousands of abandoned youth."[37]

During the Nixon years, Crip sets proliferated and gang rivalries intensified. When Washington was kicked out of Fremont and sent to Washington High on the westside, he recruited Stanley "Tookie" Williams, and Crip sets expanded into South Central Los Angeles. By 1972, where there had recently been none, there were eighteen new Black gangs.[38]

Youths on Compton's Piru Street organized themselves into groups they called Pirus or Bloods. Other Crip rivals also emerged. In 1973, the beefs turned bloody. Through the efforts of Bobby Lavender, Sylvester "Puddin' " Scott and others, Brims, Bloods and Pirus formed a Bloods confederation.[39] Gang fashion had shifted from Black power dress to an appropriation of *cholo* style—Pendletons, white tees, khakis—and when Crips began flagging blue, Bloods flagged red.

Like a national map on the night of a presidential election, the Los Angeles grid was now being tallied into columns of red and blue. In the unbreachable logic of turf warfare, sets proliferated in the Black corridor, stretching through the colored suburbs west to the beach at Venice, south to Long Beach, and north to Altadena. Soon there were so many Crip sets they even went to war with each other.

"During the late seventies it slowed down," Athens Park Bloods member Cle "Bone" Sloan says, "because niggas started working in the factories. When they took the jobs away, shit started back up. Then cocaine hit the streets and niggas were in it for real."[40] As the 1980s dawned, Raymond Washington was dead in prison, killed by a rival, and 155 gangs claimed 30,000 members across the city.[41]

THE BOTTOMS

Firestone, Goodyear and General Motors closed their manufacturing plants in South Central. In all, 131 plants shuttered during the 1980s, eliminating unionized manufacturing jobs in the rubber, steel, and auto industries and leaving 124,000 people unemployed in the center city. Job growth shifted to service and information industries located beyond the rim of the ten-mile ring. Bobby Lavender saw the effects: "Thousands of parents lost their jobs. Homes and cars were repossessed. People who had just started to become middle-class were losing everything and sinking down."[42]

In 1978, California voters, spurred by the same right-wing strategists who would soon lift Reagan from his former governorship into the presidency, passed Proposition 13, an initiative that capped property taxes and dramatically altered state and local government financing, launching a national tax revolt and permanently plunging the state into the cruelest cycle of state budget crises in the country. Passage of Proposition 13 had the kind of effect on California's cities that turning off the water might have had on its farm belt. Three decades of investment had made the state's primary and secondary education, college and university systems the envy of the nation—a model of access and quality. After Proposition 13, the state's K-12 system tumbled down all national educational indices, and as fees exploded, its colleges and universities became increasingly inaccessible to the working-class and the poor. Now that the postwar generation had gotten what it needed for itself and its children, it was pulling up the ladder.

In Los Angeles, the signs of the new mood of the state's aging white electorate read, "Armed Response." Around the downtown and at the edges of the ten-mile ring, in what Mike Davis called "post-liberal Los Angeles," security fences and security forces sprung up in commercial buildings and around gated communities. Meanwhile, Chief Darryl Gates's army locked down the interior—the vast area running south of the Santa Monica Freeway, along both sides of the Harbor Freeway and back west with the Century Freeway that had been swallowed up into the construct called "South Central," a heaving barbarian space behind the walls, the Everywhere Else at the bottom of the ten-mile ring, viewed mainly through the nightly news or from behind the surveillance camera.

During the Reagan recession of 1983, Los Angeles's official unemployment rate hit 11 percent.[43] But in South Central, it was much higher, at least 50 percent for youths.[44] The median household income there was just half the state median. While white poverty rates in Los Angeles County actually declined to 7 percent, a quarter of Blacks and Latinos and 14 percent of Asians lived below the poverty line. In South Central, the rate was higher than 30 percent. Almost half of South Central's children lived below the poverty level.[45] Infant mortality in Watts was triple the rate in Santa Monica, only twenty miles away.[46] By any index, conditions had deteriorated for the generation born after the Watts Uprising.

What the South Bronx had been to the 1970s, South Central would be for the 1980s. It was the epitome of a growing number of inner-city nexuses where deindustrialization, devolution, Cold War adventurism, the drug trade, gang structures and rivalries, arms profiteering, and police brutality were combining to destabilize poor communities and alienate massive numbers of youths.

THE SOUND OF THE BATTERRAM

Chaos was settling in for a long stay. Even an otherwise innocuous knock on one's door could bring the threat of fathomless violence. The chief symbol of the new repression was the Batterram—a V-100 armored military vehicle equipped with a massive battering ram that police used to barge into suspected crack-houses. With the drug war in full swing, the Batterram was getting a lot of action.

By the summer of 1985, nineteen-year-old rapper Toddy Tee's "Batterram" tape was the most popular cassette on the streets. Telling a story of a working-class family man whose life is interrupted by cluckheads and the Batterram, the tape was one of the first to describe the changing streets. Toddy had written and recorded the rap in his bedroom as he watched the Batterram crash through a crackhouse live on television, then duplicated the initial copies on a cheap dubbing deck, and gone out in the streets to hawk them. To his surprise, the song became a sensation, a top request on KDAY. By the end of the year, he was recutting the track in an expensive studio with a major-label budget over music produced by big-name funk musician Leon Haywood (whose 1975 hit, "I Want' a Do Something Freaky to You" would later be used on Dr. Dre's "Nuthin' But a 'G' Thing").

Toddy Tee was one of several teenagers who had hung out in the garage of a local rap legend named Mixmaster Spade. If Lonzo's empire was one center where South Central rap talent gathered, Spade's was the other major one. Spade was an older cat who had come up on '70s funk, and had developed a singing style of rap that made him a mixtape and house party legend from Watts to Long Beach. Although he never became more than a local rap hero, his style was carried on by artists like Snoop Dogg, Nate Dogg, Warren G and DJ Quik.

At Spade's house on 156th and Wilmington, right under the flight path of the two-strip Compton Airport, he held court with a kind of advanced rap school, teaching the finer points of rapping, mixing and scratching to a burgeoning crew of kids that called themselves the Compton Posse—Toddy, King Tee, Coolio, DJ Pooh, DJ Alladin, J-Ro (later of the Alkaholiks) and others. But classes ended for good one afternoon in late 1987 when L.A. county sheriffs tried to raid the house, and Spade and seven associates engaged the sheriffs in a shootout. During the fracas, one of the sheriffs plugged another in the back and sent him to King-Drew hospital. When the smoke cleared and Spade and his crew had surrendered, sheriffs confiscated $3,000 in cash, a MAC-10 and twenty-five gallons of PCP—better known in the 'hood as "sherm" or "water."[47] The local rap school had been doubling as the neighborhood narcotics factory.

These South Central rap songs were like the new blues. But the Mississippi blues culture had developed under the conditions of back-breakingly oppressive work, the toil of building a modern nation. Hip-hop culture, whether in the South Bronx or South Central, had developed under alienated play, as solid jobs evaporated into the airy buzz and flow of a network society. As Greg Brown, a resident of Nickerson Gardens, put it, "In the sixties, General Motors in neighboring Southgate was the future. In the seventies, King Hospital was the future. Now the future in Watts and South Central is jail. You see that new Seventy-seventh Street LAPD station? It's beautiful. You see anything else in the community that looks better than that jail?"[48]

Hip-hop was close to the underground economy because, more often than not, it was being made by youths who were not exploitable, but expendable. The flatland ghettos of South Central had more in common with the distant hillside *favelas* of Rio De Janeiro, hoods switched off from the global network, than with the walled estates of Beverly Hills just miles away. The main difference, though, was the proximity of the LA 'hoods to the heart of the most advanced culture industry in the world. So from homemade cassettes, grandiose dreams were swelling.

These new blues captured the feel of the serpentine twists of daily inner-city life on the hairtrigger margin. With their urban-canyon echoing drums and casual descriptions of explosive violence, the new myths of crack, guns, and gangs sounded a lot larger than life. On *Straight Outta Compton*, they reached their apotheosis.

THE ALTERNATIVE TO BLACK POWER

Bryan Turner was a young white SoCal transplant from Winnipeg. In 1981, he had set out to make a living in the Los Angeles music industry, going to work at Capitol Records' Special Markets department where he put together cheap anthologies for niche markets. He left to start his own label, Priority Records, and turned a profit from novelty records like The California Raisins. After selling two million units of the Raisins, Turner's staff swelled to ten and was securing annual sales of $5 million. Now he needed a real artist.

Eazy E's manager Jerry Heller had his offices in the same building. Despite the fact that "Boyz-N-The Hood" had begun moving thousands of copies, Heller was receiving rejection after rejection from major labels for Eazy's "supergroup." The stuff was too violent, he was told, too street. Heller walked down to Turner's office one day and told him of his new rap project. He played Turner "Boyz-N-The Hood" and a rough demo of "Fuck Tha Police." Turner could not believe his ears, and immediately scheduled a meeting with Heller, Eric Wright and the group.

As they discussed the group and the music, Wright impressed Turner as a man with a plan. Turner says, "Almost instinctively, without a lot of experience, I wanted to be in business with these kids." He signed NWA as Priority's first act, and quickly sold over 300,000 copies of "Boyz-N-The Hood."

When Jackson returned from Phoenix, he jumped back into the fold. He, Wright's neighbor from Compton, Lorenzo Patterson, who called himself MC Ren, and an associate of Dre and Wright, Tracy "The DOC" Curry, penned the lyrics for Eazy E's debut, *Eazy Duz It*. Their diminutive character inflated stereotypes to their breaking point—equal parts urban threat, hypersexed Black male, and class clown. The album was not half as compelling as "Boyz-N-The Hood," but when it came out in 1988, it went gold.

Then they turned their attention to the NWA album. Confident that they were on to something, they decided to go as far out as they could. Dr. Dre bragged to Brian Cross, "I wanted to make people go: 'Oh shit, I can't believe he's saying that shit.' I wanted to go all the way left. Everybody trying to do this Black power and shit, so I was like, let's give 'em an alternative. Nigger niggernigger niggernigger fuck this fuck that bitch bitch bitch bitch suck my dick, all this kind of shit, you know what I'm saying?"[49]

If the thing was protest, they would toss the ideology and go straight to the riot. If the thing was sex, they would chuck the seduction and go straight to the fuck. Forget knowledge of self or empowering the race. This was about, as Eazy would put it, the strength of street knowledge.

THE AESTHETICS OF EXCESS

For the album's opener, the title track, Dre looped up the drum break from D.C. funk band, the Winstons' "Amen Brother," a frenetic horn-driven instrumental funk take on the joyous hymn, "Amen," that had been revived by Curtis Mayfield and was now played with Sunday-morning abandon. The raucous and herky-jerky breakdown—which later formed the backbone for the equally frenetic drum V bass sound a decade later—was the most stable element of the track.

These were not going to be the old Negro spirituals. Under Dre's hand, the "Amen" break took on a brutal, menacing efficiency. Although Dre's production was not as minimalist as Marley Marl's, it shared the desire for streamlining. He bassed up the kick drum, cued an insistent double-time hi-hat, and added a "Yeah! Huh!" affirmation and a scratched snare to propel the beat futureward. Then he inserted an sustaining horn line and a staccato guitar riff to increase the pre-millennial tension. It sounded like the drums of death.

Dre was creating a hybrid production style, adding studio player Stan "the Guitar Man" Jones's vamps and Yella's turntable-cuts to sampled funk fragments and concrete-destroying Roland 808 bass drops. He slowed the tempo from technopop/electrodance speeds to more aggrandizing bpm's. High-pitched horn stabs lit up the tracks like rocket launchers.

Hip hop's braggadocio, too, was about to enter a new era. Jackson was exploring the contours of his new identity, Ice Cube. In "Straight Outta Compton," "Fuck Tha Police," "Gangsta Gangsta" and "I Ain't Tha 1," he portrayed himself as an untouchable rebel without a cause. Police, girls, rivals—none of them could get in Cube's game.

Reaganism had eliminated youth programs while bombarding youths with messages to desist and abstain; it was all about tough love and denial and getting used to having nothing. Even the East Coast Utopians like Rakim and Chuck talked control and discipline. By contrast, excess was the essence of NWA's appeal. These poems celebrated pushers, played bitches, killed enemies, and assassinated police. Fuck delayed gratification, they said, take it all now. "Gangsta Gangsta" was the first single released from these sessions. On it, Ice Cube hollered,

> And then you realize we don't care
> We don't "Just say no"
> We're too busy saying, "Yeah!"

Oddly enough, the album ended with a techno-pop groove produced by an uncredited Arabian Prince, "Something 2 Dance 2," more G-rated than G'ed down. It was as if the crew had hedged their bets. When the song was released as a B-side to "Gangsta Gangsta," it became a mixshow and club staple and one of the biggest urban hits of 1988 in the West and the South. In fact, "Something 2 Dance 2" pointed sideways to the dance-floor-fillers Dre and Arabian Prince were doing for pop crossover acts like JJ. Fad, Cli-N-Tel, the Sleeze Boyz, and Dre's then-girlfriend Michel'le. JJ. Fad's *Supersonic: The Album* had easily outsold *Eazy Duz It*. But all these songs were like echoes of Eve's After Dark or an Uncle Jam's party, relics of an age of innocence that the rest of *Straight Outta Compton* was about to slam the door on forever. Nobody would be dancing anymore.

THE RETURN OF THE LOCAL

After the album was officially released on January 25, 1989, it went gold in six weeks. It had been recorded for under $10,000. Radio would not dare go near it, so Priority did almost nothing to promote it. The album's runaway success signaled the beginning of a sea-change in pop-culture tastes.

Because the sound was so powerful that it had to be named, someone called NWA's music "gangsta rap" after Cube's indomitable anthem, despite the fact that he would have preferred they had paid more attention to the next line of the chorus—KRS-One's pronouncement: "It's not about a salary, it's all about reality." But the moniker stuck, naming the theatrics and the threat, the liberating wordsound power and the internalized oppression, the coolest rebellion and the latest pathology, the new Black poetry and the "new punk rock."

As young populations browned, youths were increasingly uninterested in whitewashed hand-me-downs. The surprising success of Ted Demme and Fab 5 Freddy's *Yo! MTV Raps* in 1988 made African-American, Chicano and Latino urban style instantly accessible to millions of youths. With its claims to street authenticity, its teen rebellion, its extension of urban stereotype, and its individualist "get mine" credo, gangsta rap fit hand-in-glove with a multiculti youth demographic weaned on racism and Reaganism, the first generation in a half century to face downward mobility.

"That's how we sold two million," Turner says. "The white kids in the Valley picked it up and they decided they wanted to live vicariously through this music. Kids were just waiting for it." Although MTV banned the video for the title track two months after the record's release, the album became a cultural phenomenon. Fab 5 Freddy bucked upper management and brought his *Yo! MTV Raps* crew to tour with the crew through the streets of Compton.

Like a hurricane that had gathered energy over hot open waters before heading inland, *Straight Outta Compton* hit American popular culture with the same force as the Sex Pistols' *Never Mind the Bollocks* had in the U.K. eleven years earlier. Hip-hop critic Billy Jam says, "Like the Sex Pistols, NWA made it look easy, inspiring a Do-It-Yourself movement for anyone from the streets to crank out gangsta rap tapes." All one had to have was a pen and a pad of paper, a mic, a mixer, and a sampler. Thousands of kids labored over their raps in their dark bedrooms, then stepped onto the streets to learn first-hand the vagaries of hustling and distribution—all just so that people could hear their stories.

NWA's *Straight Outta Compton* democratized rap and allowed the world to rush in. It was as if NWA overturned transnational pop culture like a police car, gleefully set the offending thing on fire, then popped open some forties, and danced to their own murder rap.

As capital fled deindustrialized inner cities and inner-ring suburbs for Third World countries and tax-sheltered exurban "edge cities," the idea of the Local returned with a vengeance. Big thinkers like Chuck D and Rakim had broadened hip-hop's appeal with revolutionary programs and universalist messages. But two years after Rakim's open invitation to join the hip-hop nation—"It ain't where you're from, it's where you're at"—gangsta rap revoked it.

"We're born and raised in Compton!" NWA bellowed, decentering hip-hop from New York forever. NWA dropped hip-hop like a '64 Chevy right down to street-corner level, lowered it from the mountaintop view of Public Enemy's re-combinant nationalism and Rakim's streetwise spiritualism, and made hip-hop narratives specific, more coded in local symbol and slang than ever before.

After *Straight Outta Compton,* it really was all about where you were from. NWA conflated myth and place, made the narratives root themselves on the corner of every 'hood. And now every 'hood could be Compton, everyone had a story to tell. Even Bill Clinton's sepia-toned videobio, aired at the 1992 Democratic Convention, could have been titled *Straight Outta Hope.*

That a hood-centric aesthetic might rise with the Reagan right's attack on big government seemed appropriate. To combat their defense-bloated deficits, Republicans had introduced a strategy of devolution shifting much of the burden of health, education and social services from federal government back to the states and cities. By the 1990s, under President Clinton, Democrats moved to the so-called center, joining Republicans in the slashing and burning of their own legacy.

Federal government would no longer be a place to seek remedies, as it had been during the civil rights and Black power era. Politics in the Beltway was becoming increasingly symbolic, just sound and fury. Nor could the courts, stuffed with Reagan appointees, be a source of relief. Many major political struggles had already shifted to the level of state and city governments, and were being waged amidst declining resources. States with older, less urban, more homogenous populations and low social service needs—usually the "red-column" Republican-dominated states—made it through this transition just fine. States with younger, browning, urban populations and expanding social service needs—usually "blue-column" Democratic-dominated states—fell into a brutal cycle of crisis and cleanup, each more severe than the last.

The gangsta rappers were more right than they ever knew. Where you were from was exactly the story.

THE WAR ON GANGS

If the new national consensus around federal government was less-is-more, the new urban consensus around local government was more-is-more, particularly when it came to attacking crime and those old social pariahs, gang members. But the War on Gangs soon soured into something else entirely. And once again, Los Angeles was the bellwether.

The shot that launched the War on Gangs was not fired in Compton, East Los Angeles, or the central city neighborhoods of the Bottoms, but in Westwood Village, amidst hip clothing boutiques, theaters and eateries a short distance from UCLA's Fraternity Row.

There on January 30, 1988, in the teeming Saturday night crowd of students, wealthy westsiders, and youths who had come from throughout the city to cruise the Village, a Rolling 60s Crip named Durrell DeWitt "Baby Rock" Collins spotted an enemy from the Mansfield Hustler Crips walking up Broxton Avenue. Two young Asian Americans, Karen Toshima and her boyfriend, Eddie Poon, were out celebrating Toshima's promotion to senior art director at a local ad agency. They unwittingly walked into the crossfire. Even as Poon tried to pull Toshima to the ground, one of two bullets intended for Collins's rival struck her in the head.[50] She died at UCLA Medical Center the next day.

City Hall leaders reacted with outrage. To many Asian Americans' dismay, Toshima became a symbol of the city's racial divide. For whites, Toshima's death was a sign that gang violence was drawing uncomfortably close. To Blacks and Latinos, one death in Westwood was apparently more important to City Hall than hundreds in East and South Central Los Angeles.

Police Chief Darryl Gates had been itching for a war. Now he would get it. In weeks, City Hall leaders voted to add 650 officers to LAPD, bringing the department to its largest size in history. LAPD held an emergency summit on gang violence and pushed for millions in emergency funds for a new military-style operation on the gangs. City Hall gave its blessing to Gates's Operation Hammer, a program of heavy-handed sweeps in Black and brown communities touted as a national model in the War on Gangs.

On August 1, in what was supposed to be Operation Hammer's crowning moment, Gates brought the War on Gangs to South Central. That evening, eighty-eight LAPD officers, supported by thundering helicopters overhead, trained their firepower on two apartment buildings at the corner of 39th Street and Dalton Avenue in South Central Los Angeles. Cops stormed through the two buildings, taking axes to furniture and walls, overturning washing machines and stoves, smashing mirrors, toilets and stereos, rounding up residents and beating dozens of them. They spray-painted LAPD RULES and ROLLIN 30S DIE on apartment walls. One resident was forced wet and naked out of the shower and forced to watch her two toddlers taken away while cops destroyed her apartment with sledgehammers.[51] "We weren't just searching for drugs. We were delivering a message that there was a price to pay for selling drugs and being a gang member," said one policeman who participated in the raid. "I looked at it as something of a Normandy Beach, a D-Day."[52]

Residents in the area had indeed complained to police of the drug dealing by Crips on the block. But none of those dealers lived in these two buildings. The raid yielded only trace amounts of crack and less than six ounces of marijuana. The Red Cross was forced to house nearly two dozen of the buildings' tenants, who had been effectively rendered homeless. One relief official termed it "a total disaster, a shocking disaster."[53]

In fact, Operation Hammer had been a massive failure from the start. In the year following Toshima's death, Gates's operation netted 25,000 arrests, mainly of youths that appeared to fit the department's gang profile. 1,500 youths could be swept up into jail in a day; 90 percent of them might be released without charge, after their information was entered into the gang database, now teeming with the names of thousands of innocents.[54] Meanwhile, hardcore bangers often tipped each other off in advance of the sweeps and escaped the LAPD dragnet.[55] The math of the Hammer did not add up. By 1992, the city was paying out $11 million annually in brutality settlements while allocating less than $2 million to gang intervention programs, and almost half of all young Black males living in South Central were in the gang database.[56]

Twilight Bey, a former Cirkle City Piru, described to hip-hop journalist and DJ David "Davey D" Cook a typically harrowing day in the life of a young male in South Central.

> One of the things that would always happen is [the police] would stop you and ask you "What gang are you from?" … In some cases, if you had a snappy answer and by that I mean, if you were quick and to the point and had one word answers they would get up in your face and grab your collar, push you up against the police car and choke you. Or they would call us over and tell us to put our hands up and place them on the hood of the police car. Now usually the car had been running all day, which meant that the engine was hot. So the car is burning our hands which meant that we would have to remove our hands from the car. When that happened, the police would accuse of us of not cooperating. Next thing you know you would get pushed in the back or knocked over. …
>
> You have to remember most of us at that time were between the ages of twelve and sixteen. Just a year ago we were ten and eleven and playing in the sheriffs basketball league where they would treat us like little kids. A year later when we are close to being teenagers we are suddenly being treated with all this abuse.
>
> In a lot of cases you had kids who had chosen never to be a gang member. … If you told them you weren't in a gang, they would look at whatever graffiti was written on the wall and put you on record as being part of that gang.
>
> DAVEY D: … It seems like it was some sort of sick rites of passage so that by the time you became a grown man you knew to never cross that line with the police.
>
> TWILIGHT: Yes, that's exactly what it was. It was some sort of social conditioning. Instilling fear is the strongest motivation that this world has to use. It's also the most negative. … What I mean by that is, if you are constantly being pushed into a corner where you are afraid, you're going to get to a point where you one day won't be. Eventually one day you will fight back. Eventually one day you will push back. When you push back what is going to be the end result? How far will this go?

THE BACKLASH

By June 1989, a right-wing backlash against NWA was in full effect. That month, the newsletter *Focus On the Family Citizen* bore the headline RAP GROUP NWA SAYS "KILL POLICE." Police departments across the South and Midwest faxed each other the song's lyrics. Tour dates were abruptly cancelled. Cops refused to provide security for NWA shows in Toledo and Milwaukee. In Cincinnati, federal agents subjected the crew to drug searches, asking if they were L.A. gang members using their tour as a front to expand their crack-selling operations. Nothing was ever found.[57]

In August, FBI assistant director Milt Ahlerich fired off a letter bluntly warning Priority Records on "Fuck Tha Police." It read:

> A song recorded by the rap group NWA on their album entitled *Straight Outta Compton* encourages violence against and disrespect for the law enforcement officer and has been brought to my attention. I understand your company recorded and distributed this album and I am writing to share my thoughts and concerns with you.
>
> Advocating violence and assault is wrong, and we in the law enforcement community take exception to such action. Violent crime, a major problem in our country, reached an unprecedented high in 1988. Seventy-eight law enforcement officers were feloniously slain in the line of duty during 1988, four more than in 1987. Law enforcement officers dedicate their lives to the protection of our citizens, and recordings such as the one from NWA are both discouraging and degrading to these brave, dedicated officers.
>
> Music plays a significant role in society, and I wanted you to be aware of the FBI's position relative to this song and its message. I believe my views reflect the opinion of the entire law enforcement community.[58]

The letter came as NWA was touring, and had the effect of further mobilizing police along the tour route. NWA's tour promoters tried to secure an agreement from the band not to perform the song. The national 200,000-member Fraternal Order of Police voted to boycott groups that advocated assaults on officers of the law. But in Detroit, where local police showed in intimidatingly large numbers, the crowd chanted "Fuck the police" all night, and the crew decided to try anyway. As Cube began the song, the cops rushed the stage. The group fled.

Music critic David Marsh and publicist Phyllis Pollack broke the Ahlerich story in a cover article in *The Village Voice*, and through their organization Music In Action, mobilized the ACLU and industry leaders to formally protest. Turner forwarded the letter to sympathetic congresspersons and the FBI backed off.

CHOOSING SIDES

But NWA's scattershot test of the limits of free speech provoked outrage even in sympathetic quarters.

"I thought NWA was Satan's spawn. I was like, fuck these Negroes for real," says hip-hop journalist Sheena Lester, then the youth and culture editor for the Black-owned, South Central-based *Los Angeles Sentinel* later an editor at *Rap Pages* and *Vibe*. "I was reading about them—who are these motherfuckers? What do you mean, 'bitch' this and 'ho' that? Fuck them. If I'm a bitch, kiss my ass. I just felt like dealing with NWA was counterproductive."

She was not alone. The political and cultural rads had become hip-hop progressives, deeply influenced by their elders' Third World liberation politics but drawn to the rapidly transforming landscape of pop culture's present. The media dam holding back representations of youths of color was near to bursting, and hip-hop gave them confidence the flood would soon come. They took over college and community radio stations, started up magazines, cafes and clubs, and created art, design and poetry with the same kind of energy they took to storming administration buildings.

NWA presented them with a thorny dilemma. There was the I-am-somebody rap rewrite of Charles Wright's Watts 103rd Street Band's "Express Yourself" and the lumpenprole rebellion of "Fuck Tha Police." But they certainly couldn't ignore the allure of lines like, "To a kid looking up to me, life ain't nothing but bitches and money," not least when the rhyme was being delivered boldly over thrilling beats that made a heart race.

The first boycotts against NWA came from community radio DJs and hip-hop writers, who were publicly outraged at the crew's belligerent ignorance, and privately ambivalent about the music's visceral heart-pounding power. Bay Area hip-hop DJs Davey D and Kevin "Kevvy Kev" Montague led a boycott of NWA and Eazy E on their nationally influential college radio shows, believing it would be contradictory to play such music while they were trying to create an Afrocentric space on the air. Both devoted hours of call-in radio to the debate, and their listeners finally supported the ban. The boycott spread to other hip-hop shows across the nation.

To the hip-hop progressives, the true believers who embraced rap as the voice of their generation, NWA sounded militantly incoherent. Their music drew new lines over issues of misogyny, homophobia, and violence. NWA had stepped up rap's dialogics; reaction was the point. They anticipated the criticisms, but silenced them by shouting them down. Defiant and confident, Yella even disclosed the in-joke, scratching in a female voice, "Hoping all you sophisticated motherfuckers hear what I have to say."

The hip-hop progressives were hearing it and were conflicted. Three decades after Baraka's call for "poems that kill," radical chic had become gangsta chic. Just as the blues had for a generation of white baby boomers, these tall tales populated with drunken, high, rowdy, irresponsible, criminal, murderous niggas with attitude seemed to be just what the masses of their generation wanted. Even more disconcerting, they lined up all the right enemies: the Christian right, the FBI, baby boomer demagogues. NWA was going to force every hip-hop progressive to confront her or his relationship to the music and choose sides.

When *Straight Outta Compton* crossed over to white audiences, things became very unpleasant. Gangsta rap was proving more than just "the new punk rock"; it became a more formidable lightning rod for the suppression of youth culture than white rock music ever had been. Yet the music was undoubtedly difficult to defend. It sometimes seemed less than a cultural effect of material realities, a catalyst for progressive discussion, or objective street reportage of social despair, than the start of further reversal.

In the photo for a 1990 *Source* cover story, Eazy E aimed his 9mm at the reader, over the cover line, THE GANGSTA RAPPER: VIOLENT HERO OR NEGATIVE ROLE MODEL? Inside, a fierce debate raged over gangsta rap. David Mills asked, "[Y]ou wonder whether things have gotten out of control, and whether, like radiation exposure, it'll be years before we can really know the consequences of our nasty little entertainments."[59]

Worse yet, the culture wars seemed to stoke the political wars—the War on Gangs, the War on Drugs, the War on Youth. As Rob Marriott, James Bernard and Allen Gordon would write in *The Source*, "The saddest thing is that these attacks on rap have helped set the stage for the most oppressive and wrong-headed crime legislation. Three strikes out? Mandatory sentences? More cops? More prisons? Utter bullshit."[60]

But the hip-hop progressives had always argued that the media needed to be opened to unheard voices. By calling themselves journalists, Ice Cube and NWA outmaneuvered the hip-hop progressives, positioning themselves between the mainstream and those voices. No one else, they claimed, was speaking for the brother on the corner but them—loudly, defiantly and unapologetically. So *Straight Outta Compton* also marked the beginning of hip-hop's obsession with "The Real." From now on, rappers had to *represent*—to scream for the unheard and otherwise speak the unspeakable. Life on the hair-trigger margin—with all of its unpredictability, contradiction, instability, menace, tragedy and irony, with its daily death and resistance—needed to be described in its passionate complexity, painted in bold strokes, framed in wide angles, targeted with laser precision. A generation needed to assassinate its demons.

Many young hip-hop progressives would thus come to have their "NWA moment," that moment of surprise and surrender when outrage turned to empathy, rejection became recognition and intolerance gave way to embrace. "I was going to a club called 'Funky Reggae,' and I remember being in the middle of the dance floor, hearing 'Dopeman' for the first time and stopping," says Lester. "And going over to the side of the dance floor and just concentrating on what they were saying—which was tough to do because the beat was so bananas. The lyrics just struck me so tough I had to step to the side and really concentrate on what they were talking about. And that's when I fell in love with NWA. There's been moments in my life when I've thought certain things or put up with certain things and felt a certain way about things and then, with the snap of a finger, clarity came. And this was one of those moments."

Suddenly the ghosts of 1965 seemed not only prescient, but present. They were gazing over Ice Cube's shoulder. They were pushing hip-hop progressives to give up the certainty of the past, to embrace their generation and its future, even if that meant coming closer to apocalypse and decay. A millennial impulse was brewing.

Richard Dedeaux's words from Watts seemed prophetic:

Ever since they passed them civil rights
Those fires have been lighting up the nights
And they say they ain't gon' stop til we all have equal rights
Looks to me like dem niggas ain't playing.

NOTES

1. Cross, *It's Not About a Salary,* 201–202 (see chap. 10, n. 39).
2. Rennie Harris, interview by Rudy Corpuz (September 16, 2003).
3. Cross, *It's Not About a Salary,* 102, 143 (see chap. 10, n. 39).
4. Alejandro A. Alonso, "Territoriality Among African American Street Gangs" (master's thesis, University of Southern California, May 1999), 8.
5. Cross, *It's Not About a Salary,* 143 (see chap. 10, n. 39).
6. Terry McDermott, "Parental Advisory: Explicit Lyrics," *Los Angeles Times Magazine* (April 14, 2002). Jonathan Gold, "N.W.A.: Hard Rap and Hype from the Streets of Compton,"

Angeles Weekly (May 5–May 11, 1989), 17. Frank Owen, "Hanging Tough," *Spin* (April 1990), 34.

. George Jackson, *Soledad Brother: The Prison Letters of George Jackson* (New York: Bantam, 1970), 250.

8. Alexander Cockbum, "What Goes Around, Comes Around," *The Nation* (June 1, 1992), 739.

9. J. Max Bond, "The Negro in Los Angeles" (Ph.D. diss., University of Southern California, June 1936), 12, 33. Keith E. Collins, *Black Los Angeles: The Maturing of the Ghetto, 1940–1950* (Saratoga, Calif.: Century Twenty One Publishing, 1 980), 13.

10. Bond, "The Negro in Los Angeles," 12, 33. This man would find an ironic counterpart seventy years later in John Singleton's *Boyz N The Hood,* in the fictional character of Furious Styles, a Black real estate agent struggling to keep his area from being gentrified by whites and overseas Asians.

11. Collins, *Black Los Angeles,* 20–22.

12. Ibid., 70.

13. Gerald Home, *Fire This Time: The Watts Uprisings and the 1960s* (New York: Da Capo Press, 1997), 35.

14. This is according to the Athens Park Blood O.G. named Bone, quoted in the cover story, *F.E.D.S. Magazine* (no date), 78.

15. James Vigil, *A Rainbow of Gangs* (Austin, Tex.: University of Texas Press, 2002), 67.

16. This is according to the Crip O.G. named Red, in *Uprising: Crips and Bloods Tell The Story* of *America's Youth in the Crossfire,* ed. Yusuf Jah and Sister Shah'Keyah (New York: Touchstone, 1997).

17. Alonso, "Territoriality Among African American Street Gangs," 74–75.

18. Richard Serrano, "Dreams of LAPD Class Become Tarnished," *Los Angeles Times* (January 21, 1992), Bl.

19. This argument has been advanced most forcefully by the scholar Greg Hise. Greg Hise, *Magnetic Los Angeles* (Baltimore: Johns Hopkins University Press, 1 997).

20. Horne, *Fire This Time,* 65.

21. Mike Davis, *City of Quartz* (New York: Verso, 1 990), 297–298. Horne, *Fire This Time,* 99.

22. Horne, *Fire This Time,* 64–69.

23. Richard Serrano. "Dreams of LAPD Class Become Tarnished."

24. Horne, *Fire This Time,* 91.

25. *Daily Chronicle* newspaper seen in *The Fire This Time* (Blacktop Films, 1993).

26. Odie Hawkins, *Scars and Memories: The Story of a Life* (Los Angeles: Holloway House, 1987), 125.

27. Davis, *City of Quartz,* 297.

28. *F.E.D.S. Magazine,* 79.

29. Ibid.

30. Elaine Brown, *A Taste of Power: A Black Woman's Story* (New York: Pantheon, 1992), 118, 165. Jack Olsen, *Last Man Standing: The Tragedy and Triumph of Geronimo Pratt* (New York: Doubleday, 2000), 38.

31. Donald Bakeer, *Crips: The Story of the L.A. Street Gang from 1971–1985* (Los Angeles: Precocious Publishing, 1987, 1992), 116.

32. Alonso, "Territoriality Among African American Street Gangs," 90.

33. Ibid., 90–93.

34. Godfather Jimel Barnes in *Uprising,* 152.

35. Bone in *F.E.D.S. Magazine,* Leon Bing, *Do or Die* (New York: Harper Collins, 1991), 149–150. Godfather Jimel Barnes in *Uprising,* 151–152.

36. Alonso, "Territoriality Among African American Street Gangs," 91.

37. Davis, *City of Quartz,* 300.

38. Alonso, "Territoriality Among African American Street Gangs," 7, 97.

39. Ibid., 95.

40. Bone in *F.E.D.S. Magazine,* 82.

41. Alonso, "Territoriality Among African American Street Gangs," 98.

42. Bettijane Levine, "An OG Tries to Make Things Right," *Los Angeles Times* (November 24, 1991), E2.

43. Research Group on the Los Angeles Economy, *The Widening Divide: Income Inequality and Poverty in Los Angeles* (Los Angeles: UCLA Urban Planning Program, 1989), 1.

44. Robin D. G, Kelley, *Race Rebels: Culture, Politics and the Black Working Class* (New York: The Free Press, 1994), 192.

45. California Legislature, Senate, Office of Research, *The South-Central Los Angeles and Koreatown Riots: A Study of Civil Unrest* (Sacramento: State Senate Office of Research, June 17, 1992), 3.

46. Sandy Banks, "Health Center: A Vital Aid in Distressed Community," *Los Angeles Times* (January 27, 1 985), Metro sect., 1.

47. "Metro Digest: Local News in Brief," *Los Angeles Times* (November 17, 1987), 2.

48. Michael Krikorian and Greg Krikorian, "Watts Truce Holds Even As Hopes Fade," Los *Angeles Times* (May 1 8, 1997), B1.

49. Cross, *It's Not About a Salary,* 197 (see chap. 1 0, n. 39).

50. John Glionna, "A Murder That Woke Up LA," *Los Angeles Times* (January 30, 1998), A1. Sandy Banks, "Fate Leads Witnesses to Focal Point of Gang Strife," *Los Angeles Times* (October 1, 1989).

51. Kenneth J. Garcia, "Residents Still Coping with Raid's Effects. Police Gang Sweep Left Families Homeless," *Los Angeles Times* (January 6, 1 989), Metro sect., 1.

52. John L. Mitchell, "The Raid That Still Haunts L.A.," *Los Angeles Times* (March 14, 2001), A1.

53. John A. Oswald, "LAPD to Investigate Raid Damage," *Los Angeles Times* (August 5, 1988), Metro sect., 1.

54. Marc Cooper, "L.A.'s State of Siege: City of Angeles, Cops From Hell," in *Inside the L.A. Riots: What Really Happened and Why It Will Happen Again,* ed. Don Hazen (San Francisco: Institute For Alternative Journalism, 1992), 15.

55. Bob Baker, "A Year After Westwood Killing, L.A. Outrage Makes Little Impact on Gang Epidemic," *Los Angeles Times* (January 30, 1989), 1.

56. Cooper, "LA's State of Siege," 14. Bill Martinez, interview (September 1 8, 2003). (Martinez is a gang intervention trainer and former community youth gang services staffer.) Wendy E. Lane, "DA's Report: Almost Half of L.A. County's Young Black Males in Gangs," Associated Press wire report (May 21,1992).

ᵗory Sandow, "What's NWA All About? Anger, Yes. Violence, No," *Los Angeles Herald* ‿*miner* (July 16, 1989), E-l, E-l 0.

Dave Marsh and Phyllis Pollack, "Wanted for Attitude," *Village Voice* (October 10. 1989), 33.

59. David Mills, "The Gangsta Rapper: Violent Hero or Negative Role Model?" *The Source* (December 1990).

60. Rob Marriott, James Bernard and Allen S. Gordon, "Reality Check," *The Source* (June 1994), 64–65.

OBJECTIVE QUESTIONS

1. What was the name of the group that O'Shea Jackson had with his friends Tony Wheatob and Darrell Johnson?
2. In the early 80s Los Angeles had its own version of Roxy and the "Wheels of Steel" called_____.
3. Where and how did Eric Wright meet Andre Young and O'Shea Jackson?
4. Ice Cube had initially written "Boyz-N-The Hood" for an East Coast group called _____, but they refused to record it. Who recorded it instead, somewhat reluctantly?
5. What prompted the Watts riots of 1965?
6. Eric Wright paid Lonzo Williams $750 to introduce him to a Jewish manager from the valley named_____.
7. At his house on 156ᵗʰ and Wilmington, he held court with a kind of advance rap school to a group of kids that called themselves the Compton Posse. Although he never became more than a local rap hero, his style was carried on by artists like Snoop Dogg, Warren G and DJ Quik.
8. What was Bryan Turner's record label? How had it become successful and how did he meet Jerry Heller?
9. According to Bryan Turner, how did *Straight Outta Compton* sell two million records?
10. What was "Operation Hammer" and who recorded "Batterram"?

QUESTIONS FOR FURTHER THOUGHT, RESEARCH, AND DISCUSSION

1. Compare the controversy surrounding East Coast/West Coast rap to the controversy about East Coast and West Coast jazz in the 1950s.
2. Do you think the fact that O'Shea Jackson was bused to Taft High in the Valley had an affect on his career? What? How? Why?
3. Research the story of George and Jonathan Jackson and compare it to the story in "Boyz-N-The Hood."

4. Listen to recordings of The Watts Prophets and compare them to West Coast rap.

5. Uncle Jam's Army was originally the way that funkmaster George Clinton referred to his fans. Research the life and career of George Clinton and trace his influence on various rappers.

6. Trace the lives and careers of the original members of N.W.A. and what happened to them after the group split up.

7. Ice T got his name from pulp novelist Iceberg Slim. Another pulp novelist who actually wrote from prison was Donald Goines. Read some of the work of either or both and compare it to "gangsta" rap.

"Gangsta, Gansta: The Sad, Violent Parable of Death Row Records" and "Bad Boy"

By Robert Marriott and Dream Hampton

Robert Marriott is a writer and journalist living in the South Bronx. He has written for *The Village Voice*, *The Source*, VIBE, *Spin* and *New York* magazine and was the cofounder of *XXL*. He is currently the executive editor of *Manifest* magazine.

Until the advent of Suge Knight and Death Row Records, one could argue that Hip Hop's connection to gangs, violence and street crime was exaggerated and somewhat metaphorical. There was nothing metaphorical about the violence at Death Row Records, however. Suge's office was painted "Blood" red and his company logo was a drawing of a hooded man in the electric chair awaiting execution. His "strong arm" negotiations and physical intimidation make the godfather's infamous "non-refusable" offers look like child's play. This rather terse article documents Death Row's history and rise to prominence with all of the appropriate facts, but leaves out much of the drama, violence and gory details that fueled the era. The most difficult thing for the journalist of course is separating the facts from the abundance of fiction. This article should be considered merely an outline of what really went on.

"GANGSTA, GANSTA: THE SAD, VIOLENT PARABLE OF DEATH ROW RECORDS"

THE GANGSTA ETHOS AND N.W.A.; DR. DRE, AND THE BIRTH OF DEATH ROW RECORDS

B Y THE EARLY '90S, the American pop consciousness was well aware of the Los Angeles Gangsta Ethos. Artists like Ice-T introduced the concept, but it was the collective of DJs and MCs known as Niggaz With Attitude who would define and refine it. Eazy-E, DJ Yella, MC Ren, Dr. Dre, and Ice Cube articulated the style, stance, and raw ghetto rhetoric that would not only capture the imagination of young people worldwide but also permanently transform American pop culture. N.W.A seared their unsettling image onto the contemporary psyche.

The genre they spawned during the late '80s—scapegoated, vilified, and marketed as gangsta rap—generated millions of dollars for a music industry still attempting to exploit hip hop's popularity and dynamism without truly acknowledging or dealing with the music's street-culture roots. Record companies set out to manufacture "safe" crossover rap, lighter in sound and subject matter, more likely to appeal to a mainstream audience. Even the highly politicized raps of the late '80s—following the lead of Public Enemy and Boogie Down Productions—were becoming more and more affected by the corporations that distributed them, and the raw edge of the music was quietly disappearing.

Gangsta music challenged all of that. It was independent minded, demanding to be heard on it own terms, and it took its cues from the streets, not the boardrooms. It was also selling big. By '91, gangsta music would not only become one of the economic focal points of an otherwise weak music industry, it would also raise the ire of the FBI and the U.S. Congress. Death Row Records—with its dark insignia, gangstafied sound, and street-level ties—appeared right as the money, the movement, and the criticism seemed to be cresting.

Seeing how much money there was to made, Marion "Sugar Bear" Knight, a former college football player turned bodyguard, seized the opportunity. Along with Dr. Dre, whose production for N.W.A was greatly responsible for this new movement, and David Kenner, a lawyer known for his Colombian and Mafia-linked clientele, Knight formed Death Row in 1991. (Among Kenner's former clients was a jailed cocaine dealer and entrepreneur named Michael "Harry-O" Harris, who claims to have provided one million dollars' worth of start-up money in exchange for partial ownership of Death Row Records; Kenner denies Harry's involvement although Kenner and Harry-O's wife, Lydia Harris, both signed legal documents in 1991 tying them to a new company called "GF Music.")

Death Row was a forced birth. Dre was still contracted to Ruthless Records, so Suge—in a room crowded with bodyguards brandishing lead pipes—"persuaded" label owner/N.W.A. founder Eazy-E to release Dre from his contract. With a certified hitmaker in Dre and the ambition and drive to demand more, Suge broke new ground on the business front by forming an alliance with emerging powerhouse Interscope Records. Interscope not only allowed Knight to operate with unprecedented autonomy and control, but gave Knight ownership of his master recordings, something extremely rare in the rap industry. Dre and Suge quickly signed a full roster of acts including Snoop Doggy Dogg, The D.O.C., Dat Nigga Daz, Lady of Rage, Jewell, Kurupt, RBX, and others.

Death Row made no bones about their ties to the L.A. streets. In fact, Knight and the label wrapped themselves in gangsta mythology, determined not just to sell it but to live and breathe it. "We named it Death Row," Suge explained to VIBE, "because most everybody been involved with the law. A majority of our people was parolees or incarcerated." Their logo was hand-drawn and ominous: a man strapped in an electric chair awaiting execution, his head covered with a bag. (The logo would seem stranger still on the cover of the 1996 *Christmas on Death Row* album.) The label's color was blood red—not coincidentally the color of the Luedis Park Pirus, a Blood gang that Suge grew up around. Such associations and the culture that comes with them deeply affected Death Row's direction, motivation, and tactics, and would come back to haunt Knight when the media, the music industry, various police organizations, and even his own artists began to turn against him and his company.

THE CHRONIC, SNOOP DOGG, AND THE INTRODUCTION OF THE G-FUNK ERA

On the title track of the 1992 *Deep Cover* soundtrack, over a beat seemingly composed from arsenic, newcomer Snoop Doggy Dogg gleeful chanted murder: *"And it's 1-8-7 on an undercover cop."* Snoop's drawl was equal parts Mississippi and L.A.: seethingly countrified urban gothic. His style unified two divergent esthetics into a singular sound, an innovation that would foreshadow the subsequent bamafication of hip hop. The Dre-Snoop chemistry embodied on the track, which topped the rap charts, would signal the beginning of Death Row's brief reign over hip hop. Still, as hot as that record was, few expected the bomb that would drop just a few months later. At the height of his powers, Dr. Dre produced *The Chronic*, a certified masterwork of LA gangsta lore.

The Chronic (the title referred to a particularly strong strain of Cali weed) continued where N.W.A's last album, *Efil4zaggin*, left off: haunted P-Funk laced with synthesized vice. They called it G-Funk. Dre and his collaborators gave body to the laid-back tension that characterizes life in the Los Angeles ghettos. It was depraved gospel: searing, uncompromised commentary over luscious production and arrangements. Knocks like "Day the Niggaz Took Over," "Lil' Ghetto Boy," and "Bitches Ain't Shit" were pure street, but with enough musicality to be acknowledged if not fully accepted by the MTV demographic. "Let Me Ride" and the definitive "Nuthin' But a 'G' Thang" had undeniable hooks punctuated with the angst and menace of atmospheric whines. The incongruity made for brilliant pop craft and massive hits. Shock remained the schtick, all part of a formula Dre concocted with N.W.A.—a group built on controversy and bad boy signifying.

By the time Snoop's first solo record, 1993's *Doggystyle,* was released, he had already been crowned rap's new king. Snoop accepted the role with a certain reluctance. Even as he spat cocky brag raps, his eyes often shifted down and away from the cameras. His cool, almost shy demeanor made him downright magnetic. But Snoop ruled over a divided kingdom. Even as *The Chronic*'s formula continued to dominate the charts *(The Chronic* was a commercial and artistic success, selling three million copies; *Doggystyle* would follow with four million), the amorphous hip hop audience—at this point an amalgam of criminals, wannabes, thugs, opportunists, musicians, and charlatans—was as fractious as it had ever been.

The East Coast–West Coast tension that had long been on simmer was brought to a boil in the aftermath of *The Chronic* and *Doggystyle*. This aesthetic quarrel between coastal conglomerates turned into a major media event, but it started earlier than most people acknowledge. In the mid-'80s the West Coast, particularly L.A. and the Bay Area, began to demand a certain respect and attention for their local musics and styles—not only from the East Coast, where the rap industry was centered, but also from their own artists. West Coast audiences grew tired of rappers from California sounding like New Yorkers and sought a distinctively West Coast sound and feel—something only artists like N.W.A., Compton's Most Wanted, and Too Short really provided.

By the turn of the decade, New York, always loath to give anyone else too much respect, was suffering from low record sales and a demoralized music community. N.Y.C. artists couldn't understand why West Coast music kept outselling them by the millions. No one considered the fact that New York rap had actually become an overcrowded field, greatly watered down and now lacking the content and creativity that originally made the city the center of innovation. Whatever the case, the tensions continued to increase as the media fanned the flames.

DEATH ROW AND SUGE SHAKE UP THE INDUSTRY; DRE IS ISOLATED FROM HIS OWN COMPANY

By 1994, Death Row, having established its unquestioned dominance, began showing signs of weakness. In the wake of several more multiplatinum-selling albums (Tha Dogg Pound's *Dogg Food*, the *Above the Rim* soundtrack), Suge became more and more notorious; the G-Funk sound was beginning to get exploited by everyone within the reach of a synthesizer; Snoop, the Row's biggest star, was put on trial for murder; and, most important, Dr. Dre was beginning to feel alienated from his own label.

At first, the black corners of the music industry respected Suge and what he seemed to be accomplishing: getting better deals for his and other artists, frightening the industry heads that made millions off the music into breaking off a bigger chunk for the people who actually created the music, and inspiring ghetto people everywhere to strive for bigger things. Suge was rich, independent, and didn't stand for the nonsense. He played the role of protective older brother, eventually luring non-Death Row big names like Jodeci and Mary J. Blige to hire him as a "consultant." But that admiration soon turned into a fearful respect and, not long after that, into naked fear. Suge always denied the violent stories (what else was he going to do?) but never shied away from his image as a thuggish CEO who wasn't above taking it *to* you. "I know the stories," he said, "but ultimately it's about *results*." Suge understood that the intimidation factor added by the more brutal rumors was a clear business advantage and started to revel in the respect and allowances afforded to a gangsta mogul. He became more and more cavalier in his various declarations and actions. He and his entourage terrorized and/or beat down many of those who dared question him. He stockpiled enemies and court cases. Rumors and allegations of how he threatened and assaulted various figures in the music industry, such as Uptown Records' Andre Harrell, were rampant.

At the second annual *Source* awards in 1995, Suge began what would be a two-year siege on the character and manhood of rival record mogul Sean "Puff Daddy" Combs. "If you don't want your CEO dancing in all your videos," he announced from the podium, "come on over to Death Row."

It was a swipe clearly aimed at Combs and his Bad Boy label, including Combs's biggest star, the Notorious B.I.G. But war was truly declared in October 1995, when Jake Robles, a good friend of Suge's, was shot to death in Atlanta at a Jermaine Dupri party. Suge felt Puff and his bodyguards were to blame for the murder; Puffy denied any connection to the shooting.

THE RELEASE OF TUPAC SHAKUR;
THE BAD BOY / DEATH ROW FEUD;
DRE LEAVES DEATH ROW

Tupac Shakur was a star pitted in a life-and-death struggle with himself. After nearly a four-year career of turmoil and conflict resulting in court cases and infamy, Shakur found himself languishing in a jail cell while his latest album, the aptly titled *Me Against the World,* topped the charts—a plight that accurately characterizes the dual nature of the volatile Mr. Shakur. Convicted on the lesser counts of a rape charge he caught in a New York City hotel, Shakur faced a sizable bid.

Knight and David Kenner came to visit Tupac at Clinton, the Upstate New York medium security prison in which he was held, and made him the proverbial offer he couldn't refuse. It was a common perception among those close to Shakur that he, in a very real sense, sold his soul to get out of that cramped cell when he signed the four-page handwritten contract they proffered in exchange for posting his bail. But few anticipated the white-hot spectacle of Tupac's final days. He was incredibly prolific recording hundreds of songs after his release; the seven-times platinum double album *All Eyez on Me* and the posthumous *Makaveli* were but a small sampling of the enormous catalog he created in a few short months.

With the addition of Tupac to the roster, Suge renamed the label "The New 'Untouchable' Death Row"—perhaps as testimony to his infallibility, perhaps as reassurance in light of mounting tensions. But the writing was on the wall. Not long after the release of Tupac's debut single on Death Row, "California Love," Dre made it publicly known that he wanted out. Even though Snoop beat the murder rap, the very public trial lent credence to gangsta music's critics: this was a music for sociopaths, they argued—just look at its icons. Suge, meanwhile, was paying out enormous settlements to his many victims, and more and more people in the industry and the underworld began to lay claim to Death Row's enormous fortune.

Meanwhile Tupac, caught up in Death Row's violent mystique, began putting in work for Suge's campaign against Bad Boy. Tupac already blamed the Bad Boy camp for setting up his shooting the previous year in the lobby of a Times Square building, so he was eager to take them on. There was a backstage showdown at the *Soul Train* Awards. Tupac released the venomous "Hit 'Em Up," a tirade against Biggie and his entire entourage. Suge, for his part, continued to assail Puffy and Biggie, attempting to goad the two into a war of words and music, not unaware that such a war would stir up publicity. But Puffy and Biggie refused to fuel the already out-of-control fire in their interviews, responding only on Big's posthumous *Life After Death* with the gothic "Downfall" and "Long Kiss Goodnight." The conflict between the East and West Coasts, though, became more open, with more and more artists recording battle songs or stating which side they were claiming. Things came to a head when Tha Dogg Pound came to Brooklyn to make the video for "New York, New York," a song many in N.Y.C. considered an insult to the city. Their trailer was shot at, but no one was hurt. The coastal rivalry was now a war of more than just words.

THE SHOOTING OF TUPAC SHAKUR AND THE END OF THE DEATH ROW ERA; THE EVOLUTION OF THE RECORD COMPANY; THE ENTIRELY POSSIBLE REDEMPTION OF SUGE

By the summer of 1996, the entire Death Row situation had degenerated into madness. Every day was a fight, a threat, an argument in a war that Tupac struggled to give meaning to. "The 'W' I throw up" he said, referring to the hand sign he and Ice Cube made famous, "don't stand for 'Wesside.' It stands for War, and until we come together and have power it's gonna be war." But on September 7, 1996, Death Row and its disorganized notions of valor were taken to their destructive conclusion. Under the flashing lights and Las Vegas glitter of the MGM Grand on a Mike Tyson fight night, Shakur and the Death Row entourage got into yet another scuffle, one that would prove to be Shakur's last. A few hours later, on a relatively quiet Vegas street, Suge and 'Pac made their way to an after party in one of Suge's fleet of cars. Without anyone noticing, a white Cadillac rode alongside Suge's black BMW and let off fifteen rounds of gunfire into the passenger seat, grazing Suge's head and fatally wounding Shakur. He died on September 13. The crime remains unsolved.

Las Vegas was a strangely appropriate setting for the violent finale of Death Row's hour upon the American stage. Tupac and Suge had fallen victim to their own Babylonian excesses, and the wholly American illusions of gangsta glamour immediately began to burn away in the wake of the fall. Dr. Dre split from Death Row, but has been relegated to a less significant role in the genre he helped create; his fledgling Aftermath Entertainment struggled to make an impact until the 1999 release of white-boy wonder Eminem's *The Slim Shady LP*. In the end, Snoop was merely a rhyme sayer, not the gangsta icon everybody wanted him to be. He too eventually broke from Death Row and joined Master P's No Limit battalion. Suge Knight, the embodiment of uncompromised power and wealth, was forced to sell his prized masters. He was now powerless against a court system that had it out for him, and was ultimately imprisoned on a parole violation charge stemming from the tussle in the MGM Grand lobby.

Death Row Records served as a sad and necessary step in the evolution of the black independent record company, an increasingly important American institution. Granted, the violent behavior, the heavy jailhouse influence, the mob-style usage of intimidation as a business strategy pointed to an inevitable conclusion, but the impact of their intentions are just beginning to be felt. In the void left in the wake of Death Row's demise, No Limit Records and a host of other southern record companies like Suave House and Cash Money are making good on the Death Row promissory note: thriving as the strong, black-owned, and street-rooted independents Death Row once was.

But it would be wrong to underestimate Suge Knight's redemptive potential once he is released from prison (and rumors regularly circulate that such release will come sooner rather than later). Master P and others have learned from Death Row's mistakes. It's hard to believe that Suge hasn't learned a few lessons himself.

DISCOGRAPHY

Snoop Doggy Dogg

Doggystyle (Death Row/Interscope, 1993). *Murder Was the Case: The Soundtrack* (Death Row/Interscope, 1994). *Tha Doggfather* (Death Row/Interscope, 1996).

[As Snoop Dogg]

Da Game Is to Be Sold, Not to Be Told (No Limit/Priority, 1998). *Top Dogg* (No Limit/Priority, 1999).

Tha Dogg Pound

Dogg Food (Death Row/Interscope, 1995). *West Coast Aftershock* (Death Row/Priority, 1998).

The Lady of Rage

Necessary Roughness (Death Row, 1997).

Various Artists

Above the Rim [soundtrack] (Death Row/Interscope, 1994). *Christmas on Death Row* (Death Row, 1996). *Death Row's Greatest Hits* (Death Row, 1996). *Suge Knight Represents: Chronic 2000* (Death Row, 1999).

OBJECTIVE QUESTIONS

1. What was Suge Knight's introduction to the rap music industry?
2. Suge Knight's initial partner in Death Row Records was a lawyer known for his Columbian and Mafia-linked clientele named_____.
3. Suge formed an alliance with emerging powerhouse _____
4. What was Snoop Dogg's first recording?
5. Where does the title to Dr. Dre's famous Lp *The Chronic* come from?
6. Who was Suge referring to when he famously announced at the annual *Source* awards in 1995, "If you don't want your CEO dancing in all your videos, come on over to Death Row"?
7. What is the story behind Tupac's "Hit 'Em Up"?
8. Why did Tupac sign with Death Row?
9. Who produced Eminem's *The Slim Shady Lp.*?
10. What was the occasion that brought Suge and Tupac to Las Vegas on September 7, 1996?

QUESTIONS FOR FURTHER THOUGHT, RESEARCH, AND DISCUSSION

1. Research the history of African American owned record companies starting with Black Swan in the 1920s and including Motown and Def Jam. How is Death Row different or similar?
2. Research and report on the attitude and atmosphere at Death Row during the recording of *The Chronic*. Research the details of the nefarious origins of the company and its business dealings.
3. Research and report on the legal problems of Snoop Dogg.
4. Research the history of the East Coast/West Coast feud. Why do you think West Coast records were outselling East Coast records?
5. Research and report on the history and influence of organized crime in the record industry. Frank Sinatra and Berry Gordy are just two tips of the iceberg.

"BAD BOY"
FROM *THE VIBE HISTORY HISTORY OF HIP HOP*

BY DREAM HAMPTON

Dream Hampton became the first woman editor of *The Source* magazine in 1990 while still a film student at NYU. As a contributing writer at *Vibe* magazine she has written articles on Jay-Z, Mary J. Blige, and D'Angelo. Her writing has appeared in the *Village Voice, Spin, The Detroit News, Harper's Bizarre, Essence, Parenting,* and other magazines. Hampton's short film *I Am Ali* was an official entry in the 2002 Sundance Film festival and won the Jury award at *Vanity Fair's* Newport Beach Film Festival. In 1994, Hampton was a founding member of the Malcolm X Grassroots Movement's Brooklyn chapter.

Historically it seems hip hop has had more trouble crossing coastal barriers than either racial or economic ones. This is the story of Sean "Puffy" Combs, Bad Boy Records and Notorious B.I.G., but once again, the expurgated version with all of the drama and most of the embarrassing details left out or glossed over. "Puff Daddy" was mentored in the music business by Andre Harrell at Uptown Records and made his mark with pop and soul remixes before starting his own company backed by Arista. A lot has been written about the East Coast/West Coast feud of the 1990s and who started it. Unfortunately, we all know how it ended. There are many who think they know what happened and why, but typically, there doesn't seem to be anyone who is willing to talk about it, at least not to the police. This article has most of the important facts, but the real fan and student will feel the need to investigate deeper below the surface.

DECEMBER 30, 1991
UPTOWN RECORDS CONFERENCE ROOM

L AWYERS ARE HERE. Puff's mentor and boss Andre Harrell is here. As president and founder of Uptown Records, Andre has a lot invested in Sean "Puffy" Combs; he recently gave Puff the high-profile, high-pressure job of shepherding the embryonic careers of Jodeci and Mary J. Bilge. Heavy D, Uptown's only bona fide star, is here because he and Puff are friends—Hev put Puff on as an intern at Uptown, they're both from Mount Vernon, and they co-sponsored the celebrity basketball game two days earlier where nine people were trampled to death.

Puff is afraid that reading from index cards will seem disingenuous, so he's trying to memorize the short speech he has prepared: "It has always been my dream to throw parties where young black people ..." The basketball game at City College was supposed to be a way to end a year in which Puff's parties—weekly events dubbed "Daddy's House" at a midtown Manhattan club called the Red Zone—had grown mammoth, uniting the New York hip hop community on a scale not seen since the legendary nights at Harlem's Rooftop in the '80s. Andre tells him "dream" sounds too

MIXED CUTS: HOW REMIXES COMPLIMENT AND COMPLICATE

by The Blackspot

IN 1996, MC LYTE's *Bad As I Wanna B* album wasn't going anywhere too fast. Then Puff Daddy was handed the next single—an otherwise-forgettable track titled "Cold Rock a Party." He hooked up a new beat underneath Lyte's rhymes—a loop from Diana Ross's disco hit "Upside Down"—and brought in rising star Missy Elliott for a cameo verse. Presto! The refurbished song was the biggest hit of Lyte's career, and *Bad* got a new lease on life. Witness the power of the remix.

For decades, artists have recorded multiple versions of the same song. Some make up creative names like the "Ego Mix" the "Baby Muvah Bump Mix," and the "Government Cheese Mix." And over the years, these souped-up versions of a song—or "remixes," as they've come to be known—have become an increasingly essential element in making hit records.

It's difficult to accurately trace the first remix in hip hop, because any change to an original recording can be classified as a remix. Early remixes like the "Vocal Dub version" of Run-D.M.C.'s 1984 "Rock Box" included minor alterations—an extra bass line, the switching of a snare drum, or an added hand clap. DJs such as Ron G and Kid Capri made their own remixes of previously released songs on mix tapes fey blending the instrumental of one song with an a capella version of another.

Later, a remix could consist of an entirely different beat and even new lyrics. One example is De La Soul's 1989 classic "Buddy." The album version fetured Q-Tip from the then up-and-coming group A Tribe Called Quest arid the Jungle Brothers. The remixed version added Monie Love and Qyeen Latifah, who all rhymed over a sample of Taana Gardner's 1981 "Heartbeat." Because of the extreme changes, "Buddy" is held up by many enthusiasts as one of the most innovative remixes in hip hop history.

Although there is a definite creative element involved, the remix is also a tool for monetary interests. "Remixes were originally used to save a record that's already out," says Deric "D-Dot" Angelettie—a member of Bad Boy Entertainment's notorious Hitmen production team, who ruled the remix universe in the latter half of the 1990s, making over hits by KRS-One, New Edition, and even the Police. "If a song was dying out, a remix would give it that edge to live an extra few months."

This was the case when Bad Boy put out "One More Chance" by the Notorious B.I.G. in 1996. The remix added a radio-friendly piano loop from DeBarge's "Stay with We" not found on the version from the *Ready to Die* album. Then Bad Boy put out yet another remix of the song, this time using a bumping, restructured sample of Craig G's "Droppin' Science." As a result, "One More Chance' stayed fresh on the streets and in clubs for months.

This tactic not only helped sales of the album but also raked in cash for the single. The remix phenomenon proved beneficial to both record companies and consumers; buying a single with multiple versions was like getting a bunch of songs for the price of one. Other notable remixes brought seemingly mismatched artists together on wax, whether live or sampled—like Eric B. and Rakim with Israeli vocalist Ofra Haza ("Paid in Full"), Marian Carey and Ol' Dirty Bastard ("Fantasy"), and Puff Daddy with Rob Zombie and Dave Grohl ("It's All About the Benjamins")—in search of the perfect blend of elements that would make or prolong a hit.

Although the multiple mix concept seemed to be painless, a downside soon became apparent: Some versions of songs were going to radio that couldn't be found on the album. Record buyers were going to stores, purchasing an album, and finding a totally different version of the hit they wanted in the first place. In 1991, urban radio was playing "Choice is Yours" by Black Sheep. Hip hop fans instantly picked up on the chorus, "You can get with this / or you can get with that ..." When they bought the *A Wolf in Sheep's Clothing* album later that year, though, and got a different version of the group's signature hit, Black Sheep's newfound fan base was left disappointed. Eventually, Mercury Records released the single that included the familiar version. This love/hate relationship over remixes remains in place—who knows how many people bought *Bad As I Wanna B* only to end up frustrated that it didn't have the hit version of "Cold Rock a Party"?

Once used as a life-support system for a record on its way out of radio rotation, remixes are being taken more seriously as an art form. In 1996, the National Association of Recording Arts and Sciences added a category to the Grammy Awards to honor the best non-classical remixer of the year. Meanwhile, thousands of hungry, unknown producers sit in studios wearing out their fingertips on recording equipment. If they're lucky, they might come across the right combination of sampled loops, sound effects, or drum sounds to create the next platinum-selling re-recording—while artists and label execs hold out hope that if you give a song enough chances, you'll find the mix that will make a new superstar.

affected, too dramatic. Puff's attorney Michael Warren—who will, years later, represent Tupac at his sexual assault trial—agrees.

"But I would say that ... wouldn't I say that?" Puff searches for an understanding face at the table. He is only twenty-two. He *is* a dreamer, and drama—well, what exactly is *too* dramatic in these surreal few days?

The local press gathers at the St. Regis Hotel. They want to know how it can be that nine people, nine young black people, died, stampeded trying to get into a basketball game. Puff and Hev have been awake all weekend trying to figure out how it happened. How to be responsible without bearing full responsibility. There was a lot of crying and pacing and phone calls; to lawyers, from friends, and finally to the families of the victims whose phone numbers they can find. Puff's girlfriend, Misa, lost one of her good friends that night. The girl's mother is inconsolable.

The night of the event inside City College's gym, when the panic threatened to create an even larger tragedy, when people around him were losing their heads, Puff scrambled from one unconscious victim to another trying to resuscitate them. "I breathed in death," he muttered as he paced Heavy D's basement that night. "I felt it happen."

The morning after the press conference, the *New York Post* blames the tragedy on a "Fool Named Puff Daddy." In the article they call him a rapper. Puff and Misa come to pick me up from work at *The Source*. It is Misa's birthday and she is still mourning her friend. She waits in the car and Puff comes up to the office. He stands in the hallway, outside the door, to avoid the magazine's other editors, who are all working on a story about CCNY and him.

His eyes are swollen from lack of sleep. He talks about death threats; people claiming to be relatives of the victims have been calling his office all day. Andre wants him to stay away from the job he loves so much for a while. He mentions suicide. By the time this registers, though, he's jumped back to the death threats. "But I feel protected. By God." He opens his black ski jacket. "See, I don't have anything on me, no guns, vests. If they kill me, they kill me. It's meant for me to die."

Puffy Combs's success—and consequently, Bad Boy Entertainment's—has always been marred by tragedy. After CCNY he began wearing a gold charm of Lazarus, the resurrected. The charm, flooded with pavé diamonds, became symbolic of Puff's own phoenixlike rise from the ashes. In the summer of 1992, Mary J. Blige's *What's the 411?* was released and it dominated the streets of New York, receiving the Jeep rotation reserved for hip hop. Mary was a raw force with an exceptional sound and a set of compelling contradictions: shy, a little rough, too trusting, mean. The marriage of who she was with the core hip hop beats Puff selected—whole bars from EPMD and Audio Two—was definitive.

Mary was accepted as the real thing, crowned the Queen of Hip Hop Soul, and Puff was considered her creator. New York buried the memory of CCNY. His peers in the music industry began to regard him with a combination of awe and envy. Hustlers in Harlem, who Puff had looked to for inspiration and sensibility, started emulating him. The weight of his links, the rims he chose, the way he wore his sweats (one leg up), the color his girl dyed her hair (honey blond, then white platinum) were all scrutinized and copied.

Bad Boy Entertainment's image began innocently enough. Puff had his precocious godson photographed wearing size 10½ Doc Martens combat boots. The preschooler had one hand on his little nuts and the other pointed toward the sky. Still vice president of A&R at Uptown, Puff hired a street promotion team to litter the hip hop party-scene with postcard-size flyers. On the back of the black and white photo was the announcement: THE NEXT GENERATION OF BAD MOTHAFUCKAS.

Puff became increasingly arrogant. He would stand in the office hallway with his shirt off and say things like, "Puff Daddy is my name as an artist, Sean Combs is my name for the movies."

In July 1993, Andre Harrell fired him. I talked to Puff that night. He was stunned. "This nigga walked into my office saying 'There can only be one lion in the jungle.'" He drove around the city in his new white BMW like a teenager who'd just been kicked out of the house, his Bad Boy business plan stuffed in the rear window, his makeshift staff, Uptown employees who had been splitting their duties, forced to choose sides.

When Puff introduces me to him, Big barely looks at me. He seems extremely shy. We are in Daddy-O from Stetsasonic's basement studio. Big is here to add a few bars to the remix of Mary's "Real Love." It is his first real recording.

It is the summer of 1992. Biggie lives around the corner from me in Brooklyn, but I didn't know him when, as an editor at The Source, *I voted for his "Unsigned Hype" submission, a raw demo where he spat lyrics with authority over a Big Daddy Kane beat. But we will see each other every day after we meet, as he is, no matter the weather, posted on Fulton Avenue when I make my way to NYU each morning.*

At 6'3" and a little more than 200 pounds, it's hard to miss Christopher "Biggie Smalls" Wallace. Plus, there is always a small crowd around him. His little niggas. He is sharp and witty, hilarious and wickedly observant. People naturally gravitate toward him. They hold down the Chinese food spot, or the wall between the laundromat and the 24-hour, Jamaican-operated weed spot, and they smoke and joke a lot. Sometimes Biggie will bogle, or pay a girl a Snapple to do the Butterfly. Crackheads maintain a respectful distance till they catch some attention. They always acknowledge Big, throwing him a "Big Chris" and a quick toothless grin. Invariably one of the kids reaches into a brown paper bag stuffed in the crevice of the wall and blesses the addict with a white top.

When Puff was fired, Biggie sank into a deep depression. "I would have rather have never come out if I'm never gonna come out," he said. His anthemic "Party and Bullshit," from the *Who's the Man?* soundtrack, was a club hit, and Puff put him on a half-dozen remixes within months of signing him to Uptown. A version of his album was almost finished. His girlfriend of four years, Jan, gave birth to a pretty baby girl, T'Yanna. Big paid friends to clean his room so he could wheel her bassinet next to his bed at night.

He and older brother figure Lance "Un" Rivera daydreamed aloud about future business plans. His best friend Damien was in and out of jail on a charge he caught defending his grandmother's life. His mother's breast cancer was always on his mind. And his entire neighborhood was counting on him to change their reality.

By the end of the year, though, the release date of Big's album was nowhere in sight. Puff made one of his rare trips to Brooklyn one night and the three of us went to Junior's restaurant. Over strawberry cheesecake, he assured Big that things were going to happen. That their dreams were going to come true. That set backs are mere challenges and together they would be unstoppable. "I'm a visionary," he said, leaning back into the circular red leather booth, decorated with Christmas lights. "You've got to trust me."

The rest, as they say, is history. Bad Boy landed a home with Clive Davis's Arista Records, and launched with Craig Mack's *Project: Funk the World*. Then, on September 1, 1994, the label released the Notorious B.I.G.'s landmark debut *Ready to Die* (copyright problems forced his official name change). And while Craig Mack's single "Flava in Ya Ear" had claimed the summer, it was Big's album that would shape Bad Boy's success.

Dr. Dre's *The Chronic* had an enormous effect on every rap album released after 1992. Previously, New York had shut out West Coast hip hop. N.W.A was virtually ignored until Cube went solo. Too Short was practically unheard of. Ultramagnetic's Tim Dog released a gimmicky single called "Fuck Compton" that was like a rallying cry during the summer of 1991.

Before, L.A. would put up with the insults. They couldn't pretend they weren't fans of New York hip hop—what else was there? But *The Chronic* presented L.A.'s languid rhyme style and murderous mentality as a challenge. And for almost two years, its superiority went uncontested. Until *Ready to Die*. It was in this sublime manner, long before it was articulated or fatally played out, that the East Coast–West Coast battle began to take form.

Puff had been aiming for a sense of album-length continuity with Jodeci and Mary when he was at Uptown. After Dre unleashed *The Chronic,* though, Puff understood exactly how cinematic 14 tracks could be. Mary's sophomore *My Life* was Dre's approach sampled and perfected; it was seamless. While Craig Mack, a producer and hip hop head from way back, shunned direction from Puff, Big became dependent on it.

With *Ready to Die,* Puff provided the proscenium arches for Big's lush narrative style. He required that the album's drama be tempered by a tone, that the action be present tense and vivid.

He encouraged Big to rhyme slower and less forcefully. Like Kool G Rap, an early influence, Big's autobiographically grafted protagonist was all criminal. Even his pitch had a violent quality; when Big said he was the illest, it didn't sound like braggadocio, but like a stickup.

Like Slick Rick's, Big's form was a storytelling style replete with costars, characters created from his own alter ego: the second shooter in "Gimme the Loot," the eavesdropping loyal homie on "Warning." He contextualized the intergenerational schism created by the drug trade with songs like "Things Done Changed." Suicide was the album's metaphor for the widespread depression, despair, and hopelessness facing the kamikaze capitalists that New Yorkers simply dubbed hustlers.

The hypermaterialism of the drug game had been transported to hip hop by a new generation, and where sales may have been less important before, now they were everything. Wu-Tang had staged an aesthetic takeover of sorts—they'd at least wrestled New Yorkers from Dre's hypnotic trance. But it would still be months before "C.R.E.A.M.," their breakthrough hit, was released. And now New York had a new hip hop hero, Brooklyn's first since Big Daddy Kane.

Unwittingly (and almost undetectably), with their classic albums, Biggie and Bad Boy and Dre and his label Death Row planted the seeds that would marry their respective futures. Ironically, Big was always aware of West Coast hip hop, always a fan. (While I can claim introducing him to Too Short—I played him ragged, boot legged copies of *Freaky Tales* early in our friendship; he loved the pornographic profanity—it was Big who illuminated some of the finer moments on N.W.A's most misogynist effort, *Efil4zaggin.*) The music affected his sensibility, making him listenable to L.A. fans where other New York rappers had failed.

In many ways, *The Chronic* and *Ready to Die* bridged coastal gaps crossing each other's audiences over. Dre's genius as a producer was undeniable. New York's legacy of brilliant lyricists descended on Biggie as if he were a cultural apex. Their influences were immeasurable. But when the tides changed, they would become binary markers.

The first week of November 1994, Puff threw himself a birthday party at Roseland ballroom. It was his first major, party since the CCNY tragedy, He shamelessly repeated a videography of all his cameos on huge monitors. Tupac, who was knee deep in a rape trial, attended. He and Biggie held court in the VIP lounge. Big introduced his wife, singer Faith Evans—whom he'd married three months before following a nine-day whirlwind romance—to 'Pac, the only nigga in the industry he considered a true friend.

A few days later, Tupac was robbed and shot in the lobby of Quad Recording Studio. He recovered rapidly and his mother wheeled him into court two days later to continue his trial. He was convicted of sexual assault and sentenced. He went to Rikers Island, then upstate to Clinton Correctional Facility. From prison, he granted *VIBE* an interview that implicated Biggie, Puff, Andre Harrell, even his best friend Stretch, who was robbed the night of the shooting. With real conviction, he asserted that his friends either had knowledge of or involvement in his shooting.

Stretch had warned Big that 'Pac was "flippin' from the stress." But Big was unprepared for the accusations, the fallout, and, more important, the media circus that ensued.

At the Hit Factory recording studio, after reading an advance copy of the story, Puff huddled with Big. "We say nothing," he told Big. "Niggas come up to you, start questioning you, reporters start asking you shit … nothing. Complete silence." Big shrugged in agreement. The whole thing had thrown him into a state of disbelief. "Man … whatever. What is there to say?"

And so it went. Bad Boy had no comment. 'Pac's accusations grew louder. Suge Knight, co-founder of Death Row Records, began listening. Knight—who blamed Puff for the murder of one of his associates at a party in Atlanta—offered Tupac a record deal (Tupac was already signed to Death Row's parent company, Interscope) and posted his bail. Tupac began a public assault on Bad Boy and Biggie. Puff and Big kept silent. Bad Boy released three R&B albums; from Total, 112, and finally from Big's immensely talented wife, Faith. They all sold well.

Big stacked up his own share of criminal cases: He was accused of breaking the jaw of a promoter who tried to stiff him, beating a "fan" with a baseball bat in front of the Palladium, and illegal possession of firearms. His marriage disintegrated. His protégé group junior M.A.F.I.A. launched Undeas Records, the company he and his partner Un formed. Lil' Kim, with whom Big was romantically involved, shone. He began building a home for his mother in a suburb of Philadelphia.

When Big arrived in Los Angeles for the 1996 *Soul Train* Awards, there was no representative or car from Bad Boy or Arista at the airport. It was the first indication to Big's core group of friends, Un and his niggas from Brooklyn, that they would have to take Big's safety in their own hands. The heated atmosphere was palpable. Big and Puff and Faith performed a medley of hits at the show wearing all white. 'Pac stormed the aisle during the performance wearing fatigues. He had a small army with him. He and Big came face to face backstage for the first time since 'Pac's conviction in 1994. "That's when I knew it was real to him," Big said later. "That he believed all this shit. Duke was just convinced." 'Pac and Lil' Cease from Junior M.A.F.I.A. threw insults at each other. A gun was fired. Then another one. The crowd dispersed.

'Pac released the most scathing dis record in hip hop history, a B-side titled "Hit 'Em Up," in which he called Big a "fat muthafucka" and yelled, "I fucked your wife!" Privately, Big became weary of it all. "The fucked-up shit is that instead of my music, the shit I accomplished, I'm gonna be remembered for this dumb shit."

But it was Tupac whose life felt the impact first. On September 6, 1996, he was shot in Las Vegas after a Mike Tyson fight. Seven days later, he died. It was truly astonishing—Tupac embodied the myth of the real nigga, an indestructible construct ("Real Niggaz Don't Die") created during one of the most violent periods in black history. And 'Pac was resilient. He had walked between bullets and, when hit, away from them.

I called Big the day after Tupac's death and asked him how he felt. "Shocked." Would he consider attending a funeral if there was one to, you know, bury the beef? "Naw, man. This nigga—he just made my life miserable. Ever since he came home. He told lies, fucked with my marriage, turned fans against me. For what?"

At the time of 'Pac's death, Big was recuperating from a car accident. Lil' Cease had crashed his Benz into a freeway median. Big's girlfriend Tiffany, whom he'd met after a concert in Philly the summer of '95 (Faith had recently given birth to their son Chris, but they were still estranged), broke her ankle. Big was unable to walk and entered extensive rehabilitation therapy. Two months later, in a wheelchair, he flew to Los Angeles to appear in the video for Puffs first single as an artist, "Can't Nobody Hold Me Down." Suge Knight, Puff's nemesis, was in jail for parole violation. And though Puff said publicly that he was simply in Los Angeles for the better film production quality, it was not lost on anyone, least of all L.A. rap fans, that his mere presence was the declaration of a quiet victory. A local DJ, Julio G, came to the set to do an interview with Big and Puff. They were diplomatic and sincere when they acknowledged 'Pac's loss.

In January 1997, Big returns to L.A. on crutches to work on Puff's debut album. He is in high spirits. He talks about his new son a lot. Advance copies of his new double album arrive on compact disc from Bad Boy's offices in New York. He plays it loudly in his rented Suburban, On March 8, he attends a party following the Soul Train *Awards, at which he was a presenter. Leaving the party in the Suburban, on Fairfax and Wilshire, he is gunned down. Damien and Cease are in the car; Gee, a friend from Brooklyn, is driving. Puff, a few cars ahead, hears the shots and runs to the truck. Big dies before they can drive him the half-mile to Cedars Sinai Hospital*

A private funeral is held on Manhattan's Upper East Side. Puff speaks, Faith sings, Big's mother reads from the Book of Job. Un and Damien and his man L are pallbearers. Big's crew—officially called Junior M.A.F.I.A., but really just very young men from Fulton Street who loved him—hold one another up in the standing room area at the back of the parlor. A motor procession drives through Brooklyn, up the block where Big was raised, St. James Place, and down Fulton Avenue.

Two weeks later, Damien, Cease, Gee, and I are in front of Big's old apartment on St. James. We pour some cognac on the makeshift altar his neighbors and fans have erected. We sit in front of the building in Big's new customized Suburban. It is completely bullet-proof and there is a stash box big enough for a .45 Ruger. It was to be shipped out to Los Angeles three days after Big was shot. Life After Death *rocks the truck back and forth. The skit that proceeds "Going Back to Cai" comes on. "You know this was playing when it happened, right?" Damien tells me. He doesn't dwell on the irony. He fast-forwards to the next track.*

* * *

Big's second album, *Life After Death,* was released just three weeks after his murder. It is a staggering achievement. In the beginning Big had been hungry, for fortune more than fame. He wanted to be rich. With Puff, he achieved that, and in many ways his life changed drastically. He went from having no car to owning four. He bought a condo in Teaneck, New Jersey, and moved his friends in. He established funds for his two children. Through Junior M.A.F.I.A. he provided an opportunity for everyone who meant something to him from his neighborhood to change their lives.

But fame had been something else. It had turned against him, or, more accurately, it had been turned against him. He felt betrayed in the most basic sense by Tupac—as undoubtedly Tupac must have felt about Big when he began to believe the stories he was being told.

Life After Death was an examination of betrayal, notoriety, excess, and greed. Big's narratives were still firmly couched in the autobiographical tradition, his first-person protagonist still our generation's everyman, the drug dealer. That hustler still thoroughly invested in the myth of the real nigga, the myth of action. But the album is in every way evolutionary. Formally, Big exercised practically every existing flow pattern. And on songs that appear quite basic at first, like the first single, "Hypnotize," he even experimented with brand-new verbal styles.

He had achieved perfection with a remix of "One More Chance" on *Ready to Die,* and on his sophomore effort he extended that perfection with "Long Kiss Goodnight," "Niggas Bleed," and "Somebody's Gotta Die." Amazingly, wordy and intricate narratives like "I Got a Story to Tell" were never committed to paper; the autodidactic practice of composing whole songs in his head had become, for him, effortless. Sonically, the album was even more cinematic than the first: full, rich, and three-dimensional.

Big had never learned to separate himself from his narrative, to inject criticism of his reality—mostly because he was living it. But if his and Tupac's lives were sacrifices, then the lessons to be garnered, the history that's documented, will be transmitted through the immediacy of their lyrics. It is this legacy—of a generation racing toward the millennium with all of the century's loaded symbols, its technology, its maddening war on young black bodies and our often inadequate response to that assault—that will be passed on.

A month after the funeral, I visit Puff at his recording studio in Midtown Manhattan, Daddy's House, There are rumors floating around that he might take a sabbatical from the music industry, postpone or cancel plans to release the solo album he'd been working on in Los Angeles, then titled Harlem World. *"There's so much to say—but what is there to say." I look at my boots, then at the walls in the office of the studio and the platinum plaques on them. "I don't know. … I think about suicide a lot." I look at the healed scars on his wrists, rumored to be an attempt but actually just the nasty marks from a shattered champagne bottle that got tangled in his bracelet and lodged in his veins. That arm is cold to touch and, he says, often numb. "But not really, not in that kind of way. … You know, not like I'm going to do it. … "*

I know he won't. And as I walk back to my hotel room it occurs to me that not only will he move forward and release the album, eventually titled No Way Out, *but that he will also become a huge star. That he will release the album he is in the studio to mix, by the Lox. That it too will be a hit and Bad Boy will keep making hits—as it turns out, by a slow-talking rapper named Mase and by Puff's producing everybody from Lil' Kim to Mariah Carey. That Puff will break and set records. That he will realize his dream to make and star in films. That while drama like his alleged assault of Nas's manager, Steve Stoute, will follow him, he will continue to invoke the kind of envy that can become violent and that he will be emulated until the day he dies.*

I think, as I walk, that he must have paid some great karmic debt, in some distant lifetime, to walk in and out of deep darkness and blinding light (and that it will be that way for this whole life), to be so protected by angels.

MARCH 9, 1997
LOS ANGELES

My phone rings. It is after mid-night and I am sleeping. I think it might be Biggie. He always calls late. But it is not. It is someone telling me that Biggie was shot, that he might be dead. I hang up on the person. Someone else calls. They tell me Biggie is indeed dead.

I hang up on them too. But I call Puff. His cellular phone is turned off. It is never turned off.

I feel the first signs of panic. I call my homegirl, who makes it to my house in a matter of minutes. We drive to Cedars Sinai, where she heard he had been taken. In front of the emergency room is the Suburban he'd rented. There is police tape around it and a tightly formed pattern of bullet holes in the passenger door, where Big would have been sitting.

The panic is real now. I call Big's best friend Damien. A girl answers the phone, tells me it's true. Damien is with Faith at her hotel and he'll meet me at Big's hotel room. He has to make all of the hard phone calls. To Un and L and Kim in New York, to Big's girl Tiffany in Philly. To Big's mom.

"This nigga, who ain't never hurt nobody" Damien keeps saying. "I could see if it was one of us." Cease stares out the window, unable to speak or move. In a few hours, he will put his arm through the window and stitches will be required to close the wound. ""One fucking bullet." That's how it happened. There were no last words. "I been shot mad times—niggas get shot." Damien sounds as if he were up pacing the room, but he's sitting on the couch, his head in his hands, exhausted. On his right arm is the psalm that Big had tattooed in the same spot a week earlier.

The hotel room floor is covered with Big's clothes. Custom-made Versace. The gator loafers he bought when he came to Detroit. Big's mother is on her way to the airport in Queens. Un is driving her. T'Yanna's mother Jan and Mann from the neighborhood are accompanying her on the flight. She hears on the early-morning radio what she would not allow herself to believe when Damien called. The sun is beginning to rise in Big's hotel room. Damien needs to sleep but promises he will not, nor will he shower, until "I get my man out of this motherfucker."

When Mrs. Wallace lands at LAX it is scorching. She thinks L.A. is the cruelest, most awful place on the planet. She vows never to return, "except to look my son's murderer in the face. To ask him 'Why?'"

"This nigga died from one ass bullet," Damien keeps repeating as if trying to find logic in the details of the absurd. Cease stares at the rising sun. Damien tilts his head back on the couch, covers his eyes with one arm, and lets his tears flow. "One ass bullet."

112

112 (Bad Boy/Arista, 1996). *Room 112* (Bad Boy/Arista, 1998).

Black Rob

Life Stories (Bad Boy/Arista, 1999).

Faith Evans

Faith Evans (Bad Boy/Arista, 1996). *Keep the Faith* (Bad Boy/Arista, 1998).

Lil' Cease

The Wonderful World of Cease a Leo (Queen Bee/Undeas/Atlantic, 1999).

THE Lox

Money, Power, and Respect (Bad Boy/ Arista, 1998).

Craig Mack

Project: Funk da World (Bad Boy/Arista, 1994).

Mase

Harlem World (Bad Boy/Arista, 1997). *Double Up* (Bad Boy/Arista, 1999).

Harlem World

Mase Presents Harlem World—The Movement (All Out/So So Def/Columbia, 1999).

The Notorious B.I.G.

Ready to Die (Bad Boy/Arista, 1994). *Life After Death* (Bad Boy/Arista, 1997).

Puff Daddy (& the Family)

No Way Out (Bad Boy/Arista, 1997). *Forever* (Bad Boy/ Arista, 1999).

Total

Total (Bad Boy/Arista, 1996). *Kima, Keisha and Pam* (Bad Boy/Arista, 1998).

Compilation

Bad Boy's Greatest Hits, Volume 1 (Bad Boy/Arista, 1998).

OBJECTIVE QUESTIONS

1. What happened at the charity basketball game at CCNY in Dec. 1991?
2. She was crowned the Queen of Hip Hop Soul. In 1992, she released *What's the 411?*
3. What was the name of the raw demo that Biggie Smalls sent to *The Source?*
4. After completing the deal with Clive Davis, Bad Boy launched with Craig Mack's_____.
5. What was the name of Notorious B.I.G.'s debut album?
6. What was Bad Boy's reaction to the charges being leveled at them by Tupac and Suge after Tupac's shooting at the Quad Recording Studios?
7. Why was Biggie Smalls in Los Angeles on March 8, 1997?

QUESTIONS FOR FURTHER THOUGHT, RESEARCH, AND DISCUSSION

1. Do more research on the murders of Tupac and Biggie and examine the several different theories of who might be responsible.
2. Does rap from the West Coast sound different than rap from the East Coast and why? Historically, how have they influenced each other?
3. What has happened in the life of Sean "Puffy" Combs since the year 2000?
4. Who are Christopher Wallace's influences? How is he unique?
5. What do you think are the reasons behind "Puffy" Combs quick rise to wealth and power?

No Malcolm X in
My History Text

By Michael Eric Dyson

Michael Eric Dyson is a professor at the University of Pennsylvania and is one of the nation's foremost public intellectuals. He has been named by *Ebony* as one of the 100 most influential black Americans and is the author of twelve books.

No one exemplifies the many inherent contradictions embodied in Hip Hop culture better than Tupac Shakur. He was truly *The Rose That Grew from Concrete* (the title of his posthumously published book of poetry). He was both an exploitive capitalist and an angry revolutionary. He was both a gangster and a social activist, a sensitive poet with an assault rifle across his lap, a seductive ladies man, devoted son, and ghetto misogynist, and all at the same time. He was a pop icon whose albums sold millions, but at the same time he was extremely "conscious" of the importance of his message. He was the first recording artist in America to top the pop charts while incarcerated. Most importantly, he spoke for a troubled generation with a unique and powerful voice. A high school dropout, he was a voracious reader and was probably the first rapper intellectual. Not even KRS-One had been able to make learning and reading as "cool" as Tupac did. Knowledge is truth and Tupac realized that the more knowledge he accrued about a broad range of topics the more easily he could express the truth of the inequities he saw surrounding him and his people. Dyson's well-researched book ambitiously tries to tackle the complex subject of Tupac's life and career in all of its dimensions. In the process, Dyson succeeds in canonizing his work and elevating Tupac to cultural sainthood. This chapter deals with Tupac's early career and his relationship with his mentor, Leila Steinberg. It also expresses his youthful but insightful ideas about education, poverty, and politics, as well as describing his love of literature, poetry, philosophy, and culture in general.

School, Learning, and Tupac's Books

WHAT DO YOU know about Winnie Mandela?" a voice called out to Leila Steinberg in November 1988. Steinberg had just cleared a space on the grass in Marin City's ghetto park to read Mandela's *A Part of My Soul Went with Him.* She remembers that she turned to find a slight, caramel-skinned boy with "beautiful eyes" standing over her. He was the youth she had danced with the night before at a club party where her husband had been the DJ.

"What do I know?" she asked in mock defensiveness. "Someone gave me this book [since] I do a lot of reading. I can't tell you what I know until I'm done." Without missing a beat, he quoted her a couple of lines from the book, verbatim.

"Okay, you read this book?" Steinberg asked.

"I read everything I can get my hands on," he replied.

Tupac Shakur was always hungry for knowledge. When he was a boy in Harlem and got out of line, his mother made him read the *New York Times* all the way through. When he hit the road as a rapper and actor, he consumed an endless diet of books and magazines. His interviews and lyrics were littered with learned allusions to ancient philosophy, mystical writings, African and European cultures, health food manuals, black literature, and pop culture. He could quote passages from cherished books and cite lines from favorite films.

"He was very clearly smart," says journalist Allison Samuels. "He could quote Shakespeare." But his knowledge didn't end there.

"You could have a conversation with him about everything," says actress Peggy Lipton, whose daughter, Kidada, Tupac was in love with when he died. She remembers playing classical music and some Kate Bush music one night when he came over. "I remember sitting there saying [to him], This is Kate Bush.""I listen to Kate Bush," Tupac replied.

Lipton was surprised, especially since he "carried this heavy-duty" reputation. "He divulged his incredible musical interests. He had wonderful musical taste, and he listened to everybody. Kidada confirmed that with me."

Tupac's lawyer, Shawn Chapman, got a firsthand sense of the variety of Tupac's musical tastes. The first time she defended Tupac occurred on a criminal charge that took them to the Los Angeles Criminal Courts Building. Tupac was accompanied by several acquaintances, who decided after court to dine at Roscoe's, the famous Los Angeles soul food restaurant. Tupac invited Chapman and elected to ride in her car. The lawyer, a fan almost exclusively of rock-and-roll music, had a tape partially lodged in her tape player. "What tape is this?" Tupac asked.

"You are never going to know who it is," Chapman replied. Tupac grabbed the tape from her deck.

"Oh, Sarah McLachlan," he said as he started singing one of her songs.

"He knew all the lyrics," Chapman remembers in disbelief. Lipton, however, argues that Tupac's interests stretched well beyond music: "You could have a conversation with him about everything. He knew about everything, and he was open to everything." Jada Pinkett Smith agrees. "He was quick to tell me what book I should be reading," says Smith. "He was a well-read brother. And I loved that because he always had something to teach me. And he didn't graduate from high school."

Tupac's high school career was ultimately short-circuited by homelessness, his mother's addiction, fierce parental spats, and a fatherless adolescence. But he gained valuable experiences in school and in the arts community that nurtured his love of learning, even as his family suffered one setback after another. For a short time after her acquittal, Afeni became a minor celebrity on the liberal speaking circuit, garnering invitations to lecture at prominent universities like Yale and Harvard. She was even set up for a while in an apartment on Manhattan's Riverside Drive. Then the tide turned against black radicalism, and her liberal allies fell away. A year after her trial, Afeni's support dried up. And her family suffered, despite her work as a legal assistant at Bronx Legal Services. "Dick Fishbein was the managing attorney there at the time," Afeni says. "He was doing a rent strike for my sister's building, and he knew about me, and he came to see me to try to help me. I had never met him before in my life. He gave me a job at Legal Services, sight unseen, no resume, no job description, no nothing." Times were still tough. Afeni had three mouths to feed with little help from her children's fathers. Eventually, Afeni, Sekyiwa, and Tupac had to go on welfare. By the time Tupac was ready for junior high school, the family had already moved nearly twenty times.[1]

Tupac displayed promise when he began writing plays at the age of six. "When they were kids, Tupac used to stage productions with his cousins," Afeni says. "He wrote plays, and they had to be the actors, and they had to do everything he said, because he would tell them that he was the director," she recalls, laughing at the memory. Tupac's earliest influences as a fledgling playwright were distinctly Asian. "He saw every single karate movie," Afeni says. "We used to travel back and forth to California, so he would go to San Francisco where they have the Kabuki theater, where they have the real Japanese movies." Inspired by what he saw, Tupac emulated their moves on his makeshift stage. "He made all the props," Afeni remembers, "and the poor people had to act in these productions." Tupac's quick mind and natural talents sometimes kept his early instructors from challenging him. One teacher complimented Afeni when she retrieved four-year-old Tupac from school. "You should be proud; he is so perfect," the teacher said. "He didn't come here to be entertainment for you," Afeni says she replied. "He came here to get an education."

When he was twelve, Tupac found a nurturing community in the West 127th Street Ensemble Company in Harlem. He didn't like his life, but he loved escaping through the characters he played. He fed off of the affirmation he absorbed from his fellow thespians. Realizing that he was homeless, members of the company treated him to a thirteenth birthday party after a company rehearsal. Noted actress Minnie Gentry, a visiting performer with the company, publicly recited Langston Hughes's poem "Mother to Son." Another member presented him with a special gift. "She went and got thirteen brand new one-dollar bills," Afeni recalls with tears. "And [she] rolled them up like a scroll, put a yellow ribbon around each one, the way you would do a diploma, and then she lined up every one of them in a box, and she presented that to him." Tupac was fortunate to have encountered people who loved him and recognized his gifts. "We might have been poor,"

Afeni says, but there was a "richness [to] the people in Pac's life," especially because "they knew he was gifted," and "what they had, they gave to him. ... There was no place that didn't happen."

The love flowed as well at the Baltimore School for the Arts after the family moved to the Maryland capital with the promise of a job for Afeni in 1986. Although it's reported that Tupac learned to act in Baltimore, he always took pride in his earlier induction into the acting guild at the age of twelve. "That season [the company] performed for a paying audience in ... an off-off-off-Broadway theater," Afeni says. "But Tupac was told by those actors and by that director—and he believed it from that day—[that] he was a professional actor. And he went to the Baltimore School of the Arts a *professional* actor." Indeed, many believe that had Tupac lived, he would have become, as Bill Maher told me, "a big movie star." As compelling a hip-hop icon as he was, says Quincy Jones, "he was a better actor than rapper."

In Baltimore Tupac prized the broad arts education he received. His interest in acting and art had already been established, the latter coming when Afeni brought home from the library prints of various artists, including van Gogh, whose *Starry Night* Tupac found particularly captivating. (In fact he also loved singer Don McLean's haunting paean to van Gogh, *Vincent*, which played continuously as he teetered on the brink of death in a Las Vegas hospital years later.) Tupac also delved into Shakespeare, ballet, jazz, and poetry, which he began writing in grammar school. It was easy enough for Tupac to move from poetry to writing raps, which he did with great skill and remarkable speed, features that added to his legend as a rapper. (Rapper Notorious B.I.G. said that when he once visited Tupac, the latter went to the bathroom, and when he emerged, he had penned two songs.) Though he thrived in school, Tupac's domestic troubles escalated, and Baltimore's mean streets got meaner. At the end of his junior year in school, gang violence claimed the life of a neighborhood boy. The boy's death and Tupac's chaotic home life thrust him onto a bus for a cross-country trek to Marin City, California, and to the equally troubled home of Linda Pratt, wife of Panther Elmer "Geronimo" Pratt.[2]

If Tupac hit his stride in Baltimore, he lost his footing in California. By his own admission, he was an outsider, especially since he couldn't play basketball, he dressed like a hippie, he was a target of street gangs, he wrote poetry, and he secretly loathed himself. When Afeni joined him in California, her drug addiction, which came at the height of the crack epidemic, put her in dangerous proximity to the drug's infamous center of distribution in northern California's black ghettos. Tupac momentarily lived with Afeni, but when she could no longer hold her house together, he left her and his sister and joined a group of boys in an abandoned apartment while working at a pizza parlor. He eventually started hustling crack, but some good friends, like Charles Fuller, who discerned his talent for bigger goals, discouraged him. Tupac enrolled at the affluent Mt. Tamalpais High School, the school in rich Marin County that overlooked the ghetto of Marin City, known as "the Jungle." Tupac gained a reputation for his riveting acting but eventually left school after forming a rap group, the One Nation Emcees, with his roommates.

Before he left school, Tupac's desperate desire for a useful, relevant education loomed large. I had the chance to see this desire dance on his countenance when Leila Steinberg showed me the video of Tupac being interviewed in high school. His handsome brown face was lit by a brightly contagious smile. At seventeen Tupac had not yet shown signs of the alopecia that would cause him to completely shave his locks. His hair was faded on the sides and higher in the top in the style of the late 1980s, with a part in the left and a brownish red tinting splashed across the top. He had a small stud in his right ear. Tupac's look could be called boho—bohemian homeboy—and featured a black tank top with two spindly arms sticking out like spider's legs.[3] His slight arms were capped with three bands on the right wrist and a sky blue watch with an inexpensive band on the left wrist. Steinberg popped the tape in, and I sat, transfixed by this highly articulate young man who spoke gently but animatedly about his views on schools, education, a curriculum rooted in real-world needs, poverty, and his difficult but rewarding upbringing. Long before he found fame, Tupac possessed a sharp intelligence and acutely observed the world around him.

Tupac readily admits that he has goofed off in school, largely because he craved popularity and being social. He gives a precocious analysis of the tension between schooling and education. "I think that we got so caught up in school being a tradition that we stopped using it as a learning tool, which it should be," Tupac says. "I'm learning about the basics, but they're not basic for me. ... To get us ready for today's world, [the present curriculum] is not helping." Tupac suggests that dull tradition is responsible for the deadening effect of passing on irrelevant knowledge from one generation to another. Seeking an escape from such unimaginative transmission of information, Tupac proclaims the practical source of his knowledge. "That's why the streets have taught me." Discussing the bland repetition of knowledge—"they tend ... to teach you to read, write, and [do] arithmetic, then teach you reading and writing and arithmetic again, then again, then again"—Tupac suggests that the purpose of such pedagogical routines is "to keep you busy." He offers instead a list of classes he thinks will benefit his peers. "There should be a class on drugs. There should be a class on sex education, a real sex education class, not just pictures and diagrams and illogical terms. ... There should be a class on scams. There should be a class on religious cults. There should be a class on police brutality. There should be a class on apartheid. There should be a class on racism in America. There should be a class on why people are hungry."

Watching this tape, I'm astounded at the thoughtful engagement displayed by this young man who is on the verge of a wildly successful life that will take him far outside the schoolroom. It is clear that Tupac believes schools should address the pressing social issues of the day, and even more specifically, they should help youth confront the ills that directly affect them. Classes on sex education, scams, and religious cults would explore general problems confronted by: youth of all colors. But police brutality, apartheid, and racism are of obvious relevance to poor black and brown youth. Tupac's pedagogical themes are linked to salient social issues that are rarely explored in rich detail in our nation's educational institutions, especially in high school. For Tupac, educational relevance is not an index of frivolous or ephemeral concerns. His list gives pride of place to the themes that he learned as a child of social protest and radical resistance. Like a good son of the Panthers, Tupac is interested in forging connections between sites of learning and the communities in which they are located. Schools should help students negotiate the worlds they occupy.

So he points out that "the things that helped me were the things that I learned from my mother, from the streets, and reading." He is grateful to school because it "taught me reading, which I love." Questioning the relevance of algebra and foreign languages, Tupac makes a forceful criticism of dishonest political rhetoric that reflects remarks made decades earlier by George Orwell. "I think [foreign languages] are important but ... they should be teaching you English, and then teaching you how to understand double talk. Politics is double-talk." Tupac makes a point that is neither xenophobic nor jingoistic. Instead, he looks beyond the abstract good of foreign-language education by questioning its comparative worth in a curriculum that should be geared to the real lives of poor youth: "When am I going to Germany? I can't afford to pay my rent in America. How am I going to Germany?" Although his query may be dismissed as an index of his parochialism, it may just as well reflect the lack of opportunity open to a desperately poor youth, even one as bright as Tupac. The real misfortune is not that Tupac appears provincial; the tragedy is that by seventeen he has not had the chance, one enjoyed by many of his wealthy peers, to experience the mind-opening, life-altering effect of foreign travel—or to imagine the international itinerary that would soon dominate his life.

Tupac appeals to traditions of learning that are older than America's, citing "ancient civilizations [that] have survived without going to schools like this." The budding rapper also delivers a stinging judgment of the nostalgia on which he believes American education is built, even as it fails to transmit values that are useful to young people. "We're being taught to deal with this fairyland, which we're not even living in anymore. And it's sad, 'cause *I'm* telling you, and it should not be me telling you. It should be common knowledge." Tupac's disgust with educational officials who overlook social misery and the willful ignorance on which it thrives is apparent. "Aren't they wondering why death rates are going up, and suicide is going up, and drug abuse? Aren't they wondering? Don't they understand that … more kids are being handed crack than they're being handed diplomas?" Tupac's insightful criticism of the social circumstances of poor youth suggests a reordering of educational priorities that values survival over repetition. It is also interesting to observe Tupac's relentless efforts to link the economic and racial contexts of learning with the pedagogical and curricular strategies that are most likely to help poor black and Latino students. Tupac's remedy, in part, for such a state of affairs is a Twain-like update on the prince and pauper exchange, a switch meant to right social wrongs by inviting the rich to see life through the eyes of the poor, and vice versa. In Tupac's case it was also the old viewing society through the eyes of youth. He contends that rich folk should trade places with the poor and that adults should go to school again. If his suggestion reflects the naivete of youth, it also captures a poor bright boy's ardent desire to combat the social ills he observes at home and in his neighborhood.[4]

One of Tupac's most revealing comments about the regulation of the poor comes when he compares the effects of society's control over youth to rats being routed through a maze and their arbitrary trapping for experimental purposes. "They'll let you go as far as you want, but as soon as you start asking too many questions, and you're ready to change, boom, that block will come." He links critical questioning to social regulation, not altogether unexpected in light of his experience as the child of a black revolutionary. "Since I'm living in a slummish area and I'm black, [my block] will come through being a statistic, you know. I'll get caught up in all of this, and one day I'll be with my friends, and they'll go, 'Let's go out partying. We don't have a car; let's steal a car.'… We'll steal a car, and I'll go to jail for sixteen years and then come out and be bitter." The math may indeed be fuzzy, but Tupac is depressingly accurate in his prediction that he will serve time and that the experience will have a damaging effect on his outlook on life. Of course what is perhaps most disheartening in Tupac's analysis is to see how already, by the age of seventeen, a poor black youth perceives his expendability. His prescient and disturbing vision of trouble for himself is nonetheless chilling: It reflects the disproportionate incarceration of young black males caught up in the criminal justice system.

In keeping with his yen for an education that is relevant, Tupac reflects on the relation between politics and class. His hopes for "a better America" were dashed when instead of electing Jesse Jackson or Michael Dukakis to the presidency, the nation chose George Bush. "I couldn't believe it because every time I asked people, 'Who would you have voted for?' … They were like, 'Well, Dukakis.' But how did Bush win? I keep wondering." Tupac's question is one that has stumped far more seasoned experts and points to a vexing feature of the electoral landscape: Citizens who are polled often publicly claim to have voted for one candidate but have privately chosen another. Bush's election makes Tupac "rebel more against society because they're supposed to represent the people." Tupac displays his acute political judgment in a withering attack on conservative politics. "I don't want Bush in government. I spent eight years of my seventeen years on this earth under Republicans, under Ronald Reagan, under an ex-actor who lies to the people, who steals money, and who's done nothing at all for me." Tupac links destructive conservative policies to class politics, carefully distinguishing personality from principle. He manages to avoid personal attack while also refusing to confuse interpersonal pleasantness with political compassion. "I don't think Bush is a bad person or a bad president, because for the upper class, he's a perfect president. And that's how society is built."

Tupac brilliantly distinguishes between discourse about politics and the real exercise of political power, a distinction that is driven by class. "The upper class runs [society] while ... the middle class and lower class, we talk about it. And for the working class, we're just lost; we're going through the motions. We're the worker bees, and they get to live like royalty." Those class distinctions flare up at his school as well, as Tupac carves up social space with an acumen that might have made Karl Marx, Max Weber, and Talcott Parsons equally proud. "There's the lower Marin City class. There's the lower white class. There's the 'middle-class' white class. There's the 'middle-class' black class and ... there's the upper-class white and the upper-class black. And it's a shame that it has to be cut in so many pieces, because it all boils down to just one piece of money." Zero-sum economics could not have found a better advocate.

Following through with his class analysis, Tupac makes an interesting suggestion: Since there is so much room in the White House, President Ronald Reagan could address a "staggering" homeless problem by opening the White House to displaced indigents. "Why can't he take some of them people off the street and put them in his White House?" Tupac yearns to know. "Because he doesn't want to get dirty. The White House would be a little tainted." Tupac's fangs are admirably flashing, a foretaste of the acerbic criticism he would wield against chosen targets in his rap career. But he displays humanity when he refuses to identify homeless people with their condition. Instead, in the best tradition of enlightened social theory, he argues that their critical importance has not been erased by their unfortunate circumstances. "They haven't been homeless forever. They've done things in society. ... They've had jobs before. ... They worked hard."

Tupac's insight into social problems grew from critical reflection on the harsh circumstances of his youth. Although he obviously had a problem with school, he displayed a deep love of learning. He brought his analytical skills to bear on his recent upbringing in Baltimore and Marin City. By his own admission, it makes him "upset to talk" about Baltimore's horrible conditions. "Baltimore has the highest rate of teenage pregnancy, the highest rate of AIDS within the black community"-an awareness that put Tupac far ahead of most leaders in black communities-"the highest rate of teens killing teens, the highest rate of teenage suicide, and the highest rate of blacks killing blacks. ... And this is where I chose to live!" Obviously the choice was his mother's, not his, but Tupac's comprehension of the clutch of social ills that ganged up on poor ghetto blacks is remarkable. But he is not willing simply to observe the pain; he seeks to relieve it, an admirable glimpse into the social compassion that will stick with him throughout his life. "So as soon as I got there—being the person I am—I said 'No, no. I'm changing this.' So I started a stop-the-killing' campaign and safe sex campaign and AIDS prevention campaign ... and then I came back, and

I felt like I did a lot of good." The good he did, however, could not stem the tide of violence that would drown his peers after he left Baltimore. "The second week I was in California, I got a call and two of my friends were shot dead in the head, two of the friends that were working with me at the time … and it's just like, why try? Because this is what happens." In sharp contrast to his later life, when hopelessness erupted in him like a volcano, Tupac is able to bounce back. "But I still try, you know."

Tupac does not miss the irony of his situation: He escaped New York's violence by heading to Baltimore, only to escape its violence by coming to California, where he encountered the violence of racism, which he "can't stand in any form, shape, or color." He also sees death and needless brutality. "I mean, this lady slashed a man's throat because he spit on her kids, and I've seen teenagers fight last night over girls." But he mostly endured the violence of poverty, an experience that, he repeatedly states, has left him bitter. "I loved my childhood, but I hated growing up poor, and it made me very bitter. You know, it's like, all right, now I got a job. I had to quit now. I had a job, and just today I got paid, and I have money in my pocket that I worked for. And that's the greatest feeling, you know, that I worked for it. … But I'm still poor. My family is still poor. I still live in a poor neighborhood. … I still see poor people."

Haunted by a sight that was invisible to most people, Tupac could no longer pretend school fit his view of the world. Neither could he reconcile the poverty he saw and the useless education he felt he got at Mt. Tamalpais, so he simply stopped going, although he had psychically withdrawn months before. His quest for learning, however, was undiminished. In a delightful twist of fate, he was about to meet someone who would help him reach his goal.

When Tupac came across Leila Steinberg that day in the park, it was a serendipitous meeting that changed both of their lives. Steinberg bridged many cultures, both in her name-"Leila" is Arabic, "Steinberg" Jewish-and in her work as a dancer and teacher who held workshops on poetry and self-expression for poor youth around the city. She was born in Los Angeles in 1960, reared in Watts, and attended all-black schools. "The black community nurtured me, raised me, and gave me a sense of where I stood on the planet," Steinberg, who is white, remembers. "I didn't even understand my North African roots or my Jewish roots, and I ran as far as I could from [them]." Under the influence of black artists in the 1960s, she came to understand "how fucked up we are in our schools, in our healing process, [and] in education." By the time she reached sixth grade, Steinberg found her mission in the arts. "It was the only place that I knew that the truth was told," she says. "You could go 500 years backwards and know what was going on with any people, because artists don't lie." Her mother, who was born in Mexico but whose roots were in the Middle East, was an activist involved in Latin and black politics. She also thrust Leila and her siblings into social protest through marching for the rights of migrant farm workers. By the time she was twelve, Leila's mother left home to pursue her activist agenda full time. She was raised by her father and influenced by her grandfather, a Latin dance teacher, who introduced her to salsa, Brazilian, and other Latin dance. Leila performed around the city and met teachers who taught her West African dance as well.

When she graduated from high school, Steinberg moved to Central America, researching various music and artists and enrolling in college in Panama. When she returned to: the United States a few years later, she moved to northern California, attended college, and started touring with well-known Congolese and Latin artists. She also went on the road with guitarist Carlos Santana's band and the soul group the Neville Brothers. During this time she met and married Bruce, who was caught up in the L.A. rap scene; had a daughter; and studied sports therapy, with the aim of exploring alternative healing as an athletic trainer, her fallback career in case she needed steady money. Her husband's involvement in rap exposed her to its powerful social critique. "Because I was so involved in African music, [rap] was the first honest voice in a long time that was very fresh." Steinberg juggled several responsibilities: her dance career, her therapy job, raising her daughter, and supporting her husband's efforts as a rap promoter. Steinberg and her family moved to the Bay area and eventually further north as her husband earned a growing reputation as a skilled DJ. When the family moved north, Steinberg began to front her husband's business ventures. As a black male, Bruce faced difficulties in renting facilities to hold rap concerts and club parties. They started promoting shows in California, drawing up to 10,000 kids in a single event.

Along with her burgeoning promotional career, Steinberg got involved in the local schools because of her expanding brood of children. "I didn't want my kids to be subjected to the same stuff that I wasn't okay with," she says. Steinberg began volunteering her time in class and eventually met a woman who ran Young Imaginations, a nonprofit educational agency. The agency focused primarily on getting artists to come into local schools to entertain the students. Steinberg spotted a larger opportunity. She helped the head of the agency reshape her organization into a multicultural arts and education agency that used artists from a variety of races, ethnicities, and cultures to help educate the children about history, culture, and politics. Steinberg began addressing assemblies in the high schools during the day and promoting rap shows with her husband at night. When she witnessed the enthusiastic response to their rap programs, she yearned to bring rap into the curriculum. "I really saw how kids resonated [with us], because we had square dancing coming in the black schools. … God, what I would have done to have some rappers and some African artists and rap artists come up and do something." But Young Imaginations was not prepared to make the leap, so Steinberg started her own nonprofit program, joining forces with a woman who had access to "white corporate money."

As Steinberg's program took off in school, her promotional work with Bruce was paying big dividends as well. But tensions flared when her name became almost exclusively associated with efforts that her husband had initiated and when her reputation rose above the artists she helped to promote. "The really messed-up thing is that every time there was success in the black community, there was always a nonblack person that came in and took credit," Steinberg says. "So I was really afraid to have myself on the forefront in an industry that deserved to be credited to what these young black men were doing." Steinberg pulled back on the promotional front and directed much of her energy into her work in the schools of Marin City and Oakland. She wanted to have a program that, "would touch these ideas and [that] would make a difference because we really care." Because she loved language, rap could be a natural ally to her efforts. "I kept saying, 'I need to find somebody who has that political connection and the social connection, but is really ready to also move past… a world of … black and white.'" Although she hadn't found the right person to fulfill her goals, Steinberg continued to hold free after-school workshops—on writing and performance—two days a week. Her reputation grew quickly. "If you want to write a poem or rap, a piece, a monologue; if you want to read the dictionary with me; if you're willing to create and be out of the streets, come on," Steinberg says in explaining her appeal to the more than 300 students who signed up for her workshops in Marin, Nevada, and Sonoma counties. And then her breakthrough came, at least in principle. "One day one of my students, Lawanda Hunter, an amazing young dancer who was also on my team of promotions and [who worked] with my husband … came to me and said,

'You know, Leila, you touch and inspire a lot of us, and your commitment to work is great, but I found somebody in Marin who just moved here, who is everything you're looking for [in a person to] collaborate with." Discounting her student's glowing recommendation—"everyone wanted to bring me their shining stars"—Steinberg brushed Lawanda off "for a long time." In the meantime Hunter was telling Tupac about Steinberg.

Several weeks later Leila and Bruce held a promotional party at a local club. Bruce was the DJ, Leila the free spirit. "He's deejaying and I'm like the life of the party," Steinberg recalls. "We are doing this thing together, and we are converting Sonoma County, [which] is very white, scared to death of rap." As Steinberg danced, "this very beautiful young person made eye contact, [and] jumped on the dance floor and started dancing with me." After their dance, Steinberg quickly turned her attention to the night's business without the chance of learning her dance partner's name. The next day she had an early afternoon workshop in Marin City and before class headed to the park to read her new book. And then she met Tupac.

"By the way what's your name?" Tupac asked after giving Steinberg a good ribbing. "I'm Leila."

"You're shitting me," Tupac gasped. "You're not Leila. I'm Tupac!"

As the two excitedly jumped up and down—because of their dance the night before, because Steinberg was reading a book Tupac had just finished, because of how destiny brought them together—they celebrated their good fortune.

"How old are you?" Steinberg asked.

"Oh, I just turned seventeen," Tupac replied. "Where are you going right now?"

"Well, I have to go teach in Marin City. Don't you have school?"

"I'm not going today."

'Does your mother know you're not going?"

"I raised my mother and sister. I'm taking care of my home. I'm the man. I don't know if you understand that."

"Well, I was the woman, and my dad did his best, but I raised my younger brothers. So I understand what it is to be the parent of your parents and have a house full."

"Would you like to come with me to my class?"

"Yes, I would. I want to talk to you."

As Steinberg did her workshop, Tupac sat silently and observed her every move, squirming in his seat. He made faces and was anxious to speak but refrained from talking since Steinberg asked him not to interrupt her. After class Tupac opened up. "I appreciate what you're doing," he said. "I feel you. But I've got a lot to tell you about what you do." As she was to learn later, this was classic Tupac. "He was very challenging," Steinberg recalls. "Because as brilliant as he was, Tupac would challenge everybody and anything. That was his nature." After her workshop Steinberg phoned home to tell Bruce that she was bringing a guest who would be attending her evening workshop. Tupac went home with her, attended the evening workshop, and almost instantly had a big impact on Steinberg. His aggressive questioning about her pedagogical methods forced her to rethink her approach. "I've been teaching now for the last fourteen years," Steinberg says. "And Pac changed my teaching. He changed who I am as a woman and as a parent, because as Pac entered our group, he took a lot of my infantile thought processes to the next level." At seventeen, Tupac was a formidable intellectual presence in the life of this formally educated artist and teacher. If he shook her brain up, he did the same to her household: He moved in with Steinberg's family shortly after meeting her.

Tupac and Steinberg began to tour the schools together. She taught; he rapped. Their success forged a profound bond between the two. Tupac told her almost immediately that he was soon going to be a famous artist selling millions of records and that she was going to be his manager. As it turns out, Tupac was right on both counts, although Steinberg handed Digital Underground manager Atron Gregory the reins to Tupac's career as he was getting started. But she remained a crucial presence in his life. She argued with him about his ideas and career direction. She supported him through his personal and career crises. She listened to his boyish pride in his famous conquests (he once called her with a white female pop star in his bed). She provided unflagging love to an artist she saw rapidly transform from a sweet-faced teen to an internationally recognized rap superstar. But above all she believed in the mythological power of his life and career, a belief that has only enlarged since his tragic death.

Perhaps the most important role Steinberg played in Tupac's life was that of literary soul mate. Steinberg encouraged Tupac's ample literary talents in her workshops. She kept the many efforts he made there, especially his poems, which were published after his death in a volume entitled *The Rose That Grew from Concrete,* a project Steinberg oversaw. But it was as reading partners that Steinberg and Tupac most profoundly shaped each other's lives. They incessantly shared, reflected on, responded to, and argued about the written word. When Steinberg met Tupac, he was already well read. "He could recite sonnets that I couldn't understand how this seventeen-year-old could memorize," she says. "He did a class project that blew me away, where he did his own 1990s version of one of Shakespeare's plays." In fact the Bard played a significant role in Tupac's rapidly expanding self-mythologization. "The way these kids study Shakespeare in class now, they will study my work, too," Tupac told Steinberg. To many observers this may have come off as the delusion of a poor black youth who felt relatively powerless and therefore projected his fame as a means to compensate for his lowly status. But Steinberg quickly became a true believer. "This is why I'm so committed to his work," she says. "Because I knew it was true then. … That's why I think we have to study Pac in every university." Steinberg contends that Tupac's poetry and life can be a means to the critical self-reflection that Tupac believed should be taught in the nation's classrooms. "Most of his documenting and his [artistic] process was really an internal process lived out loud, publicly, for you to question everything you do, for you to question … how you live, what's right and wrong and who decides it. That's really who he was in all these fragments."

Tupac and Steinberg spent hours reading books at their favorite haunt, L.A.'s Bohdi Tree Bookstore, especially after Tupac moved to Los Angeles in the early 1990s. Located on Melrose Avenue, Bohdi specializes in spiritual literature and revolutionary tomes. "He did it on his own," Steinberg says. "He was totally self-educated." Tupac wanted to get everyone in the country reading. "Oprah got going what Pac wanted to do," Steinberg says. "He was going to use rap to get kids reading again. They were going to analyze and destroy all the great theorists and philosophers." Tupac's literary interests were impressively catholic. He read novelist, Kurt Vonnegut and political theorist Mikhail Bakunin. He read books on anarchy and Platonism. He read Teilhard de Chardin's *Phenomenon of Man.* "He loved that book," Steinberg tells me. "We would go in [to Bohdi], and he would want them to refer books to us." But it was Steinberg's teacher Peggy Shackleton who was the primary reference librarian of their growing archive. When Tupac asked Steinberg where she got the books in her library, she told him about Shackleton. "He wanted to talk to Peggy"

Steinberg recalls. "He was like, 'Whoever this lady is that's sending you these books [is great]. I know some of those books; I found them on my own,'" Steinberg was impressed, since she hadn't found "Khalil Gibran on my own. ... So he just had this love affair with this now sixty-five-year-old woman and wanted every book Peggy ever gave me, which was his introduction to a whole new world of reading." Shackleton gave Steinberg lists of books to feed Tupac's insatiable intellectual appetite, a pattern that continued until his death. Steinberg has kept Tupac's books. "It's the only thing I ever travel with [when I move]. ... If you come to my house, you'll see."[5]

Taking advantage of Steinberg's offer, I visit her cozy Santa Monica bungalow, recessed in a manicured cove on a dimly lit street. I want to lay my eyes on the books, finger through them, and get a sense of the rapper's intellectual habits rising from the ruffle of pages rabidly perused. Steinberg leads me to one of many bookshelves tucked in crevices and along the walls of her house. I drink in the sea of books and wade through the volumes Tupac consumed. There is J. D. Salinger's *Catcher in the Rye,* Robert Pirsig's *Zen and the Art of Motorcycle Maintenance,* Richard Wright's *Native Son,* and Maya Angelou's *I Know Why the Caged Bird Sings.* (In prison Tupac said, "I read a lot of good books; I read a lot of Maya Angelou's books.") There are novels by Hermann Hesse, Gabriel Garcia Marquez, and Henry Miller. Homer's *Odyssey* pops up, as does the well-regarded anthology of Friedrich Nietzsche's work edited by Walter Kaufmann. My eyes run across books by Sigmund Freud—"He read Freud to discredit him. ... He thought Freud was a frustrated homosexual who never [fully] formulated his opinions," Steinberg tells me—and Carl Jung. The sight of Robin Morgan's *Sisterhood Is Powerful: Anthology of Writings from the Women's Liberation Movement* strikes me. "Did he really read this?" I ask. "He read a lot of feminist writings," Steinberg replies. There's work by Alice Walker, including *In Search of Our Mothers' Gardens,* and George Orwell. (Perhaps he *had* read Orwell's celebrated essay "The Politics of the English Language" before he made his powerful comments on political double-talk during his interview.)

I spot E. D. Hirsch's *Dictionary of Cultural Literacy: What Every American Needs to Know,* an Interesting choice to be sure. "When we did our assemblies in the high schools," Steinberg says, "he said that this was a white supremacist perspective on cultural literacy. He wanted to use the second edition to define how whites define what cultural literacy is. Pac paid for this to attack it." As if to counter Hirsch, there is a volume by Jonathan Kozol, *Savage Inequalities: Children in America's Schools.* There are tomes by John Steinbeck, Alex Haley—"He read *Roots* at least two or three times," Steinberg says—and Jamaica Kincaid, Including her *At the Bottom of the River.* I notice Eileen Southern's *Music of Black Americans: A History* and Herman Melville's *Moby Dick.* Ira Peck's edited *Life and Words of Martin Luther King, Jr.* is there, and so are Anais Nin and Aldous Huxley ("He was fascinated with Aldous Huxley and the whole sixties psychedelic time period, [which covered] the drugs Afeni did before the crack that almost destroyed her.") Dick Gregory is present, and so is Derrick Bell. "Our friend worked with Derrick Bell and gave us both copies," Steinberg says. I see William Styron's *Confessions of Nat Turner* and Sun Tzu's *Art of War,* as well as George L. Lee's *Interesting People: Black American History Makers,* a collection of the original illustrative biographies syndicated in the National Black Press, 1945 to 1948 and 1970 to 1986. And there is the riveting corpus of Donald Goines, the Detroit writer who specialized in brutal tales of black street life and who died prematurely and violently.

Across the room I spot a familiar book: UCLA professor Susan McClary's *Feminine Endings: Music, Gender and Sexuality,* but Steinberg gently removes it from my hands. "Pac did not read this. But she likes his work." When I see Amiri Baraka's *Blues People,* I reflect on the intriguing similarities that bind the writer and the rapper: huge gifts, fearless out spokenness, and poetically phrased rage. There is Donald Passman's *All You Need to Know About the Music Business* and Fox Butterfield's *All God's Children: The Boskett Family and the American Tradition of Violence.* (When I later talk to Stanley Crouch about Tupac, he mentions Butterfield. "I don't know if you read this book; you probably did. It's called *All God's Children!*" "Oh, Butterfield," I reply. "Yeah, right," Crouch says. "A book, by the way, that Tupac read," I say "Well, he didn't make much of it that I know of," Crouch retorts. He thinks for a moment and then backs up a bit. "Well, maybe he didn't get a chance to. I'm glad to know he did read it.")

There's poetry by black women. "He loved Maya Angelou, Nikki Giovanni, and Sonia Sanchez," Steinberg says, as I pore over *Black Sister: Poetry by Black American Women, 1746 to 1980,* edited by Earlene Stetson. I also see William H. Harris's *The Harder We Run: Black Workers Since the Civil War,* as well as *Bulhwhip Days: The Slaves Remember* and *Souls of Black Folk,* the classic volume by master black intellectual W. E. B. DuBois. *Monster,* Sanyika Shakur's scary gang autobiography, rides the shelf. "They were going to do stuff together," Steinberg says. "They were in touch quite a bit." There is Nathan McCall's *Makes Me Wanna Holler* and Jack Gratus's *Great White Lie: Slavery, Emancipation and Changing Racial Attitudes.* The oversized pictorial *Songs of My People* sticks out, as does *The New Our Bodies? Ourselves* and *The State of the World Atlas,* part 1, by Michael Kidron and Ronald Segal. There is a copy of *The Meaning of Masonry* by W L. Wilmshurst. "He was very fascinated by masonry by secret societies and the white elite and their control. He definitely was going, to dissect [it] and tear [it] down, so he studied." I also notice quite a few volumes on crime and notorious criminals. "He was obsessed with reading about black crimes and white crimes," Steinberg says. "He would read serial-killer books and talk about white crimes related to lots of sick things. And then black crimes as a completely different world of crime [related to] economic struggle." (That Insight, however, did not stop Tupac from defending at least one white criminal. In outtakes from an interview that he and Snoop Dogg did for MTV in 1996, Tupac discusses the fact that prosecutors on famous murder trials can write books and make money, but not the criminals. "How can they put a book out and Charles Manson can't put a book out?" he asks. "He did the murders. They didn't do shit. They just talked about what another nigga did. Charles did that shit.")

There is a great deal of spiritual literature, much of which I know, some of it unfamiliar to me. There is Thomas a Kempis's *Imitation of Christ* and several books on Buddhism, including jack Kornfield's *Teachings of the Buddha.* There are other classics, such as *St. John of the Cross* and *Cloud of Unknowing,* as well as noteworthy contemporary volumes, including Thomas Merton's *No Man Is an Island* and Evelyn Underbill's *Mysticism.* I recognize A. N. Watts's *Wisdom of Insecurity* and Gershem Scholem's edition of the *Kabbalah,* the compendium of Jewish mystical writings. And the *Bhagavad Gita* rests easily against its neighbor, *Tears and Laughter* by Khalil Gibran. *The Tibetan Book of the Dead* sits next to *Secret Splendor by* Charles Essert. The preface to this book, written by David Raffeloc, says, "For many years, Charles Earnest Essert believed that the only reality was experience. And true to his conviction, he sought a varied life." (I think to myself that experience was a huge theme in Tupac's work; maybe this book helped establish its primacy in his thinking.) I pick up *Life Is Corolla* by Joan Grant. "Pac loved her books. … She would do stories about other lives, and she would take characters from Egypt." There is also *Serving Humanity* from the writings of Alice A. Bailey. I glance at the table of contents: "The True server;" "The Inertia of the average spiritually minded man;" "The law of service;" "The need for service;" "What is service?" "Forces of enlightenment;" "Preparing for the reappearance of Christ;" "Mystical perception;" "Meditation;" "Discipleship;" "Requirements needed by aspirants." I turn next to *Messages from Maitreya* volume 1: *100 Messages,* and then Ruth Montgomery's well-known books, including *Life After Life.* There are literally hundreds of other books-on garlic ("Pac was a great cook, and everything had to have garlic and onions in it, 'cause if you didn't have medical insurance, you ate potato tacos with garlic. That was always our joke"), psychic science, yoga, alternative health, metaphysical science, painting ("He read every book you can imagine on every major ... visual artist, not just musical or fine arts"), philosophy, psychology, and meditation. The range is more than impressive for a poor, black high school dropout and autodidact who never had the benefit of formal higher education.

Tupac's voracious reading continued throughout his career, a habit that allowed him to fill his raps with acute observations about the world around him. "As an artist, I was initially impressed with his skills and his lyrical ability," says manager Atron Gregory "And as time went on I got to know him as a human being. He was very inquisitive. He wanted to know as much about everything as he could. I noticed he did a lot of reading." Tupac's profound literacy rebutted the belief that hip-hop is an intellectual wasteland. "There's very little in rap where these kids even encourage people to read books," Stanley Crouch says. Tupac helped to combat the anti-intellectualism in rap, a force, to be sure, that pervades the entire culture. His reading not only gave depth to his lyrics, but it influenced his fellow rappers as well. "I feel what Pac gave to me and gave to a lot of these cats is that you can be street, but you can be smart, too," says rapper Big Syke, who appeared on many of Tupac's last records. Beyond that, Tupac inspired many of his rap mates to read seriously, many for the first time. "He had the words, and he was articulate," Syke says. "That's what made me start reading books. I wasn't reading no books, but the more I started dissecting him, the more I started seeing what all his game was coming from." When Tupac adopted his Makaveli persona and renamed some of his fellow rappers, he spurred their interest in discovering the intellectual roots of the names they bore. "He changed his name to 'Makaveli,'" Syke remembers. "He named me 'Mussolini.' He gave Eddie the name 'Castro,' and [somebody else he named] 'Napoleon.' Gave all of us our names. Now, I had to get a book on Mussolini. And then I got to dissecting Machiavelli. How am I going to find out about him if I don't read?"

Producer Preston Holmes, who worked with Tupac at the beginning of his career (on *Juice)* and at the end (on *Gridlock'd),* believes that Tupac yearned to use his enormous learning and fame to encourage youth to think about big social issues. "He wanted to do a film about Nat Turner and had given it a lot of thought." Holmes told Tupac the idea had two strikes against it: it was black, and it was a period film. But Tupac insisted that the way to make it successful was to include popular young actors who would draw a big audience. "He just thought it was important that he use his celebrity to get young people to think about and learn about some things they might not otherwise [consider]." Holmes points to Tupac's love of literature and art as examples of his open-mindedness and his multifaceted personality. "These kids need to know that this was somebody who loved poetry before he discovered rap. And there is nothing wrong with that. Maybe a little bit of that will rub off on some of these kids running around wanting to be gangsters."

NOTES

1. Bruck, "The Takedown of Tupac," *The New Yorker.*
2. Anson, "To Die Like a Gangsta," *Vanity Fair;* Bruck, "The Takedown of Tupac," *The New Yorker.*
3. George, *Buppies, B-Boys, Baps and Bohos: Notes on Post-Soul Culture.* I borrow the term "boho" from George's book.
4. Twain, *The Prince and the Pauper.*
5. Teilhard de Chardin, *The Phenomenon of Man.*

OBJECTIVE QUESTIONS

1. What was Leila Stenberg reading when she encountered Tupac and who wrote it?
2. What was Tupac's reply when she asked him if he had read it?
3. According to the author, what short-circuited Tupac's high school career?
4. What was the name of the rap group that he formed?
5. By the time Tupac was ready for junior high school, the family had already moved more than _____ times.
6. According to his mother, what were Tupac's favorite movies as a child?
7. How and when did Tupac become a *professional* actor? What did Quincy Jones say about his acting?
8. While Tupac teetered on the brink of death in a Las Vegas hospital, what music was playing continuously?
9. What happened when Notorious B.I.G. was visiting Tupac and he went to the bathroom?
10. How does Dyson describe Tupac's look when he was in high school?
11. What were the classes that Tupac believed high schools should be offering?
12. What did Tupac have to say about Ronald Reagan? How did he think he should address the homeless problem?
13. What did Tupac say about his Baltimore upbringing?
14. After Leila Steinberg, who became Tupac's manager and with whom did he first tour and record?
15. How does Leila Steinberg describe Tupac's attitudes about crime, particularly white and black crime?
16. What was it that Big Skye said Tupac gave to him?

QUESTIONS FOR FURTHER THOUGHT, RESEARCH, AND DISCUSSION

1. Research the history and use of the name Shakur in the Black Panther movement.

2. Tupac's tragic life and career has often been compared to Elvis Presley. Mostly, because their fans don't want to believe they are dead. Perhaps a better comparison would be Jimi Hendrix, or better still, Charlie Parker. Compare Tupac's tragic life, influence, and career to any or all of these three, or perhaps other tragic heroes. Where do the analogies breakdown?

3. Tupac spent much of his young life homeless. Tupac argues that those unfortunate circumstances should not necessarily prevent an artist from becoming critically important and socially significant and productive. Can you name others who have become famous after being homeless?

4. Reseach Tupac's career as a movie star and his training as an actor. Watch all of his movie roles and write a critique of his acting abilities.

5. Research and outline the history of Tupac's legal problems and try to explain why he was always running up against the law and the authorities.

6. Discuss the life and background of Leila Steinberg and how she influenced Tupac's career.

7. What does Leila Steinberg say about art?

8. Leila Steinberg describes Tupac's raps as "critical self-reflection," a means to pose internal questions out loud. What are those questions? How do we answer them? Where did Tupac get theses questions? Why is it important that we ask them?

9. List and discuss the books that the author found in Tupac's library. How do you think each or any of these books may have affected Tupac's raps?

10. What does Tupac mean by "Thug Life"? What was his acronym for nigga?

11. Tupac wanted to make a movie about Nat Turner. Who was Nat Turner and why did Tupac want to make a movie about his life?

12. Read *The Rose That Grew from Concrete* and compare Tupac's poetry to his rap lyrics.

PART FIVE

Crossover and Diversity

Black Owned

By Nelson George

The debate over the extent of hip hop's "blackness" is often a spirited one, with good points to be made on both sides. African Americans, naturally, are prone to claim it entirely as their own, but all of African Americans' aesthetic "gifts" to American culture have been by necessity, mixtures of African and European traditions. Hip hop is no exception. The important roles of Puerto Ricans, Jamaicans, and other ethnic groups in hip hop's development—especially in the early development of the elements of breaking and tagging—are well-documented. On the other hand, the oral traditions that hip hop MCs most often model and borrow from have their origins, more often than not, in black prison "toasts," the "dozens," and the rhetoric of the NOI and the Five-Percenters. Even raps in other languages often make awkward attempts at translating Ebonics.

Louis Armstrong once wrote that some of the best advice he ever received as a young black man growing up in the racial crucible of New Orleans was to make sure that he always had a respected "white" man who would stand up for him and vouch for him. In the last and perhaps happiest phase of Louis's career, that role was capably filled by the ex fight promoter and notoriously politically incorrect Joe Glaser. Likewise, Duke Ellington enjoyed the sponsorship and patronage and—depending on your point of view—was perhaps in turn exploited by the powerful Irving Mills. Count Basie and Billie Holiday benefited from the national exposure given them by the influential John Hammond. R&B was literally named and then marketed to the world by Jerry Wexler at Atlantic Records and other like-minded whites at small independent labels, like Leonard Chess and Syd Nathan. At Def Jam, Russell Simmons had Rick Rubin: twenty years earlier, Berry Gordy at Motown had the marketing expertise of Barney Ales, which enabled his black artists to "crossover" to the white pop charts.

Here again it is Nelson George and his insight and familiarity with the inner workings of the music business that illuminates us. His well-documented contention here is that like jazz and R&B, the commercial success of hip hop has always required the patronage and sponsorship of white—most often Jewish—entrepreneurs and idealists. The real irony here, of course, is that the target audience of P.E.'s black nationalism and N.W.A.'s garish descriptions of gangs and ghetto-life is primarily white teenagers.

A time of tension, racially fenced in I came off (and all the brothers blessed him)
— 3rd Bass, "Product of the Environment"

SOMETIME IN THE mid-'80s charles stettler, then manager of the Fat Boys, charged me with racism. "You don't like me," he scolded, "Because I'm a white and I manage a black group." Stettler was the balding, glib European who'd skillfully masterminded the marketing of three overweight Brooklyn boys into rap stars. Under his guidance Prince Markie Dee (Mark Morales), Kool Rock-Ski (Damon Wimbley), and the Human Beat Box (Darren "Buffy" Robinson) amassed significant hits ("In Jail," "All You Can Eat," "Can You Feel It") and won major commercial endorsements.

Stettler convinced the Swiss makers of Swatch watches, then struggling to penetrate the American youth market with their colorful timepieces, to underwrite a national hip hop tour for the Fat Boys in a national television spot, a historic breakthrough in terms of corporate support and national exposure for hip hop. After the Fat Boys costarred with Run-D.M.C. in the 1985 feature *Krush Groove,* Stettler negotiated a deal for a starring vehicle called *Disorderlies,* perhaps the crummiest of many crummy rap flicks.

Stettler, who had renamed the trio the more comic Fat Boys after they'd won a New York talent show as the Disco 3, cannily exploited the boys' hefty waistlines to make them lovable clowns and not what they were—health-endangered kids from East New York in Brooklyn, one of the city's toughest 'hoods. He was the ringmaster orchestrating a lucrative merchandising and media circus based primarily on the group's weight, particularly the unhealthy looking Buffy, and that same teenager's gift for creating polyrhythms with his mouth.

If I had any real beef with Stettler it was because of his style, not his skin color. I have no inherent dislike of hustlers. It goes with the business—my good friend Russell Simmons is hardly shy about hyping his clients. Stettler and I just didn't vibe. Mind you, our bad chemistry didn't hurt his career any—over a decade later, Stettler's still in the game, as the manager of the nationally syndicated hip hop radio jocks Dr. Dre and Ed Lover—but our interactions are still chilly.

Yet Stettler's charge of antiwhite racism has lingered with me. Not because I felt he was justi-fied, but because it dramatized for me how much antiwhite feeling Stettler must have encountered in his moves through the black music world. Antiwhite rhetoric flows through hip hop, and he had no reason to think I felt any different.

One of the prevailing assumptions around hip hop is that it was, at some early moment, solely African-American created, owned, controlled, and consumed. It's an appealing origin myth-but the evidence just isn't there to support it. Start with who "invented" hip hop: In its days as an evolving street culture, Latino dancers and tastemakers—later internationally know as breakers—were integral to its evolution, because of the synergy between what the mobile DJs played and what excited the breakers. Also, Caribbean culture clearly informed hip hop's Holy Trinity—Afrika

Bambaataa, Grandmaster Flash, and Kool Herc. Two of them, Flash and Herc, were either born in the Carribean or had close relatives from there. In Bam's case, non-American black music had been essential to his aesthetic.

More heretically, on the owner front, I'd argue that without white entrepreneurial involvement hip hop culture wouldn't have survived its first half decade on vinyl. It is indisputable that black-owned independents like Sugar Hill, Enjoy, and Winley cultivated and supported hip hop from 1979 to 1981. But it was white small-businesspeople who nurtured it next. Scores of white stepmothers and fathers adopted the baby as their own and many have shown more loyalty to the child than more celebrated black parental figures.

The list of these folks is long and includes Tommy Boy founder Tom Silverman and president Monica Lynch, the late manager-producer Dave (Funken) Klein, publicist Bill Adler, artist and A&R man Serch (Michael Benin), record executive-producer Dante Ross, Jive's Barry Weiss and Ann Carli, Select's Fred Munao, Tuff City's Aaron Fuchs, Priority's Brian Turner (a tremendous champion of West Coast and non-New York rap) and of course the Fat Boys' Charles Stettler. Lyor Cohen, Russell Simmons's longtime partner, first in Rush Management and later at Def Jam, has long been a behind-the-scenes force. Def Jam itself was founded by the adventurous producer Rick Rubin. Booking agent Cara Lewis has been a longtime champion in the shark-infested waters of concert appearances.

Interestingly, the majority of these men and women were Jews who carried on a long tradition of black and white collaboration in grassroots music that stretches back, at least, to the '40s when Jewish record men like Leonard and Phil Chess in Chicago and Jerry Wexler in New York led the pioneers who put electrified blues and R&B on vinyl. All of these people poured a great deal of time and passion into hip hop and, of course, many were handsomely rewarded. And, I say, why not? They believed when so many others didn't.

In 1989 Public Enemy was widely accused of anti-Semitism because of public statements given by its Minister of Information Professor Griff (William Griffen). This flap, which generated plenty of hand-wringing and column inches in the music press, resulted in Griff's removal from the group. Later lyrics in one of the band's greatest records, "Welcome to the Terrordome" on the 1990 *Fear of a Black Planet,* were interpreted to be anti-Semitic—again generating much morning talk show fodder. The great irony of these two infamous is-Public-Enemy-anti Semitic controversies was how many Jews were working for and with the band at the time. Public Enemy were signed to Def Jam by the Jewish Rick Rubin. Their tours were organized by the Jewish Lyor Cohen at Rush Management in conjunction with agent Cara Lewis. Much of their spin doctoring at the time was done by the Jewish Bill Adler at Rush Management. And Chuck D and Hank Schocklee were partners in Rhythm Method Productions with two Jews, Ed Chalpin and Ron Skuller. If P.E. hated Jews, then they must have been applying the gangster ethos: "Keep your friends close and your enemies closer."

The truth is, during 1981 to 1985, hip hops developmental period, African-American executives at black music departments and at black urban radio were not supportive. The buppies of the business who peopled the black music departments of the early to mid '80s and programmed radio stations were still putting time into Michael Jackson clones or the latest act from Minneapolis with keyboards programmed like Prince.

They didn't understand, respect, or support hip hop.

Kurtis Blow, signed to Mercury in 1979, was the only rap star with a major label deal at the time. His contract didn't come through the black department—he was signed by a white English A&R executive. There was a real class schism working against hip hop at the time. This dislike of the music was hardly limited to blacks in the business, but of course their lack of enthusiasm had real practical consequences. If you're looking for *one* of those crucial turning points where the adult black population began to profoundly disconnect from its kids, where the foundations of the intergenerational tension rampant in the '90s began, you can find it in the attitudes of black music industry figures of the early '80s toward hip hop. During my tenure as black music editor at *Billboard*, I regularly interviewed the buppies, and psuedo-buppies, who populated the offices of CBS, Warner Bros., PolyGram, RCA, MCA, and the other corporate imprints. The closer they drew to the top the stronger their attitude of "How long will this last?" They saw rap records, at best, as a fad and, at worst, as a blotch on African-America. This profound mistake occurred because these executives, armed with expense accounts and suburban homes, had fallen out of touch with—or deliberately rejected—black urban youth culture and were skeptical of any talent not recommended by attorneys and managers they hobnobbed with at the Jack the Rapper and Black Radio Exclusive conventions.

The corporate record companies had been committed to producing black talent a little over a decade when hip hop on small labels began appearing regularly on the charts. Because it was perceived as juvenile, unmusical, and with a limited audience, it didn't fit the prevailing crossover orthodoxy then epitomized by Michael Jackson and Lionel Richie. The twist is that hip hop prospered without them—by figuring out a whole different way to attract white music fans.

WALK THIS WAY

It is a fallacy that there ever existed a time when hip hop buyers were exclusively black. The first rap hit, "Rappers Delight," was voted single of the year by the National Association of Record Merchandisers, hardly a collective interested in celebrating singles sold just to black teenagers. "The Breaks" was only the second 12-inch single ever to sell 500,000 copies, a format originally designed for disco. You've got to be deluded to think that no whites purchased "The Breaks" in large numbers. The same can be said of Afrika Bambaataa & the Soul Sonic Force's "Looking for the Perfect Beat" and Grandmaster Flash & the Furious Fives "The Message." The numbers betray the myth. All these records were crucial building blocks for the music, artistic triumphs, and multicultural successes—just the crossover market the big labels lusted for.

In fact, a straight line can be drawn from "Rapper's Delight" to the hip hop present by looking at popular rap hits whose sales testify to the devotion of the white teen audience for nearly twenty years.

Sugar Hill Gang "Rapper's Delight" 1979
Stayed on the *Billboard* pop chart for 12 weeks, though it only reached #36. The charts at that time were heavily skewed by pop radio play, which the record didn't get a lot of. Still, its 12-week stay reflected the record's appeal. Because sales were balanced out by pop air play during this period, the position of rap singles on the chart weren't always true barometers of their crossover sales. In Canada and several foreign territories "Rapper's Delight" was a top 5 record.

Kurtis Blow "The Breaks (Part I)" 1980

Only the second 12-inch single to be certified gold. For perspective, it should be noted that the first was the Barbra Streisand–Donna Summer duet, "Enough Is Enough."

Grandmaster Flash & the Furious Five (featuring Duke Bootee)
"The Message" 1982

Social commentary that first made rock critics respect rap lyrics and inspired a generation of MCs. A gold single.

Herbie Hancock (with Grandmixer DST) "Rockit" 1983

Though it only reached #71 on the pop chart, it went gold in large part because the still-young MTV network adored its gimmicky video.

Chaka Khan (with Melle Mel) "I Feel for You" 1984

The first hugely commercial collaboration between a rapper and an established vocal star. It went to #3 on the pop chart, then went gold and pushed Khan's album, *I Feel for You,* to platinum. Adapted from a Prince song.

Run-D.M.C. "Rock Box" 1984

A hit MTV video helped propel this first rap-rock success. Helped make the trio s debut album, *Run-DM.C.,* gold.

Run-D.M.C. (with Aerosmith) "Walk This Way" 1986

As culturally significant as "Rapper's Delight." Made Run and his crew superstars, revived the career of Aerosmith by remodeling one of their classics, and made the rock world pay attention to Rick Rubin's production skills. Run-D.M.C.'s *Raising Hell* sold three million copies.

Jazzy Jeff & the Fresh Prince "Parents Just Don't Understand" 1988

Everything that Will Smith (aka the Fresh Prince) has accomplished, from his television series to his movie stardom, flows out of this song and video.

Beastie Boys "Fight for Your Right to Party" 1986

This frat-party anthem led the landmark album *Licensed to Ill* to sales of four million plus, which at the time was the most albums sold by any rap act.

L.L. Cool J "I Need Love" 1987
L.L. created the rap ballad and rode it to #1 on the black singles chart, one million sales, and a two-million-selling album, *Bigger and Deffer*.

Salt-N-Pepa "Push It" 1987
This single sold one million copies and the accompanying album, *Hot, Cool & Vicious,* went platinum, both firsts for female rappers.

Rob Base & DJ E-Z Rock "It Takes Two" 1988
A genius, left-field dance hit with great sampled hooks and a quick silver rhyme from Rob Base that sold one million copies.

Tone Loc "Wild Thing" 1989
Another great dance single. Reached #2 on the pop chart and stayed on 25 weeks. The album *Locked After Dark* went #1 on the pop chart and contained another huge single, "Funky Cold Medina," that hit the #3 spot.

Digital Underground "Humpty Dance" 1989
If you wanna be nostalgic for when hip hop was fun, this record makes your case. Fun, funny, and sure to rock any house party. One million satisfied customers purchased it.

Young MC "Bust a Move" 1989
Went to #7 on the pop charts behind a brash, lively video by Tamra Davis (who'd already done Tone Loc's two hits).

MC Hammer "U Can't Touch This" and "Pray" 1990
By sampling Rick James and Prince, and making kinetic dance-driven videos, Hammer created a formula that's worked in hip hop ever since—familiar samples and movement-driven visuals. As a result *Please Hammer Don't Hurt 'Em* sold 10 million copies, more than twice what the Beasties did just a few years before.

Vanilla Ice "Ice Ice Baby" 1990
The Osmond Brothers to Hammer's Jackson Five, Vanilla Ice enjoyed a #1 single and a seven-times platinum album, made a movie, was threatened by Suge Knight, and dated Madonna. It was his fifteen minutes, and they were action packed. Now stands as the universal symbol of hip hop wackness.

Naughty By Nature "OPP" 1991

Lead rapper Treach had a hard delivery over pop melodies, an infectious blend that led this clever record to #6 on the pop chart and two million sales.

L.L. Cool J "Around the Way Girl" 1990

No rapper has loved women more than L.L., and this celebration of urban womanhood went gold and set up L.L. s best album, *Mama Said Knock You Out.*

Salt-N-Pepa "Let's Talk About Sex" 1991

Playful, cute, and yet frank. A gold girl-group record for the '90s.

Arrested Development "Tennessee" 1992

A true one-album phenomenon that led the group to the 1992 Grammy for best new artist. The *3 Years, 5 Months & 2 Days in the Life Of* … sold two million copies.

House of Pain "Jump Around" 1992

Another white rap one-hit wonder, but a damn good one.

Sir Mix-A-Lot "Baby Got Back" 1992

A #1 pop single that rapped the praises of the African-American backside. Who says hip hop isn't a force for good?

Kriss Kross "Jump" 1992

Teen appeal duo with backward gear, an undeniable pop hook, and shrewd production by young Jermaine Dupri. Atlanta's emergence into the hip hop game.

Naughty By Nature "Hip Hop Hooray" 1993

A hip hop anthem for the time capsule with an irritatingly memorable chorus and a simple, arm-waving dance move that replaced the wave at sports arenas nationwide. Spike Lee's biggest video.

Tag Team "Whoomp! (There It Is)" 1993

Inspired by the activities at an Atlanta strip club, it went on to be one of the biggest-selling singles of all time at four million sold. It is one of the records that people will forever identify with the '90s.

Dr. Dre "Nuthin' But a 'G' Thang" 1993/Snoop Doggy Dogg "Gin & Juice" 1994

The power of street knowledge manifested. Two massive hits that illustrate the intense, spacious, funk-based production of Dre and the singing, sinister, melodic voice of Snoop. Dre's *The Chronic* sold three million and Snoop's *Doggystyle* eventually sold four.

Coolio "Gangsta's Paradise" 1995

Employing the Hammer formula and an unusual hairstyle, this ex-gang banger found a new career as a pop star with a bite of Stevie Wonder's "Pastime Paradise" from the *Dangerous Minds* soundtrack.

Salt-N-Pepa "Shoop" 1995

Not a great hip hop group, but a fantastic pop singles act, the Queens from Queens rule again.

Puff Daddy (featuring Mase) "Can't Nobody Hold Me Down" 1997

In the wake of the Notorious B.I.G.'s murder and at the height of Puff's synchronicity with the age, this three million seller became the "Ain't No Stoppin' Us Now" of the '90s.

These records share plenty of similarities. They are overwhelmingly dance-oriented with up-beat lyrics and catchy, simple choruses that appealed to teenage girls and kids (the notable exceptions are the down tempo L.L. Cool J's "I Need Love" and Coolio's "Gangsta's Paradise"). Most sample a musical or vocal hook from a well-known R&B or pop song of the 70s or '80s. "Rapper's Delight" is one of the few that actually had musicians re-create the musical source—in this case Chics "Good Times"—by employing a band. Quite a few in the '80s used rock guitar riffs in their hooks, a trend that has become as played out as lace-less sneakers.

From "Rockit" on, the records were aided by vivid, fun videos that gave the performers larger-than-life personas and featured great dancing or some combination of both. The publics embrace of the kinetic, dance-oriented videos for innocuous records like "Ice Ice Baby" or "Bust a Move" was crucial in driving them to million-selling status. Listening to Young MC and Vanilla Ice's records without recalling the videos *is* like imagining hip hop DJing without the mixer.

To hard-core purists almost all the records on my list are crossover crap and not "true hip hop," a stance that, like a great many purist positions in all art, is short-sighted and ahistorical. Throughout the last twenty years these hits kept the general population excited or at least aware of the music and, within the industry, constantly proved nonbelievers wrong.

Bubblegum rap records, often made by one-(or perhaps two-) hit wonders, just one angle of intersection between hip hop and white buyers. The reception given "The Message" by rock media (*Rolling Stone* gave the song a five-star review) foreshadowed a long-standing kinship between the teenage male rock audience and hip hop. Perhaps the chief exploiter of this relationship has been Def Jam Records head Russell Simmons. Starting with "Rock Box," produced by Simmons with Larry Smith, Run-D.M.C. was promoted as a rock band. There was a rebellious, nonconformist attitude in rap that Russell saw as analogous to the rock attitude he experienced hanging out at punk clubs like the Mudd Club, Hurrahs, and the Peppermint Lounge in Manhattan.

The white hipsters who had been intrigued by hip hop in its graffiti and break dancing forms also became fans of the music, influencing the coverage of early rap records in periodicals like the *Village Voice, SoHo Weekly News,* and other Lower Manhattan journals. Early national television exposure on ABC's *20/20* was also catalyzed by this community. However, Russell, who left Queens to become a habitue of this downtown world, was after bigger game. He wanted mall America to become hip hop America, and in Rick Rubin—NYU student, long-haired guitarist, hardcore rap aficionado, and product of Long Island—Russell found a partner who shared his vision of rap as rock.

Rubin "reduced" rap tracks, moving the music away from the R&B that supported Kurtis Blow and the Furious Five to a hard, stark aural assault with antecedents in AC/DCs "Back in Black" and Billy Squier's "The Big Beat"—the last of which had been an old-school break beat in the Bronx, The Rubin-reduced sonic masterpieces created with Run D.M.C. (*Raising Hell*) and on several Def Jam acts (L.L. Cool J's *Radio,* the Beastie Boys' *Licensed to Ill*) added heavy metal timbres to the beat emphasis of old-school DJs, creating a new way of hearing hip hop. Moreover, encouraged by Russell and Rubin, their artists proved that hip hop albums could be more than a collection of singles and filler, they could be complete artistic statements in a way rock fans understood.

One of the peculiar things about African-American culture is that white interest in black art is what sometimes incites proprietary interest in that art within our community. Prime example: the emergence of the Beastie Boys, The rapid rise of this Manhattan-based trio of white MCs, whose debut, *Licensed to Ill,* sold four million copies, generated a racial chauvinism among black folks, making the Beasties the first whites (but hardly the last) to be accused of treading on 100 percent black turf.

The irony is that these young men were managed and zealously promoted by Russell Simmons. It was one of the rare moments in pop history that a successful white group practiced a black music style with a black person so intimately involved in guiding their careers. (The next most prominent example is Boston-based producer-writer Maurice Starr's grooming of teen idols New Kids on the Block and their subsequent management by Dick Scott, another black man.) While Rubin provided the production punch, Russell gleefully encouraged the various little acts of adolescent outrage that the band perpetrated to promote *Licensed to Ill,* for which the trio became justly notorious and now, happily, have matured out of.

Public Enemy, signed by Rubin and hyped by Russell, found its own unique balance of rap danceablity and rock aggression. Black people used to wonder how a problack nationalist group like P.E. garnered a large, loyal, white fan base. It was simple: Public Enemy rocked and rebelled, literally, against the status quo. There is an endearing part of the white American mind that as teenagers (and less often as adults) detests the outward manifestations of this nation's mainstream culture. To be sure, this youthful rebellion is often superficial, not politically astute, and can be highly hypocritical—but it sells a lot of records.

This limited rebellion led white teenagers to pump *It Takes a Nation of Millions to Hold Us Back* in 1988, Ice Cube's *AmeriKKKa's Most Wanted* in 1990, N.W. A's *Niggaz 4 Life* in 1991, and Snoop Doggy Dogg's *Doggy style* in 1993. N.W.A (Niggaz with Attitude) and its West Coast cousins (Cube, Dr. Dre, Snoop, Tupac Shakur) inherited P.E.'s rebel status sans the consistent political critique. In its place was a more general antiauthoritarianism, coupled with a celebration of those two most American of obsessions—the gun and revenge as lifestyle—and a cartoonish misogyny that has never failed to titillate teenage boys, whether espoused by rockers or rappers.

While pop-rap hits appealed to kids and girls, and rap as rebellion attracted suburban males, there *is* a third aspect to hip hop s relationship with white buyers. Out *of* New York in the late '80s and early '90s a number of acts received much love from the rap cognoscenti. The *Source* magazine, for example, heaped praise on Brand Nubian (awarding *its One for All* in 1990 four mikes), its renegade member Grand Puba, and Queens-native Nas (Nasir Jones). If you read the reviews, you'd think these rappers were not just God's gift to hip hop but repositories of all that was true, urban, and black.

Brand Nubian, Grand Puba, and Nas all received recording contracts via white executives, canny signings not based merely on a reading of the market. The whites involved in giving them a platform were very much products of the same musical culture as the acts themselves. They were also, intriguingly enough, all alumni of the Rick Rubin-Russell Simmons axis, who worked out of 298 Elizabeth Street, once the Greenwich Village home of both Def Jam and Rush Management.

While crackheads got high across the street, inside the building a new generation of record executives was learning by doing. Bill Stephney, Dante Ross, Lisa Cortez, Sean "Captain Pissy" Casarov, Faith Newman, Dave (Funken) Klein, Hank Schocklee, and Lindsay Williams were among the many who moved through the building as interns or low-paid staffers and assistants. Within five years, all would be vice presidents at major labels, owners of their own boutique labels, or both.

Brand Nubian were recruited to Elektra by Dante Ross, an edgy, lanky New York native with the style of a new jack Bowery Boy. Known in hip hop circles for his love of basketball and his notorious temper, Dante started his career at Def Jam as a messenger and then moved up to the role of assistant to Rush management VP Lyor Cohen. Dante developed a rep as a producer-writer on several underground acts—one quite appropriately named Uptown—before Elektra head Bob Krasnow scooped him up to handle rap A&R in 1989. Krasnow is a white executive with great taste in black music based on an involvement that dates back to the Ike & Tina Turner Revue on Blue Note records. Although white, Dante's taste was of a New York rap snob who disdained pop-rap and rock-rap for an aesthetic based on dirty sounding old-school beats and lyrical flow. This sensibility lead Dante to sign Brand Nubian, a quintet who found inspiration in the teachings of the Five Percent Nation, a splinter off-shoot of the Nation of Islam with a strong following in the New York area that spilled over into hip hop.

OF GODS AND DEVILS

The Five Percenter theology was inspired by "Lost Found Moslem Lesson #2," penned by Nation of Islam founder W.D. Fard in 1934. In the Q&A-formatted essay Fard wrote that 85 percent of the earth was populated by "uncivilized people, poison animal eaters, slaves from mental death and power"; that 10 percent were "slave makers: of the poor who lie by teaching that the almighty true god is a spook and cannot be seen by the physical eye"; and that the remaining 5 percent were "poor, righteous teachers [who knew] that the living god is the Son of Man, the supreme being, the black man of Asia."Clarence 13X (Clarence Jowars Smith), a renegade from the Nation of Islam, founded the Five Percent Nation and, along with his excerpts from Fard, used concepts such as "Supreme Alphabet" and "Supreme Mathematics" to explain the universe. In his cosmology, his Harlem base became Mecca and Brooklyn, where he would relocate, was labeled Medina. Woman were variously known as Moons or Earths who circled around their men and were intended as the soil in which black Gods planted their seed.

Since at least the '70s, Five Percenters have been a strong underground force in the northeast, due both to the comfort their beliefs give to young black men and their less rigorous demands regarding clothing and discipline in comparison to the Nation of Islam or traditional Islam. Since Clarence 13X's unsolved shooting in 1969, the Five Percenters have had no formal leader so believers could readily follow the religion as they saw fit. Next door to me in East New York a house full of rowdy brothers converted to the Five Percent religion and changed their names to True God, Powerful, and other one or two word combinations that they felt were empowering. It didn't make them any less rowdy, but it did give them an enhanced sense of pride and community.

Rakim is probably the most prominent Five Percent rapper, and he has used the religions imagery to inform his writing throughout his career. A slew of other New York rap stars (Lakim Shabazz, the Poor Righteous Teachers, King Sun, Big Daddy Kane) have also pledged some form of allegiance. In much of hip hop, the Five Percenter belief that white men are devils, which it shares with the NOI, and that black men are Gods here on earth echos as loudly as a drum sample. As opposed to the white Jesus of Christianity, the Five Percenter finds power and truth in *himself*, a philosophy that lends itself easily to egotism and spirituality.

A white man would seem to be the last person in the world to give a group spouting such beliefs a platform, but Dante Ross was a dedicated supporter, sticking by Brand Nubian (even after Grand Puba split) and supporting other band members in their own solo efforts.

An act Dante worked with at Def Jam was 3rd Bass, a white rap duo fronted by Pete Nice (Peter J. Nash) and MC Serch (Michael Berrin). Serch is as white a b-boy as the definition will allow. He was raised out in largely black Far Rockaway, Queens, and spent most of his teenage weekends at the Latin Quarters, a legendarily treacherous Times Square club where great MCing and chain snatchings thrived simultaneously. Despite initially hostile crowds, Serch continued getting on the mike, eventually earning respect for his rhyme skills and pugnacious attitude (a respect denied the bizarrely titled Young Black Teenagers, a white group who recorded for Hank Schocklee and Bill Stephney's short-lived SOUL label).

As a result, when 3rd Bass debuted on Def Jam in 1989 the duo had real credibility within New York's rap community. And its "Steppin to the A.M." and subsequent singles, such as "The Gas Face," found favor primarily in the northeast. The duo's chance for a national breakout arrived in 1991 with "Pop Goes the Weasel," a sharp skewering of white rap rival Vanilla Ice. However, the duo's momentum was sabotaged when Serch and Pete Nice began bickering and eventually split up. Pete Nice kept the 3rd Bass name and, with DJ Richie Rich, released an ill-fated album, while Serch—after his own unsuccessful solo disc—moved fulltime into management and production.

It was in that capacity that Serch came into contact with Nas, a small framed, sleepy-eyed kid considered by many hip hop heads to be one of the best lyricists ever. Nas debuted as a guest vocalist on Main Source's 'Live at the BBQ," a memorable performance that made him an instant Big Apple cult figure. Serch ran into him at a Manhattan studio and, after having him do guest vocals on the 3rd Bass single "Back to the Grill Again," inquired as to whether Nas had a record deal. The teenage protege had been approached by a few people but hadn't signed anywhere yet.

Acting as Nas's manager, Serch brought demos to the Madison Avenue offices of Sony A&R executive Faith Newman in 1991. Five years earlier Faith, a soul fanatic raised in a Philadelphia suburb, had come to New York to attend NYU, but her real education came first as an intern and then A&R executive at Def Jam. When Serch handed her the tape, it turned out that Faith had been trying to locate Nas for months. For Faith, who has since moved to Jive, it was her first major signing; for Nas, it was the beginning of a career that has spawned two platinum albums and one of hip hop's most devoted followings.

BMOC

While Ross, Serch, and Newman all received progressive educations at Def Jam U, this trio involved with New York hip hop's cutting edge wasn't an anomaly. They were part of a new generation of white hipsters, not the folks from the Roxy, but younger people for whom hip hop wasn't a curiosity, for whom rap was their first musical language. Two other young people for whom "true hip hop" would be a calling were Jon Schecter and David Mayes.

As an underclassman at Harvard University Schecter recorded a rap album, *BMOC (Big Men on Campus),* that was picked up by a label owned by Brett Ratner, another rap-loving white kid who had a distribution deal with Sire Records. (Ratner would become a top video director, later handling the 1997 Chris Tucker comedy *Money Talks?)* Despite the prestige of ex-Chic member Nile Rodgers's providing some production, wack songs like "Play That Funk" made *BMOC* seem more like a novelty effort than an authentic rap record.

Schecter, with David Mayes, another Harvard student who DJed at the campus radio station, and a low-key black man named Ed Young, made a more enduring impact on hip hop by founding the *Source* in 1988. The magazine began as a two-page newsletter published for $2.50 out of a Cambridge dorm. By the time the *Source* moved to New York in the early '90s, it had grown into a color monthly. Mayes supervised advertising and promotion, Schecter supervised the editorial, and together they put together a talented, African-American-majority staff of writers, photographers, and designers. The *Source* became known for its record-rating system, which used microphones instead of stars *to* signify quality (five mikes was a masterpiece), and the best ongoing coverage of hip hop and its ever-multiplying cultural off-shoots. The *Source* became such a crucial piece of the culture that Quincy Jones and Time-Warner tried to buy it. Mayes and Schecter wouldn't sell. So in 1992 the would-be buyers turned around and created *Vibe,* which became the *Source's* chief competitor.

The *Source* suffered a major blow in 1994 when the editorial staff, supported by Schecter, battled with Mayes over his fierce loyalty to the mediocre Boston rap crew the Almighty RSO. Mayes had been close to the group since college, a relationship that created tension because most of the magazine's editors didn't respect them. Moreover, members of the Almighty RSO camp, aware of the low regard in which they were held and frustrated that Mayes couldn't help them more, were accused of threatening several members of the editorial staff.

This soap opera came to a conclusion when an article written by Mayes on the Almighty RSO was published in the magazine behind the backs of the editorial staff. After some nasty open letters and much shouting, Schecter and the editorial staff quit en mass while Mayes and Young retained control of the magazine. The battle over the *Source* wasn't pretty; it completely fractured the original team and, for a time, weakened the editorial product.

Still, and it speaks to hip hop's broad cultural appeal, the *Source* weathered that storm and has been able to find a new collection of young journalists obsessed enough with the culture to work for the *Sources* low wages. By 1997, the editorial staff was entirely black and Hispanic, with an average age of twenty-five. That same year, the magazine's relevance and vitality was confirmed when it sold more magazines via newsstands than any other music periodical in America, averaging 317,369 copies per issue compared to *Rolling Stones* 169,625. The *Source* continues on because it represents a keep-it-real alternative to the glossy, photo-driven coverage that has defined *Vibe.*

In 1997, several of the key African-American editors who'd fled the *Source,* including Reginald Dennis and James Bernard, began publishing an impressive competing mag, *XXL,* on a quarterly basis, only to again run afoul of a publisher in a dispute over control and feel compelled to resign.

THE MOST IMPORTANT WHITE MAN IN HIP HOP

When antirap activist C. Dolores Tucker (whom I will discuss later) attacked white executives whom she viewed as irresponsible or insensitive because they promoted rap music, she could have been talking about Barry Weiss. From a stereotypical point of view (and nothing C. Dolores Tucker says verges very far from stereotype), Barry fits the part-he's a white adult male who has supervised the signing of scores of hip hop artists for over fifteen years. Moreover, he's Jewish and from New York, which for the conspiracy-minded would confirm the venal nature of his career. Even worse, his father, Hy Weiss, owned Old Town Records in the '50s and '60s, a prolific doo-wop–R&B operation, which makes his son a legacy member of the record industry's permanent business. With the possible exception of Tommy Boy founder Tom Silverman, no white businessman has been in rap music longer, more consistently, or more successfully than Weiss.

Jive Records, an off-shoot of the highly successful U.K. publishing company Zomba, made Weiss its first U.S. employee in 1982. One of Jives first domestic projects was a compilation of break beat records to which Zomba owned the publishing rights. The modest yet impressive sales of this compilation awakened him to this developing scene. Weiss wanted to record a 12-inch with Mr. Magic, whose overnight weekend show—*The Rap Attack,* on low frequency WHBI—was rap's first regularly scheduled radio broadcast. When Mr. Magic backed out at the last minute his assistant, Jalil Hutchins, and the assistant's friend Ecstasy (John Fletcher) cut "Magics Wand" at a hastily put together session. Weiss himself named the duo Whodini and, supported by flashy DJ Grandmaster Dee (Drew Carter), they went on to enjoy several platinum albums.

Subsequently, Weiss either signed or helped woo a broad spectrum of rappers, from the iconoclastic KRS-One, the pop-rap poster boys DJ Jazzy Jeff & the Fresh Prince, the smooth Kool Moe Dee, native tongue standard-bearer A Tribe Called Quest, pimp-rap godhead Too Short, West Coast homicide chronicler Spice I, Oakland mogul E-40, and many others. It was *Weiss's* support that allowed Jive staffer Ann Carli and myself to get the Stop the Violence Movement's "Self-Destruction" recorded and released in January 1989. This was after several of the most prominent African-Americans in hip hop were asked to help put together an antiviolence record for charity and either declined or didn't respond.

Weiss has been involved with hip hop from its earliest days on record, through its national expansion, to its ongoing regionalization in the '90s. The reason Weiss has been so agile in rolling with rap's changes is that he's never had an artistic agenda. Unlike Suge Knight, Andre Harrell, and Russell Simmons, Weiss has shrewdly never let his personal taste intrude on his business decisions. Key to Jive's philosophy has been to carefully scrutinize retail sales around the country in search for breaking records on indie labels. Weiss would then make contact with the label or artist, either signing the act directly to Jive or making a deal with the indie label for master rights.

Boogie Down Productions' historic first album, *Criminal Minded,* was on Bronx-based B-Boy Records in 1987 before Jive snatched them up. Weiss had also been monitoring the record sales out of Philly in the late '80s and signed a number of groups from the city of brotherly love, including Jazzy Jeff & the Fresh Prince. Moe Dee had recorded for Harlem's Rooftop Records prior to joining Jive. Too Short had recorded three albums of material celebrating the joys of pimping and macking on the Oakland-based Dangerous Music before joining Jive in 1988. E-40, who succeeded Too Short as the king of the Bay Area's hyperactive hip hop scene, had recorded several successful albums before inking a deal with Jive both as an artist and for his label, Sick-Wit-It. Even R. Kelly, the most gifted R&B singer-songwriter of the '90s, was picked up by Jive after he'd recorded and released his debut, *R. Kelly & the Public Announcement,* out of Chicago. Now this strategy isn't foolproof. Around 1990 with much chest pounding Jive signed members of Oakland's Hirogifics Posse—Casual, Souls of Mischief, and the Prolific—none of whom made much of a dent nationally. But in the trend-conscious hip hop world Weiss and the label's hip hop hit-to-miss ratio is extraordinary. The troubling side of Jive's nonjudgmental vision is that it can seem as amoral as Mrs. Tucker would suggest. By signing Too Short, Weiss and his company gave national exposure to ad infinitum rants about screwing perpetually horny females. When blood-soaked West Coast rap began flourishing, Jive didn't blink, signing the homicidal tales of Oakland based Spice I. In fact, the soundtrack to *Menace II Society,* compiled with considerable input from directors Allen and Albert Hughes, is as representative a document of the nihilistic gangsta genre as anything recorded. Jive's best defense is its eclectic nature. Unlike Death Row, whose thuggish vision was announced by its logo, Jive has always let the audience dictate its direction. Because Jives A&R department is so driven by what has already been proven in the market, at least regionally, they have followed their taste to places that many black adults detest, places that are embraced by African-American entrepreneurs and hip hop audiences. Blaming the messenger, a popular American pastime, in no way invalidates the message.

For me, the single most important thing about Weiss's tenure has been his commitment to KRS-One. In ten years Jive has released eight Boogie Down Productions–KRS-One albums. These records have spawned no crossover singles, few MTV videos, and a small white audience. Weiss and Jive's involvement with such an uncompromising, non-pop, non R&B, hardheaded, contentious, rarely platinum act has no other precedent in hip hop history. No MC, with the exception of L.L. Cool J, has made as many albums or been with the same label as long. By supporting KRS-One, Weiss has given creative license to the genre's most complex mind.

LABOR DAY

I can't leave the topic of rap and white folks without offering up this memory. It is summer 1995 and I am spending the long Labor Day weekend at a house out on the tip of Long Island. To my surprise, in a local publication I spot an ad for a Run-D.M.C. gig at the Bay Club in the Hamptons' town of East Quoque. Along with two other old school hip hop colleagues, Ann Carli and Bill Stephney, I drive to the club where we encounter a large drunken crowd of college-age and young adult whites. The club is jam-packed and the narrow stage swollen with equipment.

When Run, D.M.C, and Jam Master Jay arrive onstage, the building rocks. The 99.9 percent white audience knows the words to every song. "My Adidas," "Rock Box," and "King of Rock" are not exotic to this crowd. It is the music they grew up on. I flash back on Temptations–Four Tops concerts that are '60s nostalgia lovefests. Well, for these twenty somethings, Run-D.M.C. is '80s nostalgia. They don't feel the music like a black kid from Harlem might. No, they feel it like white people have always felt black pop—it speaks to them in some deep, joyous sense as a sweet memory of childhood fun. In a frenzy of rhymed words, familiar beats, and chanted hooks the suburban crowd drinks, laughs, and tongue kisses with their heads pressed against booming speakers. It may not be what many folks want hip hop to mean, but it is a true aspect of what hip hop has become.

OBJECTIVE QUESTIONS

1. Who accused Nelson George of "racism" and what was the group that he managed?
2. According to the article, hip hop wouldn't have survived its first half decade on vinyl without _____.
3. What is the great irony of Public Enemy's controversies with anti-Semitism?
4. During hip hop's developmental period (1981–1985), African American executives at black music departments and at black urban radio were _____.
5. How did black record executives initially view hip hop and who epitomized their prevailing crossover orthodoxy?
6. What was the second 12-inch single to be certified as gold? What was the first?
7. This record revived the career of Aerosmith by remodeling one of their classics and made the rock world pay attention to the production skills of _____.
8. By sampling Rick James and Prince and making kinetic dance-driven videos, he created a formula that has worked in hip hop ever since—familiar samples and movement driven visuals.
9. According to the article, he "now stands as the universal symbol of hip hop whackness."
10. The records in George's list share several similarities. What are they?
11. To hard-core purists, almost all of the records on the list would be considered ____.
12. What was different about the way that Russell Simmons promoted and marketed Run-D.M.C.
13. According to George, West Coast rap celebrated the two most American of obsessions—the gun and revenge as lifestyle—and _____.
14. He is probably the most prominent Five Percent rapper, and he has used the religion's imagery to inform his writing throughout his career: _____.
15. Who worked with 3rd Bass at Def Jam and what made them different?
16. What was Nas's debut recording? Who was his manager, and who signed him to Sony?
17. Who are Jon Schecter and David Mays and what is their background?
18. According to George, who is the most important white man in hip hop and how does he differ from Suge Knight, Andre Harrell, and Russell Simmons?

19. In George's view, the most important thing about Weiss's tenure has been his commitment to_____.
20. What was George's epiphany on Labor Day 1995?

TOPICS FOR FURTHER THOUGHT, RESEARCH, AND DISCUSSION

1. Discuss and argue the extent of hip hop culture's "blackness." Include the contributions from other cultures, the African American origins of much of its rhetoric, its role as the voice of black nationalism (the black CNN), and the extent of its globalization.
2. Research and report on the careers of R&B producers like Leonard Chess, Jerry Wexler, and Syd Nathan.
3. How do you feel about George's list of recordings. Would you add any or subtract any?
4. "One of the peculiar things about African American culture is that white interest in black art is what sometimes incites proprietary interest in that art within our community." What does that mean? George uses the Beastie Boys as an example. How many others can you name?
5. "There is an endearing part of the white teenage American mind (and, occasionally the adult one) that detests the outward manifestations of this nation's mainstream culture. To be sure this youthful rebellion is often superficial, not politically astute, and can be highly hypocriti-cal—but it sells a lot of records." Do you believe this to be true, now and historically? What other styles, groups, or recordings exemplify this statement?
6. How do white hip hop artists and white blues singers or jazz artists get credibility in the African American community? What other white artists have successfully and unpretentiously worked in genres dominated by or created by African Americans without appearing exploitive?
7. Report on the beginnings, growth, and ultimate demise of *The Source* magazine. Report on the beginnings of *Vibe* magazine and how it is different than *The Source.*
8. Report on the life and background of C. Delores Tucker, her involvement in politics and her attacks on rap.
9. Research the careers of Barry Weiss and his father and the music that they have promoted.
10. George maintains that white kids from Long Island feel the music differently from black kids from Harlem. If so, how so?
11. How do the career and recordings of Eminem fit into this discussion?

Ladies First

By Laura Jamison

Laura Jamison is a writer and critic living in New York. Her interview subjects for *Vibe* have included the Notorious B.I.G., Too Short, and Savion Glover. She has also contributed to *Rolling Stone* and the new *York Times.*

There is certainly no greater controversy surrounding hip hop than its portrayal of women and its infamous sexism. Indeed, there are several entire volumes and several college courses that are specifically devoted to this issue alone. Despite rappers' reputations for priapic posturing, and the recurrent sexist and homophobic lyrics, the question hip hop culture must answer is: "Is hip hop culture more sexist than other traditionally male-dominated forms of show business like rock n' roll and the blues? Or, even is it more sexist than American society in general?" Again, there are good arguments to be found on both sides of the question. This article from *The Vibe History of Hip Hop* sidesteps the controversy entirely and simply traces the important roles that women have played in its history. With several notable exceptions of course, rappers and MCs have always been predominantly male. There has never seemed to be a shortage, however, of women entrepreneurs, record executives, and journalists in hip hop's history, including Laura Jamison, the author of this article. In this respect alone, there is evidence of much social progress in our culture generally, and in this area, hip hop may actually be somewhat ahead of the curve. Of course, hip hop evolved as a celebration of adolescence and part of the human mating ritual. Therefore, in spite of the rarity of traditional romance in its history, it has really always been about bringing the sexes together. The misogynist and homophobic lyrics so often encountered in hip hop recordings are again remnants of the all-male prison culture and are sometimes unfortunately dismissed as pure entertainment.

The sad lesson of the minstrel shows of the 19th century is that these caricatures and stereotypes—created initially solely to be funny and entertaining—can leave a negative legacy that stubbornly persists and permeates the social fabric for generations. While there may be a dearth of hip hop lyrics about heartbreak and romance, rappers are not the least bit shy about lyrics expressing their love for their mothers—in most cases, single mothers. A good argument could be made that prison misogyny and by extension the misogyny in hip hop, stems from what in the ghetto is often a matriarchal society—where unemployed males lack self esteem and kids grow up without father figures. Of course, hip hop lyrics are not the first references to *bitches* and *hoes* in American popular song. In 1952, for example, Big Mama Thornton—who was probably at least bi-sexual and often performed dressed in men's clothes—popularized lyrics written by two Jewish teenagers (Jerry Lieber and Michael Stoller) that said, *"You ain't nothin' but a hound dog. You can wag your tail, but I ain't going to feed you no more."* There's not a lot of difference between a metaphor that describes your lover as a "hound dog" and referring to him or her as a "bitch." And of course there is no shortage of blues lyrics with euphemisms for prostitution, pandering and drug use as well. Not to be ignored here is the fact that at a time when male blues singers were being ignored by the recording industry, the blues "queens" of the 1920s not only did a great deal to proliferate and popularize the blues, but perhaps even more important, expressed a decidedly female point of view.

RAP, AS ERICK Sermon of EPMD once said, "has always been about bullshit: my shit is betta than yours, your shit sucks." Macho antics like posturing, bragging, and throwing attitude are the heart and soul of the rhyming tradition which is probably why rap is usually considered an inherently male form (rump shakin' videos and bee-yatch-laden lyrics probably don't help dispel the idea, either). Female MCs have traditionally been viewed as interlopers—either butchy anomalies or cute novelties who by some fluke infiltrated a boy's game. But the fact is, while fewer in number than men, women have been integral to rap since its formative years (a claim that can't be made for the other dominant postwar pop music form, rock 'n' roll). Indeed, females have rocked mikes alongside the boys since the beginning.

Even before "Rapper's Delight" brought the beat to the rest of America in 1979, when rap was still a local phenomenon storming the South Bronx, female MCs were already on hand—and according to one of them, these women were no less important in creating the new form than the men involved. Ms. Melodie, a female rapper who was part of the Boogie Down Productions crew (and was married to KRS-One), states. "It wasn't that the male started rap, the male was just the first to be put on wax. Females were always into rap, and females always had their little crews and were always known for rockin house parties and streets, school yards, the corner, the park, whatever it was."

Though this pre-wax era is poorly documented, some venerable names that live on from that time are Little Lee, a woman who rhymed with Kool DJ AJ, and Sweet & Sour, who dropped rhymes with Grandmixer D.S.T. Lady B was the first woman rapper to record, with "To the Beat Y'all" in 1980 before going on to DJ at Philadelphia's WUSL and to serve as editor-in-chief of *Word Up!*, an early rap 'zine. The Mercedes Ladies appeared on "Don's Groove" by Donald D., but this female rap posse never received official credit. Women also took part in other aspects of the burgeoning culture called hip hop: breakdancing produced an all female breaking troupe called the Dynamic Dolls, as well as b-girls like Daisy Castro, who busted her moves as part of the predominantly male Rock Steady Crew. On the graffiti front, women artists such as Lady Pink and Lady Heart made their names with their illicit public art.

Perhaps there's no better evidence that women hold a righteous place in hip hop's genesis than the fact that it was a female who first thought to cash in on the then underground "fad." Sylvia Robinson, a middle-aged sometime R&B singer, was the woman

who enlisted a group of young men to record a playful rap over Chic's "Good Times," and "Rapper's Delight" was born, forever changing music history. The overwhelming success of that now historic song prompted her to start Sugar Hill Records, a label that turned out most of the significant rap acts of the early 1980s. (And she was soon followed by such prominent female executives as Monica Lynch at Tommy Boy and Carmen Ashurst-Watson at Def Jam.; again in contrast to rock, women were firmly established in positions of power in the rap business from the early days.)

Robinson was an entrepreneur, however, not a crusader for women's rights, and when she formed Sugar Hill, she signed whoever she thought would bring in some dollars. And, tellingly, a few of those acts happened to be female: Sequence, a flashy, disco-influenced trio, sang and rapped on. the 1979 classic "Funk You Up" and "Monster Jam." Their danceable music prefigured some of the hip hop-soul hybrids of the late 90s. Another label, Enjoy Records, put out the first record by the legendary Funky Four + One—the "One" being a pretty young woman named Sha Rock. Hailing from the Bronx's Edenwald Projects, this group earned a rep for Temptations-style choreography, for riffing on the *Gilligan's Island* theme, and for putting on four-hour shows. After its first record, "Rappin' and Rockin' the House," the group went to Robinson's Sugar Hill, where it recorded the towering "That's the Joint." In 1981, they took their rowdy feel good party vibes to the set of *Saturday Night Live,* making them the first rap act ever to perform on that show.

Sha Rock earned her props not only as an MC, but as an innovator on the beat box. She didn't have a lot of female company in that arena, however. In a tradition that still stands, only a handful of other women worked on the production side in the early days (DJ Jazzy Joyce, and later Salt-N-Pepa's Spinderella). A variety of social and economic conditions made this true: then and now, men have more access to electronic equipment, both financially and culturally. As MC Lady "D" recalled, by limiting herself to rhyming, she "didn't have to worry about getting her equipment ripped off, coming up with the cash to get it in the first place, or hauling it around on subways to gigs—problems that kept a lot of other women out of rap in the early days." In other words, it was simpler and safer for women to leave production to the boys.

But rhyming was open to anyone with a smart mouth, and plenty of women opened theirs and let loose. Lisa Lee, the front-woman for Cosmic Force, a crew that formed in the Bronx in the late '70s, later broke off and joined Afrika Bambaataa's Zulu Nation in 1980. After ditching Cosmic Force, Lisa teamed up with Sha Rock and Debbie Dee from Mercedes Ladies to form the short-lived all-star team Us Girls, who recorded a track for Harry Belafonte's 1984 film *Beat Street* Sweet Trio featuring Jazzy Joyce cut "Non Stop" on Tommy Boy in 1986; Joyce (who remains a popular New York DJ to this day) subsequently teamed up with Sweet Tee, a former dancer with Davy D who had also worked with producer Hurby "Luv Bug" Azor, to create "It's My Beat," an entirely female-created rap record that topped the charts.

Women still lagged behind men in hip hop, just as female rockers lagged behind their male counterparts, but there was a moment in hip hop history when it looked as though women might have the chance to even the playing field: the infamous dis (or response) records craze of the 1980s blew up the careers of several female MCs. The firestorm started in 1985, when an unsuspecting trio of male rappers called U.T.F.O. cut a song called "Roxanne, Roxanne" about a stuck-up girl who had the nerve to resist their charms. Suddenly, out of nowhere, a record featuring a 14-year-old with a high voice and debilitating wit slammed U.T.F.O.: She was Roxanne Shante, from Queensbridge, New York.

Pretending to be the Roxanne they were talking about, this pudgy-cheeked, merciless young MC (with the production help of New York radio DJ Marley Marl) blasted onto the rap scene, instantly becoming the preeminent Mistress of the Dis—though immediately female MCs started battling to snatch away her title (and share some of her profits). As soon as producer Spyder D heard Roxanne Shanté's track, he called on his protegee, Sparky D, to verbally slay Shante. Within two weeks she too had landed a record deal. Then the Real Roxanne, until then a waitress in New York named Joan Martinez, came out with yet another response to U.T.F.O. Over 100 Roxanne-related records were eventually cut.

The popularity of the response record was a huge boon to female MCs. They allowed women to brag, dis, and employ their cutting wit without alienating the largely male rap audience—probably in part because a lot of these records sounded like straight-up cat fights or everyday battle-of-the-sexes brawls. JJ. Fad (M.C.J.B., Baby-D, and Sassy C), the L.A.-based group who made their name with a quasirap dance record called "Supersonic" (produced by Dr. Dre during his N.W.A days), got dissed hard by the fresh-mouthed Roxanne Shante on her record "Wack It." J.J. Fad came back with "Ya Coin' Down," which dogged Roxanne Shante's weight and sexuality. Meanwhile, Pebblee Poo answered the Boogie Boys' popular song "A Fly Girl" with her own "A Fly Guy," and E-Vette Money exacted "E-Vette's Revenge," her answer to L.L. Cool J's "Dear Yvette." As late as 1992, Roxanne Shanté (who by then had changed her name to simply Shante) shredded a slew of female MCs, including Queen Latifah, MC Lyte, and Yo Yo on the scathing, no-holds-barred track "Big Mama."

It was a response record that launched the careers of rap's longest-enduring female act, Salt-N-Pepa. Cheryl James and Sandy Denton met at Queensborough College; both also worked at a Sears department store, where they met Hurby "Luv Bug" Azor. Still a student himself, Azor was making a record for a school project, so his new friends recorded "The Show-stopper (Is Stupid Fresh)," an answer to Doug E. Fresh and Slick Rick's "The Show." Azor took the song to a small label, Pop Art, which signed the group under the name Super Nature. Later Azor met Pamela Greene, and brought her on as DJ Spinderella.

After changing their name to Salt-N-Pepa, their 1986 debut album, *Hot Cool & Vicious,* went double platinum after two years, making the group the first female act to achieve that honor. After the first album, Greene left the group, and Dee Dee Roper took her place as Spinderella. In 1987, S-N-P released "Push It," which went gold, as did their albums *A Salt with a Deadly Pepa* and *Blacks' Magic.* Their 1993 release *Very Necessary* has sold over five million to date, buoyed by the smash singles "Whatta Man," featuring En Vogue, and "Shoop."

But Salt-N-Pepa's big sales were an anomaly. The fact is, women were still not selling a lot of records. As late as 1992, the only women to have a gold rap single or album were S-N-P and J.J. Fad—who are often discounted by those who don't consider "Supersonic" to be a real rap song. One reason women artists sold such measly numbers is that the core rap audience was (and is) male, and men simply weren't ready to hear women copping the tough posture that defined rap. By the same token, female listeners preferred more melodic music to rap's hard beats, something

Salt-N-Pepa wisely recognized and capitalized on: They dropped their pro-women, pro-sex rhymes over R&B melodies, a combination that won them countless female fans. But the majority of women artists had a tough time; like women everywhere, female MCs faced garden variety gender bias. In 1994, Queen Latifah pointed out in VIBE: "People wonder why girls don't go platinum, but a lot of the time we don't get the same money [for marketing and promotion], and that's just a straight-up fact."

Success would become even more elusive for female MCs as rap took a crucial turn. In its first stages, the music had been about dissing and bragging, but there was an element of playfulness and glitzy artifice—in short, "show biz." Think back to early photos of Grandmaster Flash in his spacesuits and sequins or Sequence with their gold lame clothes and coiffed dancing-queen hair. Likewise, the sound reflected vestiges of disco and electric boogie: It was party music. But things started to change when "The Message," with its bleak portrait of ghetto desperation, hit in 1982, and Run-D.M.C. hit arena stages in street clothes, with stark rhymes and beats like "Hard Times" and "It's Like That." Ironically, Run-D.M.C.'s members were middleclass kids from Hollis, Queens, to whom ghetto life was as much a boyish fantasy as it was to the white suburban kids they appealed to. "With Run-D.M.C. and the suburban rap school," said producer and cofounder of Def Jam Recordings Rick Rubin, "we looked at that [ghetto] life as a cowboy movie. To us, it was like Clint Eastwood. We could talk about those things because they weren't that close to home."

Together with a harder, more brash rock sound, Run-D.M.C.—and L.L. Cool J soon after them—captured the ears of a huge number of listeners, converting millions to the form only recently considered a passing fad. The tenor of rap was changing. Hard guys and street life were selling, and that's what the record companies wanted. Now it wasn't about Hollywood dreams it was about keepin' it real. And women, who for obvious reasons would have a difficult time posing as menaces to society were getting pushed further aside in the rap game.

One exception was MC Lyte, who arrived on the scene at the tender age of 16 with her 1986 single "Cram to Understand," Raised in Queens and Brooklyn, Lana Moorer learned to rhyme from her paternal half-brothers, a pair called Audio Two who blew up with the masterful single "Top Billin'." Their shrewd father Nat Robinson decided to start a label for them called First Priority but he was later enticed to cut a deal with Atlantic on the condition that the mega record company agreed to grant his daughter Lana a record contract too.

Lyte's first complete album, *Lyte as a Rock,* followed in 1988, producing songs that have since become classics, including "10% Dis," a preemptive strike at rival rapper Antoinette, who was rumored to be planning a dis record about Lyte, and "Paper Thin." Lyte's voice was raspy, raw, and young—she couldn't be too threatening—little tomboy that she was, but she was dead serious when she rhymed, earning her respect (Chuck D later rapped, "MC Lyte, that's right /She could win a rhyme fight").

In "Paper Thin"—which sold 125,000 copies in its first six months with virtually no airplay— she dogged a cheating boyfriend. Lyte projected herself as a proud young woman who held herself above such low-down antics. "I'm not the kind of girl to try and play a man out/ They take the money and they break the hell out / … But if it doesn't work out, yo, it just doesn't / It wasn't meant to be, you know, it just wasn't / So I treat all of you like I treat all of them/ What you say to me is just paper thin." Lyte was hard, tough—but clearly she was at heart a respectable girl.

Lyte's popularity continued to build with her 1989 album *Eyes on This* which featured "Cha Cha Cha," a raucous record made with DJ K-Rock that shot to the top of the rap charts. But just two years later, Lyte imprudently attempted to change her ways: Her next album, *Act Like You Know,* was a collection of softer, sweeter, more romantic songs, which alienated fans of her tough-girl image. She underwent a makeover too, replacing the tomboy look with grown-up clothes and makeup. *Act Like You Know* bombed. Yet that failure may have spawned a historical occasion in rap, because with her next effort, she returned to her old hard ways with a vengeance. In 1993 *Ain't No Other* produced "Ruffneck," the first rap tune by a solo woman to go gold. In 1996, she released *Bad as I Wanna B,* her fifth album, which included songs by Jermaine Dupri and R. Kelly and "Cold Rock a Party," which Puff Daddy remixed over a sample of Diana Ross's "Upside Down," giving Lyte her biggest hit yet. But in 1998, she released *Seven and Seven,* a disappointment both critically and financially. Even so, MC Lyte has enjoyed greater longevity than nearly all of the men who debuted when she did.

Lyte cracked rap's new keepin'-it-real mandate by walking a fine line between tough girl and good girl, a model that also applied to Yo Yo, who was still a high school cheerleader when Ice Cube discovered her in an L.A. mall in 1989. Cube brought Yo Yo into the studio to trade snaps with him on "It's a Man's World," and the spunky but still feminine image she established went on to carry her through four albums in the '90s.

Queen Latifah created yet another alternative to the men's club with her regal bearing, Afrocentric garb, and positive rhymes (Latifah means "fine and delicate" in Arabic). A native of East Orange, New Jersey, Dana Owens performed at her high school as the human beat box for a group of girls who called themselves Ladies Fresh. She then met DJ Mark the 45 King, who produced a demo with her that caught the attention of Tommy Boy Records. At the age of 19, she put out *All Hail the Queen* (1989). The second single from that album, "Ladies First" which introduced British rapper Monie Love to the American audience, became an anthem—it exalted women but didn't dis black men (interestingly, Latifah's homeboy Apache penned the lyrics to this supremely womanist song—the same guy whose own big hit was called "Gangsta Bitch").

From the start, Latifah was a phenomenon: her natural charisma, warmth, and sense of dignity appealed to round-the-way kids and suburban rap fans alike. Stalking the stage with her husky self and big smile, Latifah could move any crowd; she was a born entertainer. Early in her career, she hooked up with the Native Tongues, the loose-knit crew of peace-and-love hip hoppers that included De La Soul and Jungle Brothers, which gave her an extra boost of exposure. Even though her next effort two years later, *Nature of a Sista,* didn't even sell as well as the critically lauded but commercially disappointing *All Hail,* Latifah's personality continued to buoy her in the public eye. She was called on to appear in Spike Lee's *Jungle Fever,* as well as the films *juice* and *House Party* 2.

It was 1993's *Black Reign* that finally earned Latifah her due as an MC. She recorded it after her beloved brother died in a motorcycle accident, so the songs reflected a new dark side as well as her stock-in-trade positivity. (Either the album's darkness or its lack of focus prompted Tommy Boy to drop her but Motown snatched up Latifah and released the album.) *Black Reign* went gold, and won a Grammy for the single "U.N.I.T.Y. (Who You Calling a Bitch?)"

Queen Latifah embodies the hip hop spirit in ways that go beyond rhyming: A highly successful entrepreneur, she co-heads Flavor Unit management and Flavor Unit Records; she also penned an inspirational book *(From the Heart of a Queen)* and has been developing a talk show. As an actress, Latifah played the role of sarcastic Khadijah, the founder and editor of a VIBE-like hip hop magazine, on the long-running television sitcom *Living Single.* In the 1997 film *Set It Off,* she played a lesbian bank robber, which not only won her critical acclaim but piqued questions about her own sexuality. More recently she has moved further into the Hollywood mainstream with roles in *Sphere* and *Living Out Loud.*

It's not surprising that both MC Lyte and Queen Latifah have been rumored to be gay since they first came to fame. Whether or not the murmurs are true is irrelevant; what's significant is that they point to the perceived contradiction of women in hip hop. If the figure of the MC is one of power-over money, sex, the streets, whatever then by its very nature it's unwomanly, at least to the minds of some. But thankfully that kind of thinking is changing: Just consider the wildly successful careers of such bold, blunt females as Lil' Kim, Missy Elliott, and Lauryn Hill, who owe much to the skills and tenacity of these early women MCs. Surely none of these pioneers set out to become the Susan B. Anthonys of rap. They were women who, like their brothers were moved by the big beat and a love of the rhyme to create music, laying claim for all women on this thing we call hip hop.

DISCOGRAPHY

J.J. Fad
Supersonic (Atco/Ruthless, 1988). *Not Just a Fad* (Ruthless, 1990).

MC Lyte
Lyte as a Rock (First Priority/Atlantic, 1988). *Eyes on This* (First Priority/ Atlantic, 1989). *Act Like You Know* (First Priority/Atlantic, 1991). *Ain't No Other* (First Priority/Atlantic, 1993). *Bad as I Wanna B* (First Priority/ Elektra, 1996). *Seven and Seven* (Eastwest/Elektra, 1998).

Queen Latifah
All Hail the Queen (Tommy Boy, 1989). *Nature of a Sista* (Tommy Boy, 1991). *Black Reign* (Motown, 1993). *Order in the Court* (Flavor Unit/Motown, 1998).

The Real Roxanne
The Real Roxanne (Select, 1988).

Roxanne Shanté:
Bad Sister (Cold Chillin', 1989). *Def Mix#1* (Cold Chillin', 1989). *The Bitch Is Back* (Cold Chillin', 1992). *Roxanne Shante's Greatest Hits* (Cold Chillin', 1996).

Yo Yo
Make Way for the Mother Lode (EastWest, 1991). *Black Pearl* (EastWest, 1992). *You Better Ask Somebody* (EastWest, 1993). *Total Control* (EastWest, 1996).

Compilations

Fat Beats and Bra Straps: Women of Hip Hop Volume 1: Classics (Rhino, 1998). *Volume 2: Battle Rhymes and Posse Cuts* (Rhino, 1998). *Queens of Rap* (Priority, 1989).

OBJECTIVE QUESTIONS

1. After working with Grandmaster D.S.T., she became the first women rapper to record, with "To The Beat Y'all" in 1980, before going on to DJ at Philadelphia's WUSL and to serve as editor in chief of *Word Up,* an early rap 'zine.
2. Breakdancing produced an all female breaking troupe called _____.
3. In the legendary Funky Four + One, the + One was female rapper _____.
4. Lisa Lee, formerly of Cosmic Force and the Zulu Nation, teamed up with Debbie Dee, from the Mercedes ladies and Sha Rock to form the short-lived all-star team, _____, who recorded a track for Harry Belafonte's 1984 film, *Beat Street.*
5. It was a response record to Doug E. Fresh's "The Show" that launched the careers of rap's longest-enduring female act: _____.
6. How did Cheryl James and Sandra Denton meet Hurby "Luv Bug" Azor, and what prompted their first recording?
7. As late as 1992, the only women to have a gold rap single or album were _____ and _____.
8. Jazzy Joyce teamed up with ex-dancer Sweet Tee to create _____, an entirely female created rap record that topped the charts.
9. Who said, "People wonder why girls don't go platinum, but a lot of the time we don't get the same money [for marketing and promotion], and that's just a straight up fact?"
10. What is MC Lyte's real name? What was her brothers' group called?
11. What was the first rap tune by a solo woman artist to go gold?
12. What does "Latifah" mean in Arabic?
13. On Queen Latifah's single "Ladies First," she introduced to American audiences British rapper _____.

QUESTIONS FOR FURTHER THOUGHT, RESEARCH, AND DISCUSSION

1. Do you think hip hop culture is more sexist and misogynist than American culture in general? Do you think it is more than the music business in general? Do you think hip hop lyrics accurately portray the truth about gender relations in African American culture? All things considered, has hip hop helped or hindered women's struggles for gender equality and equal rights?

2. Tricia Rose, Gwendolyn D. Pough, Cheryl L. Keyes and others have all written prolifically and profoundly about the subject of women in hip hop culture. Read, research, report, and comment on their writing, opinions and observations.

3. There has never been a shortage of women journalists and entrepreneurs in hip hop history. Research and report on the careers of women entrepreneurs like Monica Lynch, Sylvia Robinson, or Carmen Ashurst-Watson. Research and report on the careers of hip hop journalists like Danyel Smith, Dream Hampton, Elysa Gardener or Laura Jamison.

4. Report on the blues "Queens" or "Divas" of the 1920s and how they affected the direction of the record business and the proliferation of the blues. Why do you suppose that female, as opposed to male, blues singers became so popular in the 1920s?

5. Research and report on the history of women in jazz and/or rock. What hurdles did they have to face? How are their struggles different from or similar to those of women in hip hop?

6. Research and report on the systematic destruction of African American families and family values, starting with slavery and continuing through the institutionalized poverty of the 20th century. Does this mean that African American culture is more misogynist and sexist than American culture in general, or is it just a product of poverty and ignorance that has little or nothing to do with race and culture?

7. Do you think that some of the teachings of the NOI and the Five Percenters are inherently sexist, and may in part be responsible for rappers' sexist lyrics?

Hip Hop Chicano: A Separate but Parallel Story

By Raegan Kelly

As stated earlier, the important role of Puerto Rican culture on the beginnings of hip hop in the boroughs of New York has been well-documented. Perhaps not quite as well documented is the influence of Hispanics, particularly *chicanos*, on the development of hip hop on the west coast and the importance of the *varrio*. This article traces the beginnings of the *Chicano* gangs in Los Angeles back to the early 1930s and traces the rise of "lowriders" and "zoot suits" in the 1940s. The author compares the making of custom cars, or "lowriders," out of scraps from the junkyard to hip hop rhythm tracks pieced together from samples of often-discarded funk and salsa records. Kelly also traces the origins of *Calo*, the *chicano* slang and street language that is the origin of familiar hip hop terms like "Loc" and "homeboy." Also included is a history of the first *chicano* DJs and sound systems; the first bilingual rap records; and the stories of Kid Frost, The Boo Yaa Tribe and Cypress Hill.

What's up Homie? Don't you know me?
Si mon.
Ain't you the brother of mass chingon?
Straight up, and I'm down with the Raza
Kid Frost got my back
Boo Yaa's en la casa
Cause every day things get a little crazier
As I step to the microphone area
First I call my city
Puro Los Angeles

[lights up & cops a hit] Yeah homes
That's what the ganga says …

—Cypress Hill, "Latin Lingo"

LAYING CLAIM TO the gangsta persona is a favorite theme in hiphop. Reading the wax, Toddy Tee, Schooly D, and NWA get major props … but for the concepts of *carnelismo, calo* terminology (homebody, OG, etc.), the pachuco/cholo/gangsta style of dress, and the lowered ride, proper respect is due the *varrio.*

Chicoano gangs, or "street syndicates," have been a fact of life in LA since the early 1930s (some claim earlier); accordingly their history, memory, and culture are long and strong. Defined by Martin Sanchez Jankowski as (roughly) adaptational organizations whose primary goal is survival through self-reliance[1], "gang youth," while always a target of the media and law enforcement, have become, in LA at least, social pariahs without peer. To take pride visibly in this position is one way of inverting it, but the presence of colors, oversized Dickies, pendeltons, street lingo and fire power within the language and style of hiphop is only in small part fantasy-fulfillment—many of those who talk the talk have walked the walk.

Paralleling the development of gang culture were the rise of the lowrider and the zoot suiter in LA. In the *varrio,* self-reliance and brown pride go hand in hand, and a large percentage of brown hiphop integrates commentary on race and cultural difference into straightforward narratives of life on the streets. Sen Dogg of Cypress Hill exemplifies the West Coast B-boy in "Latin Lingo"—he declares his homies, his Raza, his hood, LA hiphop (and, of course, a phat blunt) in a particularly West Coast combination of English, *pachuquismo,* and hiphog slang. Both linguistically and stylistically, aspects of the West Coast gangsta, whether it be Kid Frost, Ganxsta Ridd (of the Boo Yaa Tribe) or Ice Cube in a Pendleton, Dickies and a lowered '63S.S., originated with *pachucos* and Zoot Suiters of 1940s *varrios* of east Los Angeles.

Like the "Teddy Boy" of Harlem, the *pachuco* was the ultimate expression of cultural resistance, anarchy, and (in) difference in the North American south west of the 1940s. Generally identified as Chicano gang members (although most were not)[2] *pachucos* sported pompadours, wide-shouldered extra-long fingertip coats, high-waisted "drape" pants with pegged ankles and reat pleats, wide-brimmed hats, long watch chains, and *fileros.* Much has been written in detail about the "Zoot Suit Riots" that took place in Los Angeles in 1943, but what matters is precisely what caused civilians and sailors to roam the streets in mobs looking for young Chicanos to beat down. In the *Zoot-Suit Riots,* Mauricio Mazon describes their hatred as being comprised of a mixture of patriotic fervour and fear (mixed with envy) of difference, and of themselves.

To the good citizens of LA, "[Zoot Suiters] seemed to be simply marking time while the rest of the country intensified the war effort."[3] *Pachucos* openly smoked marijuana, spoke their own tongue, had their own style of music, dance and dress. Most infuriating, however, was that *pachucos* and zoot suiters spent so much time developing their own insular culture while good "patriotic" Americans built bombers 9-to-5 and went off to war. *Pachucos* didn't have a good "work ethic." They didn't seem to care, had their own set of priorities, and this pissed people off. The attacks weren't completely symbolic, of course—it was around this time that the California Youth Authority camps were established, and an increasingly militant approach to law enforcement in Los Angeles was adopted.[4]

THE LOWERED RIDE

Although the east side of Los Angeles was generally regarded as being overrun by gangs, violence, and an undocumented workforce,[5] what was to become one of the largest *varrios* in the south west had its own fast developing political, musical and street culture. In the early fifties a "basic car plan" was initiated by the First Street Merchants and the sheriff's department, and the tradition of car clubs began among east Los Angeles youth.[6] Originally designed to provide an alternative to gangs, car clubs became a focal point for social life in the *varrio*, providing a place to work, hang out, listen to music, gain knowledge of self-expression and cultural identity through the art of car customizing.

Chicanos have been customizing cars since the forties. The concept of a fully customized car, top to bottom, front to back, inside and out, took years to develop, but from the very beginning it was treated as an art form. Generally starting with a used American standard, a clay model, and much ingenuity and love, customizers take bits and pieces off different automobiles out of scrap yards, alter them and put them together to create a totally new and unique car. Bill Hines is one of *Lowrider* magazine's "Legends of Lowriding"; his first custom was a '41 Buick convertible with "chopped top" and a Cadillac front end. Known to some as the "King of Lead" for his ability totally to rework a body with a lead paddle and a spray gun, he was also one of the first to design a hydraulic lift system for raising and lowering custom cars (using modified aircraft landing gear parts), California-style, in 1964. (The first lifted custom was purportedly done by the Aguirres of San Bernardino, California, on a 1956 Corvette).[7] Hydraulics served a dual function—to raise a lowered vehicle for driving long distances (protect the underside), and to keep the cops away (riding too slow was a ticketable offense). "I remember a guy with this candy turquoise '63 Ford … that wanted to fool the cops. So, he had me juice it in front and back. He'd cruise with it laid until the cops spotted him. They couldn't figure it out. They didn't know what a lift was."[8]

To drive a beautifully customized ride low and slow down one of LA's main thoroughfares is an expression of pride, pride in being different, taking one's time, being Chicano. Jesse Valdez, another of the original lowriders and former leader of one of LA's best-known car clubs, The Imperials, remembers the heyday of lowriding: "In '66, '67, '68—we'd cruise Downey, Paramount, Whittier. That's when everybody was lowriding; Chicanos, black guys, white guys.[9] Whittier Boulevard, a unifying site for east LA through to the mid-seventies, was the site of the Eastside Blowouts, the Chicano political protests of '71–72; it provided a focal point for the muralista movement of the same time and Luis Valdez's 1979 movie Boulevard Nights. (Valdez's film, a classic Hollywood document of varrio street Life in LA, opened ironically just after the boulevard was permanently closed to cruisers). Favorites of the car culture tended to be instrumentals with sparse lyrics and heavy basslines—"Whittier Boulevard" by Thee Midniters, "Lowrider" by WAR (previously Senor Soul), "More Bounce" by Zapp.

LATIN LINGO

Calo is the privileged language of the Mexican-American barrio … (It) was neither a *pachuco* nor a new world contribution. Calo has its ancient roots buried deeply in the fertile gypsy tongue (Calé, Romano, Zincalo and Calogitano…) … fractured in spelling, crippled in meaning; mutilated French, English, Italian, and the dead languages of Latin, Greek, and Hebrew, plus medieval Moorish, Calo, originally *Zincalo,* was the idiom of the Spanish Gypsies—one of the many minorities in Spain. The *conquistadores* brought Calo to the New World. Already identified by the upper classes as the argot of the criminal, the poor, and the uneducated, Calo and its variants became well known to the conquered Indian…

Mauricio Mazon, The Zoot-Suit Riots, p. 3

To followers of scat and the spoken-word traditions of jazz and bebop, Calo probably sounds little different than the jive scat of Cab Calloway or the inverted *Vout* language of Slim Gaillard. In some ways today it operates much like early hipster phraseology—hip Calo terms like homeboy and loc have completely penetrated hiphop and gang culture. But for the *pachucos* of the forties and in the *varrios* of today, Calo is also an important way to mark cultural difference/peripherality through language, Frequently referred to as "Spanglish" (half English, half Spanish) Calo is in fact a tongue all its own, a "living language" whose words and meanings change from location to location and person to person.

> Muy Loco, Crazy
> Ever since I come from Mexico
> I don't want to do the Mambono
> All I want to do is go to go
> When the crazy band she starts to blow
> All the *señoritas* say to me
> Come on Pancho dance with me
> Pancho Pancho don't go the Rancho
> Til you do the Pancho Rock with me
>
> Lalo Guerrero and His Orchestra, "Pancho Rock"

The great Latin bandleader Lalo Guerrero was one of the first to incorporate Calo into the Los Angeles club scene in the forties. *Pachuco* and zoot cultures gravitated towards the big band sound, which Guerrero fused with the structures of swing and rumba in songs like "Chuco Suave, " "Marijuana Boogie, " and " Vamos a bailar."[10] Another Calo favorite was the Don Tosti band's "Pachuco Boogie," characterized by Johnny Otis as Chicano Jump Blues, "which consisted of a jump type shuffle with either Raul [Diaz] or Don [Tosti] rapping in Calo about getting ready to go out on a date. Very funny stuff and another candidate for the title of the first rap record."[11]

Through the fifties and sixties East Los Angeles developed an active recording and club scene, which, as Steven Loza explains in *Barrio Rhythm*, "was integrally related to the black music experience, for musical as well as economic reasons."[12] The influence went both ways, and in 1952 African American saxophonist Chuck Higgins released the hit single "Pachuco Hop, " Loza quotes Ruben Guevara's description of the east LA music scene in the late fifties and early sixties at El Monte Legion Stadium, which reads like an early description of Go-Go:

> A lot of Anglo kids copied not only the styles (hair, dress) but the dances, the most popular of which were the Pachuco Hop, Hully Gully, and the Corrido Rock…the Corrido was the wildest, sort of an early form of slam dancing. Two or three lines would form, people arm in arm, each line consisting of 150 to 250 people. With the band blasting

away at breakneck rocking tempo, the lines took four steps forward and four steps back, eventually slamming into each other (but making sure that no one got hurt)… After the dance, it was out to the parking lot for the grand finale. Where's the party? *Quien tiene pisto? Mota?* Who's got the booze? Weed? Rumors would fly as to which gangs were going to throw *chingasos*—come to blows, The Jesters Car Club from Boyle Heights, which dominated the Eastside, would parade around the parking lot in their lavender, maroon or gray primered cars, wearing T-Timer shades (blue or green colored glasses in square wire frames).[13]

Latin and Afro-Cuban rhythms seem to have penetrated the early hiphop scene at least a decade before we hear any bilingual or Calo phraseology. In the early seventies, at the same time as lowriders in Califas were bumpin' the sounds of Tierra, Señor Soul, and Rulie Garcia and the East LA Congregation, Jimmy Castor was creating hiphop beats in New York using a fusion of "one-chord riffing, a Sly Stone pop bridge, fuzz guitar, timbales breaks, and an idealistic lyric applicable to any emergent movement."[14] David Toop credits Jimmy Castor with being a hiphop innovator, at the center of the Latin soul movement in the sixties and highly influenced by Latin masters like Cal Tjader, Chano Pozo, and Tito Puente.[15] Seven years later Afrika Bambaataa would redefine "influence," straight cutting Slim Gaillard's unique *Vout* lyrics into the mix.

In *Hip-Hop: The Illustrated History,* Steven Hager describes the early tagging and writing scene in 1970s New York as being racially integrated: the first tagger on record, Taki 183, was Greek, the second, Julio 204, was Chicano; and Tracy 168, a young white kid living in Black Spades territory, founded one of the scene's largest crews, "Wanted," in 1972.[16] The internationally known Lee Quinones and Lady Pink(stars of *Wild Style*)[17] were both Puerto Rican, as were the members of the all-time great breaking group, the Rock Steady Crew.

In the Bronx, funk and early hiphop entered the already hot Puerto Rican street and dance scene around 1977–78, with members of the Zulu Nation schooling Puerto Ricans in the ways of breakdancing and Puerto Rican DJs like Charlie Chase spinning funk and sporting early B-boy styles at their then disco-dominated block parties.[18] Rammelzee (Ramm-elevation-Z—Z being a symbol of energy which flows in two directions)[19] and RubyD, recently dubbed the Puerto Rican Old School by West Coast Puerto Rican funkster Son Doobie of Funkdoobiest, rocked the mike all over NYC. The 1983 hit "Beat Bop" (Rammelzee vs. K-Rob) showcases what Rammelzee is known best for—what he dubbed "slanguage,"[20] an ingenious combination of freestyle metaphor and over-the-top hiphop drops delivered in the Shake Up King's particular nasal drawl.

> Just groovin' like a sage y' all
> Break it up, yeah, yeah, stage y'all
> Like a roller coaster ride that can make ya bump
> Groovin with the rhythm as you shake yer rump—rock rock ya don't stop
> You got it now baby—ya don't stop
> Just hiphop the day, yeah doobie doo
> Yeah scoobie doo, whatcha wanna do crew?
> Just freak it, ya baby, just freak up, ya ya baby
> Drink it up here, I know my dear
> I can rock you out this atmosphere

Like a gangster prankster, number one bankster
Got much cash to make you thank ya
Rock on to the break a dawn—Keep it on now keep it on
I know Zee Zee that can rock quick
Like a high kind a class
Hand yer rhythm to the stick. …

"Beat Bop." Rammelzee vs. K-Rob

In 1980 a young Samoan dancer named Sugar Pop would move west from the streets of New York to bring breaking to the poplockers of south central, Venice and Hollywood in Los Angeles. One of the groups Sugar Pop encountered was the Blue City Crew, a group of Samoan poplockers coming out of Carson in south LA. In Topper Carew's movie *Breakin and Entering* about the early eighties breaking scene in LA, the crew talks about how the advent of street dancing correlated with a drop in gangbanging in the hoods and *varrios* of LA—homies were taking their battles to the dance floor. "In LA it ain't like that … If you got the moves, you can hold down. That's all it is."

It was also around this time that hiphop started to penetrate the LA Chicano dance scene. In the mid-to late seventies Chicanos were throwing giant dance parties at Will Rogers State Beach, Devonshire Downs and in parks and roller rinks in the San Fernando Valley, completed with battling mobile DJs, hundreds of Curwen Vegas, MCs to keep the crowd hyped and, of course, circling helicopters. Precursors of today's massive rave scene (which are approximately 75 percent Chicano in Los Angeles), the music of choice at these parties was alternative/new wave, disco, and early techno-based hiphop (Egyptian Lover, Magic Mike, Melle Mel, Grandmaster Flash). Due to popular demand, in 1983–1984 Uncle Jam's Army set up special Valley-side gigs at the Sherman Square roller rink in Sherman Oaks. Young Chicano, Latino, and Samoan MCs, many of them former dancers, were working their way through the LA house party scene at this time, but one of the earliest to make it to wax was Arthur Molina, Jr.(aka Kid Frost) in 1984 with the single "Rough Cut." The music, written by David Storrs of Electrobeat Records (the same Storrs who wrote the music for Ice T's "Body Rock"),[21] has a decidedly early West Coast flavor, but lyrically the song bears a strong resemblance to Run DMC's "It's Like that" also released in 1984.

Sometimes you wait around
Rockin' cold hard streets
People strugglin' hard
Just tryin' to make ends meet
I just stand tough
Hold down my feet
Never understand the meaning
of the word Defeat
So you see it's like that
And that's the way it is
But when I'm on the microphone, it goes something like this:
Body breakin' Booty shakin'
Good money for the makin'
You just put it in my pocket

Cause you know I got talent
It's Rough, it's Tough
Let me see if you can handle my stuff
It's Rough Rough Rough Rough Rough…

Kid Frost, "Rough Cut"

The earliest bilingual hiphop song that I've heard on record is out of New York—Carlos T (aka Spanish Fly) and the Terrible Two's hit "Spanglish."[22] Rapping over a classic Grandmaster Flash beat the Terrible Two dominate the song in English, with Carlos T coming in short and fast. "This is the way we harmonize, everybody, everybody, I said Danse funky danse, y que danse, todo mundo, todo mundo."

In 1989 the Cuban-born Mellow Man Ace kicked bilingual lyrics throughout his album *Escape from Havana*, generally alternating line for line between English and Spanish, as in "Mentirosa," or verse for verse, as he does in "Rap Guanco," over the Kool and the Gang bassline from Lightnin' Rod's[23] cut "Sport" on the *Hustlers Convention* album of 1973:

…. I'm the lyrical, miracle founder of the talk style
Put together intelligently wild
And what I came up with is called Rap Guanco
Different than house, nothing like GoGo
And if you're wonderin' damn how'd he start this
Well, last year I opened my own market
Cause it was time for somethin' new to come along and I thought
A bilingual single, that can't go wrong …
…
Ahora si que vengo [And now yes I'm coming]
Sabroso si caliente … [Flavor very hot] …

Mellow Man Ace, "Rap Guanco"

A year later, Kid Frost hit the streets with his classic adaptation of the Gerald Wilson/El Chicano tune "Viva La Tirado," "La Raza," matching in syntax and lingo the Pachuco street slang (Calo) of East LA.

Quevo
Aqui' stoy MC Kid Frost
Yo estoy jefe [I am in charge]
My *cabron* is the big boss
My *cuete* is loaded [pistol/rod]
It's full of *balas* [bullets]
I'll put it in your face
And you won't say *nada*. [nothing]
Vatos, cholos, call us what you will [Chicano homeboys, lowriders]
You say we are assassins,
Train ourselves to kill

It's in our blood to be an Aztec warrior
Go to any extreme
And hold to no barriers
Chicano and I'm brown and proud
Want this *chingaso?* [smack, wack, as in "beat down"]
Si mon I said let's get down

...

The foreign tongue I'm speaking is known as Calo
Y sabes que loco? [And you know what, loc?]
Yo estoy malo [I am mean/bad]
Tu no sabes que I think your brain is hollow? [Don't you know that ...]

...

And so I look and I laugh and say *Que pasa?* [What's happening?]
Yeah, this is for La Raza.

Kid Frost, "La Raza," Hispanic Causing Panic

"La Raza" is important for several reasons. It marks a radical change in Kid Frost's work—the distance between the non-committal "So rough, so tough" of "Rough Cut" and "It's in our blood to be an Aztec warrior/Go to any extreme" marks a change in consciousness, at least of his perception of hiphop as a language of consciousness. Frost's use of Calo is an appeal to the authenticity of the streets and the *pachuco* lifestyle, but within the context of the song it is also a nod to Chicano pride, as is the claim "Chicano and I'm brown and proud." The term Chicano, derived from *mechicano* and once considered derogatory and indicative of lower-class standing, applies to all people of Mexican descent/all people of indigenous descent. To call yourself Chicano is to claim La Raza, to locate your origin within the struggle of a people for land and for cultural, political and economic self-determination. Also, Frost's use of an El Chicano hit, as opposed to the less culturally specific beat of "Rough Cut," is a nod to the *veteranos* (who to this day remain partial to Oldies over hiphop).

The early nineties have been watershed years for Chicano hiphoppers—a peak moment being the 1991 release of Cypress Hill's first album. Showcasing the combined talents of Mellow Man Ace's brother Sen Dogg, B-Real, DJ Muggs, *Cypress Hill* integrates the best of Rammelzee's hiphop tricknology, the Calo rap of Don Tosti and Raul Diaz, bad-ass West Coast gangsta mythology, humor, and trademark beats.

Gangsta Rid, What's up Y'all?
"It's a tribe thing ..."

...

"Hey where you from homies?"
It's on
He sees em reach for his gun
Buckshot to the dome
He jumps in the bomb
Homies in tha back but she just wants to go home
But he trips to the store

Homeboy needs a 40
White boy's at the counter
Thinkin' "O Lordy Lordy"
Pushin' on the button
Panickin' for nuttin'
Pigs on the way.
Hey yo he smells bacon …
…
Scooby doo y'all, Scooby doo y'all
A Scooby doo y'all
A doobie doobie doo y'all …

Cypress Hill, Hole in the Head, 1991

It's a Tribe Thing

I am a revolutionary … because creating life and death is a revolutionary act. Just as building nationalism in an era of imperialism is a   life-giving act. … We are an awakening people, an emerging nation, a new breed.

Carlos Munoz, Jr., Youth Identity, Power, p.76

Corky Gonzales's Crusade for Justice in 1969 brought people from every corner of the *varrio* together in the name of self-determination and La Raza. One of the concepts put forth during the course of the conference was that Chicano students, needing "revolutionary role models, would do well to emulate their brothers and sisters in the streets, the *vatos locos* of the *varrio*, *Carnelismo* or the code of absolute love in Chicano gangs, was to be adopted by radical student nationalists as the locus of their developing ideology.[24]

The Chicano hiphop that has made it to wax in the last two years frequently assimilates some combination of street mentality and nationalist politics, whether it be as simple as giving the nod to brown pride, or as complex as the cultural nationalism of Aztlan Underground. The gangsta presently dominates brown hiphop, good examples being Proper Dos (west LA), RPM (Valley), Street Mentality (Pico/Union), The Mexicanz (Long Beach) and Brown Town(east LA), to name a few. The music: generally simple beats, frequently scary, down with ganga, *rucas* and *cuetes*, sometimes intentionally educational, and occasionally hilarious. Groups like Of Mexican Descent represent a new generation of lyrical wizards, working in two tongues, with breath control, and kicking knowledge of self.

Cypress Hill are at the center of one of LA's finer hiphop posses, the Soul Assassins. The more recent group Funkdoobiest (consisting of Puerto Rican and Sioux MCs and a Mexican DJ) are down, as well as the Irish American group House of Pain, and allied are the Samoan brothers of the Boo Yaa Tribe, Mellow Man Ace, and Kid Frost. For me, the Soul Assassins represent some of the most radical (and difficult) aspects of living in Los Angeles. On one hand they describe the celebration of difference through hiphop (and the fierce potential in collaboration and in the music), on the other, their lyrics frequently demarcate territorial and personal boundaries (BOOM-in-your-face). But at its most elemental, the beats of hiphop are about walking all over those boundaries with no apologies.

Out of the east we've heard from groups like the Puerto Rican Powerrule (New York), and Fat Joe the Gangsta (Bronx), there's a Brewley MC in Puerto Rico, and reggae español posses in Panama and Mexico, but brown hiphop seems to be coming to fruition on the West Coast. Although the Latin Alliance project didn't hold, hopefully the concept was not outmoded but a little ahead of its time. In a city where 10 per cent of the world's population of El Salvadorans lives around MacArthur Park (downtown), the possibilities for cross-cultural collaboration and unity seem, well, massive. And with cats like Kid Frost, Cypress, AUG, Proper Dos, and OMD sharpening their skills in every corner of LA, hiphop is where to make it happen. After all, it still remains true that (referring back to the Samoan brother from Carson City) in LA hiphop if you are down, you can hold down.

Special Thanks to Bulldog and Tate:

NOTES

1. Martin Sanchez Jankowski, *Islands in the Street*, Berkeley, Los Angeles and Oxford 1991, pp. 25–7.
2. Mauricio Mazon, The Zoot-Suit Riots; *The Psychology of Symbolic Annihilation*, Austin, 1984, p.5.
3. Ibid, p.9.
4. Ibid, p. 108
5. Steven Loza, *Barrio Rhythm; Mexican American Music in Los Angeles*, Urbana and Chicago, 1993, p.42.
6. Ibid.
7. Dick DeLoach, "Bill Hines: The King of Lead," *Lowrider Magazine,* April 1992, p.52
8. Ibid, p. 53.
9. Dick DeLoach, "Jesse Valdez and Gypsy Rose," *Lowrider Magazine*, October 1992, p. 56.
10. Barvio Rhythm, p.71
11. Ibid, p. 81
12. Ibid.
13. Ibid, p. 83.
14. David Toop, *Rap Attack 2: African Rap to Global Hip Hop*, London and New York, 1991, p. 22.
15. Ibid, p. 24
16. Steven Hager, *Hip-Hop: The Illustrated History*, p. 21.
17. *Wild Style*, Charlie Ahearn, 1981. A 35mm rap-umentary about the early integration of the different elements of hiphop culture in New York. Also starring Fred Braithwaite and Patty Astor.
18. *An Illustrated History of Hip Hop*. P. 81.
19. *Rap Attack 2*, p.122.
20. Ibid.
21. Billy Jam, liner notes on *West Coast Rap, The First Dynasty*, Vol. 2, 1992, Rhino Records.
22. *On Greatest Hits to the Zulu Nation*, circa 1982.
23. AKA Jalal of the Last Poets.
24. Carlos Munoz, Jr., *Youth, Identity, Power: The Chicano*, Verso, 1989, p.76.

FURTHER READING

Rodolfo F. Acuna, *A Community Under Siege: A Chronicle of Chicanos East of the Los Angeles River*, 1945–1975. Monograph no. 11/Chicano Studies Research Center Publications, Los Angeles: University of California 1984.

Rodolfo F. Acuna, *Occupied America; A History of Chicanos*, New York: HarperCollins 1988.

Dick DeLoach, "Bill Hines: The King of Lead," *Lowrider Magazine* 14, 1992, pp.52–3.

Dick DeLoach, "Jesse Valdez and Gypsy Rose," *Lowrider Magazine* 14, 1992, pp.56–8.

Willard Gingerich, "Aspects of Prose Style in Three Chicano Novels: *Pocho*, *Bless Me, Ultima* and *The Road to Tamazunchale* in ed. Jacob Ornstein-Galicia, Form and Function in Chicano English, Rowley, Massachusetts: Newbury House 1994.

Steven Hager, *Hip-Hop: The Illustrated History, Rap Music and Graffiti,* New York: St. Martin's Press, 1984.

Martin Sanchez Jankowski, *Islands in the Street*, Berkeley, Los Angeles and Oxford: University of California Press 1991.

George Lipsitz, *Time Passages: Collective Memory and American Popular Culture,* Minneapolis: University of Minnesota Press 1990.

Steven Loza, *Barrio Rhythm: Mexican American Music in Los Angeles*, Urbana and Chicago: University of Illinois Press 1993.

Mauricio Mazon, *The Zoot-Suit Riots: The Psychology of Symbolic Annihilation*, Austin: University of Texas Press 1984.

Carlos Munoz Jr, *Youth, Identity, Power: The Chicano Movement*, London and New York: Verso 1989.

Harry Polkinhorn, Alfredo Velasco and Mal Lambert, *El Libro De Calo; Pachuco Slang Dictionary*, San Diego: Alticus Press 1983.

Stan Steiner, *La Raza: The Mexican Americans*. New York, Evanston and London: Harper & Row 1970.

David Toop, *Rap Attack 2: African Rap to Global Hip Hop*, London and New York: Serpent's Tail 1991.

OBJECTIVE QUESTIONS

1. Both linguistically and stylistically, aspects of West Coast gangsta, whether it be Kid Frost, Ganxsta Ridd, or Ice Cube originated with _____ and _____ of 1940s *varrios* of east Los Angeles.

2. Chicanos have been customizing cars since the 1940s, and the fully customized car took years to develop, but right from the beginning, it was considered _____.

3. Luis Valdez's 1979 movie, a classic Hollywood document of *varrio* street life in LA, opened ironically, just after the boulevard was permanently closed to cruisers.

4. Where do the roots of *Calo* come from?

5. The great Latin bandleader Lalo Guerrero was one of the first to incorporate Calo into the Los Angeles club scene in the forties. What were his hits?

6. Who was Don Tosti, what was his big hit and how did Johnny Otis describe his style?

7. David Toop credits him with being a hip hop innovator, at the center of the Latin soul movement of the sixties, and highly influenced by Latin masters like Cal Tjader, Chano Pozo, and Tito Puente: _____.

8. Who was Charlie Chase?

9. What is Kid Frost's real name and what was his first hit? It has a decidedly early West Coast flavor, but lyrically the song bears a strong resemblance to _____ by _____, also released in 1984.

10. The earliest bilingual hip hop record is out of New York, by Carlos T and the Terrible Two, called _____.

11. In 1989, the Cuban-born _____ kicked bilingual lyrics throughout his album *Escape from Havana.*

12. Kid Frost's hit "La Raza" is rapped over an adaptation of *Viva Tirado,* an instrumental by jazz musician _____ and made into a hit by _____.

13. They integrate the best of Rammelzee's "tricknology," the Calo rap of Don Tosti and Raul Diaz, bad-ass West Coast gangsta mythology, humor and trademark beats: _____.

TOPICS FOR FURTHER THOUGHT, RESEARCH, AND DISCUSSION

1. Research and examine in depth the underlying causes of the "Zoot Suit" Riots and the resulting fallout.

2. Compare Calo and its contribution to hip hop with Ebonics and the phraseology and rhetoric of the Five Percenters.

3. Research and report on the history of car clubs and "lowriders" in East Los Angeles and the music they inspired.

4. Listen to the recordings of Cab Calloway and Slim Galliard and compare the language to hip hop lyrics.

5. Report on "Reggaeton," its history and popularity.

6. Report on contemporary rap records and groups that rap in Spanish.

"Rap Goes Pop" and "Walking the Line: Rap and Censorship"

By Alex Ogg and David Upshal

Alex Ogg is also the author of *Standing On The Edge* (Radiohead) and *Def Jam: The Radical Rise of Russell Simmons and Rick Rubin*. In 2006 Alex published his new book about the punk years, *No More Heroes* and in 2009 his exhaustive history *Independence Days*, a complete overview of UK independent record labels from 1976 to 1987. Alex has also written for several encyclopedias, dozens of magazines, newspapers and websites and compiled more than 100 album sleeves.

David Upshal is an executive producer for Lion Television, one of Britain's largest independent television companies. Prior to joining Lion he was best known for directing and producing the BAFTA and Emmy nominated series *The Hip Hop Years* and the landmark BBC series *Windrush*. Originally a print journalist, he began his career at the BBC in n1989 as a production trainee.

There are plenty of arguments and discussions about the racial, ethnic, and gender diversity of hip hop, but perhaps the most heated discussions about hip hop revolve around its economic and aesthetic diversity. It's the old art vs. commerce or art vs. entertainment dilemma. Should the message of hip hop recordings be primarily political, sociological, religious, pornographic, or merely harmless entertainment? The answer, of course, is all of the above. Hip hop's main message, whether it be for spiritual exaltation or commercial exploitation, is still about surviving in a threatening and unfair environment and expressing the truth about the lives of societies disenfranchised and neglected. Survival in the ghetto, of course, often includes adopting a serious party mentality as well as chasing the allure of riches, whether from crime and drug sales or the commercialization of the record business. It seems that rap itself has been victimized by the same kinds of negative stereotypes that have plagued African Americans in general for 150 years. The truth, of course, is that rap is extremely diverse in its cultural influences, artistic depth, style, message and genre. Whatever your current beliefs and tastes, whether spiritual or carnal, you can probably find someone who's rapping about them and an audience consuming it. At about the same time the mainstream media was vilifying "gangsta" rap, there emerged two of the most mainstream and child-friendly rap acts in its history—MC Hammer and Vanilla Ice. The first of these two chapters tells their stories and speculates about their importance. The second of these two chapters recounts the censorship trials of 2 Live Crew and their controversial Lp, *As Nasty As They Wanna Be*, as well as the boycott of Time Warner in response to the Ice-T produced "Cop Killer" from their heavy metal album *Body Count*. In contrast to some of the more literary, academic, or journalistic writing styles encountered in this anthology, you should find the writing here to be simple, clear, concise, and unaffected. But also very effective, especially for the book's target audience, adolescent hip hop fans.

TONE LOC—WILD THING

IN 1989, RAP DELIVERED its first quantifiable pure pop hit, "Wild Thing", written by Young MC (Marvin Young) and performed by Tone Loc (Anthony 'Toco' Smith), The producers were Matt Dike and Michael Ross of Delicious Vinyl, one of LA's most distinctive early rap labels. It reached number two in the US charts and became, behind "We Are The World", the second biggest selling single of the decade, Alongside samples from Van Halen's "Jamie's Cryin", this easy-going novelty rap featuring a memorable *basso profundo* performance from Loc, and set a new benchmark for hip hop's commercial viability,

However, Tone Loc attracted the wrath of media elements hostile to rap when the innocent party sentiments of "Wild Thing" were confused with the term 'wilding', at that time a buzzword for black criminality. A white female banker had been brutally raped while out jogging one night in New York's Central Park by a gang of non-white teenagers. One of the accused youths dismissed the horrific attack as a recreational pastime called 'wilding'. Tone Loc was suddenly thrust into the dock simply because a journalist mis-spelt and therefore misconstrued the title of his song.

Tone Loc was perplexed by the fuss.

'It's a joke. Please, there's no comparison that they could put to the song or anything. I have nothing to do with that. That's way over in Central Park on the whole other side of the country, I have no control over that whatsoever.'

The song's author was Young MC, a successful rapper in. his own right. The concept had been put forward by Delicious Records.

They had given Loc a chance to write it and they didn't like what he wrote. They didn't feel what he wrote was appropriate' for what they wanted to do. They asked me to write it, and first draft I gave them, they did their thing. I wrote the record in about half an hour, and out of the four verses I wrote they used three of them. … There was a specific record that they wanted for Loc—he was a great writer in his own right—but they thought I would be better for him. So they just had me write those two songs ["Wild Thing" and "Funky Cold Medina"].

Young MC believes the media hysteria was partially fuelled by resentment at rap's success.

'I personally think that there was a big element of that. There was a lot of jealousy from traditional musicians and traditional artists. Seeing kids that had very little or no musical training, they could not hold a note to save their lives, and they are selling millions of records. So there was a lot of disrespect.'

For Mike Ross at Delicious Vinyl the scare stories over 'wilding' were just the bizarre outcome, of ill-informed journalism.

'For a minute there the media tried to tell me to correlate the two things, but it was just for a moment and we didn't really feel it. It didn't really have any effect on what was going on because if you really paid attention they had nothing to do with each other. The whole incident, the whole sociology behind "wilding" is an ill thing, and definitely needs to be dealt with It was a scary aspect of life in New York, but it was a New York kind of thing, it had nothing to do with "Wild Thing."'

The Rev. Calvin Butts, soon to be an outspoken opponent of rap music, viewed the reporting as profoundly racist.

'I thought that was a terrible exploitation of young African American men. I thought it was a terrible exploitation of hip hop. It was a cheap shot, yellow journalism. It served to stigmatise not only the people, but the medium.'

After one further hit single, 'Funky Cold Medina' (according to Young MC an attempt to write a rap 'Love Potion No. 9'), Tone Loc retreated to obscurity and acting roles, as Ross recounts.

It took a couple of years to make [follow-up album *Cool Hand Loc*] And after Hammer blowing up with "U Can't Touch This" and then Vanilla Ice—a terrible period of rap was at hand at that point. I didn't want to try and make Tone come out that way. So we went with this ballad, "All Through The Night". No one probably remembers the song. But at that time the scene was in a different place. We'd had our fifteen minutes of fame with Tone.'

Delicious Vinyl were then submerged by the west coast gangsta rappers, a movement they steered clear from, preferring to promote acts like the Pharcyde and Masta Ace. As Ross notes, this maintained the label's integrity, but might have been the wrong fiscal decision.

'We can't get arrested. Nobody wants to talk to me but you guys now!'

The success, of "Wild Thing" meant that major record labels were now on the lookout for malleable artists who could deliver some of that market.

U CAN'T TOUCH THIS—MC HAMMER

In 1990, the music industry was turned inside out with the emergence of two child-friendly pop stars, MC Hammer and Vanilla Ice, Both harvested unprecedented levels of criticism within the hip hop community whilst attaining astonishing sales figures. The careers of both have followed similar trajectories—huge success, followed by a sharp drop in their fortunes and sometimes farcical attempts to re-invent themselves. Both have had run-ins with Suge Knight, the notorious head of Death Row Records. Hammer released a new record in 1999 after his Death Row deal failed to materialise. Vanilla Ice, whose publishing money allegedly funded Death Row, is currently fronting a hard-rock band.

'U Can't Touch This' was the summer hit which launched Oakland rapper Hammer, whose public endorsement of Christianity reflected his roots in gospel entertainment.

'I would actually rap in church, that was around '84 and '85. I started to write what would then become MC Hammer records. Previously our group was called the Holy Ghost Boys. There was two of us and I started to develop the MC Hammer style of rapping in my bedroom. It only took from '85 and '86. It took me about twelve months to get that record out because I did it myself. I pressed the record, I engineered the record, recorded the record, programmed the record and went to the recording studio. Did the whole nine yards and then began to market the record myself. So I started getting my record out at the end of '85, and mid-'86 it took off.'

The young Stanley Burrell had switched to rap from a promising career in baseball, but retained his sporting nickname.

'As a young kid I resembled Hank Aaron [Henry "Hammerin' Hank" Aaron] the world famous home run king. I worked for the Oakland A's as a bat boy so all the ball players, Reggie Jackson and all the Oakland A's, the world champions in those days, they called me the Little Hammer. So as a rapper, a friend of mine named Sam suggested I go by MC Hammer, instead of just the Holy Ghost Boy or so forth. So I became my nickname since I was a kid, MC Hammer.

For Hammer, hip hop had lost the compositional skills evident in its earliest days.

'I was into the dance scene when I began to rap, so naturally I brought in that dancing element right through my performance. I was always a big fan of group choreography, way back in the days, with the Jackson 5 and the Temptations and all the groups back then. I brought everything in it that I loved and of course the rappers at that time also brought in real music. If you listen to "Rapper's Delight", it's based on a Chic record, which was a musical record, very much so. Then you go into Grandmaster Flash and the Furious Five, those were musical productions. Grandmaster Flash and the Furious Five and the Sugarhill Gang and Melle Mel and Kurtis Blow—all of those rappers all had music, complete productions. Contrary to what a lot of rappers like to say today, music minus the real chords and music is not real rap. The real rap that came along before they ever even existed was put down with real music, before there was ever a so-called underground or what you would call hip hop today. Before some of the artists were eight or nine years old, this started off with real music.'

Hammer believes his appeal lay in those old-fashioned entertainment virtues which his main competitor, Michael Jackson, personified.

'My music is really grounded in performance, dance, responsible fun. Just having a good time and dancing. People like having a good time. Then if you throw in responsibility and understanding, these songs touch a lot of people. You capture that through your music, then you are doing what I call soul music and that is what I am making. I'm making soul music. Hip hop reflects soul from a real perspective, good days, bad days, and expresses all of it within the concept of the album.'

Hammer's breakthrough single was "U Can't Touch This," an innocuous, hook-dominated, rap over a Rick James sample. The idea took shape while Hammer was waiting at an airport.

'The idea came from sitting on the runway thinking about music, being in a creative mode, and the phrase "U Can't Touch This" just came to my mind. Those creative things happen like that and being a big fan up to this very day of just about everything that Rick James has done musically—it was just an instantaneous marriage.'

Hammer became a fixture on global pop charts, dominating MTV with his flamboyant choreography and heavily, stage-managed videos. His Capitol Records, debut album, *Let's Get It Started,* sold millions worldwide. Alan Gordon believes he deserved the sales.

'He was received very well because there was no mistaking Hammer for, say, Ice Cube. There's room for every type of rap in hip hop. A lot of people didn't like it, because some people just want their rap hardcore, but if you like to dance then you had to own a Hammer album. And the larger part of Hammer, besides just the music, was the live show or the video. Hammer made everybody upgrade their videos.'

Others, both inside and outside of hip hop, charged him with demeaning their art form. But for Hammer, being popular was not something he needed to justify.

'It is impossible for a rapper to make rap into pop. Pop is just short for popular, which means a lot of people love the record. Every artist that ever makes a record hopes to be pop. They hope that their record will be popular. Nobody makes a record saying: ""You know what, I want an under-ground hit. I only want to sell 10,000 records.""

His credibility wasn't helped by the occasion when President George Bush adopted his 'U Can't Touch This' signature as a fighting slogan. Contrast this with Bush's 1991 response to *Newsweek* about Ice Cube's controversial solo debut: I've never heard of them (sic), but I know that rap is the music where it rhymes.' Military staff also employed Hammer's album for motivational purposes in the early 90s Gulf conflict.

'All the military guys were saying we were utilising the album out there to motivate us, and things like that. So from the White House down to the jail house, people would quote different terms from the album, different phrases.'

VANILLA ICE—UNDER PRESSURE

Hot on Hammer's heels came the first commercial white rap artist, Texan, Vanilla Ice, who had opened shows on Hammer's tours. Before that, he claimed, he had won his spurs as an original hip hop B-boy.

'I went to this club called City Lights a lot, an all-black club. I just liked the music there and I was accepted there because I had so-many friends that I knew that took me there. It was an all-black club. It really wasn't acceptable for a white-guy to come in there. But I was embraced there, everybody knew me. I was always there. People accepted me there, it was really cool, I felt loved and comfortable there. I got drunk really bad one night and got up on stage, 'cos my friend dared me to at this little talent contest. I thought it was just a joke. So I got up there and I did my little thing, and the crowd went nuts. I kinda liked it I was like: "Wow, this is really cool." And I did it the next week and then the week *after* that, and I just started really liking it. The response was great, the crowd was liking it, I fed off their energy. So I kept doing it and then all of a sudden, one day I did this one contest and Epic and Warner Brothers and Motown and MCA was in the house, I didn't believe these people. A lot of people come and see you and perpetrate and say: "Yeah, I work for this record company," or "I do this and that," and they really shine shoes or something, they're just full of it. So I didn't believe 'em, even though they had the cards and everything. So I landed a small record deal out of that with Ichiban Records out of Atlanta. So I had this record [*Hooked*] that I did at sixteen years old. I had this manager that wanted to change my image and change direction and all this stuff, so it wasn't so hardcore. But if you had heard the first version of *To The Extreme*—I had to take out tons of stuff and change the lyrics and all kinds of things, because it was just too hardcore, too X-rated. We sold 48,000 copies over three years. I opened up for Ice-T, Stetsasonic, EPMD, Sir Mix-A-Lot. I did the whole Stop The Violence tour.

According to Vanilla Ice, he didn't expect things to turn out the way they did.

I signed with SPK Records, and they said: "We're going to take your hip hop record and we're going to cross it over to this pop market." I said: "No way, man, I don't even listen to pop music.

What are you talking about? It's not going to work." And they were like: "Well, we're so sure it'll work, to change your mind … here's a cheque for a million-five." And I saw it, it had my name on it and everything, a million-five. I was three payments behind on my car, and I was nineteen at that time, it was like I won the lottery, man, it was like "Fuck! What do you want me to do? I'll do whatever." So at that point I started playing a puppet. But I couldn't see, there was no way anybody could see selling fifteen, twenty, however many millions I sold of that record. No way I could see that I didn't expect that, didn't see anything that was going to come from it.'

'Ice Ice Baby' was an amiable rap built wholesale on the bass line of Queen and David Bowie's Under Pressure'. Yet its success brought him to the brink of self-destruction.

'After my drug phase from '92 to '94, in '94 I found out that basically it wasn't about the money. Because I had millions of dollars in the bank. I had a million-dollar house, boats in the back yard, Porsches in the garage, and everything materially anybody could ever want. And I tried to commit suicide in '94.'

Chuck D, who before Vanilla Ice went pop considered signing him, believes much of the criticism he took was unjustified.

"White boy just doing rap. I wasn't one of the attackers. Matter of fact, I very rarely have attacked anybody in rap music. When he first came it was 1990, we're playing in the United States, yet another tour, and I'm in Jackson, Mississippi. I hear everybody go crazy over this cut. Nobody knows what this kid looks like, but they love the record. Everybody loved the record, until they saw this kid. And they saw this white kid actually rapping. Two years before, he had opened up for us. He was a white kid from Dallas with a whole black crew, and he had opened up for us in Dallas. Actually, we tried to sign him. 'Cos I said, if there's gonna be an Elvis in hip hop, I wanna own it.'

Alan Gordon was less impressed.

'Vanilla Ice never fit. Vanilla Ice had a great beat with the first single and he was a white dude that could really, really dance which was amazing to watch. But those album sales were generated outside of the hip hop community. He probably went gold with hip hop, but the rest of the nine million or whatever that he sold were to people who were just fascinated with the fact that it was a white dude that was dancing. But Vanilla Ice really couldn't rap, his rap was very, very weak … Vanilla Ice was a cartoon—the hair-do, the outfits. He was just trying to be like Hammer, which didn't really fit because Hammer was a far better rapper and his subject matter was more endearing to the black community. Vanilla Ice was what he was. He blew up and then that was the end of him. But Vanilla Ice was the worst thing that could happen to white rappers at the time, because MC Serch [of Def Jam group 3rd Bass] was a very good dancer and a very good rapper. On the first album they just came out and they were who they were, but on the second album they tried to distance themselves from Vanilla Ice to prove that they were a different type of white dude than Vanilla Ice. That's where they failed.'

Ice-T, who claims to like Vanilla Ice's new rock band, was nevertheless deeply suspicious of his authenticity as a rapper.

Vanilla Ice's mistake—he should have never said he was street, that was his mistake. If he had just came out and said: "Hey, I'm a white kid trying to rap," he probably would still be around today rapping. But when you come out and you say street, street is a rite of passage. Every black person isn't street. When you say you're street that means you may have had to live on the street. That means you may have been homeless, you might have been out there really living. All of us didn't come from the street. I personally came from the street, I used to sleep in my car, I was out there' going hand to hand, making my money off of the street, not a job, the streets. That's different. So when he came but, he insulted a lot of people by saying that: "I'm from the street." I'm like: "What street? *Sesame Street?*"'

As to the whole MC Hammer/Vanilla Ice competition whipped up by the press, Vanilla maintains that's all it was.

'We were friends. It was just the record company stirring up all this media, and It worked, and we both ended up selling millions and millions and millions of records. To this day we still have more hip hop records sold than any other artist, and I really don't think anybody's gonna ever match that, because that was a phenomenon.'

One of the principal reasons that Vanilla Ice became 'the most hated figure in hip hop history' had to do with his unfortunate comments at an American Music Awards ceremony, where he invited the audience to 'kiss my white ass'.

'That was a regret. I have ADD [Aggression-Driven Depression], I'm very spontaneous. I said that because some guy in the balcony goes: "Wannabe!" And I go: "Kiss my white ass." I was kinda relating it to him, one guy. I didn't think all these millions of people are watching. It was an idiot moment for me, man. I look back at it and go: "Why did I say that?"'

Another high profile blunder was appearing in Madonna's *Sex* book.

That was a regret too. I was going out with her on and off for a little period of time. I was over at this house she was renting. She said: "We're going to take some pictures." And I was like: "OK, whatever." I'm not thinking too much about it and she starts taking her clothes off and everything and running out in the street and stopping traffic. I was kinda going along with it and everybody's laughing. The next thing you know, book comes out—metal jacket, hundred bucks, *Sex*. I'm looking through the pages and I'm going: "Oh, my God!" And there I am. She put me in her slutty package, and I just did not want to be a part of it. I have a lot of regrets. Taking the money and turning it into a puppet in a novelty act—that was a regret—instead of maybe staying with the roots, the hip hop thing, instead of going pop and all that you know, but … you can't change history, man.'

Years on, Vanilla Ice hasn't completely lost the arrogance that was a major source of irritation among his hip hop peers.

'People today that are selling hip hop records, like Puff Daddy or whatever, they owe a lot of their record sales to me. They really do, because I put hip hop in front of people's ears who really never considered listening to it at all. If it took a white guy to do it, so what? I still did it'

Rumours about Vanilla being extorted for money by Suge Knight, in order to found Death Row Records, are common currency in hip hop circles. The story goes something like this. Mario Lavelle Johnson, aka Chocolate, was a young rapper befriended by the D.O.C., an artist whose career prefigured N.W.A's but whose impact was dissipated when he was involved in a car crash. The D.O.C brought Chocolate to Suge Knight. In 1990, Chocolate heard a record on the radio he claimed to have written for Vanilla Ice two years previously—'Ice-Ice Baby'—while both rappers were working crowds at Tommy Kwon's City Lights venue in Houston. When 'Ice Ice Baby' became a million-seller, Suge Knight decided his client should be paid his dues. After a brief telephone conversation with Kwon, Vanilla Ice's manager, it was arranged that Chocolate would return to Texas to help write songs for Vanilla's album. However, despite selling eighteen million copies, Chocolate believed his authorship of seven songs wasn't fairly credited on *To The Extreme*.

Vanilla Ice had a touring engagement in LA and learned that Suge Knight was keen to meet him. He tracked him down to the Ballage Inn in Beverley Hills,' Knight asked Vanilla to sign over the publishing rights to *To The Extreme*. Whatever means he employed rumours persist that he held Vanilla over a balcony fifteen floors up—Knight got his signature.

Vanilla has always denied these stories.

"Suge Knight and I have really not much of a relationship *at* all. I've only seen him a few times in my entire life. The rumours about him beating me up never happened. Rumours about him hanging me over a balcony never happened. I keep having to repeat myself over and over but I Just don't want people to get the wrong impression, because I heard a lot of rumours going around and they're not true. You can look at it like I'm an investor in Death Row Records without a return on my money. And that's it, because it ain't about money with me, so there's no bitterness. He took a lot of money from me or whatever. No bitterness whatsoever, 'cos I ended up with way more than I ever thought I'd end up with.'

When pressed, Vanilla's explanation of events seems somewhat odd, as if he's attempting to excuse Suge's behaviour.

'He just approached me with some paperwork and I got the idea that he knew where I was at all times. He ran off a roster of people that pay him, from Eddie Murphy to so many other people. I was in LA, his town, and this is what he wanted from me. So I gave it to him, I pictured what was going on. I'm not an idiot … He knew where we were at all times. He showed up at the Palm Restaurant. I was eating there, he showed up at another restaurant. He had informers everywhere, in the restaurants, in the airport. They knew I was coming through, so … If I wanna play I gotta pay, so that's what I did. No big deal, I've no bitterness whatsoever.'

Whatever the truth, the tale serves as an indication of rap's descent into something altogether more sinister than the teenage innocents who bought 'Ice Ice Baby' in their millions could possibly have imagined.

OBJECTIVE QUESTIONS

1. According to this author, rap had its first quantifiable pure pop hit in 1989, written by Marvin Young and performed by Anthony "Toco" Smith: _____. Why was this recording controversial?
2. In 1990, the music industry was turned inside out with the emergence of two child-friendly pop stars, _____ and _____.
3. How did MC Hammer get his name and what was his first group called?
4. Hammer believed his appeal lay in those old entertainment virtues which his main competitor, _____, personified.
5. According to Vanilla Ice, what is the reason his work is not more "hardcore?"
6. What did Chuck D say about Vanilla Ice? What did Alan Gordon say? What did Ice-T say?
7. Recount the story of Vanilla Ice, Suge Knight and Death Row Records.

TOPICS FOR MORE THOUGHT, RESEARCH, AND DISCUSSION

1. Examine the very complex relationship between art, entertainment, show business, commerce, politics, religion and the quality of our lives. How have other styles of music or other art forms dealt with this same dilemma?
2. The spiritual roots of most rap is the NOI and the Five Percenters. Trace the history and current popularity of Christian rap or rap expressing other spiritual values. Report on other diverse styles of rap, for example: Asian rap, German rap, Middle-Eastern rap, gay rap, etc.
3. Report on, and give examples of how aspects of hip hop culture, once considered "underground" or even "dangerous" have now become mainstreamed and accepted. Compare this to similar aspects of jazz and rock, now considered mainstream.
4. Compare the role, career, personality and life of Vanilla Ice and his analogous character in rock and roll history, Pat Boone.

"WALKING THE LINE: RAP AND CENSORSHIP"
FROM *THE HIP HOP YEARS*

CASH RULES EVERYTHING AROUND ME
THE 2 LIVE CREW—AS NASTY AS THEY WANNA BE

ON 6 JUNE 1990, a federal district court judge in Florida deemed 2 Live Crew's *As Nasty As They Wanna Be* 'obscene.' It was the first album in American legal history to achieve such infamy. Many commentators would agree that it wasn't the most meritorious record ever released, but the obscenity charge marked a major departure in authoritarian responses to provocative art. Although the charge was eventually overturned by a federal appeal court in 1993, the original judgement temporarily laid artists open to prosecution over their lyrics. 2 Live Crew's case drew support from such unlikely sources as Donny Osmond, Sinead O'Connor and Bruce Springsteen as they defended their first amendment rights to freedom of speech—no matter how objectionably they abused the privilege.

Rap acts were not unique in being subjected to censorship attacks. In the late 80s, extreme rock acts like the Dead Kennedys were scrutinised by the PMRC (Parents Music Resource Center). 'Washington Wives' Tipper Gore and Susan Baker (Al Gore and James Baker's 'better halves') were backed in their moral purge by TV evangelists Pat Robertson, Jimmy Swaggart and Jerry Falwell. One of their proposals was the labelling of offensive albums, an idea based on film classification. Hence the 'Parental advisory: Explicit lyrics' stickers which bedeck most modern rap albums, and a number of rock and R&B releases. That move ensured the records were instantly more attractive to younger consumers.

Comprising Luther 'Luke Skyywalker' Campbell, Kid Ice (Christopher WongWon), Brother Marquis (Mark Ross) and Mr Mixx (David Hobbs), 2 Live Crew formed in 1985 in Miami,

Florida. Their songs and skits were written in the tradition of foul-mouthed comics like Blowfly and Richard Pryor. Campbell, who was sued by George Lucas over his appropriation of the name Luke Skyywalker, was also their label manager.

They had released a number of records before *As Nasty As They Wanna Be,* employing the Miami bass sound of deep 'jeep beats' while boasting relentlessly of their sexual accomplishments. It was crude party music, and no one paid it much heed outside Florida. Then in 1989 they released 'Me So Horny', using a sample from the film *Full Metal Jacket* (specifically, dialogue from a Vietnamese prostitute). The album housing it, *As Nasty As They Wanna Be,* contained eighty-seven separate references to oral sex. Some of their other charming efforts included 'The Fuck Shop' and 'Face Down, Ass Up' (from their appropriately titled 1990 follow-up album, *Banned In The USA).*

Brother Marquis began his interview by asking if he looked good, 'so I can get me some English pussy.' According to his colleague Kid Ice, 2 Live Crew was simply a reflection of what was happening in their area.

We represent Miami, Florida, the south, and what the south was all about. It's all about partying and having a good time and at that time we were the only thing coming out the south. The criticism and the press and the people coming at us, we didn't expect that.'

Two retailers were arrested for selling the 2 Live Crew record, and the band itself was cautioning for performing explicit songs at a Florida venue. They faced a further court appearance over a skit on Roy Orbison's 'Pretty Woman' on the 'censored' version of the album, entitled *As Clean As They Wanna Be.* This time they ended up in the Supreme Court, defending an artist's right to parody the work of others. Like the obscenity case that preceded it, they won. Journalist Chuck Phillips notes that 2 Live Crew helped wake up the recording industry to the rap phenomenon, and also to the possible consequences of censorship.

'I think it galvanised the industry, because a lot of people didn't like rap at the time. A lot of white executives didn't like rap, the Recording Industry Association didn't like rap. They were forced to take a stand because this group was going to get arrested for these lyrics. They got arrested, in concert, and then a store owner got arrested—which was, a real threat to the record industry. If the store owner gets sent to jail then he can't stock the records, he can't sell 'em, they can't make any money.'

2 Live Crew's most vocal opponent was Jack Thompson, a former golf pro turned high-profile right-wing lawyer.

'On New Year's Day 1990 a friend gave me the transcribed lyrics of 2 Live Crew's album *As Nasty As They Wanna Be.* I was stunned to find what was being uttered on that record was available in main street stores in America. I found out shortly thereafter it was being bought primarily by children. Because I'm a lawyer who has represented sexually abused women and children, that's why I had this concern about what I was looking at—this glorification of the abuse of women on this record. I contacted, ultimately, all sixty-seven sheriffs in the state of Florida and provided transcribed lyrics of the album. The first Judge who found the album in the legal parlance 'probably obscene' was in Fort Myers. Luther Campbell, who was the head of 2 Live Crew, was contacted by the media and told that this has happened and Luther said: "Well, the Judge is a racist and he must be a clan member." To which the news reporter pointed out, this Judge is black.'

Thompson tested his theory that 2 Live Crew's 'pornography' was freely available to children.

'I asked a minor and his parents to go into one of the largest record store chains in South Florida and make the purchase. The album was sold, no questions asked, to this minor, there was no effort to "ID" the boy to see if he was a minor.'

Kid Ice and the rest of the band were unrepentant

'They wasted their time trying to ban a record on 2 Live Crew instead of going after the drug dealers or something like that, It's ridiculous, but it helped in a way. It brought the group to the forefront, and we kept doing our thing and just kept having fun.'

Many in the hip hop community, like Rick Rubin, believe that without the controversy, 2 Live Crew would never have been heard of.

When the 2 Live Crew record came out there was all this hubbub about it. I remember thinking: "I wouldn't put that out." But I wouldn't put it out because I didn't think it was a good record, not because I was offended.'

Joe Levy at *Rolling Stone* concurs.

'What happened to them arguably made their career, made them bigger and more important artists then they ever would have been otherwise. They're a "booty" band. It's about rump-shaking and champagne in a hot tub. That music is party music. But all of a sudden they were a first amendment test case, and they made one of the strongest records of their career in reaction to the controversy.'

Kid Ice denies the group were one-trick ponies, pointing to their sales profile prior to national exposure.

'Before they started protesting against us, we had gold records and platinum records. All they did was just brought us more media attention, 'cos we had our core fans.'

COP KILLER—TIME WARNER GETS COLD FEET

The censorship debate exploded in 1992 when Ice-T's spin-off heavy metal band, Body Count, released their eponymous debut. Alongside songs such as 'KKK Bitch' nestled 'Cop Killer', with, lyrics about the protagonist being ready 'to dust some cops off. However, as Joe Levy points out, the song was more measured than some have suggested.

'"Cop Killer" included lines that clearly showed that [Ice-T] was not on a mission to wipe out every cop—things like: "I know your family's hurting/But I'm hurting too." He's a feeling, thinking man.'

Others saw it differently. Jack Thompson began to network with several right wing hard-hitters, including conservative poster boy Oliver North, who couldn't resist fuelling the debate with some ill-conceived moral indignation.

'Oliver North was the head of a group called Freedom Alliance which took certain public positions on issues of the day including the culture wars—the distribution of offensive illegal material through the entertainment industry. He called and asked me to represent his Freedom Alliance at the Time Warner shareholders meeting scheduled for June 1992 because Time Warner was distributing rapper Ice-T's album *Body Count,* the most offensive cut on that album being "Cop Killer," which describes how to kill police officers.'

In June, police groups nationwide co-ordinated a call to boycott Time Warner products unless Warner Bros withdrew 'Cop Killer' from the album. The following month, rap's old friend

President George Bush weighed into the debate, calling the song 'sick'. The clampdown on Ice-T, according to the artist, was simply an act of corporate racism.

'When rock 'n' roll first came out, it was a serious problem because the white kids liked it. This is the issue that goes on with, hip hop music—white kids like it. You think there is not going to be a problem in the south with little white girls singing "Me So Horny" with Luke Skyywalker on the stage? So forget about the words. The problem is not Luke or 2 Live Crew,' it's, your little daughter, the little white daughter looking at Eazy-E and saying: "I like him, Mommy." And taking down their little Donnie Wahlberg [New Kids On The Block] poster and putting Ice-T up, in shackles, over their bedroom. Back in the days, little white girls screamed for Chuck Berry, they screamed for Little Richard. Now they are screaming for DMX. This is dangerous, right. So I look deeper than the word "censorship." If you're gonna censor, then there's enough rock. I've been on tour with Cannibal Corpse and Crowbar. I've been on tour with death metal bands and black metal bands that are saying stuff that you can't imagine a rapper saying.'

An 'outraged' Charlton Heston read out the lyrics to 'KKK Bitch' to shareholders at Time Warner's annual general meeting. Jack Thompson recalls events.

'I sat there at this shareholders meeting watching Charlton Heston do a reprise of his role as Moses confronting a new Pharaoh, Gerald Levin (Time Warner CEO). It was the most stunning public oratory I had ever seen, because as Heston stood up he was booed and hissed because of what he was about to say and by the end of his speech he had captured the crowd and sat down to thunderous applause. I spoke after him, which was not a particularly enviable thing to be doing, but I made the legal point that what Time Warner was doing in distributing this was illegal. It was criminal, literally, and I predicted that Time Warner was opening itself up to civil lawsuits by people who would be third parties harmed by the advocacy of killing police officers. I mentioned specifically the likelihood that any trooper or police officer killed by an individual who could be proven to have been motivated at least in part by "Cop Killer" would have a cause of action to bring against Time Warner. The *Wall Street Journal* had an article shortly thereafter which said that although it was Heston's oratory which made the news it was my warning of what Time Warner was looking at in damages and possible civil litigation that persuaded the board to take my advice and pull the album off the shelves worldwide.'

Accountants began to look nervously at Time Warner's stock price. To many in the hip hop community, it felt like war was being waged. The theme of 'Cop Killer' was brought into sharp relief by the beating of Rodney King, and the acquittal of the four officers concerned on 30 April 1992, sparking the LA riots. Ice-T recalls how Heston's intervention escalated the furore.

'I thought he was dead first off, when he popped up out of nowhere bitching at me. Charlton Heston is nothing but a politician. The cat rails against me but at the same time he lobbies to keep a bullet called the Cop Killer legal, because he is the president of the NRA [National Rifle Association]. So he's got his shit twisted. But the problem with Charlton Heston is, due to the fact that he's been in a couple of wack movies, people think he's Moses. And if he says something really heavy, somebody thinks fucking God spoke. But he's a twisted old man, probably catch him' at a peep [strip] show anytime soon, because I know he's not getting no pussy. But he's nothing to me. For him to step out and come up against me like he knew me, like he was familiar with my work, like he ever heard that record before, that was very wrong. He was brought in to go up against me politically. If I felt he, deep down inside, really felt this song, I might even have some compassion for him. If somebody calls me up and says they want me to go up against something, I'm like:

"What about?" "Just go, because we know your voice carries." That's bullshit. I learned that when you speak up, if you start a fight, be prepared to fight it by yourself.'

Chuck Phillips interviewed Charlton Heston several times during the affair.

'He thought it was terrible that lyrics like this should be allowed to be put out on a record by a company of Time Warner's stature. If you're a company like Time Warner, which puts out children's literature and puts out supposedly good movies and things like that, their argument was you should not put out things that are filthy or encourage violence. They probably believe that. I have to give 'em the benefit of the doubt, if you look at their careers that's what they've always said. The problem with that argument is that, and I really agree with the rappers on this—it's a convenient argument for the rappers but it's true—Scorsese can make a very violent movie that can come out of mainstream production. Or a John Wayne movie can be a very violent movie, and no one really thinks of that. They separate John Wayne from the character he's playing, they separate Robert De Niro from the character he's playing. They never separate the rappers from the lyrics they're performing. In some cases it's the rappers' own fault because they promote that image, but in other cases—like Ice Cube—he's an artist, he's not a guy that's going out and shooting people. He's an artist that talks about things and writes about things and now does movies. So on that level I think it was hypocritical of Heston, I'm sure he was in a violent movie at some point in his life. If a sheriff gets shot in a cowboy movie, or a police officer gets shot in a TV show that's put out by Time Warner, then no one thinks that show should be taken off the air.'

Eventually, some sort of compromise had to be reached. There was talk of death threats against Time Warner staff, and Ice-T thought it was unfair to put the lives of his record company's employees at risk over his stance.

'It's not up to Warner Brothers to have the same political beliefs that I have, and if you are gonna be heavily political, be prepared, if you cross that line, for them to say: "Hey, we can't back you on this." I'm not mad at Warner Brothers. People get mad at Warner Brothers. Warner Brothers didn't do nothing, Warner Brothers put the record out They got in trouble, so I said: "Look, I'm sorry. Let me get a release." It was a point in time where it was just out of control. The president was after me, they were talking about charging me with sedition. You know what sedition is? That's treason, it's punishable by death. So I'm like: "Yo! I'm not gonna die over no fucking record," Wasn't like "Cop Killer" was written as a rally call to go kill cops, it was just a song out of thirteen songs. It was just a move where I had to make a business decision, whether I was going to stand that ground and just totally be destroyed, because they was trying to take me out. I got tax audited three times, it was serious, It ain't really worth it. Simply because people aren't backing me the way they should be. So we pulled it. We wrote a letter to Time Warner and I said: "Look, Time, at this moment I feel I am a liability to you, but in the same sense I feel that you are a liability to me. Because if I change my stance that is my integrity and that is all I got So, let me go, can I get a release? I owe you all three more albums, let me go my way, I'm not mad at you, just give me a release," And they released me, I put out *Home Invasion* on my own shit and we moved on. But the way the press interpreted it—like Chuck D said, if you ain't in the war, don't comment on the battle, 'cos you don't really know what's going on, The fact that "Cop Killer" was a rock record and they called it a rap record was definitely the way they were able to rally people behind. Because if you say a rock record came out called "Cop Killer", a lot of the white people with power would say: "Well, I like Aerosmith, I like Fleetwood Mac, maybe I like this song. But if you say rap, that means niggers, and I don't like it." Immediately.'

Events, according to Ice-T, went into a surreal but sinister spiral,

We're sitting at the house one day playing Sega and a homeboy calls me up. He's like: "Yo, Ice, you on TV!" So we switch the channel and there is Dan Quayle, the vice-president, saying Ice-T this and Ice-T that. We're like: "Oh shit! It's on." I don't know how many people know what it's like to have the vice-president yell your name in anger, but it's at that point, and it was crazy to us. Because, like we said, it was just a record,'

Fab Five Freddy, like Chuck Phillips, widens the context of censorship to include mainstream film entertainment, and questions why rap has been the subject of such a witch hunt.

It's inherently racist, because you have motion pictures with huge white stars that kill, shoot and maim dozens of people, Bruce Willis. Arnold Schwarzenegger, Mel Gibson, go down the list. With sound, as well as picture. And with just the sound from records, they wanna ban this thing, The same corporation, Time Warner, who have bad guys killing, cops and doing this and saying whatever, but when it's the voice of young, black, angry youth, it became this whole nightmare.'

Ice-T is still bemused by the whole affair.

'I've been listening to Ozzy Osbourne my whole life. I ain't looking for no bats to eat, I ain't done no rituals. Some kids are weak and they will, but that's not the fault of the music. Johnny Cash said: "I shot a man in Reno, just to watch him die." Sounds like the Geto Boys to me.'

PARENTS JUST DON'T UNDERSTAND

2 Live Crew and Ice-T were the two most celebrated examples of rap's brush with censorship, but there were others. In July 1992 Tommy Boy dropped Paris, a highly politicised San Franciscan rapper. An employee had leaked details of his song 'Bush Killa' and the artwork for his forthcoming *Sleeping With The Enemy* album, which featured a scene best described as a Bush assassination fantasy. Monica Lynch at Tommy Boy concedes:

'We've had our run-ins with controversies in rap. Specifically the Paris album was something that was problematic for us. It came not too long after Ice-T's controversy. During that time there was this real sort of moral outrage and a lot of political pressure being directed towards what was perceived as gangsta rap. As a result there was a lot of pressure on corporate America to tone down its involvement in rap.'

The hysteria reached a farcical high point in June 1993, when the Rev. Calvin Butts pledged to steamroller 'offensive' rap records at a New York City protest rally. Having grown up in the South Bronx, Butts knew his hip hop—he can recall seeing the documentary *Beat Street* and enjoyed records by Grandmaster Flash (he incorporated parts of The Message' into his sermons), Kurtis Blow and the Fat Boys. But gangsta rap was a whole new ball game. It was 2 Live Crew who first caught his ire. Then members of his flock starting playing him gangsta rap records.

'This is not social commentary, this is not trying to bring people to a greater and higher awareness of some of the problems. This is a glorification of a gangster culture that we certainly don't need to be a part of. Now this is a money-maker to be sure, and whenever you appeal to the lowest' element in a human being you're going to get a response. But this is not what we should be doing, this is a prostitution of the music'

He stresses his distance from some right-wing conservative thinkers who have attacked rap.

'I'm not of the William Bennett school. I wasn't dumping on 'em. I didn't want to destroy their dreams and kill their music.'

One of his many confrontations came on a TV chat show when he was put up against Ice-T, the most eloquent of rap's defenders.

'I had a fight with Ice-T on a TV programme once—not a fight but a debate—and he agreed to appear with me. Ice-T said at first there would be some things we could work out. But then he started talking about his music and how he wasn't going to change. So I exploded and said: "It's my thing to shut you down then." And it's not my thing to shut him down, that's not what I meant. In the heat of that I probably spoke too soon. What I was talking about was, it's my thing to try to get you to see even more clearly.'

After Rev. Calvin Butts, the biggest advocate of censorship in rap music was Dr C. Delores Tucker—who adopted her title despite not holding any recognised post-graduate diploma. Tucker became the highest-ranking black woman in state government in the early 70s as Pennsylvania's Commonwealth Secretary. However, she embarrassed her local party with dubious financial dealings and real estate ventures. Eventually, after being accused of accepting large sums of money for speeches actually written by state employees, she was sacked by Governor Sharp. Her profile slumped, until she was approached by Dionne Warwick at the 1993 'brunch' of the Congressional Black Caucus. Tucker, previously ignorant of rap music, formed the National Political Congress of Black Women. Warwick and Melba Moore (a former R&B singer) became co-chairs.

Dionne Warwick initially connected hip hop with MC Hammer ('It was easy to accept and easy to listen to, and most pleasant to dance to.'), but her views quickly changed.

'Gangsta rap represented a very pointed, unacceptable idiom where my ears and my being—just as a civil human being—were being assaulted and insulted. Having no control whatsoever over the verbiage that was being used, with regards to descriptions of people—women specifically—graphic and demonstrative. Not only adjectives, but activity. Demonstrating what can and will and has been done inside the privacy of four walls, which should be confined to the bedroom and is nobody's business but those that one participating. The use of curse words, just liberally used, without any regard for the ears that were going to be listening to it, and the lack of responsibility of those who were perpetuating this. That's what it did to me and it still does.'

She has heard nothing since to convince her of the worth of rap music.

'I don't think that rap has become the new black American music at all. I don't consider rap [to be] music. I consider it as a form of communication. When you talk about American black music, you talk about Ray Charles and Gladys Knight and Aretha Franklin. You talk about those who are making music. That's American black music and this is rap. It has its own niche it has carved out in our world of entertainment and in the record industry. I really don't call it music.'

C. Delores Tucker can at least make a distinction between hip hop and rap.

'Hip hop music I have no problem with. Gangsta rap I do, because gangster defined by Webster [the dictionary] is "activity engaged in criminal behavior." As we know, the media, especially music, inspires, it motivates. It's something that our children love to imitate and it has a powerful influence on them. You're teaching children how to become a gangster, because that's what gangsta rap does, it tells them how to engage in the culture of the gangster lifestyle. And that is criminal behaviour which leads them into places where they need not go and they are going at tremendous rates.'

These are legitimate concerns, some of which resonate with voices from within the hip hop community.

'No one should use any negative stereotypical images about anybody, and I support the Jewish people and I just condemn African American people for not doing what our Jewish friends have taught us—never let anybody denigrate you with these stereotypical images that you've fought for years to get rid of. Now you're gonna have children come back and use the term nigger, use the name bitch, call us that, when we are super women, what we had to do to raise those children.'

One of the old school originals, Melle Mel, is an example of someone who has concerns about gangsta rap's celebration of the ghetto and its perversion of the hip hop ideal.

I ain't trying to go back to the ghettos, just to be in the ghettos and live in some fuckin' tenement with some roaches and all that stupid shit. I ain't trying to be out with niggers drinking beer, smoking blunts—I did that. That don't get you from point A to point B.'

For Chuck Phillips, Delores Tucker at least came from the community which rappers attacked more than any other—black women.

'That was really the beauty of Delores Tucker in the beginning. There *are* very offensive, sexist, terribly misogynist lyrics in a lot of rap songs, and you had a black woman standing up saying that. That's a lot different than Tipper Gore saying it. You couldn't just say it's a white conservative going after a black rapper or black artist, you could say it's a black woman who had marched with Martin Luther King. She had a pretty good history, even though it was chequered.'

Whilst sharing some of her convictions, the Rev. Calvin Butts disapproved of Tucker's hectoring methods.

'Dolores Tucker is someone that I have great regard for, but I had another approach. 'My approach was to call the young men and women into conversation, because I believe that only through conversation, dialogue, debate, sometimes argument, will you really get to where each other is coming from.'

Tucker claims that her objections to rap music arose from observing her thirteen-year-old niece's behavior.

'We had her in a private school and we heard from the teacher that she was doing a lot of things that thirteen-year-olds were doing. She was taking little boys in the bathroom. Then she came home and asked me: "What is a bitch?" The little boys were calling her the "b" word. We even had to take the male Barbie doll away from her because as soon as she got the dolls, she's undressing them and putting them on top of each other. So it affected her in such a tremendous way.'

Sensible observers would dispute the logic of trying to explain her niece's experiments with Ken and Barbie simply by pointing to a rap record she may or may not have heard. Whatever the ideological aversions to censorship may be, the withdrawal or amendment of records is invariably counter-productive, as Kid Ice of 2 Live Crew can attest.

'Our records were meant for adults, eighteen and over with the explicit lyrics and stuff. We also made clean versions' for the kids, but somehow the kids got hold of the dirty versions and they liked the dirty version more than the clean versions. So that's when the whole thing started, when parents got a hold of it. That's what started the censorship stuff against 2 Live Crew. We weren't going for that, but it happened, we accepted it and we moved on.'

Joe Levy of *Rolling Stone* believes that America has a pre-disposition to violence that gangsta rap simply exploited.

Why was '*Goodfellas* a big hit? Why is *Lethal Weapon* a big hit worlds wide? Why does Sylvester Stallone still have a career? These are questions for the ages. I can't answer them simply, but people like violence. Americans like violence more than your average world citizen. It's sad but it's true.

You put a gun on television, you put a gun in the movies, you put a gun on a record and people pay attention.'

OBJECTIVE QUESTIONS

1. On June 6, 1990, a federal district court judge in Florida deemed it "obscene." It was the first album in American legal history to achieve such infamy: _____.

2. Who started the PMRC, name some of its backers, what was their motivation and what was the end result?

3. Where does the sample for "Me So Horny" come from?

4. *As Nasty As They Wanna Be* contains _____ references to oral sex. (It only took Lenny Bruce 18 references to get arrested.)

5. According to journalist Chuck Philips, how did 2 Live Crew's obscenity trial affect the record industry? What was his reaction to the controversy? What was Ice-T's reaction?

6. When Luther Campbell told a reporter that the judge who found his album obscene must be a racist, what was the reporter's response?

7. Who was 2 Live Crew's most vocal opponent and where did he come from?

8. What was the target of the boycott of "Cop Killer?" Who read the words to "KKK Bitch" to the shareholders at Time Warner's annual general meeting?

9. Who said, "I've been on tour with death metal bands and black metal bands that are saying stuff that you can't imagine a rapper saying?"

10. What was the essence of the legal argument that Jack Thompson made to the shareholders of Time Warner?

11. Who was the chairwomen of the National Political Congress of Black Women and who were her co-chairs?

12. How did "gangsta" rap supposedly affect the behavior of C. Delores Tucker's thirteen year-old niece?

TOPICS FOR FURTHER THOUGHT, RESEARCH, AND DISCUSSION

1. Research the life and career of C. Delores Tucker and her relationship to rap and hip hop.
2. Compare the obscenity trial of 2 Live Crew to other famous obscenity trials, like the trial of Larry Flynt and those involving William S. Burrough's *Naked Lunch* or Allen Ginsberg's "Howl."
3. Research and report on the history of Tipper Gore, Susan Baker, the PMRC.
4. Report and research on other controversial records that have been banned or boycotted for various reasons. Some examples would be: "Sixty Minute Man," "Roll With Me Henry," "Louie, Louie," "Eight Miles High," etc.

5. Report and research the history of sexually explicit humor, including limericks and continuing through the careers of people like Lenny Bruce, Redd Foxx, Richard Pryor and Sam Kineson.
6. Do you think 2 Live Crew and Ice-T were judged differently or unfairly because they were black rap artists rather than white rock stars?
7. Charles Manson claimed his mass murders were motivated by the Beatles' song "Helter Skelter." Can you name other famous crimes supposedly connected to pop music or songs? In what ways have your actions, attitudes and beliefs been affected by the music you listen to? How should society protect children from graphically violent and sexual materials, or should it even try?
8. We all understand the innately human reasons for the commercial appeal of sexuality; but why is the depiction and portrayal of graphic violence so commercially rewarding in our society's popular entertainment? Is it again part of our innate human nature? Discuss how the portrayal and glorification of violence can be found in every strata and layer of our society.
9. Compare the concerns of parents in the 1990s over the negative effects of rap on their children's morals and values to similar concerns by parents of older generations about the negative influence of ragtime, jazz and every new style of rock and roll.

APPENDIX

Timeline
by Jeff Chang

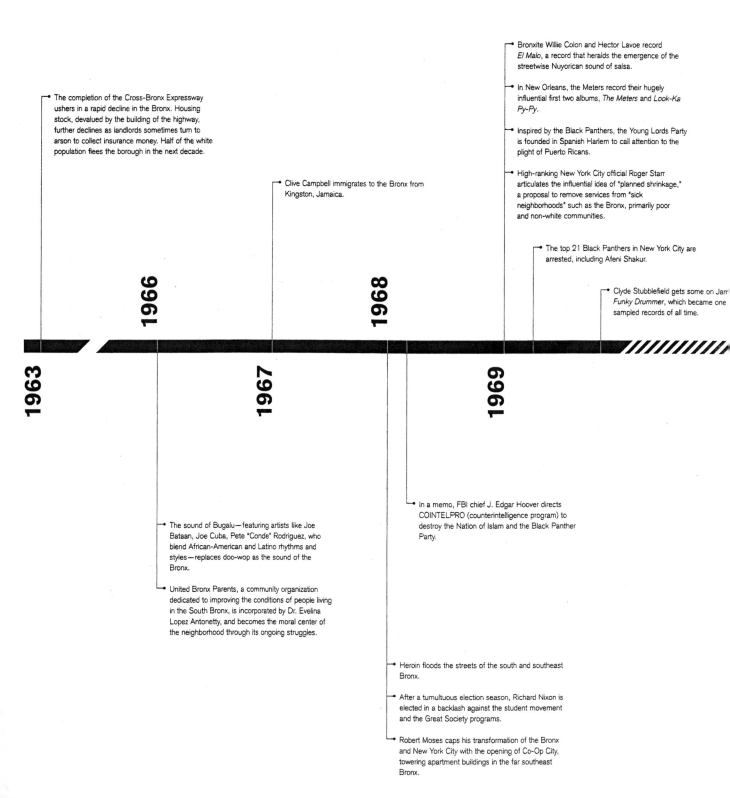

The completion of the Cross-Bronx Expressway
ushers in a rapid decline in the Bronx. Housing
stock, devalued by the building of the highway,
further declines as landlords sometimes turn to
arson to collect insurance money. Half of the white
population flees the borough in the next decade.

Clive Campbell immigrates to the Bronx from
Kingston, Jamaica.

Bronxite Willie Colon and Hector Lavoe record
El Malo, a record that heralds the emergence of the
streetwise Nuyorican sound of salsa.

In New Orleans, the Meters record their hugely
influential first two albums, *The Meters* and *Look-Ka
Py-Py*.

Inspired by the Black Panthers, the Young Lords Party
is founded in Spanish Harlem to call attention to the
plight of Puerto Ricans.

High-ranking New York City official Roger Starr
articulates the influential idea of "planned shrinkage,"
a proposal to remove services from "sick
neighborhoods" such as the Bronx, primarily poor
and non-white communities.

The top 21 Black Panthers in New York City are
arrested, including Afeni Shakur.

Clyde Stubblefield gets some on Jam
Funky Drummer, which became one
sampled records of all time.

1966

1968

1963

1967

1969

The sound of Bugalu—featuring artists like Joe
Bataan, Joe Cuba, Pete "Conde" Rodriguez, who
blend African-American and Latino rhythms and
styles—replaces doo-wop as the sound of the
Bronx.

United Bronx Parents, a community organization
dedicated to improving the conditions of people living
in the South Bronx, is incorporated by Dr. Evelina
Lopez Antonetty, and becomes the moral center of
the neighborhood through its ongoing struggles.

In a memo, FBI chief J. Edgar Hoover directs
COINTELPRO (counterintelligence program) to
destroy the Nation of Islam and the Black Panther
Party.

Heroin floods the streets of the south and southeast
Bronx.

After a tumultuous election season, Richard Nixon is
elected in a backlash against the student movement
and the Great Society programs.

Robert Moses caps his transformation of the Bronx
and New York City with the opening of Co-Op City,
towering apartment buildings in the far southeast
Bronx.

1970

Many families begin moving from the arson-devastated South Bronx to the West Bronx.

With the Panthers behind bars and the Young Lords retreating to Puerto Rico, gangs increase their influence on the streets of the Bronx.

DJ Kool Herc invents the "merry-go-round," a form of spinning breakbeats back-to-back, and forms the Herculords with his pal, the first hip-hop era rapper, Coke La Rock.

The OPEC oil crisis results in long gas line chaos and economic downturns across the U.S.

A front-page article in the *New York Times* discusses tagger TAKI 183, and suddenly hundreds of youths want to be taggers too.

Richard Goldstein's "This Thing Has Completely Gotten Out of Hand" in *New York Magazine* offers the first serious coverage—and defense—of the subway graffiti movement.

1972

New York City's two largest gangs—the largely African-American Black Spades and the largely Nuyorican Savage Skulls—go to war.

Cindy Campbell throws a back-to-school party at Sedgwick & Cedar; her brother DJ Kool Herc spins records.

After the killing of a gang peacemaker from the Ghetto Brothers, representatives of 42 gangs come together to sign an unprecedented peace treaty. While gang violence continues to be a serious problem into the mid-70s, the circumstances of the Bronx peace treaty make the emergence of hip-hop culture possible.

Afrika Bambaataa's Zulu Nation forms and begins actively recruiting outcast black and Latino youths in the south and southeast Bronx under a banner of "Peace, Love, Unity, and Having Fun."

1974

1971

Daniel Moynihan writes in a memo to President Richard Nixon, "The time may have come when the issue of race could benefit from a period of 'benign neglect'."

James Brown brings in the Collins brothers to record new versions of "Sex Machine" and "Give It Up Or Turn It Loose" that define the sound of the classic funk breakbeat, a new fusion of clave- and blues-based rhythms.

Youth gangs proliferate in south and southeast Bronx neighborhoods already devastated by deindustrialization, disinvestment, white flight, and widespread arson.

The Young Lords and members of the Savage Skulls, Savage Nomads, and Ghetto Brothers join to take over Lincoln Hospital for a day to bring attention to the terrible quality of health care provided to Bronx residents.

1973

DJ Kool Herc takes his parties indoors into West and East Bronx clubs like The Twilight Zone and The Hevalo.

Norman Mailer's ode to tagging, *The Faith of Graffiti*, is published.

The first-ever graffiti exhibition is organized by Hugo Martinez at City College of New York.

Joe Conzo takes his first photograph.

The Ghetto Brothers release their album, *Power Fuerza*.

Michael Viner's Incredible Bongo Band records a wild version of "Apache" featuring Bahamian bongo player King Errisson. It bombs everywhere but the Bronx, where it is later picked up by a young DJ named Kool Herc.

The writer's corner at 149th Street begins, started by writers like PHASE 2, BLADE, PISTOL, and others. Stylistic innovation explodes on the subway trains over the next year.

SUPER KOOL 223 does the first masterpiece and top-to-bottom car.

Afrika Bambaataa's cousin Soulski is killed by police, firming his resolve to advance peace efforts through Zulu Nation.

Grandmaster Flash, using his Clock Theory and Quickmix technique, perfects the art of mixing and blending breakbeats.

Grandwizzard Theodore discovers the scratch.

Charlie Chase begins DJ-ing in the Bronx, bringing together African-American funk crowds and Puerto Rican disco crowds at his parties.

The warm months after the riots bring the peak of the Bronx block party era.

The Rock Steady Crew is founded in the Bronx by Jo Jo and Jimmy D.

Music journalist Robert Ford makes the first mention of the rap phenomenon in club reports in his R&B column for *Billboard* magazine.

Women's crews and stars abound: the Zulu Queens B-Girl Crew, the Mercedes Ladies, as well as DJ Wanda Dee, and MCs Lisa Lee, Sha-Rock, Little Lee, Sweet and Sour, Debbie D, and Pebblee Poo.

According to Johan Kugelberg, the first breakbeat record is made: a 45 single credited to Yvette and the Kids that is simply a loop of "Funky Drummer."

Jimmy Carter visits Charlotte Street.

"Rappers Delight" explodes as an international hit.

Freeway Rick buys his first bag of cocaine.

The Fatback Band's *King Tim III (Personality Jock)* becomes the first rap record to chart in Billboard.

Joe Bataan's "Rap-O Clap-O" becomes the first rap hit in Europe. It fails to catch on in the U.S.

Mr. Magic hosts the first rap radio show *Mr. Magic's Disco Showcase* on WHBI 105.9 in New York City.

Academic Nathan Glazer's article "On Subway Graffiti in New York" in *Public Interest Journal* becomes the foundation for neoconservative "broken windows" theory and what becomes urban "quality of life" policies and "zero tolerance" policing during the '90s in American cities.

Cold Crush lineup is finally set: Charlie Chase, Tony Tone, Grandmaster Caz, JDL, Almighty KG.

Grandmaster Flash and the Furious 4 crush the Brothers Disco and The Funky 4 at the PAL. The Funky 4 temporarily dissolve and Raheim becomes a member of the newly renamed Furious 5.

Backed by Ford, Moore, and Russell Simmons, Kurtis Blow secures first rap major label deal for "Christmas Rappin."

After the President refuses to help New York City resolve its massive municipal bankruptcy crisis, the *New York Daily News* headline reads, "Ford to City: Drop Dead!"

The great blackout of New York initiates riots throughout the city.

The Yankees win the World Series behind a historic performance by Reggie Jackson in the Bronx.

1976

1978

1980

1977

1979

Afrika Bambaataa's first official party as DJ at the Bronx River Community Center.

Grandmaster Flash packs the Audobon with DJ AJ opening.

The film *Assault on Precinct 13* ushers in racial urban horror genre. The genre reaches its apotheosis in *The Warriors*.

Grandmaster Flash and the Three MCs—Cowboy, Kid Creole, Melle Mel—take up residency at the Black Door club.

Lenny Roberts introduced to the breakbeats by his son who is a member of Zulu Nation, goes on to sell Cutout Break records, then produces the Octopus Breaks then Ultimate Breaks and Beats series with the help of Afrika Bambaataa.

B-boying undergoes changes, from styles practiced by African-American dancers like the Twins to styles rooted in Afro-Latin dance traditions practiced by Puerto Ricans like Spy.

Bambaataa mixing it up with Fela, Kraftwerk.

The original cast soundtrack of the Broadway play *Runaways* features what may be the first modern rap on record.

DJ Hollywood, Pete DJ Jones, Reggie Wells, June Bug, Eddie Cheeba, and Grandmaster Flowers mark the heyday of the disco rap DJs, particularly in Uptown clubs like Club 371 and Harlem World, and venues like the Audubon Ballroom, and Brooklyn Soundsystems.

Charlie Chase, Cisco, RC, T-Bone, Grandmaster Caz, Whipper Whip, Tony Tone, Easy AD, and Dota Rock form the Cold Crush Brothers.

Whipper Whip and Dota Rock leave the Cold Crush to join Kevie Kev (Waterbed Kev), and L Brothers (Mean Gene and Grandwizzard Theodore) to form the Fantastic Romantic 5.

Inspired by Phase 2, Buddy Esquire designs his first flyer. Other important flyer artists include Eddie Ed, Beck, and Aton E.

Charlie Ahearn works on super 8 martial arts movie *The Deadly Art Of Survival* with Nathan Ingram with murals by Lee Quiñones, which leads to the making of *Wild Style*.

The Cold Crush Brothers play Joe Conzo's grad prom at South Bronx High School.

Henry Chalfant holds an exhibition of his subway art photographs at the OK Harris Gallery, giving movement important exposure in liberal art circles.

Countercultural collective Colab mounts the *Times Square Show* in an abandoned brothel, one of the first major shows for Jean-Michel Basquiat, Keith Haring, Fab 5 Freddy and Lee Quiñones.

At the *Times Square Show*, Charlie Ahearn, Fab Freddy, and Lee Quiñones meet and agree to work on the first hip hop movie, *Wild Style*.

The People's Convention opens on Charlotte St. Its organizers include future politician Jose Rivera.

Ronald Reagan visits Charlotte Street, using the words Jimmy Carter had uttered 3 years before.

Freeway Rick cuts cocaine with baking soda to "ready rock," later named "crack" by the media.

Kurtis Blow, the first rapper signed to a major label sees his single, "The Breaks," become the first to be officially certified gold.

In an October 1980 *Soul Train* appearance, Kurtis Blow becomes the first rapper on U.S. TV. Funky 4 + 1 follow soon after with an appearance on *Saturday Night Live*.

Bronx Puerto Ricans and African-Americans launch protests against the Paul Newman movie, *Fort Apache: The Bronx*.

→ Shooting begins on *Wild Style*—Busy Bee, Cold Crush Brothers, Fantastic 5, Grand Master Flash, and the Rock Steady Crew participate.

→ DJ Whiz Kid becomes the first winner of the New Music Seminar DJ Battle.

→ Afrika Bambaataa begins using the term "hip hop," popularized in parties by Lovebug Starski, to refer to the street youth cultures emerging from the Bronx and other New York communities of color.

→ Kool Lady Blue starts hosting "Wheels of Steel" night at Negril nightclub, downtown Manhattan.

→ ABC's *20/20* airs "Rappin' To The Beat." The piece is an in-depth look into hip-hop culture, featuring a young Rock Steady Crew.

→ One of the most famous old-school battles: the Cold Crush Brothers take on the Fantastic 5 at Harlem World.

→ ABC's *20/20* news program covers the Lincoln Center battle between Rock Steady Crew and the Dynamic Rockers, the first instance of national network coverage of hip-hop.

→ Feature stories on hip hop's explosion at The Roxy appear in *Rolling Stone*, *Life*, and *People* magazines.

→ After creating a huge buzz in New York City, Charlie Ahearn's *Wild Style* goes into national release.

→ *Wild Style* world premiere in Tokyo, Japan, with Cold Crush Brothers, Busy Bee, Double Trouble, Rock Steady Crew, Fab 5 Freddy, Charlie Ahearn, Futura, Dondi, among others.

→ Run DMC's first single, "It's Like That"/"Sucker MCs," heralds a new sound in rap music, an end to the old school.

→ In Los Angeles, Freeway Rick Ross standardizes the sale and distribution of crack cocaine to the masses.

→ With appearances by members of the Rock Steady Crew, *Flashdance* becomes the first Hollywood movie to feature b-boying.

→ Tagger Michael Stewart is killed by MTA police in the New York subway.

→ The widely-panned Sidney Janis Gallery exhibition *Post-Graffiti* marks the end of the art world's short-lived flirtation with graffiti writers.

→ Jesse Jackson announces his first presidential bid.

→ Brian DePalma's *Scarface* is released.

→ A new hardcore sound hits the streets in the form of Philadelphia rapper Schoolly D's "P.S.K." and Los Angeles rapper Toddy Tee's "Batteram."

→ Crack cocaine use reaches epidemic proportions in Los Angeles, Miami, and New York City.

→ LL Cool J's *Radio* becomes the first album released by a label called Def Jam through a major label distribution deal with Columbia Records.

1982

1984

1986

1983

1985

→ Run DMC's self-titled debut album becomes the first rap album to be officially certified gold.

→ Bernhard Goetz shoots 4 black male teens on a New York subway.

→ The New York City Rap Tour—featuring Afrika Bambaataa, the Rock Steady Crew, Futura, Dondi, Grandmixer D.St., Rammellzee, and Fab 5 Freddy and organized by Roxy promoter Kool Lady Blue— goes to England and France.

→ The *Fresh Fest* tour featuring Run DMC, Kurtis Blow, the Fat Boys, Newcleus, Whodini, Dynamic Breakers, and the Magnificent Force becomes the first major national rap tour, hitting 27 cities and grossing $3.5 million.

→ Grandmaster Flash and the Furious 5's record "The Message," actually written and performed by Sugarhill songwriter Duke Bootee and Melle Mel, becomes a huge hit.

→ The Roxy, a massive roller rink on the Westside, opens for *Wheels of Steel* night.

→ Afrika Bambaataa and the Soulsonic Force release *Planet Rock* on Tom Silverman's Tommy Boy Records. It goes on to sell 650,000 copies.

→ The first Reagan recession brings widespread joblessness to inner cities across the U.S.

→ *Wild Style* screened for the first time in 16mm.

→ The pilot of Michael Holman's *Graffiti Rock*, a hip-hop take on *Soul Train* and *American Bandstand*, debuts. It doesn't get picked up.

→ Tony Silver and Henry Chalfant's documentary *Style Wars* airs on PBS across the country, prompting sporadic protests from some angry viewers.

→ In Los Angeles, ground-breaking 24 hour rap radio station KDAY goes on the air.

→ The publication of first important books on hip-hop include Steven Hager's *Hip Hop* and David Toop's *Rap Attack*, followed closely by *Fresh* co-written by Nelson George, Sally Banes, Susan Flinker, and Patty Romanowski.

→ Run DMC's *Raising Hell* becomes the first rap album to be officially certified platinum.

→ During their triumphant *Raising Hell* tour, Run DMC encounter a full-blown gang melee in progress at the Long Beach auditorium.

→ Mandatory minimum sentencing is established for crack cocaine users through the Federal Anti-Drug Abuse Act of 1986. The result is a racially disparate explosion in the prison population in the U.S.

Breinigsville, PA USA
14 December 2010

251365BV00002B/3/P